More and more restaurants in my neighborhood have started delivering, and I have every intention of supporting them with my stomach. Even if that comes at the cost of my waistline.

This is *World Trigger* volume 23.

—Daisuke Ashihara, 2021

Daisuke Ashihara began his manga career at the age of 27 when his manga *Room 303* won second place in the 75th Tezuka Awards. His first series, *Super Dog Rilienthal*, began serialization in *Weekly Shonen Jump* in 2009. *World Trigger* is his second serialized work in *Weekly Shonen Jump*. He is also the author of several shorter works, including the one-shots *Super Dog Rilienthal*, *Trigger Keeper* and *Elite Agent Jin*.

WORLD TRIGGER VOL. 23
SHONEN JUMP Manga Edition

STORY AND ART BY DAISUKE ASHIHARA

Translation/Caleb Cook
Touch-Up Art & Lettering/Annaliese "Ace" Christman
Design/Julian [JR] Robinson
Editor/Marlene First

WORLD TRIGGER © 2013 by Daisuke Ashihara/SHUEISHA Inc.
All rights reserved.
First published in Japan in 2013 by SHUEISHA Inc., Tokyo.
English translation rights arranged by SHUEISHA Inc.

The stories, characters, and incidents mentioned
in this publication are entirely fictional.

Printed in Canada

Published by VIZ Media, LLC
P.O. Box 77010
San Francisco, CA 94107

10 9 8 7 6 5 4 3 2 1
First printing, March 2022

viz.com

PARENTAL ADVISORY
WORLD TRIGGER is rated T for Teen and
is recommended for ages 13 and up. This
volume contains fantasy violence.

SHONEN JUMP

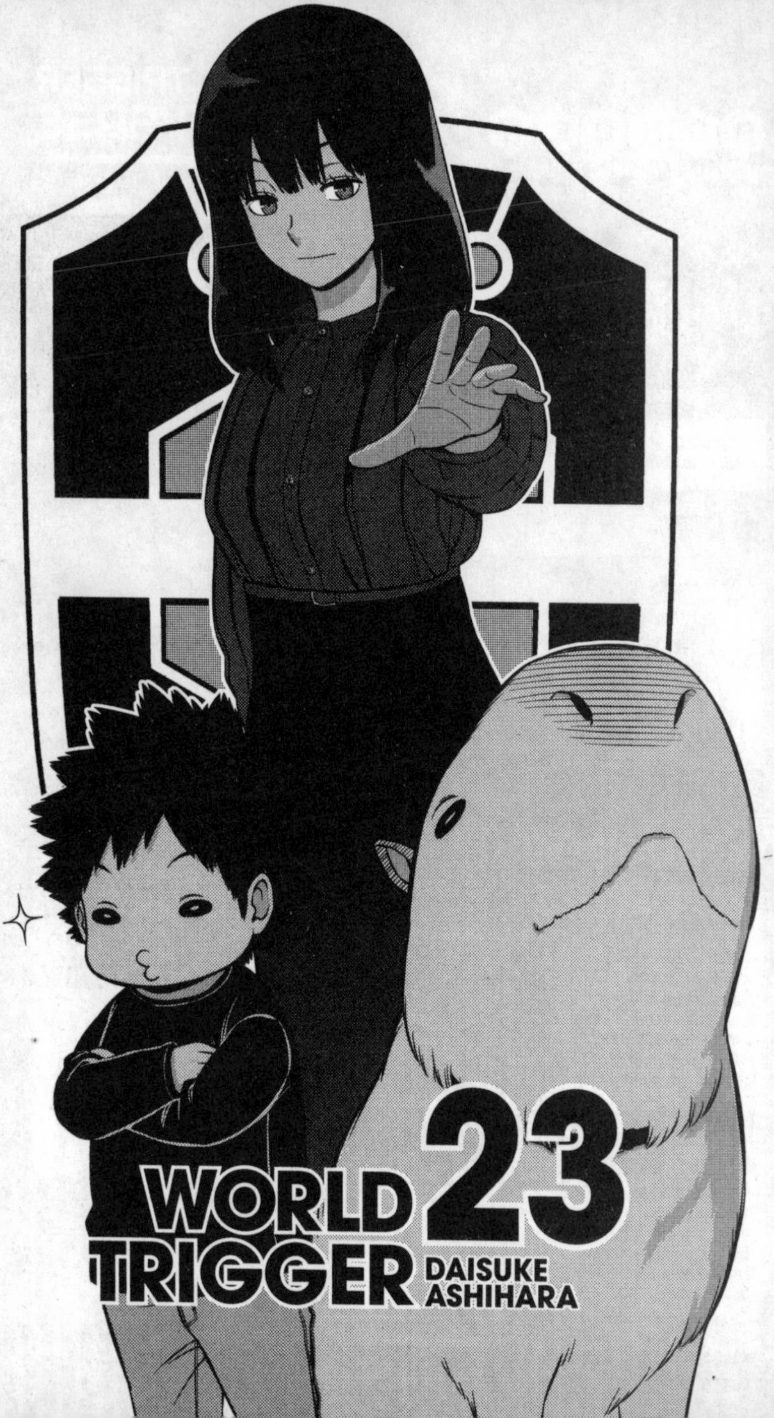

WORLD TRIGGER
23
DAISUKE ASHIHARA

WORLD TRIGGER DATA BASE

BORDER

An agency founded to protect the city's peace from Neighbors.

S-Rank Black Trigger Users (i.e. Tsukihiko Amo)

A-Rank (Elite) — Away teams selected from here (Arashiyama, Miwa squads)

Promoted in Rank Wars

B-Rank (Main force) — Agents on defense duty must be at least B-Rank (Tamakoma-2)

Promoted at 4,000 solo points

C-Rank (Trainees) — Use trainee Triggers only in emergencies (Izuho Natsume)

TRIGGER

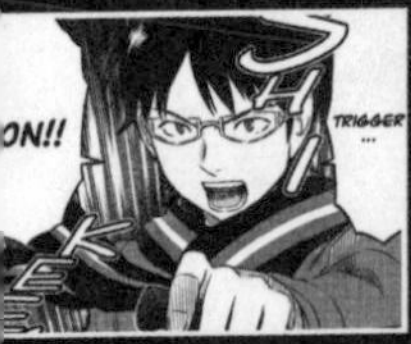
ON!!
TRIGGER...

A technology created by Neighbors to manipulate Trion. Used mainly as weapons, Triggers come in various types.

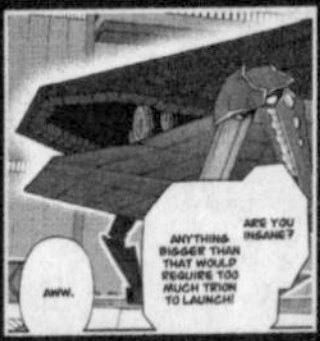
ARE YOU INSANE?
ANYTHING BIGGER THAN THAT WOULD REQUIRE TOO MUCH TRION TO LAUNCH!
AWW.

◀ A miss ships also run Trion

POSITIONS

Border classifies them into three groups: Attacker, Gunner and Sniper.

Attacker

Close-range attacks. Weapons include: close-range Scorpions that are good for surprise attacks, the balanced Kogetsu sword, and the defense-heavy Raygust.

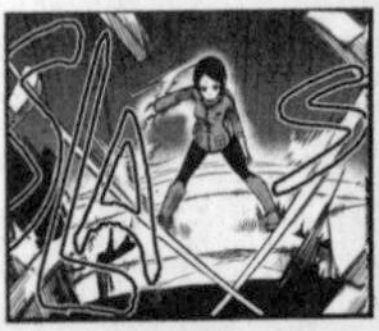

Gunner

Shoots from mid-range. There are several types of bullets, including multipurpose Asteroids, twisting Vipers, exploding Meteors, and tracking Hounds. People who don't use gun-shaped Triggers are called Shooters.

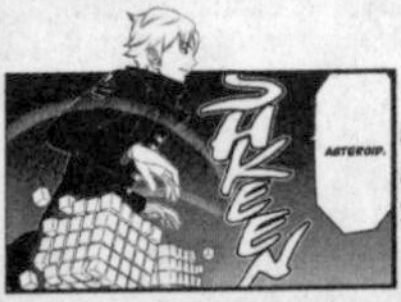
ASTEROID.

◀ Osamu and Izumi are Shooters.

Sniper

Fires from a long distance. There are three sniping rifles: the well-balanced Egret, the light and easy Lightning, and the powerful but unwieldy Ibis.

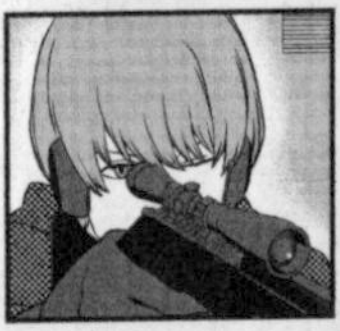

Operator

Supports combatants by relaying information such as enemy positions and abilities.

RANK WARS

Practice matches between Border agents. Promotions in Border are based on good results in the Rank Wars and defense duty achievements.

B-Rank agents are split into top, middle, and bottom groups. Three to four teams fight in a melee battle. Defeating an opposing squad member earns you one point and surviving to the end nets two points. Top teams from the previous season get a bonus.

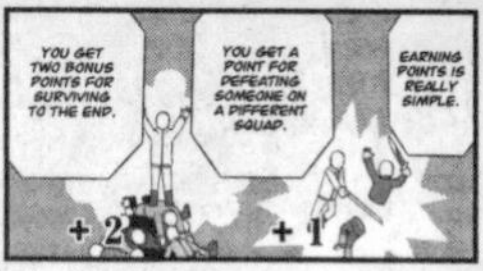
EARNING POINTS IS REALLY SIMPLE.
YOU GET A POINT FOR DEFEATING SOMEONE ON A DIFFERENT SQUAD.
YOU GET TWO BONUS POINTS FOR SURVIVING TO THE END.
+ 1
+ 2

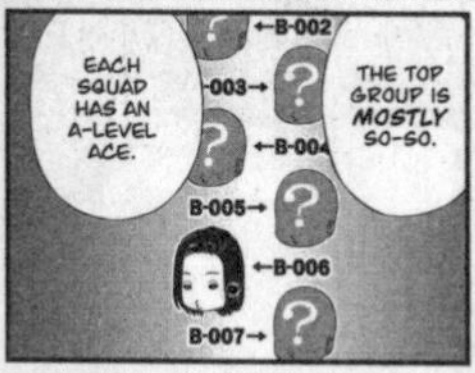
THE TOP GROUP IS MOSTLY SO-SO.
EACH SQUAD HAS AN A-LEVEL ACE.
B-002
003
B-004
B-005
B-006
B-007

B-Rank middle groups have set strategies. Top groups all have an A-Rank level ace.

The lowest-ranked team in each match gets to pick the stage.

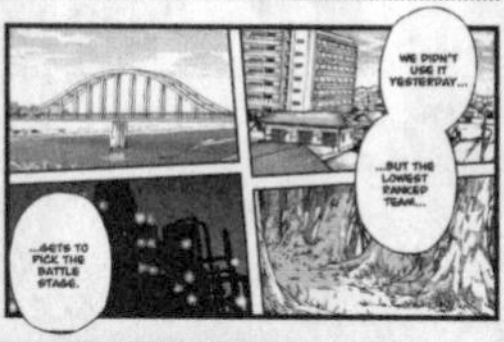
WE DIDN'T USE IT YESTERDAY...
...BUT THE LOWEST RANKED TEAM...
...GETS TO PICK THE BATTLE STAGE.

A-Rank

Top two B-Rank squads get to challenge A-Rank.

B-Rank

Agents ▶ (B-Rank and above) can't fight trainees (C-Rank) for points.

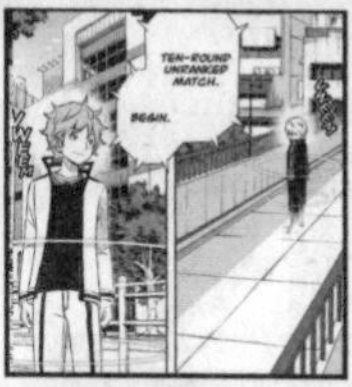
TEN-ROUND UNRANKED MATCH.
BEGIN.

C-Rank Wars are fought through solo matches. Beating someone with more points than you gets you a lot of points. On the other hand, beating someone with fewer points doesn't get you as many.

C-Rank

STORY

About four years ago, a Gate connecting to another dimension opened in Mikado City, leading to the appearance of invaders called Neighbors. After the establishment of the Border Defence Agency, people were able to return to their normal lives.

Osamu Mikumo is a junior high student who meets Yuma Kuga, a Neighbor. Yuma is targeted for capture by Border, but Tamakoma branch agent Yuichi Jin steps in to help. He convinces Yuma to join Border instead, then gives his Black Trigger to HQ in exchange for Yuma's enlistment. Now Osamu, Yuma and Osamu's friend Chika work toward making A-Rank together.

Hoping to be chosen for the away missions, Osamu and his squad are aiming for B-Rank No. 2 or higher. Hyuse, the neighbor captured from Aftokrator, was added to the squad, but in round 8, the key question was, "Can Chika shoot people or not?" And it turned out she could! Beating the Ninomiya Squad and reaching No. 2 in the ranks won Tamakoma-2 a ticket to the away mission selection test. In the meantime, the B-rank midtier final match has begun, and Katori, Suwa, and Nasu Squads

WORLD TRIGGER CHARACTERS

TAMAKOMA BRANCH

Understanding toward Neighbors. Considered divergent from Border's main philosophy.

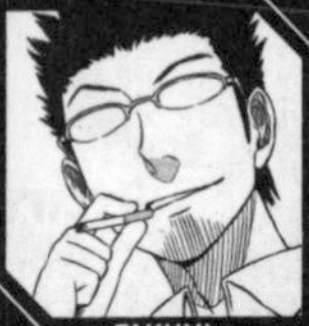

TAKUMI RINDO

Tamakoma Branch Director.

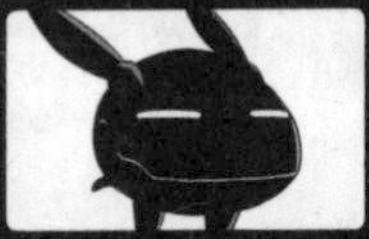

REPLICA

Yuma's chaperone. Missing after recent invasion.

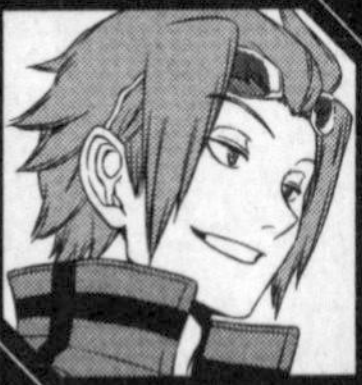

YUICHI JIN

Former S-Rank Black Trigger user. His Side Effect lets him see the future.

TAMAKOMA-2

Tamakoma's B-Rank squad, aiming to get promoted to A-Rank.

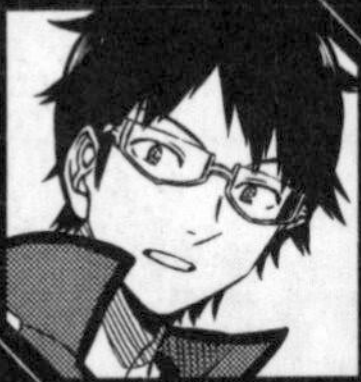

OSAMU MIKUMO

Ninth-grader who's compelled to help those in trouble. Captain of Tamakoma-2 (Mikumo squad).

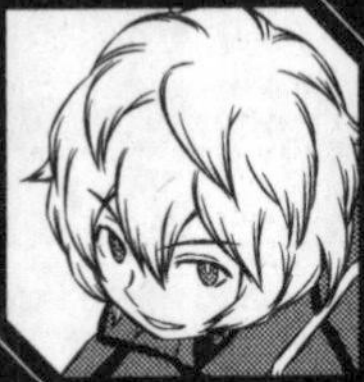

YUMA KUGA

A Neighbor who carries a Black Trigger.

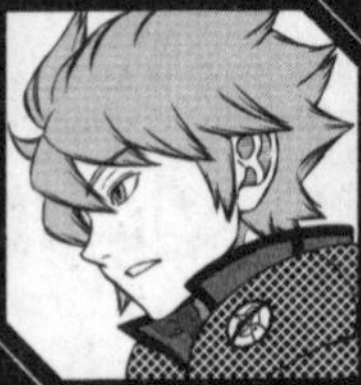

HYUSE

A Neighbor from Aftokrator captured during the large-scale invasion.

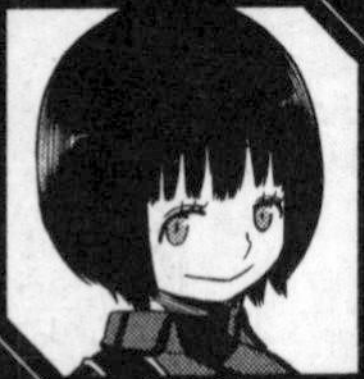

CHIKA AMATORI

Osamu's childhood friend. She has high Trion levels.

TAMAKOMA-1

Tamakoma's A-Rank squad.

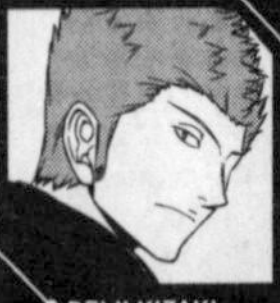

REIJI KIZAKI

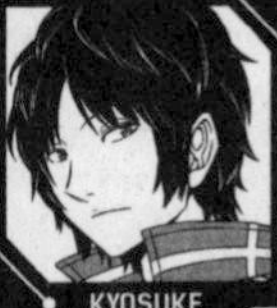

KYOSUKE KARASUMA

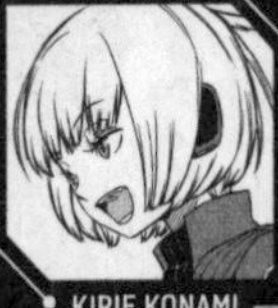

KIRIE KONAMI

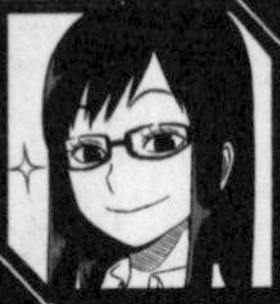

SHIORI USAMI

Famous operator now supporting Mikumo and pals.

KATORI SQUAD

Border HQ B-Rank #9

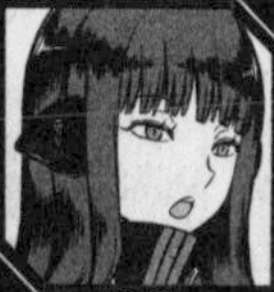
YOKO KATORI

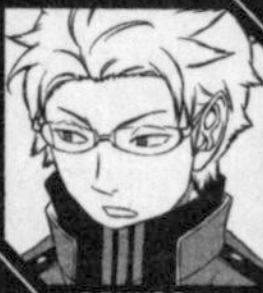
ROKURO WAKAMURA

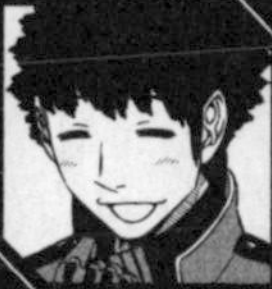
YUTA MIURA

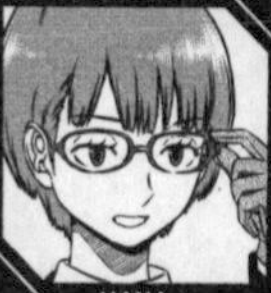
HANA SOMEI

SUWA SQUAD

Border HQ B-Rank #10

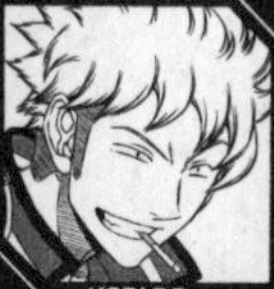
KOTARO SUWA

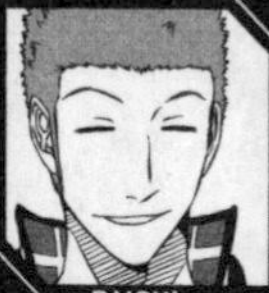
DAICHI TSUTSUMI

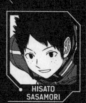

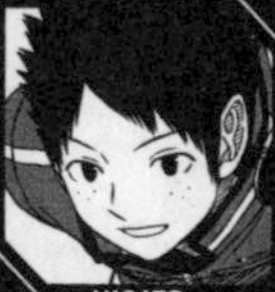
HISATO SASAMORI

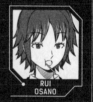

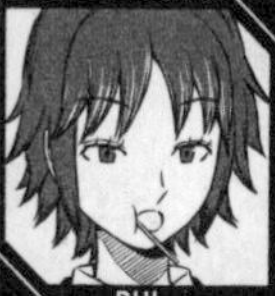
RUI OSANO

NASU SQUAD

Border HQ B-Rank #12

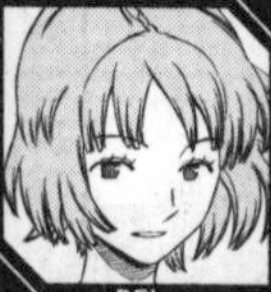
REI NASU

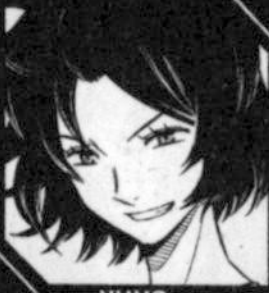
YUKO KUMAGAI

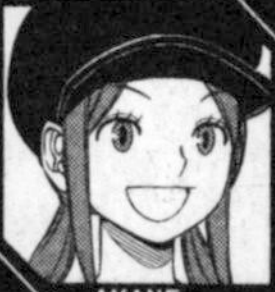
AKANE HIURA

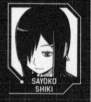

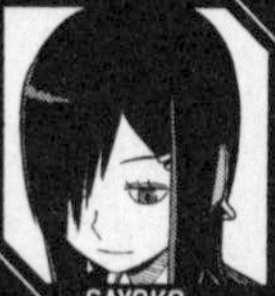
SAYOKO SHIKI

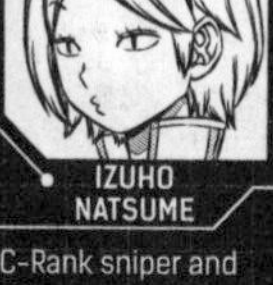
IZUHO NATSUME

C-Rank sniper and Chika's friend.

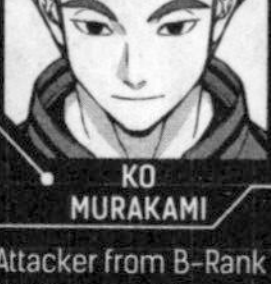
KO MURAKAMI

Attacker from B-Rank #8 Suzunari-1.

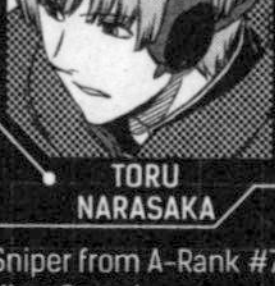
TORU NARASAKA

Sniper from A-Rank #7 Miwa Squad.

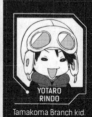

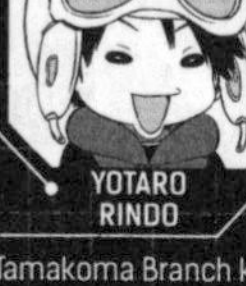
YOTARO RINDO

Tamakoma Branch kid.

WORLD TRIGGER
CONTENTS

23

Chapter 197: B-Rank Midtier Final Match ••••••••••••• 9

Chapter 198: B-Rank Midtier Final Match: Part 2 •••• 35

Chapter 199: B-Rank War's End ••••••••••••••••••••••• 59

Chapter 200: Ruka Shinoda •••••••••••••••••••••••••••• 83

Chapter 201: Yotaro Rindo: Part 3 •••••••••••••••••••• 99

Chapter 202: Galopoula: Part 14 ••••••••••••••••••••• 123

Chapter 203: The Away Mission Test ••••••••••••••••• 147

Chapter 204: The Away Mission Test: Part 2 •••••••• 167

Chapter 205: The Away Mission Test: Part 3 •••••••• 187

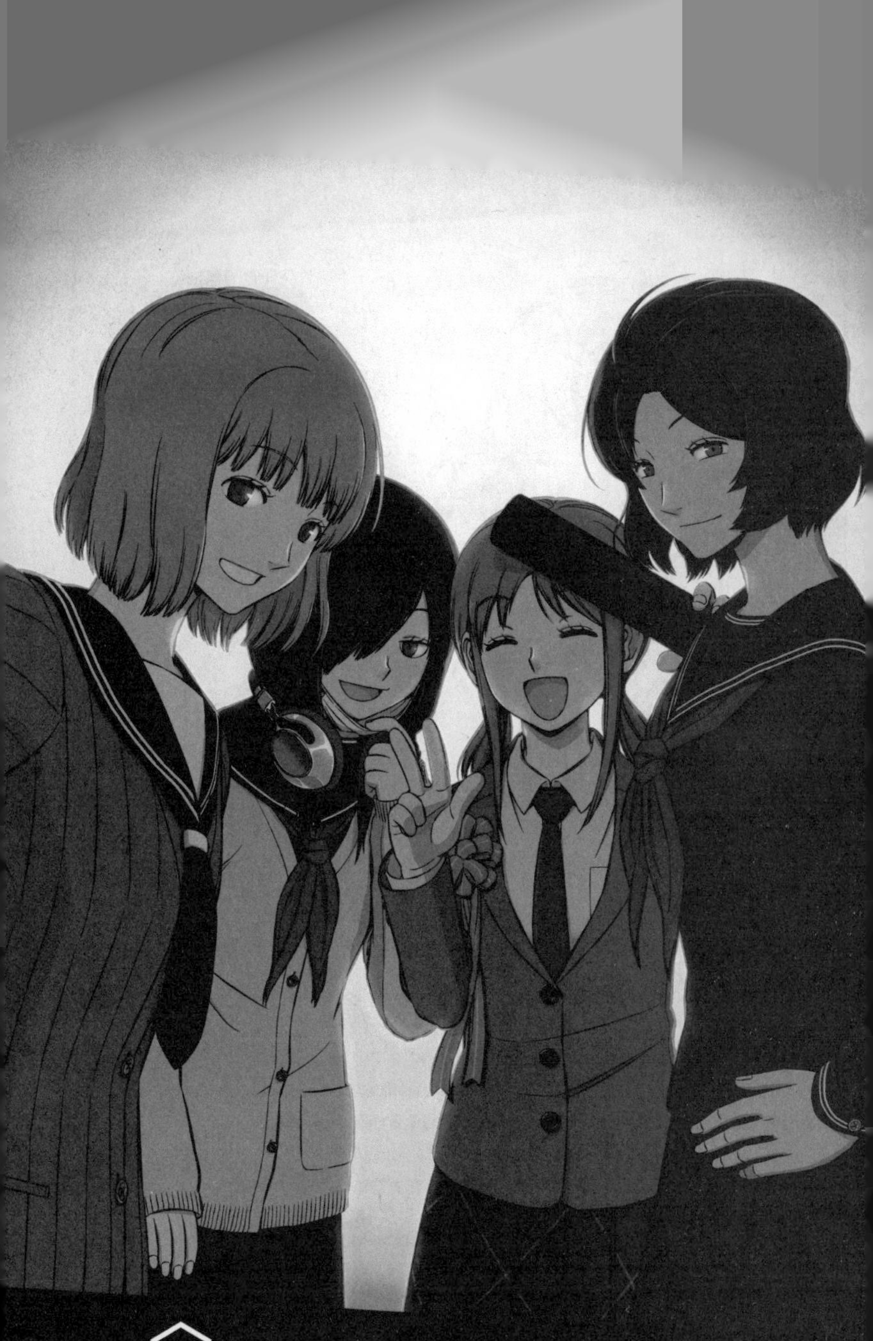

Chapter 197 B-Rank [illegible] Final Match

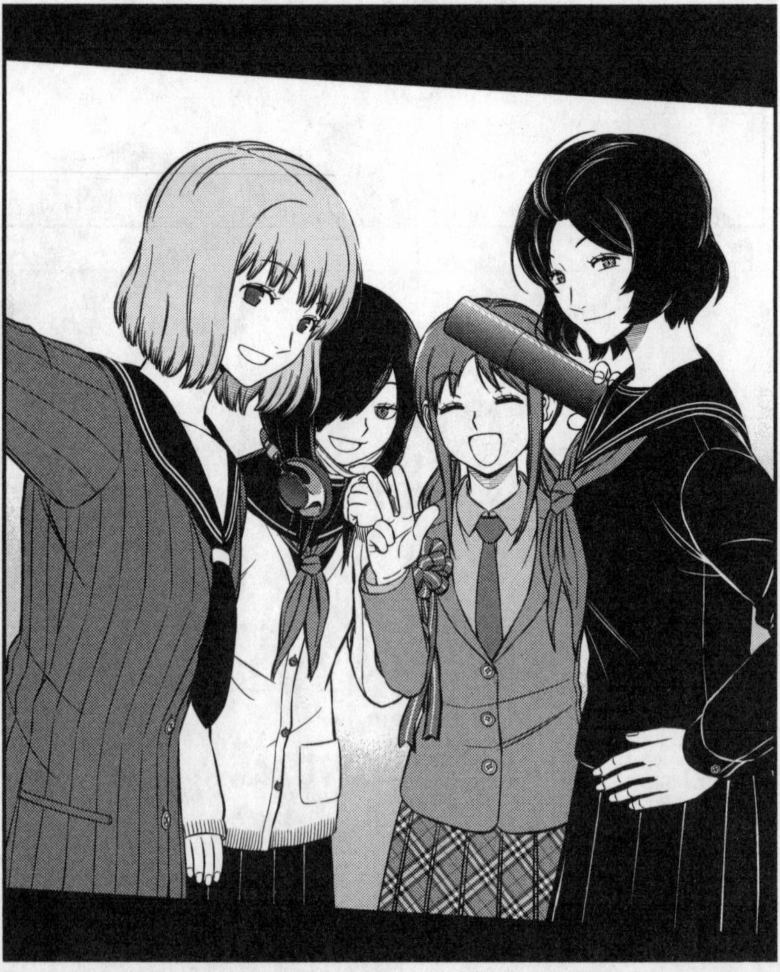

■ *Jump SQ* July 2020 issue center color (originally in color)

This feels like it would be the scene after Akane graduates. Whenever there's a meeting, a parting is sure to follow. We all hope that Akane is doing well in her new home. And Sayako somehow looks cuter than usual...

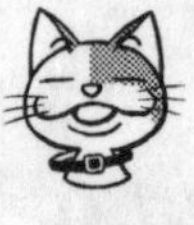

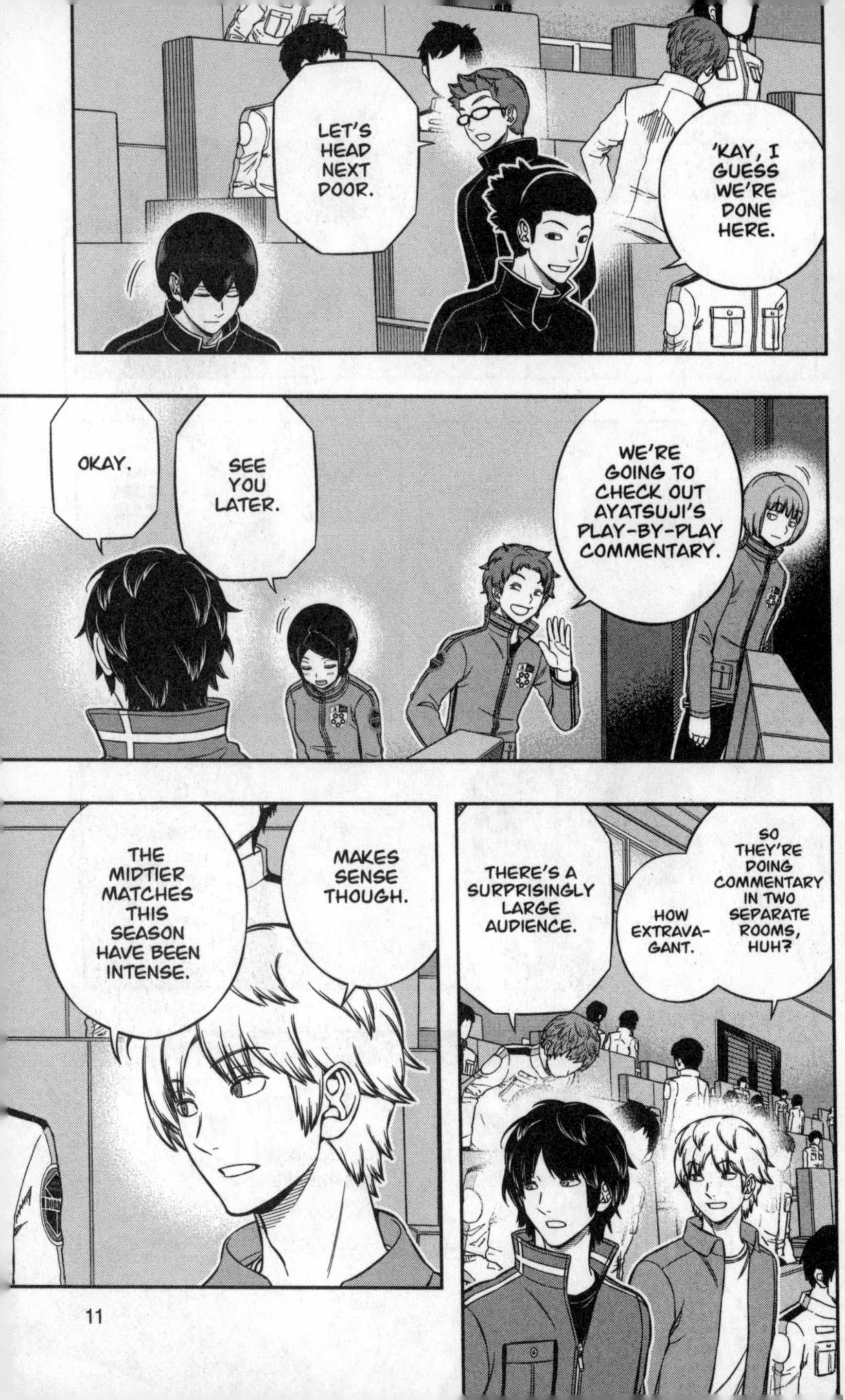
'KAY, I GUESS WE'RE DONE HERE.
LET'S HEAD NEXT DOOR.
WE'RE GOING TO CHECK OUT AYATSUJI'S PLAY-BY-PLAY COMMENTARY.
SEE YOU LATER.
OKAY.
SO THEY'RE DOING COMMENTARY IN TWO SEPARATE ROOMS, HUH?
HOW EXTRAVA-GANT.
THERE'S A SURPRISINGLY LARGE AUDIENCE.
MAKES SENSE THOUGH.
THE MIDTIER MATCHES THIS SEASON HAVE BEEN INTENSE.

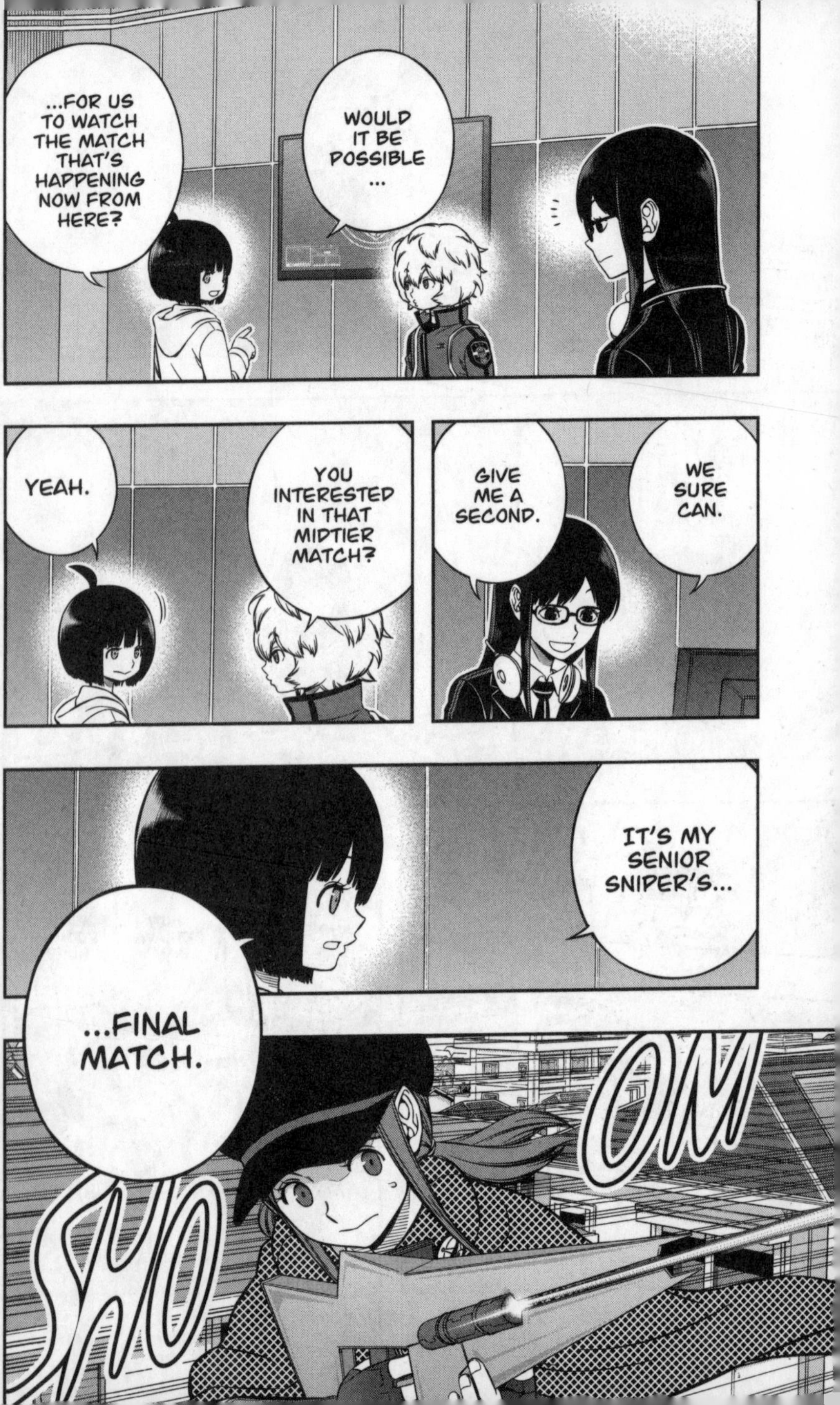
WOULD IT BE POSSIBLE ...
...FOR US TO WATCH THE MATCH THAT'S HAPPENING NOW FROM HERE?
WE SURE CAN.
GIVE ME A SECOND.
YOU INTERESTED IN THAT MIDTIER MATCH?
YEAH.
IT'S MY SENIOR SNIPER'S...
...FINAL MATCH.
SHO
OM

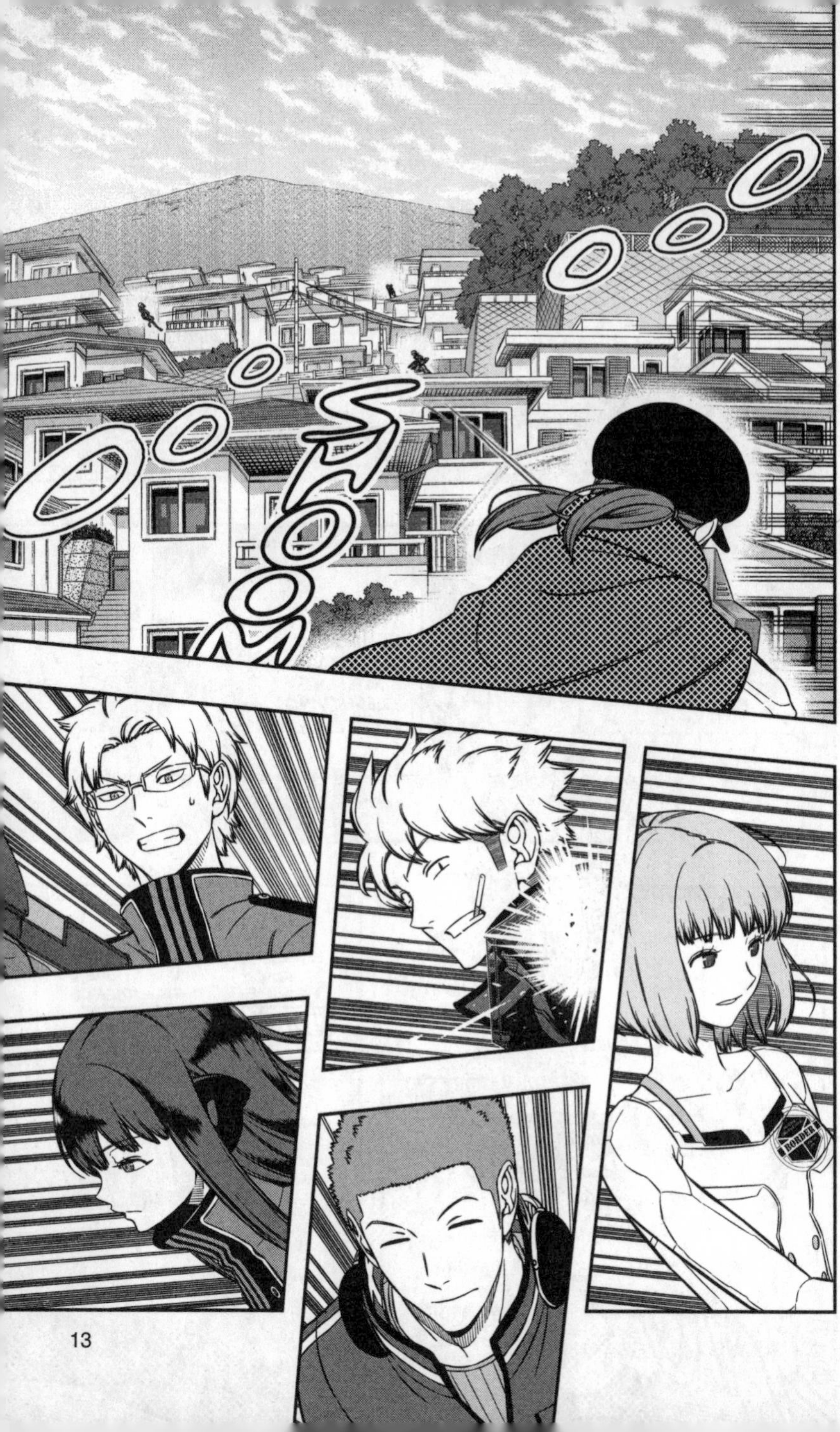
SHOOOM

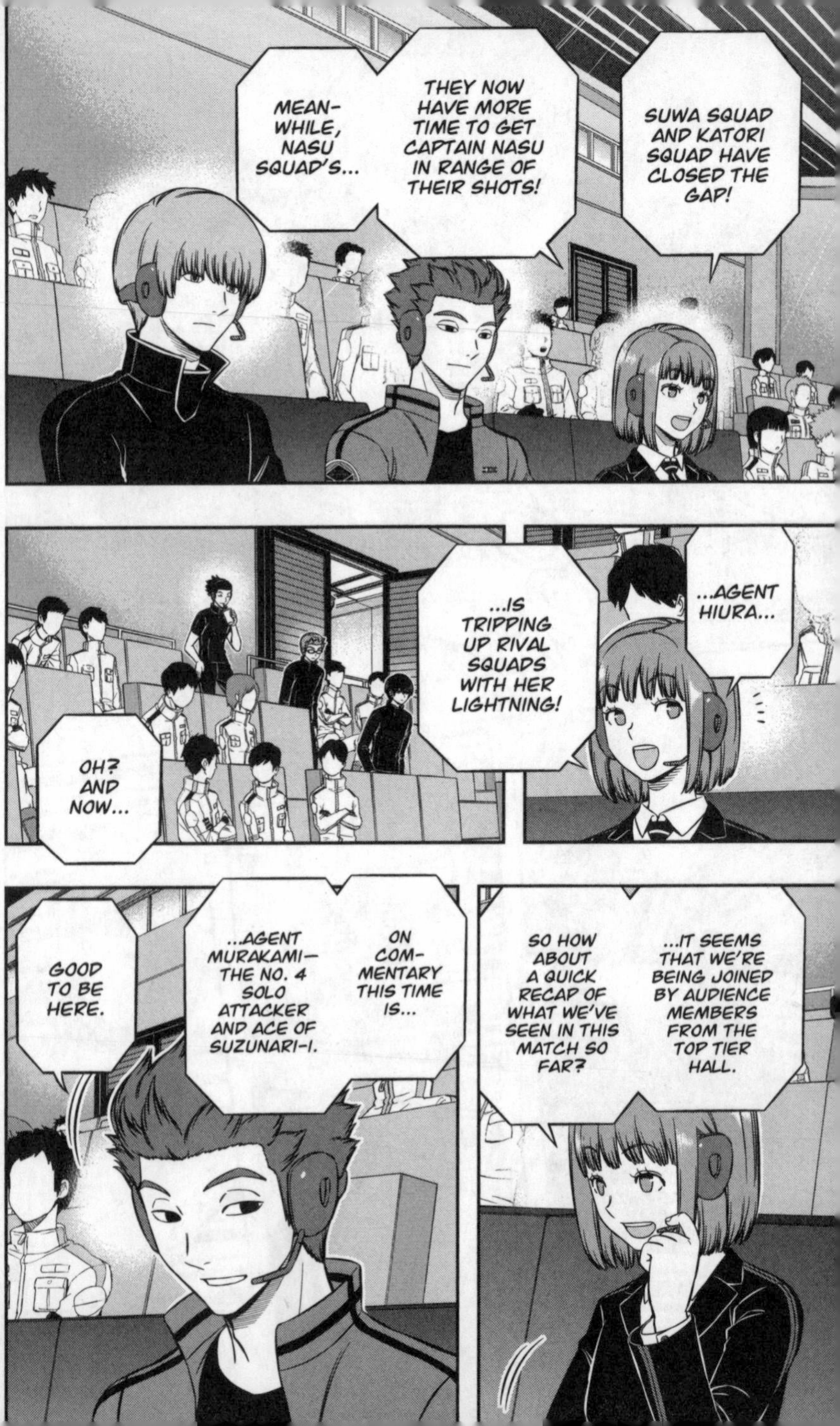
SUWA SQUAD AND KATORI SQUAD HAVE CLOSED THE GAP!
THEY NOW HAVE MORE TIME TO GET CAPTAIN NASU IN RANGE OF THEIR SHOTS!
MEAN-WHILE, NASU SQUAD'S...
...AGENT HIURA...
...IS TRIPPING UP RIVAL SQUADS WITH HER LIGHTNING!
OH? AND NOW...
...IT SEEMS THAT WE'RE BEING JOINED BY AUDIENCE MEMBERS FROM THE TOP TIER HALL.
SO HOW ABOUT A QUICK RECAP OF WHAT WE'VE SEEN IN THIS MATCH SO FAR?
ON COM-MENTARY THIS TIME IS...
...AGENT MURAKAMI— THE NO. 4 SOLO ATTACKER AND ACE OF SUZUNARI-1.
GOOD TO BE HERE.

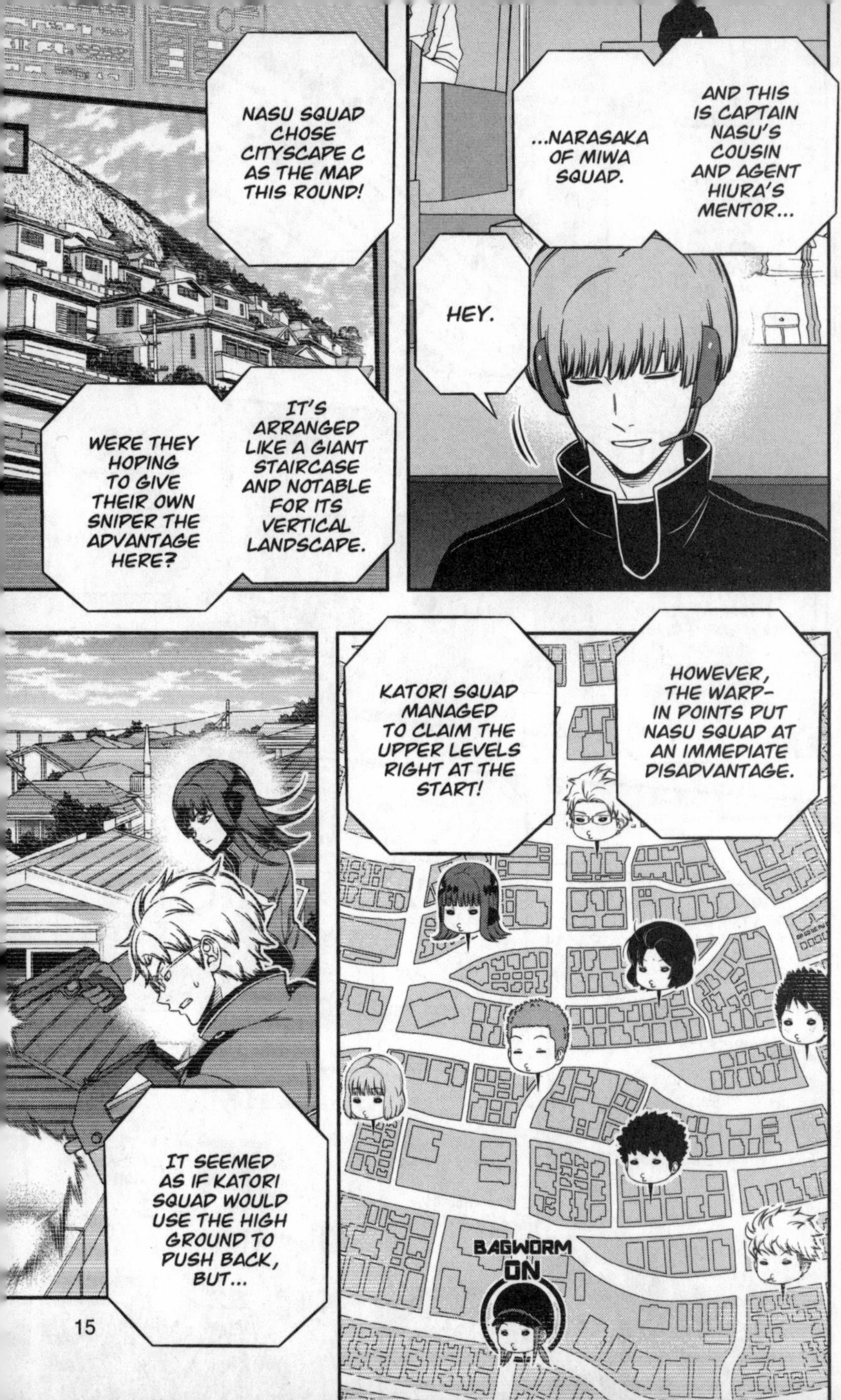
AND THIS IS CAPTAIN NASU'S COUSIN AND AGENT HIURA'S MENTOR...
...NARASAKA OF MIWA SQUAD.
HEY.
NASU SQUAD CHOSE CITYSCAPE C AS THE MAP THIS ROUND!
IT'S ARRANGED LIKE A GIANT STAIRCASE AND NOTABLE FOR ITS VERTICAL LANDSCAPE.
WERE THEY HOPING TO GIVE THEIR OWN SNIPER THE ADVANTAGE HERE?
HOWEVER, THE WARP-IN POINTS PUT NASU SQUAD AT AN IMMEDIATE DISADVANTAGE.
KATORI SQUAD MANAGED TO CLAIM THE UPPER LEVELS RIGHT AT THE START!
BAGWORM ON
IT SEEMED AS IF KATORI SQUAD WOULD USE THE HIGH GROUND TO PUSH BACK, BUT...

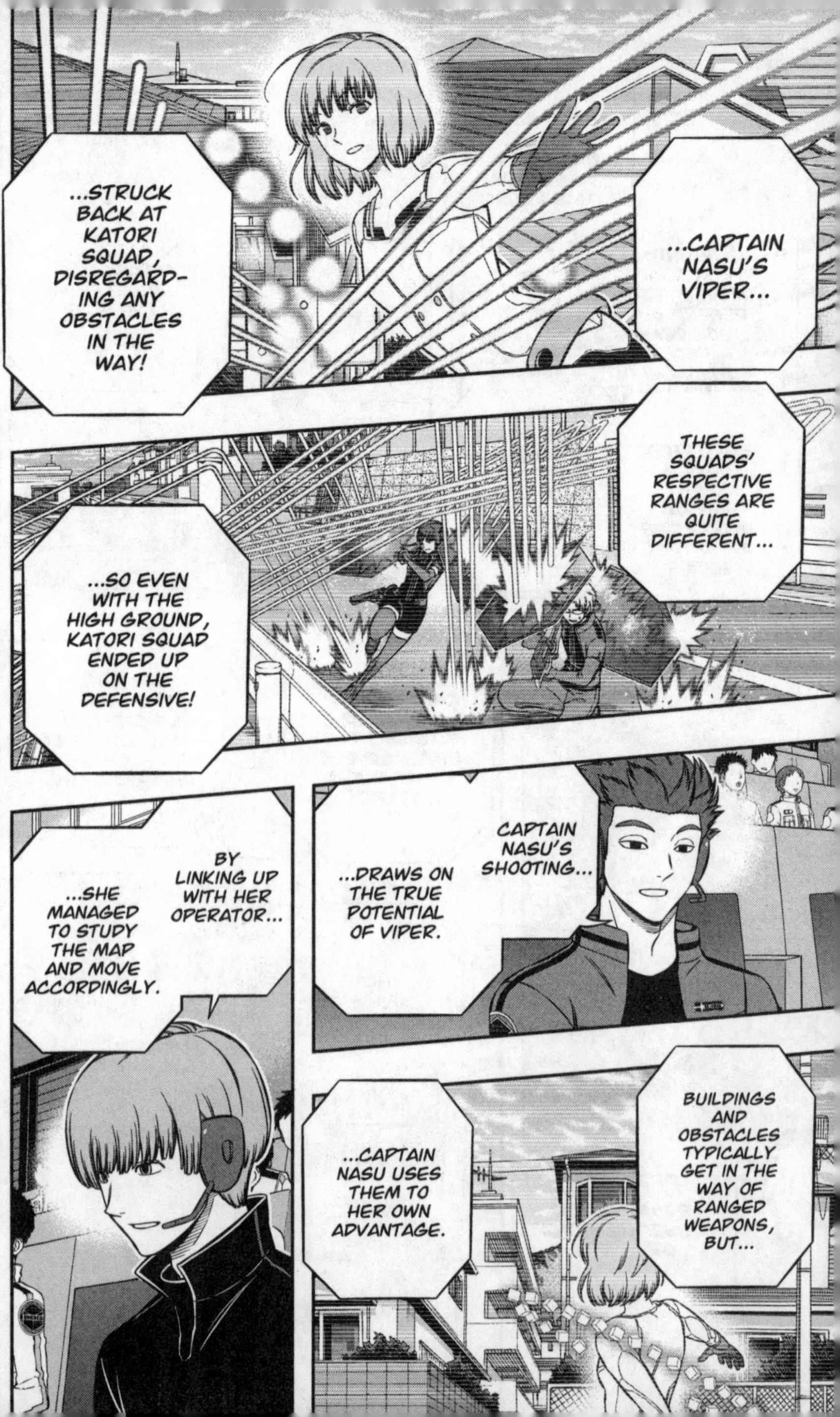
...CAPTAIN NASU'S VIPER...
...STRUCK BACK AT KATORI SQUAD, DISREGARDING ANY OBSTACLES IN THE WAY!
THESE SQUADS' RESPECTIVE RANGES ARE QUITE DIFFERENT...
...SO EVEN WITH THE HIGH GROUND, KATORI SQUAD ENDED UP ON THE DEFENSIVE!
CAPTAIN NASU'S SHOOTING...
...DRAWS ON THE TRUE POTENTIAL OF VIPER.
BUILDINGS AND OBSTACLES TYPICALLY GET IN THE WAY OF RANGED WEAPONS, BUT...
...CAPTAIN NASU USES THEM TO HER OWN ADVANTAGE.
BY LINKING UP WITH HER OPERATOR...
...SHE MANAGED TO STUDY THE MAP AND MOVE ACCORDINGLY.

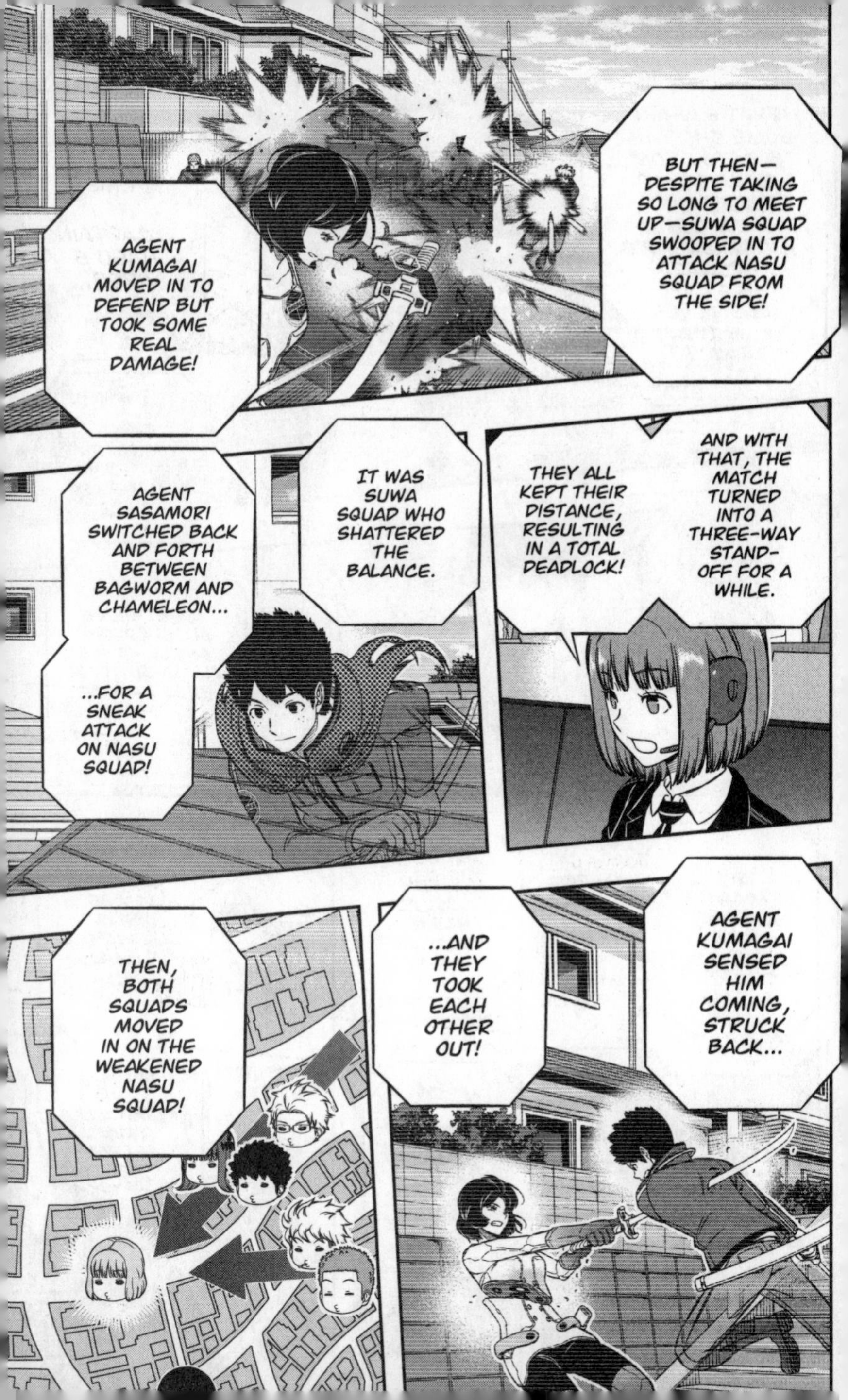
BUT THEN—DESPITE TAKING SO LONG TO MEET UP—SUWA SQUAD SWOOPED IN TO ATTACK NASU SQUAD FROM THE SIDE!
AGENT KUMAGAI MOVED IN TO DEFEND BUT TOOK SOME REAL DAMAGE!
AND WITH THAT, THE MATCH TURNED INTO A THREE-WAY STAND-OFF FOR A WHILE.
THEY ALL KEPT THEIR DISTANCE, RESULTING IN A TOTAL DEADLOCK!
IT WAS SUWA SQUAD WHO SHATTERED THE BALANCE.
AGENT SASAMORI SWITCHED BACK AND FORTH BETWEEN BAGWORM AND CHAMELEON...
...FOR A SNEAK ATTACK ON NASU SQUAD!
AGENT KUMAGAI SENSED HIM COMING, STRUCK BACK...
...AND THEY TOOK EACH OTHER OUT!
THEN, BOTH SQUADS MOVED IN ON THE WEAKENED NASU SQUAD!

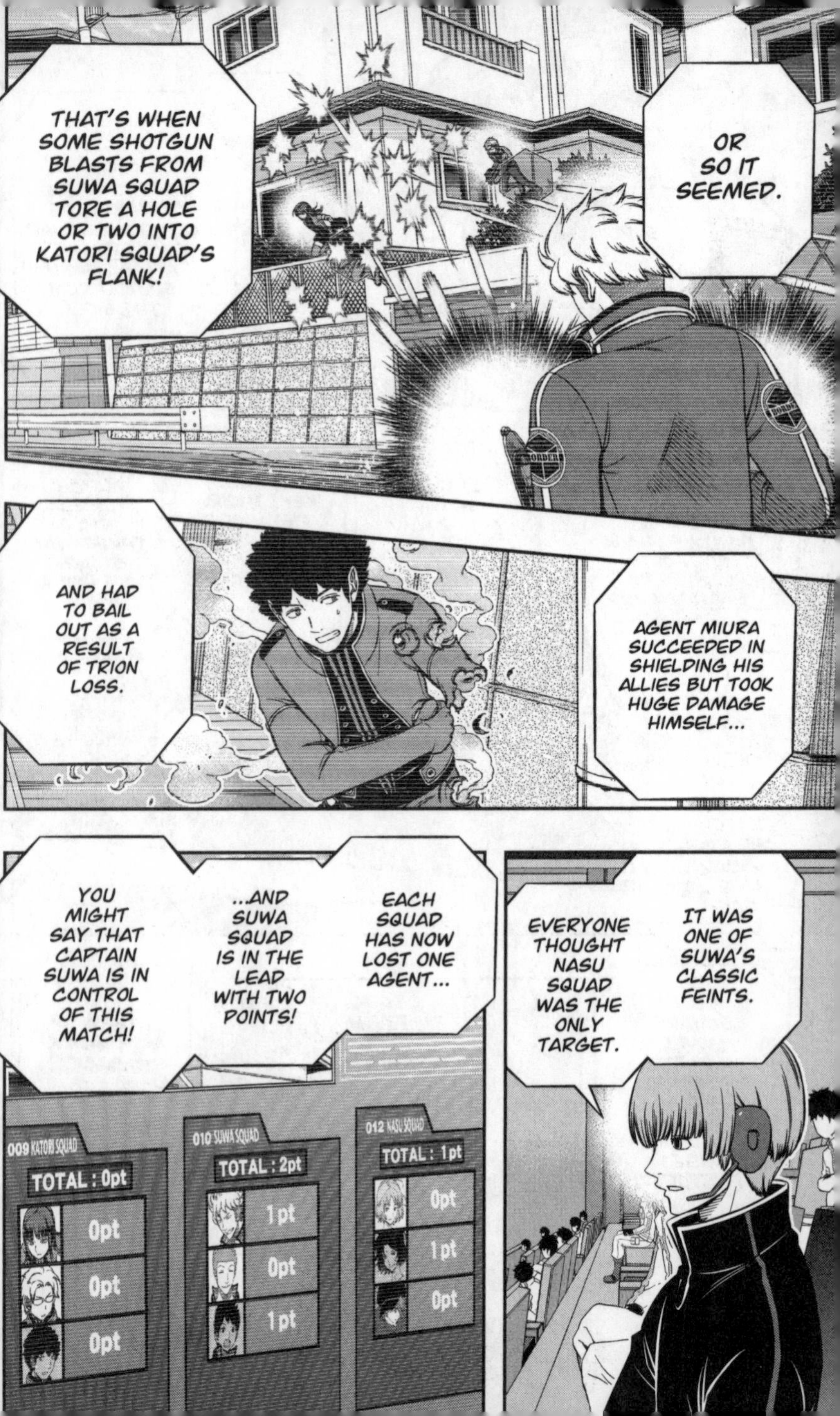
OR SO IT SEEMED.
THAT'S WHEN SOME SHOTGUN BLASTS FROM SUWA SQUAD TORE A HOLE OR TWO INTO KATORI SQUAD'S FLANK!
AGENT MIURA SUCCEEDED IN SHIELDING HIS ALLIES BUT TOOK HUGE DAMAGE HIMSELF...
AND HAD TO BAIL OUT AS A RESULT OF TRION LOSS.
IT WAS ONE OF SUWA'S CLASSIC FEINTS.
EVERYONE THOUGHT NASU SQUAD WAS THE ONLY TARGET.
EACH SQUAD HAS NOW LOST ONE AGENT...
...AND SUWA SQUAD IS IN THE LEAD WITH TWO POINTS!
YOU MIGHT SAY THAT CAPTAIN SUWA IS IN CONTROL OF THIS MATCH!
012 NASU SQUAD
TOTAL : 1pt
0pt
1pt
0pt
010 SUWA SQUAD
TOTAL : 2pt
1pt
0pt
1pt
009 KATORI SQUAD
TOTAL : 0pt
0pt
0pt
0pt

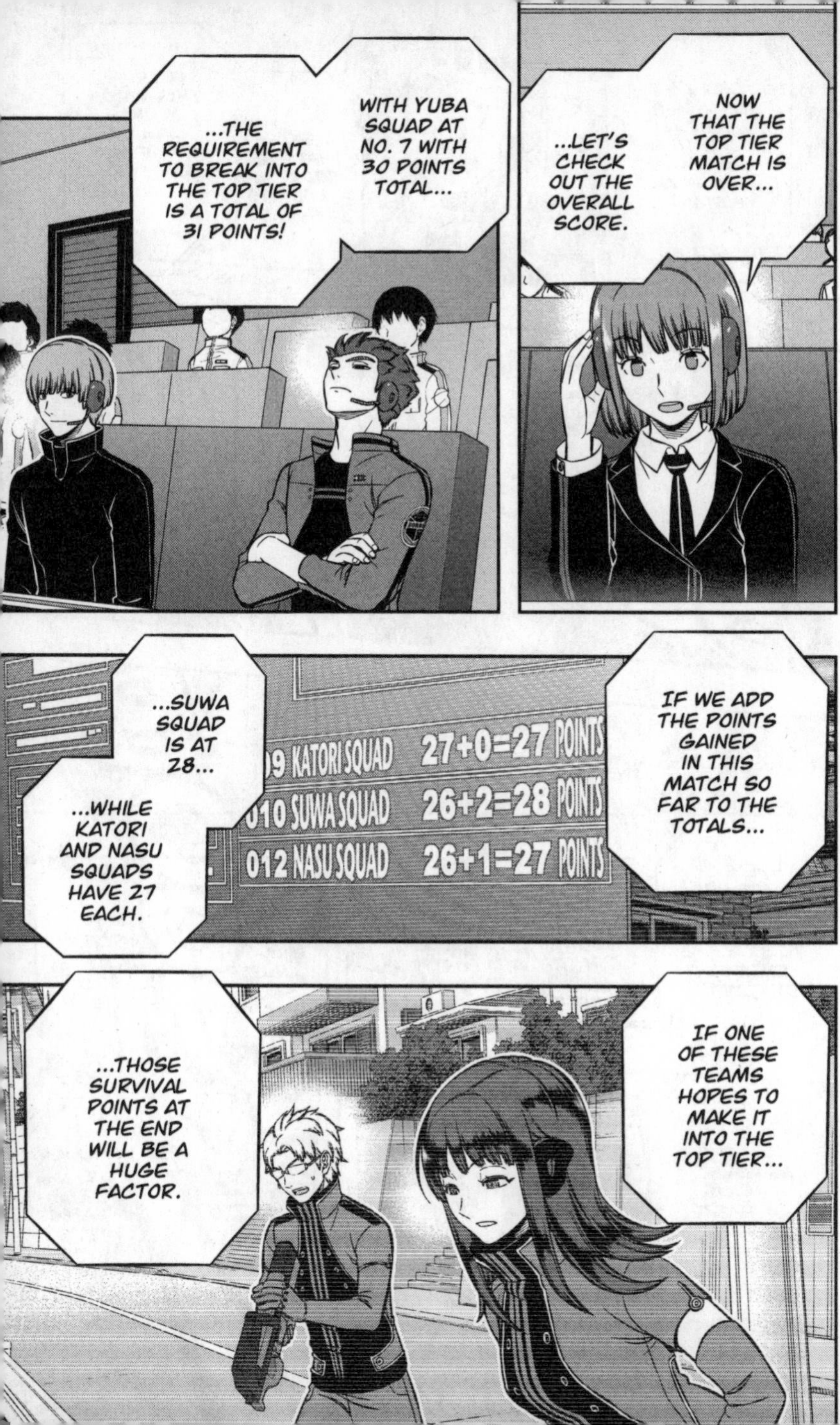
NOW THAT THE TOP TIER MATCH IS OVER...
...LET'S CHECK OUT THE OVERALL SCORE.
WITH YUBA SQUAD AT NO. 7 WITH 30 POINTS TOTAL...
...THE REQUIREMENT TO BREAK INTO THE TOP TIER IS A TOTAL OF 31 POINTS!
IF WE ADD THE POINTS GAINED IN THIS MATCH SO FAR TO THE TOTALS...
09 KATORI SQUAD 27+0=27 POINTS
010 SUWA SQUAD 26+2=28 POINTS
012 NASU SQUAD 26+1=27 POINTS
...SUWA SQUAD IS AT 28...
...WHILE KATORI AND NASU SQUADS HAVE 27 EACH.
IF ONE OF THESE TEAMS HOPES TO MAKE IT INTO THE TOP TIER...
...THOSE SURVIVAL POINTS AT THE END WILL BE A HUGE FACTOR.

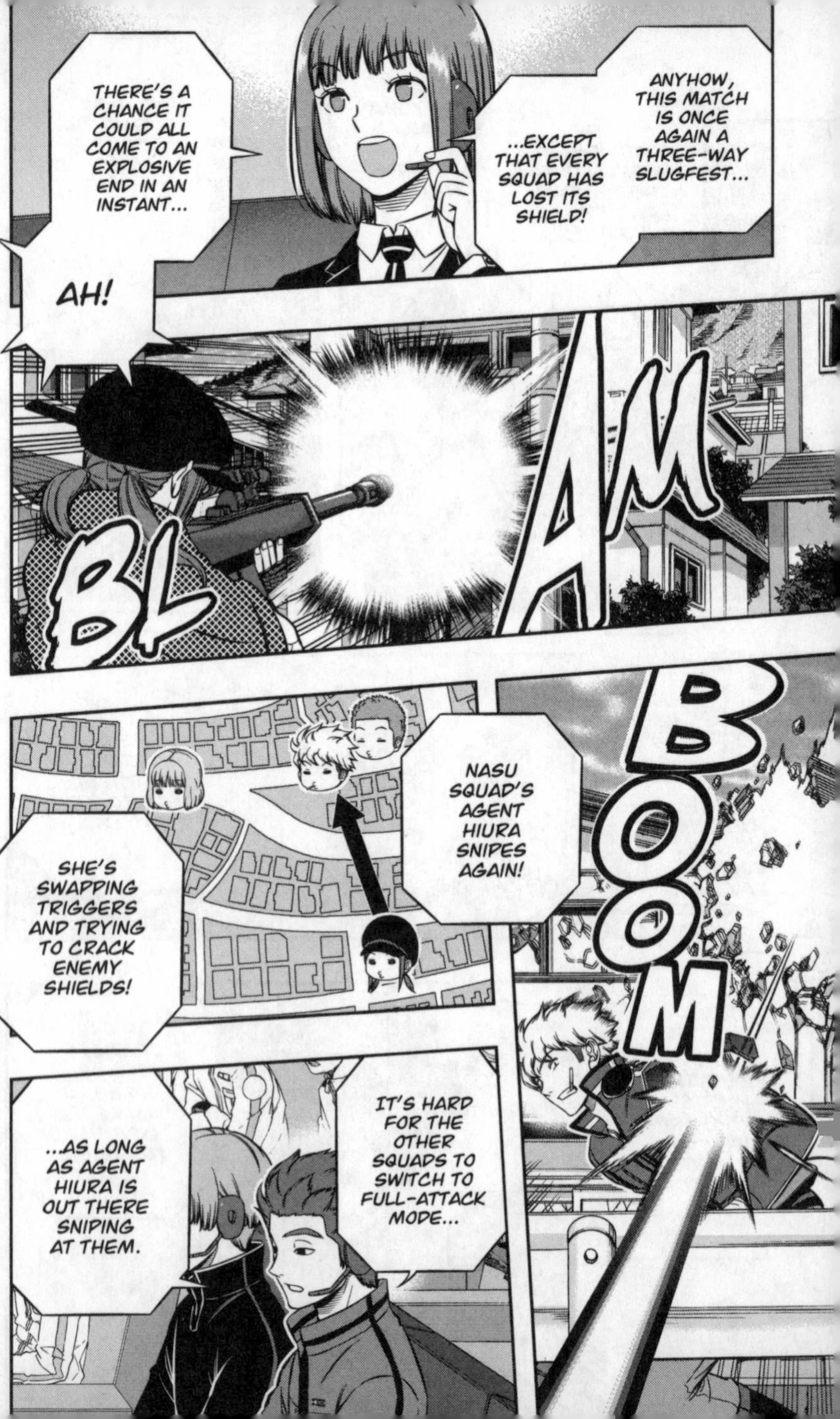
ANYHOW, THIS MATCH IS ONCE AGAIN A THREE-WAY SLUGFEST...
...EXCEPT THAT EVERY SQUAD HAS LOST ITS SHIELD!
THERE'S A CHANCE IT COULD ALL COME TO AN EXPLOSIVE END IN AN INSTANT...
AH!
BLAM
BOOM
NASU SQUAD'S AGENT HIURA SNIPES AGAIN!
SHE'S SWAPPING TRIGGERS AND TRYING TO CRACK ENEMY SHIELDS!
IT'S HARD FOR THE OTHER SQUADS TO SWITCH TO FULL-ATTACK MODE...
...AS LONG AS AGENT HIURA IS OUT THERE SNIPING AT THEM.

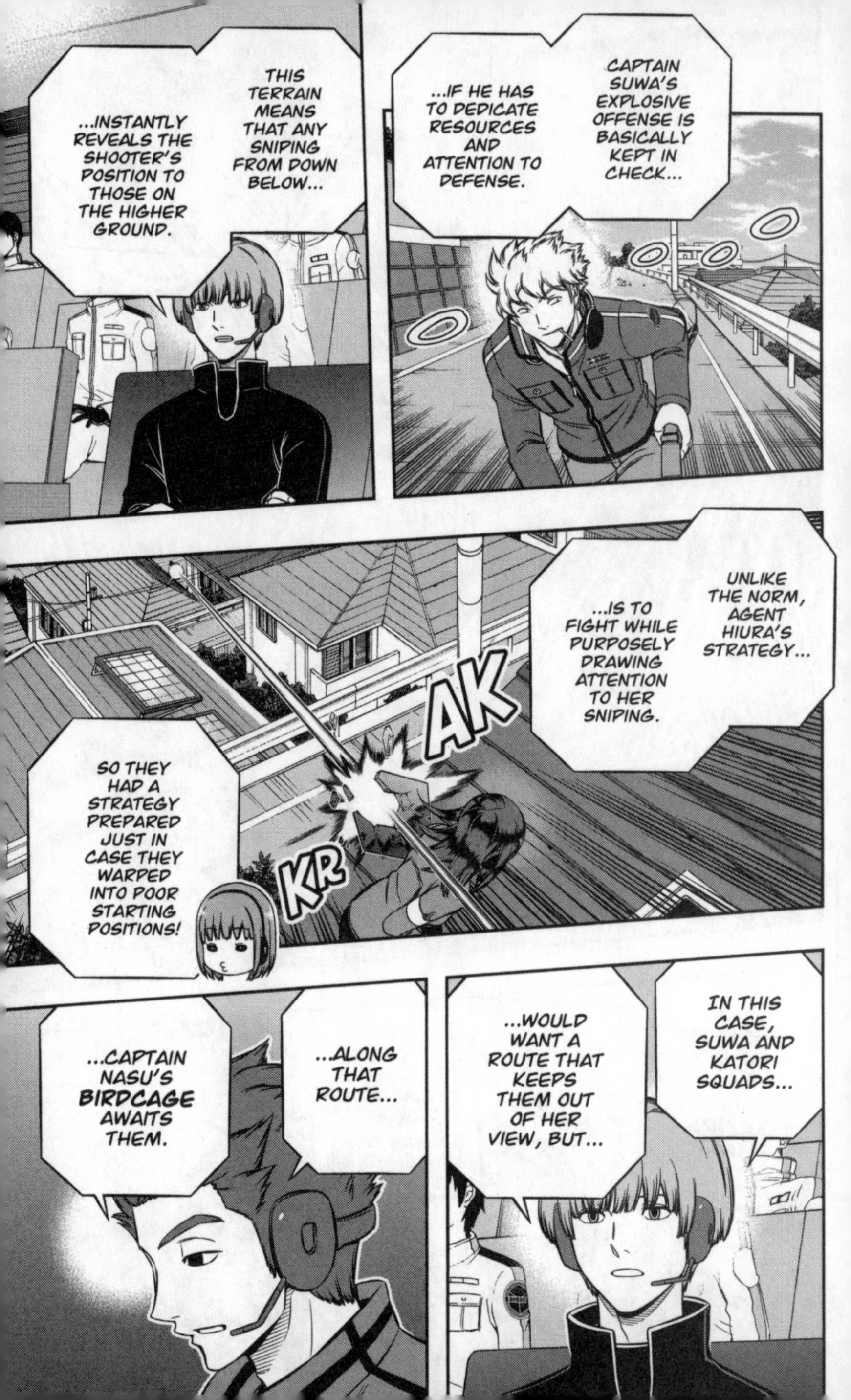
CAPTAIN SUWA'S EXPLOSIVE OFFENSE IS BASICALLY KEPT IN CHECK...
...IF HE HAS TO DEDICATE RESOURCES AND ATTENTION TO DEFENSE.
THIS TERRAIN MEANS THAT ANY SNIPING FROM DOWN BELOW...
...INSTANTLY REVEALS THE SHOOTER'S POSITION TO THOSE ON THE HIGHER GROUND.
UNLIKE THE NORM, AGENT HIURA'S STRATEGY...
...IS TO FIGHT WHILE PURPOSELY DRAWING ATTENTION TO HER SNIPING.
AK
KR
SO THEY HAD A STRATEGY PREPARED JUST IN CASE THEY WARPED INTO POOR STARTING POSITIONS!
IN THIS CASE, SUWA AND KATORI SQUADS...
...WOULD WANT A ROUTE THAT KEEPS THEM OUT OF HER VIEW, BUT...
...ALONG THAT ROUTE...
...CAPTAIN NASU'S BIRDCAGE AWAITS THEM.

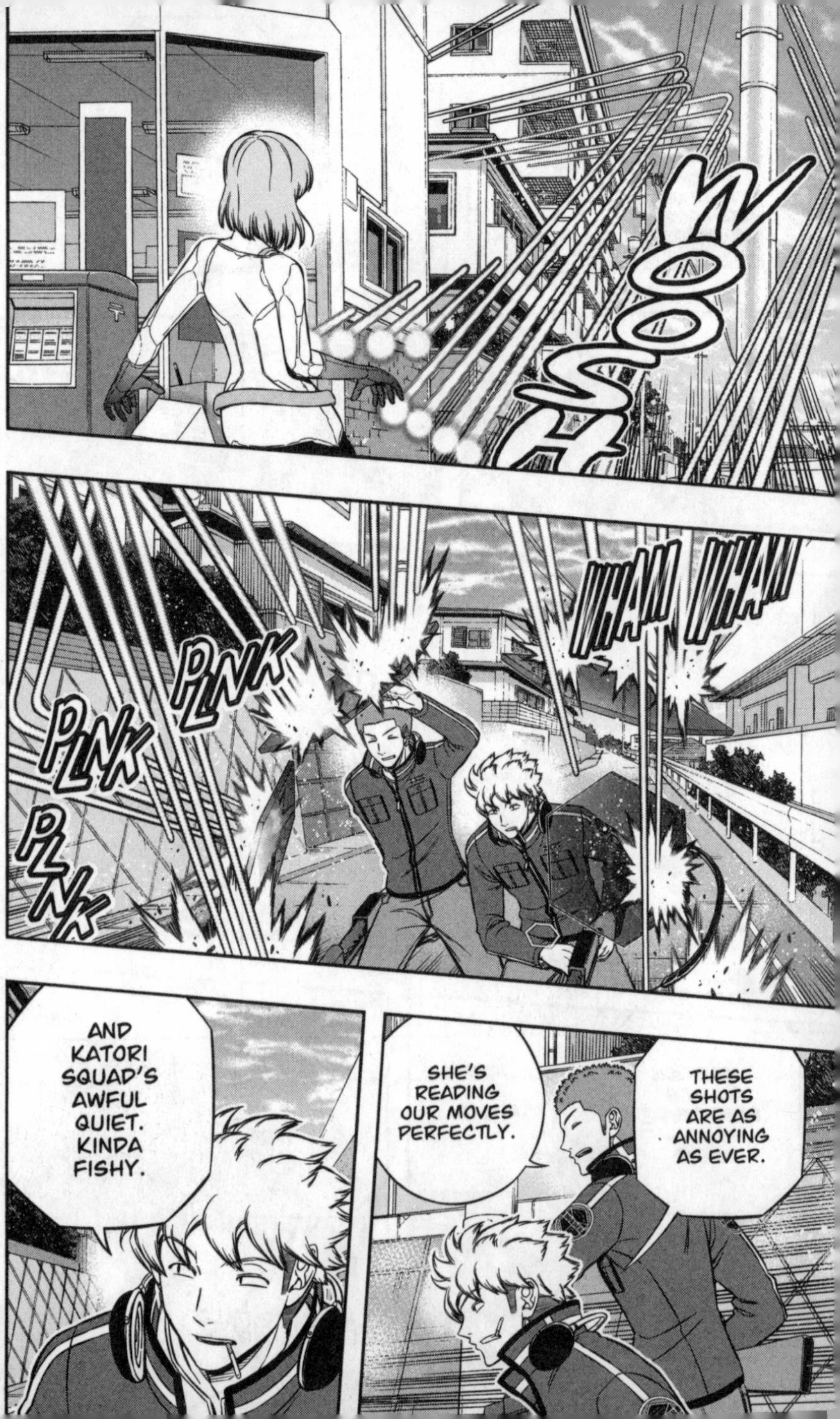
WOOOSH
WHAM WHAM
PLNK
PLNK
PLNK
THESE SHOTS ARE AS ANNOYING AS EVER.
SHE'S READING OUR MOVES PERFECTLY.
AND KATORI SQUAD'S AWFUL QUIET. KINDA FISHY.

THEY DO SEEM UN-MOTIVATED.

ARE THEY NOT FEELING IT TODAY?

YEAH, IT'S LIKE KATORI'S GOT NO PRESENCE AT ALL.

OR IS THAT WHAT SUWA SQUAD WANTS?

PERSONALLY, I'D JUST CHARGE IN WITH A SHIELD UP.

HANG ON.

LET'S NOT BE HASTY!

WE CAN'T GET NEAR NASU SQUAD, BUT...

...WHAT DO YOU THINK, ROKURO?

SURE.

HANA, CAN YOU BRING UP THE 3D MAP OF THE AREA?

HOW MANY TIMES'RE YOU GONNA CHECK THE MAP?

	POINTS	SURVIVAL	TOTAL
KATORI SQUAD	4		4
SUWA SQUAD	2	2	4
KAKIZAKI SQUAD	3		3

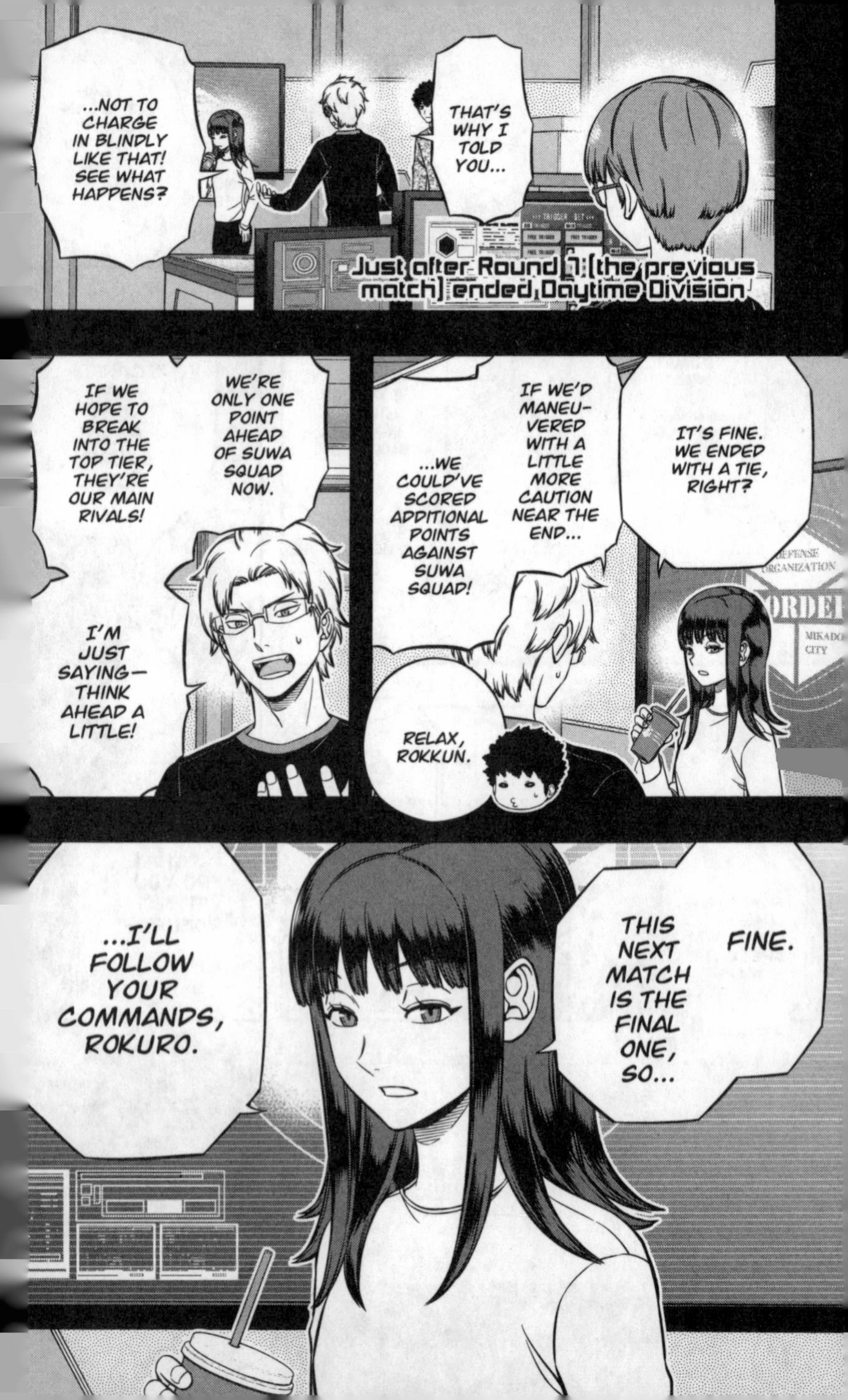
THAT'S WHY I TOLD YOU...
...NOT TO CHARGE IN BLINDLY LIKE THAT! SEE WHAT HAPPENS?
Just after Round 1 (the previous match) ended Daytime Division
IT'S FINE. WE ENDED WITH A TIE, RIGHT?
MIKADO CITY
IF WE'D MANEUVERED WITH A LITTLE MORE CAUTION NEAR THE END...
...WE COULD'VE SCORED ADDITIONAL POINTS AGAINST SUWA SQUAD!
RELAX, ROKKUN.
WE'RE ONLY ONE POINT AHEAD OF SUWA SQUAD NOW.
IF WE HOPE TO BREAK INTO THE TOP TIER, THEY'RE OUR MAIN RIVALS!
I'M JUST SAYING—THINK AHEAD A LITTLE!
FINE.
THIS NEXT MATCH IS THE FINAL ONE, SO...
...I'LL FOLLOW YOUR COMMANDS, ROKURO.

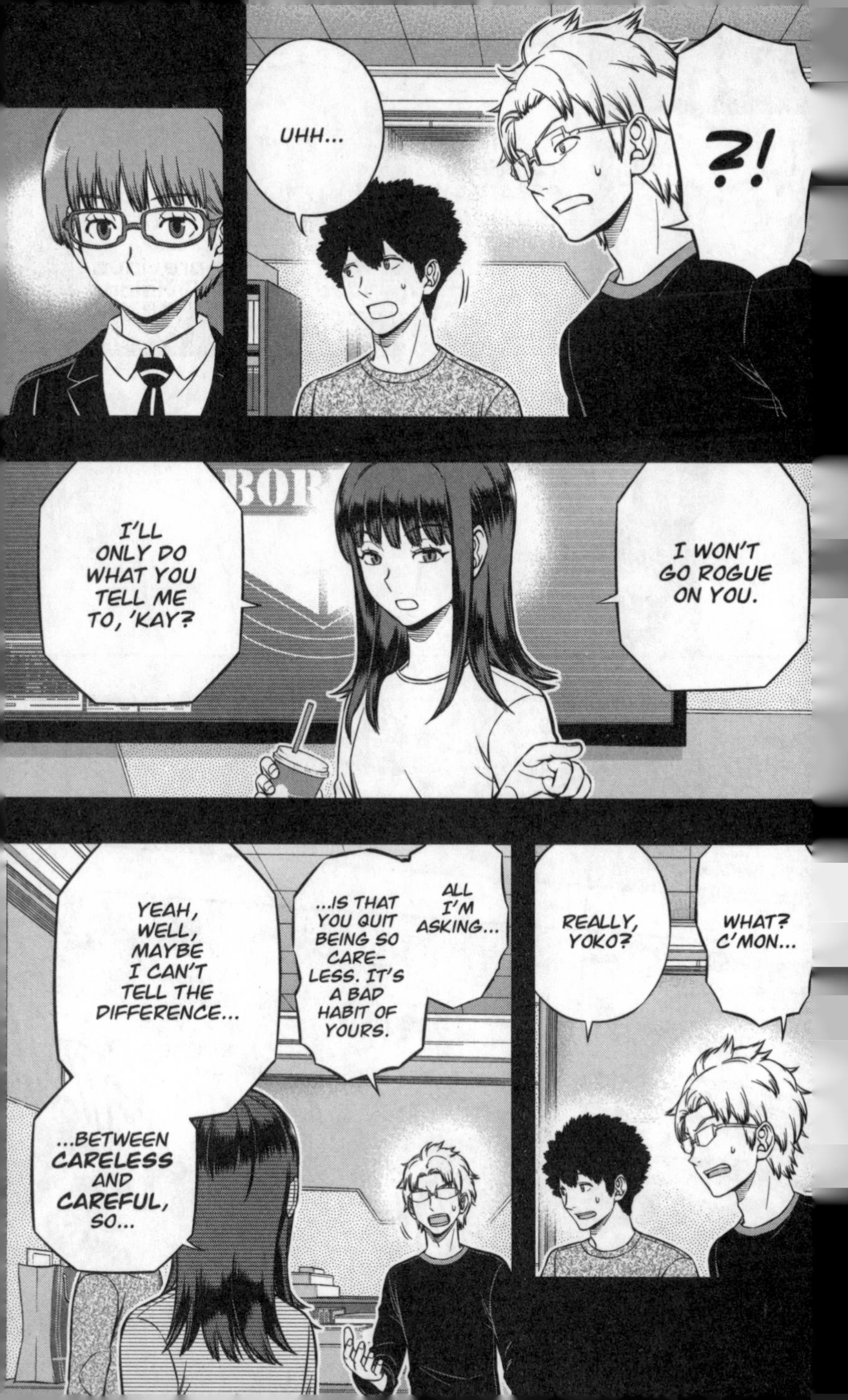
?!
UHH...
I WON'T GO ROGUE ON YOU.
I'LL ONLY DO WHAT YOU TELL ME TO, 'KAY?
WHAT? C'MON...
REALLY, YOKO?
ALL I'M ASKING...
...IS THAT YOU QUIT BEING SO CARE-LESS. IT'S A BAD HABIT OF YOURS.
YEAH, WELL, MAYBE I CAN'T TELL THE DIFFERENCE...
...BETWEEN CARELESS AND CAREFUL, SO...

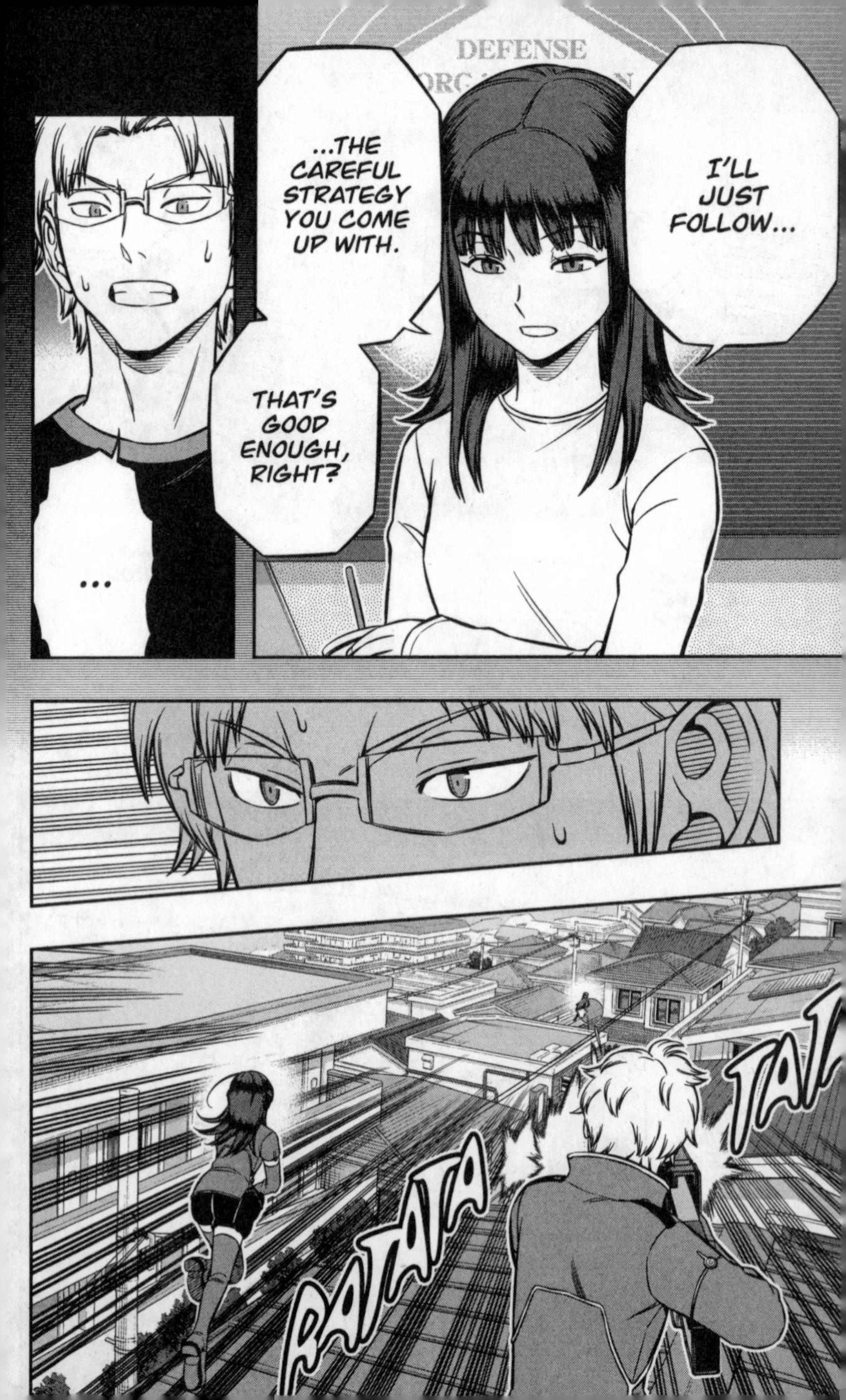
DEFENSE
I'LL JUST FOLLOW...
...THE CAREFUL STRATEGY YOU COME UP WITH.
THAT'S GOOD ENOUGH, RIGHT?
...
TAT
RATATA

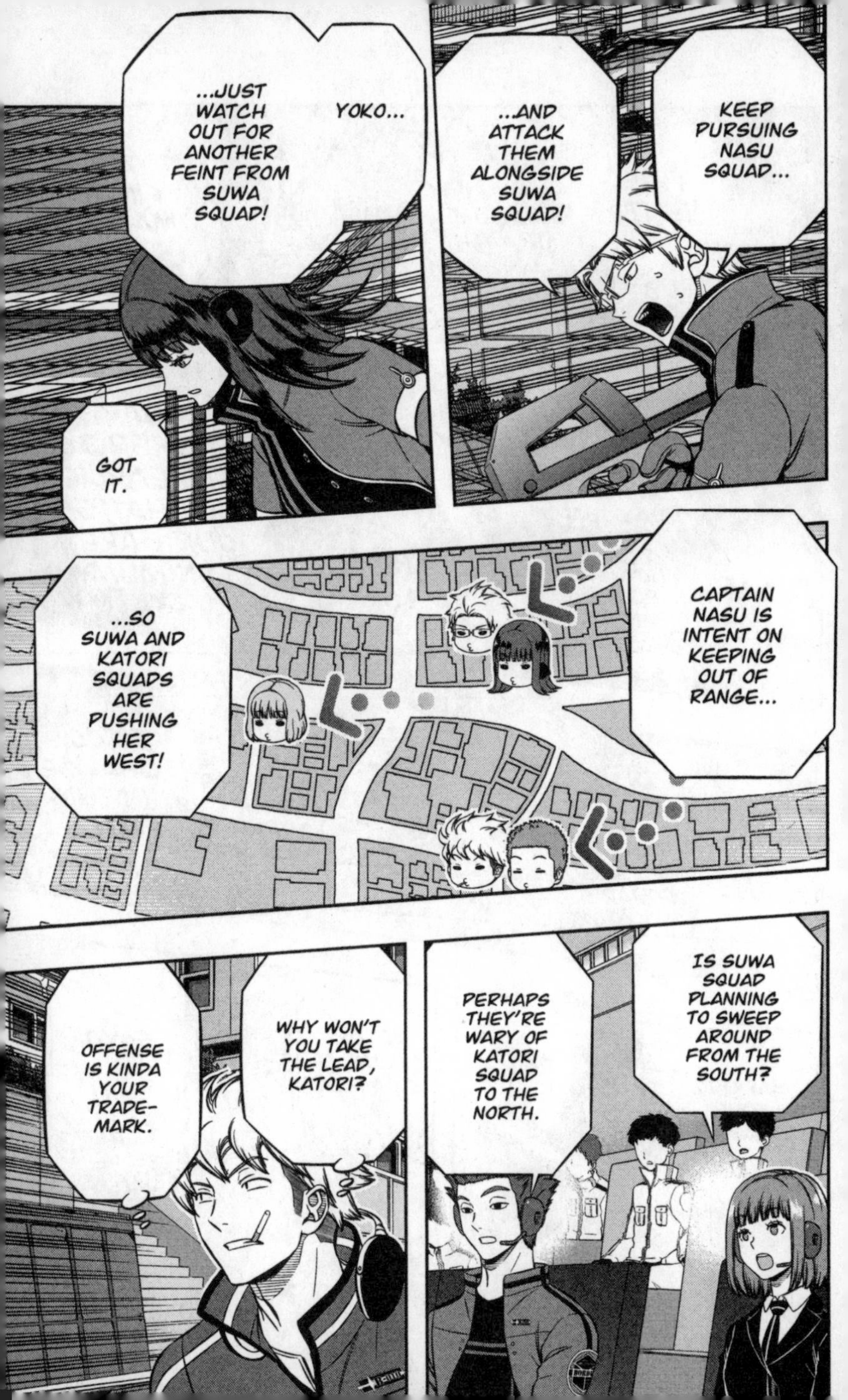
KEEP PURSUING NASU SQUAD...
...AND ATTACK THEM ALONGSIDE SUWA SQUAD!
YOKO...
...JUST WATCH OUT FOR ANOTHER FEINT FROM SUWA SQUAD!
GOT IT.
CAPTAIN NASU IS INTENT ON KEEPING OUT OF RANGE...
...SO SUWA AND KATORI SQUADS ARE PUSHING HER WEST!
IS SUWA SQUAD PLANNING TO SWEEP AROUND FROM THE SOUTH?
PERHAPS THEY'RE WARY OF KATORI SQUAD TO THE NORTH.
WHY WON'T YOU TAKE THE LEAD, KATORI?
OFFENSE IS KINDA YOUR TRADE-MARK.

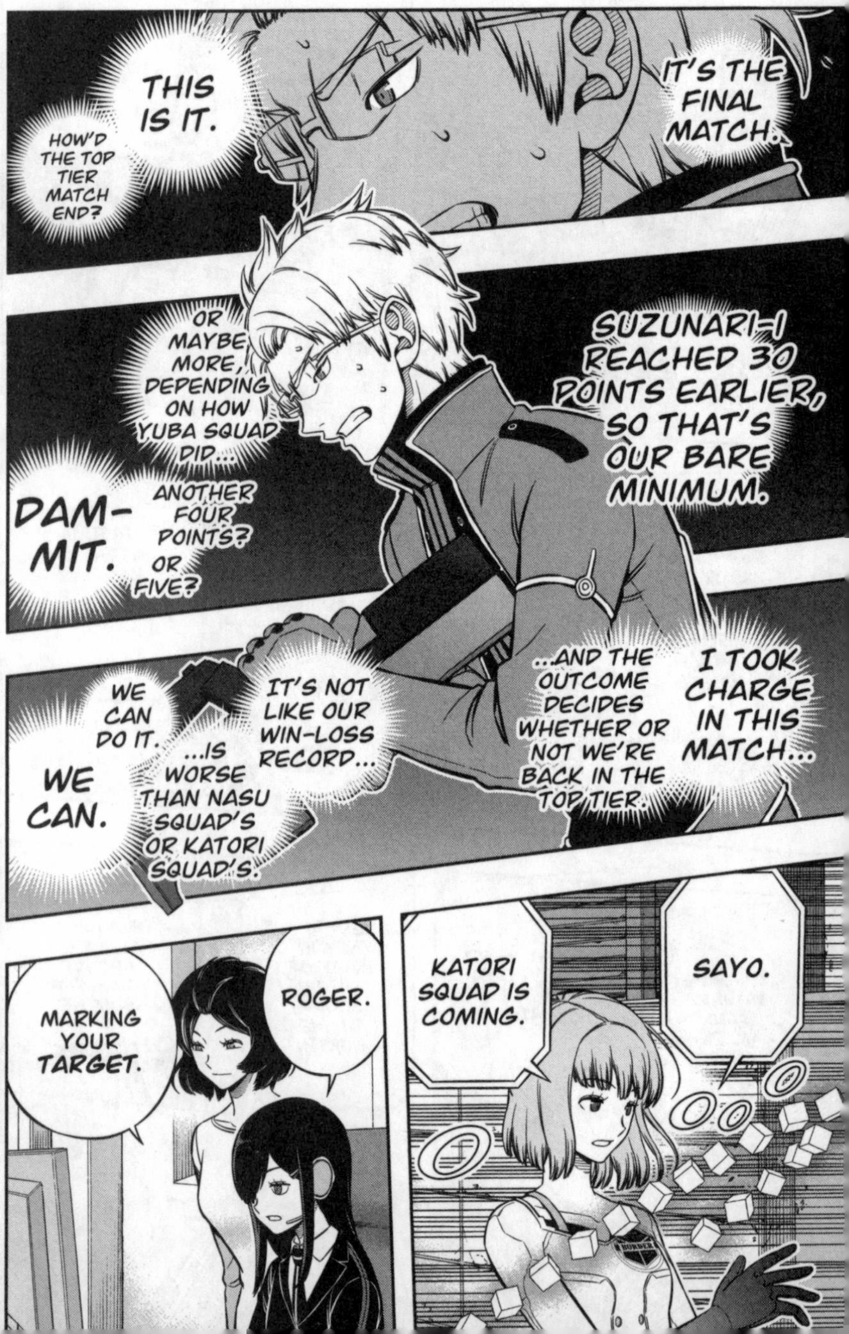
IT'S THE FINAL MATCH.
THIS IS IT.
HOW'D THE TOP TIER MATCH END?
SUZUNARI-1 REACHED 30 POINTS EARLIER, SO THAT'S OUR BARE MINIMUM.
OR MAYBE MORE, DEPENDING ON HOW YUBA SQUAD DID...
ANOTHER FOUR POINTS? OR FIVE?
DAM-MIT.
I TOOK CHARGE IN THIS MATCH...
...AND THE OUTCOME DECIDES WHETHER OR NOT WE'RE BACK IN THE TOP TIER.
IT'S NOT LIKE OUR WIN-LOSS RECORD...
...IS WORSE THAN NASU SQUAD'S OR KATORI SQUAD'S.
WE CAN DO IT.
WE CAN.
SAYO.
KATORI SQUAD IS COMING.
ROGER.
MARKING YOUR TARGET.

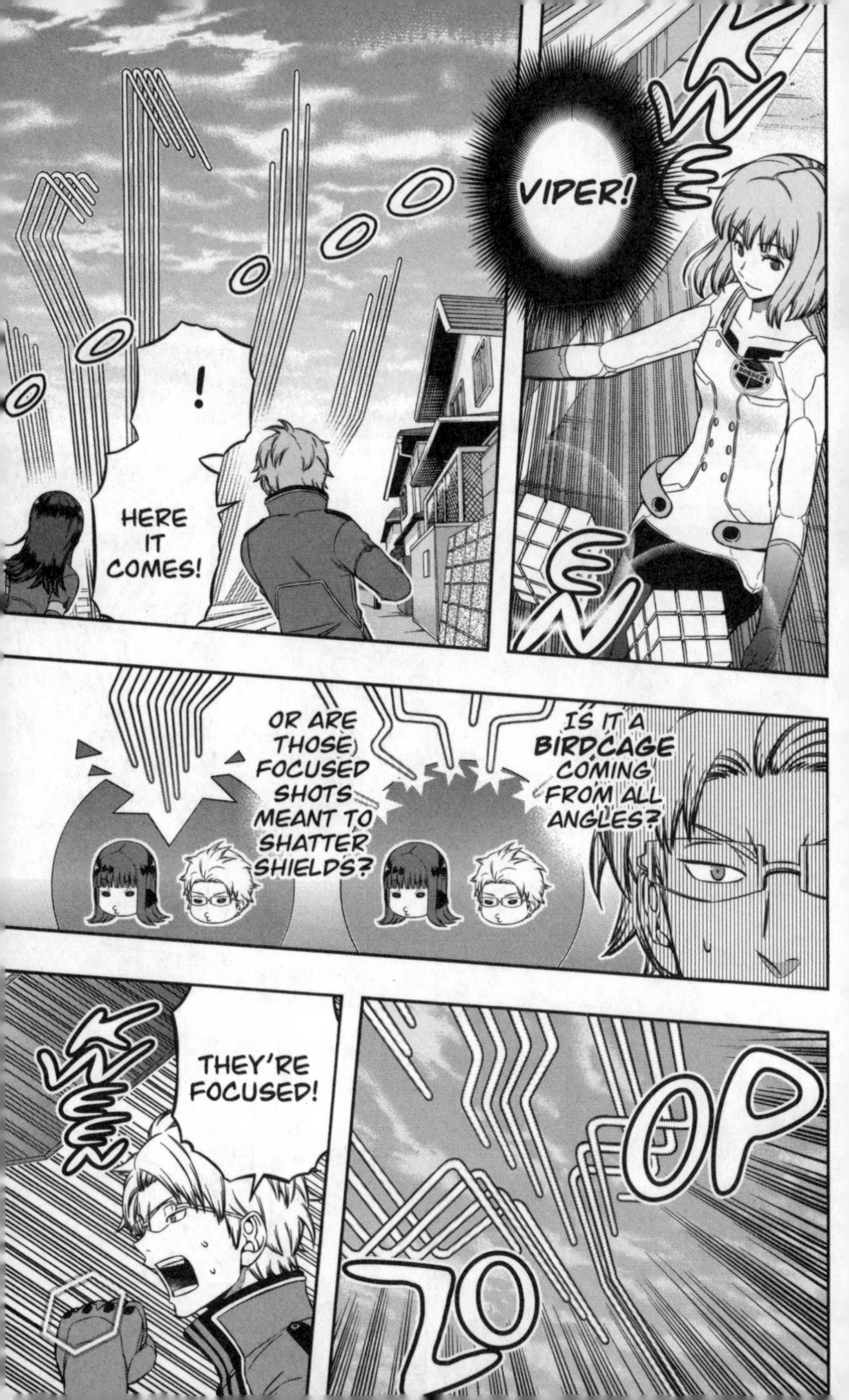
VIPER!
HERE IT COMES!
IS IT A BIRDCAGE COMING FROM ALL ANGLES?
OR ARE THOSE FOCUSED SHOTS MEANT TO SHATTER SHIELDS?
THEY'RE FOCUSED!

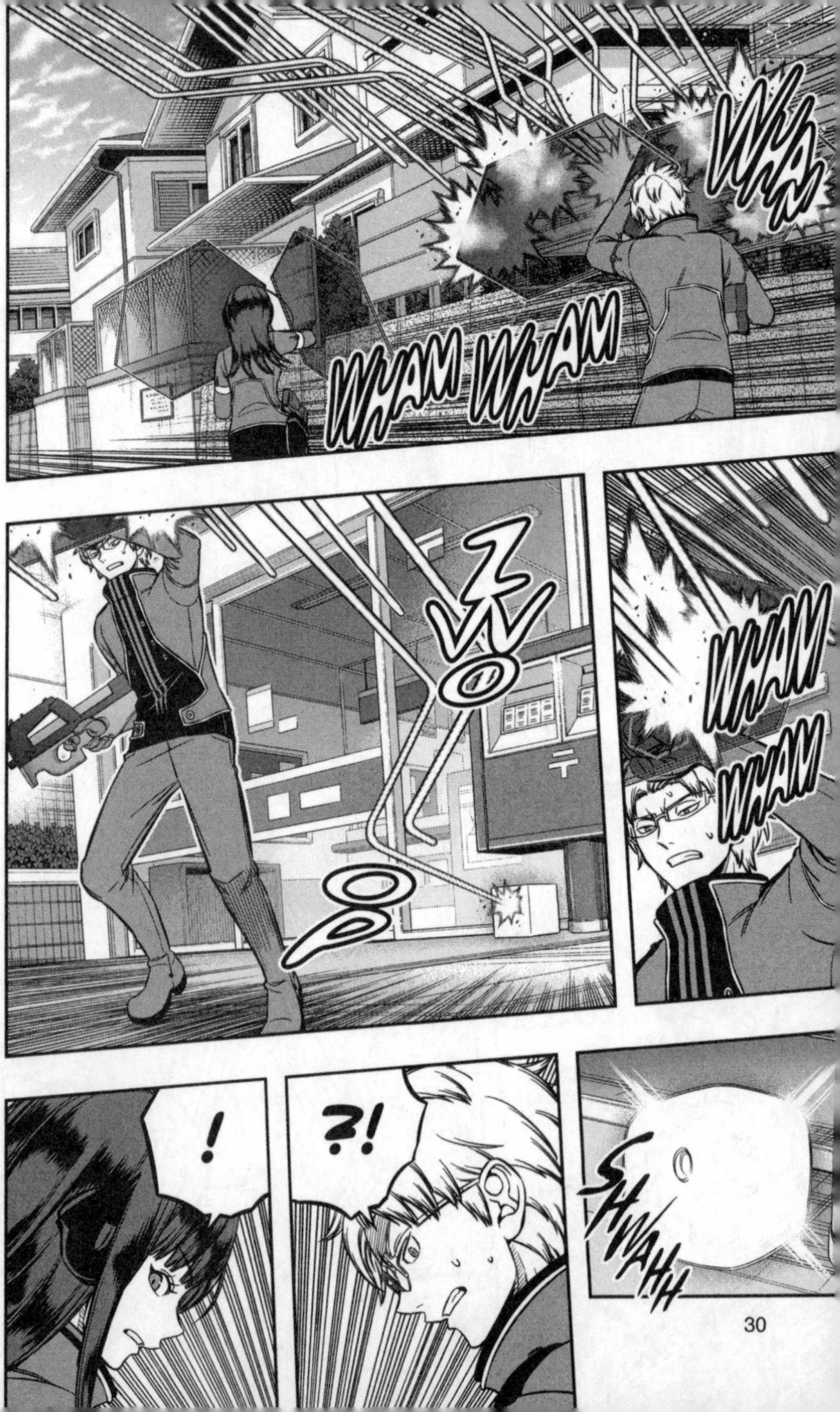
WHAM
WHAM WHAM
WHAM
WHAM
ZWOOO
SHWAHH
?!
!

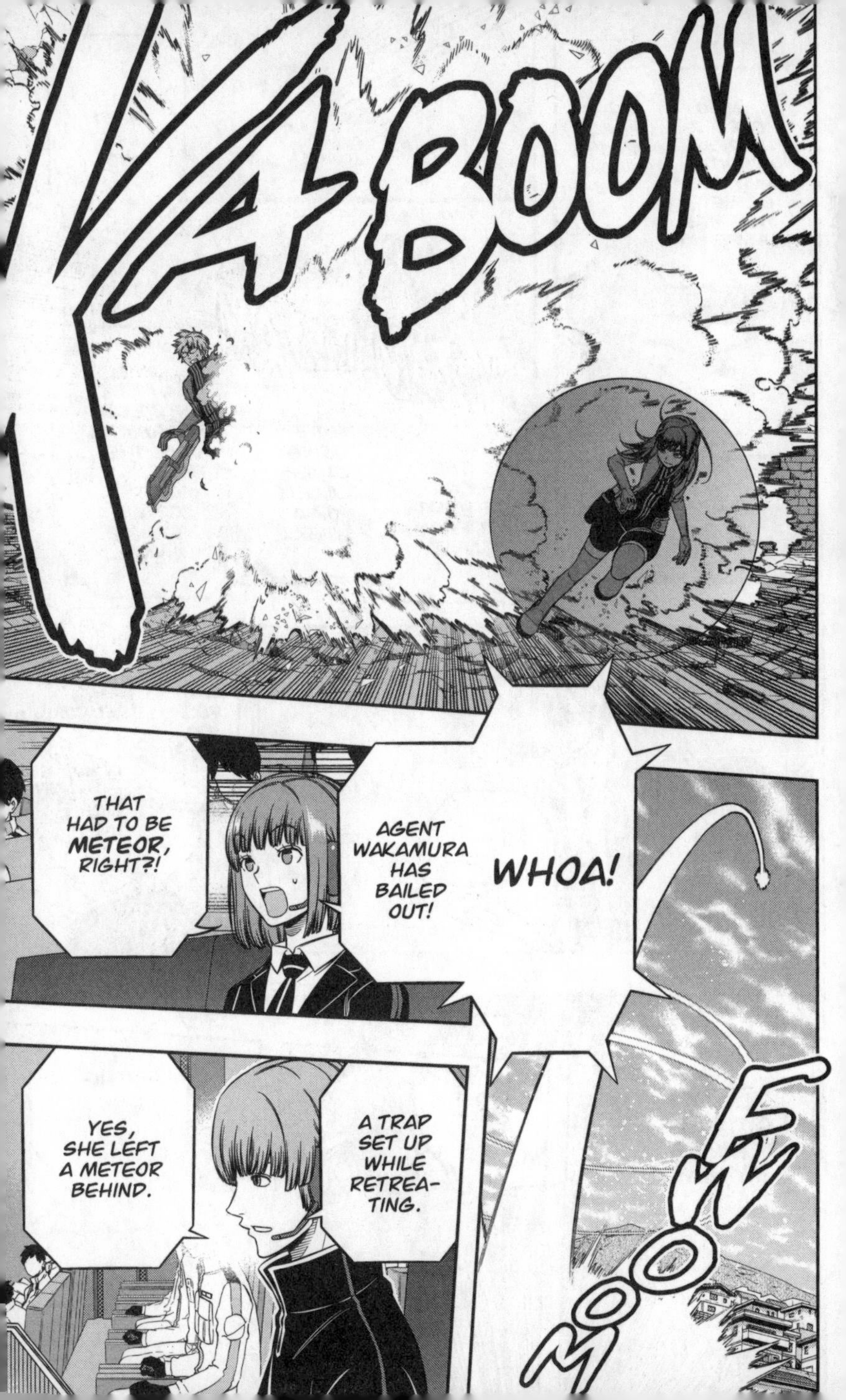
KABOOM
WHOA!
FWOOM
AGENT WAKAMURA HAS BAILED OUT!
THAT HAD TO BE METEOR, RIGHT?!
A TRAP SET UP WHILE RETREA-TING.
YES, SHE LEFT A METEOR BEHIND.

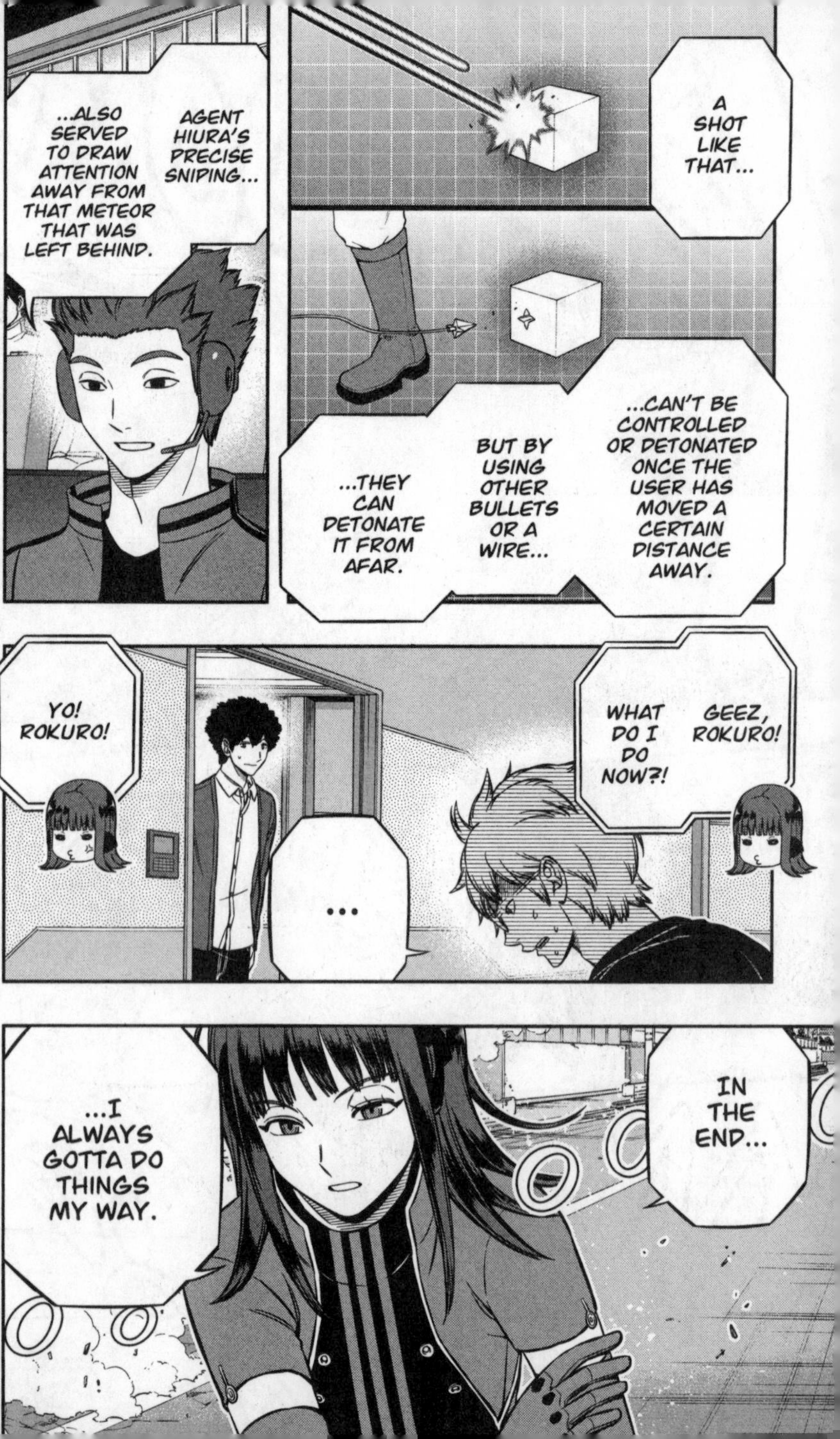
A SHOT LIKE THAT...
...CAN'T BE CONTROLLED OR DETONATED ONCE THE USER HAS MOVED A CERTAIN DISTANCE AWAY.
BUT BY USING OTHER BULLETS OR A WIRE...
...THEY CAN DETONATE IT FROM AFAR.
AGENT HIURA'S PRECISE SNIPING...
...ALSO SERVED TO DRAW ATTENTION AWAY FROM THAT METEOR THAT WAS LEFT BEHIND.
GEEZ, ROKURO!
WHAT DO I DO NOW?!
...
YO! ROKURO!
IN THE END...
...I ALWAYS GOTTA DO THINGS MY WAY.

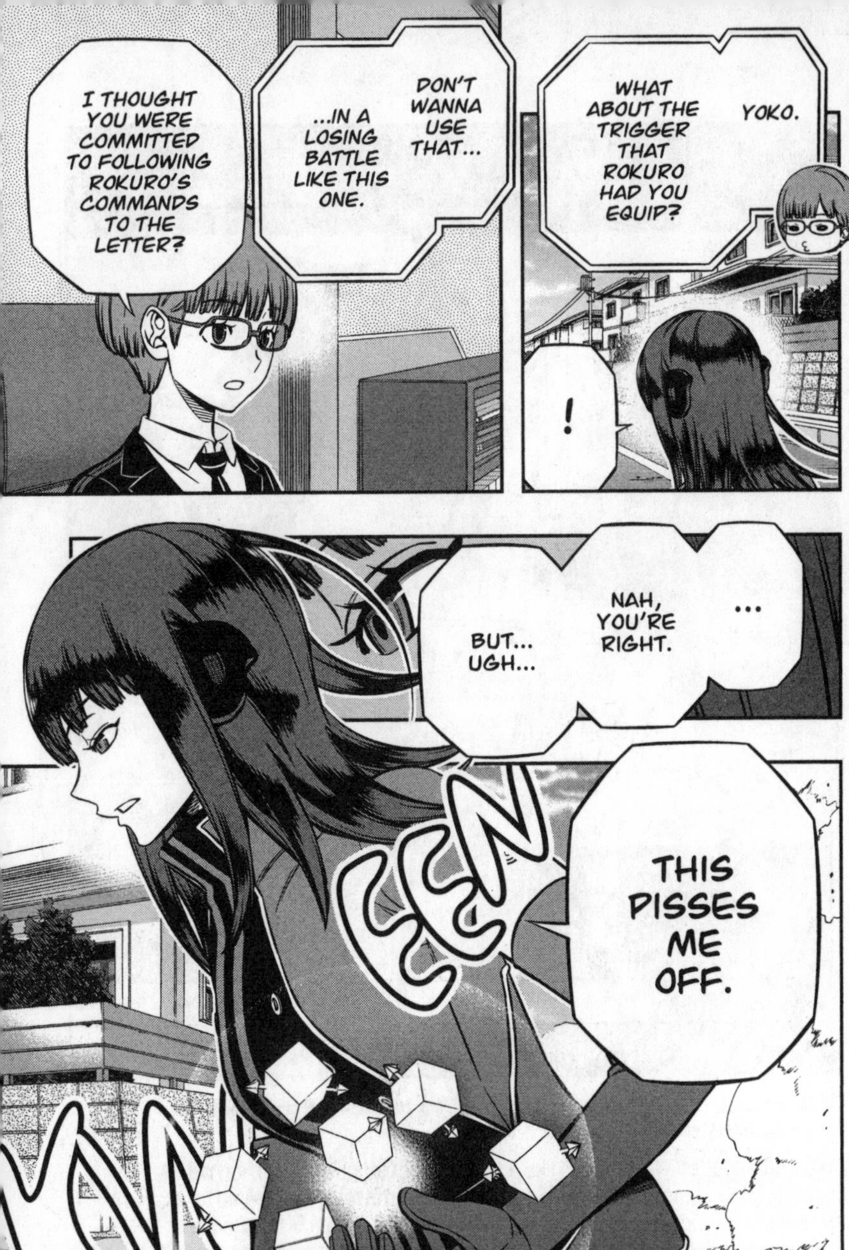
YOKO.
WHAT ABOUT THE TRIGGER THAT ROKURO HAD YOU EQUIP?
!
DON'T WANNA USE THAT...
...IN A LOSING BATTLE LIKE THIS ONE.
I THOUGHT YOU WERE COMMITTED TO FOLLOWING ROKURO'S COMMANDS TO THE LETTER?
...
NAH, YOU'RE RIGHT.
BUT... UGH...
THIS PISSES ME OFF.

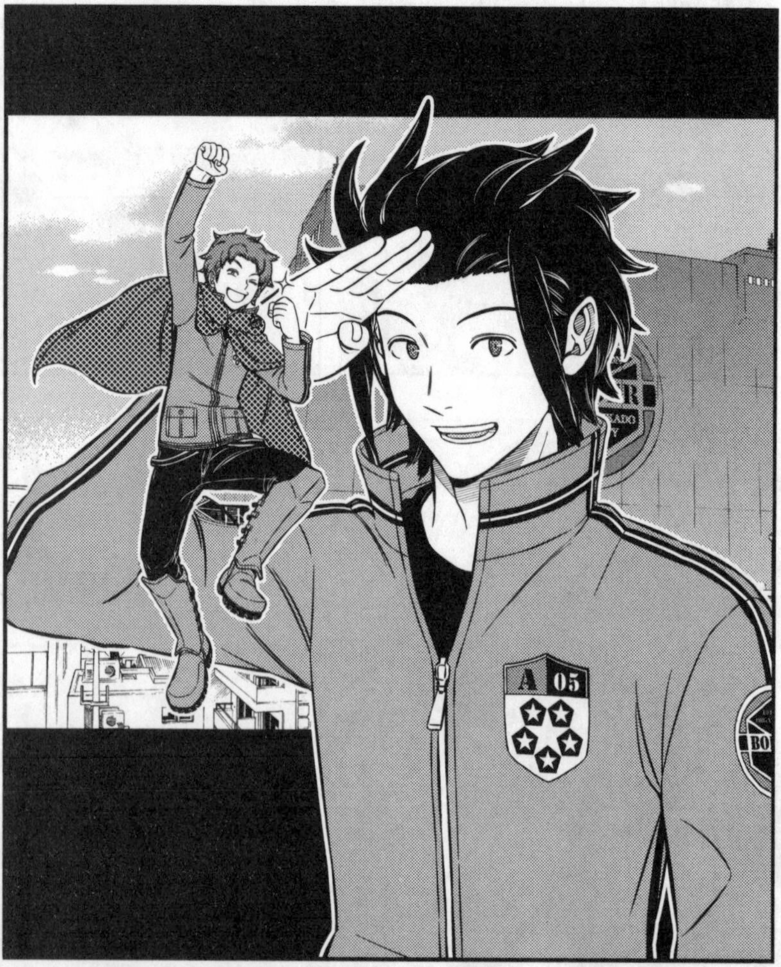
A 05

Illustration on promotional *uchiwa* fan for recruiting Border agents [July 2020 Issue] [Originally in color]

This started out as a fan shaped like a speech bubble, which would've had some notable quotes on it. That's what they asked me todo, but I talked to my editor and suggested that it could look like a recruiting tool that Border might hand out in front of a train station, which led to this Arashiyama Squad design. Somewhere in Mikado City, you've definitely got versions floating around that replace Satori with Kitora, Mitsuru, or Ayatsuji.

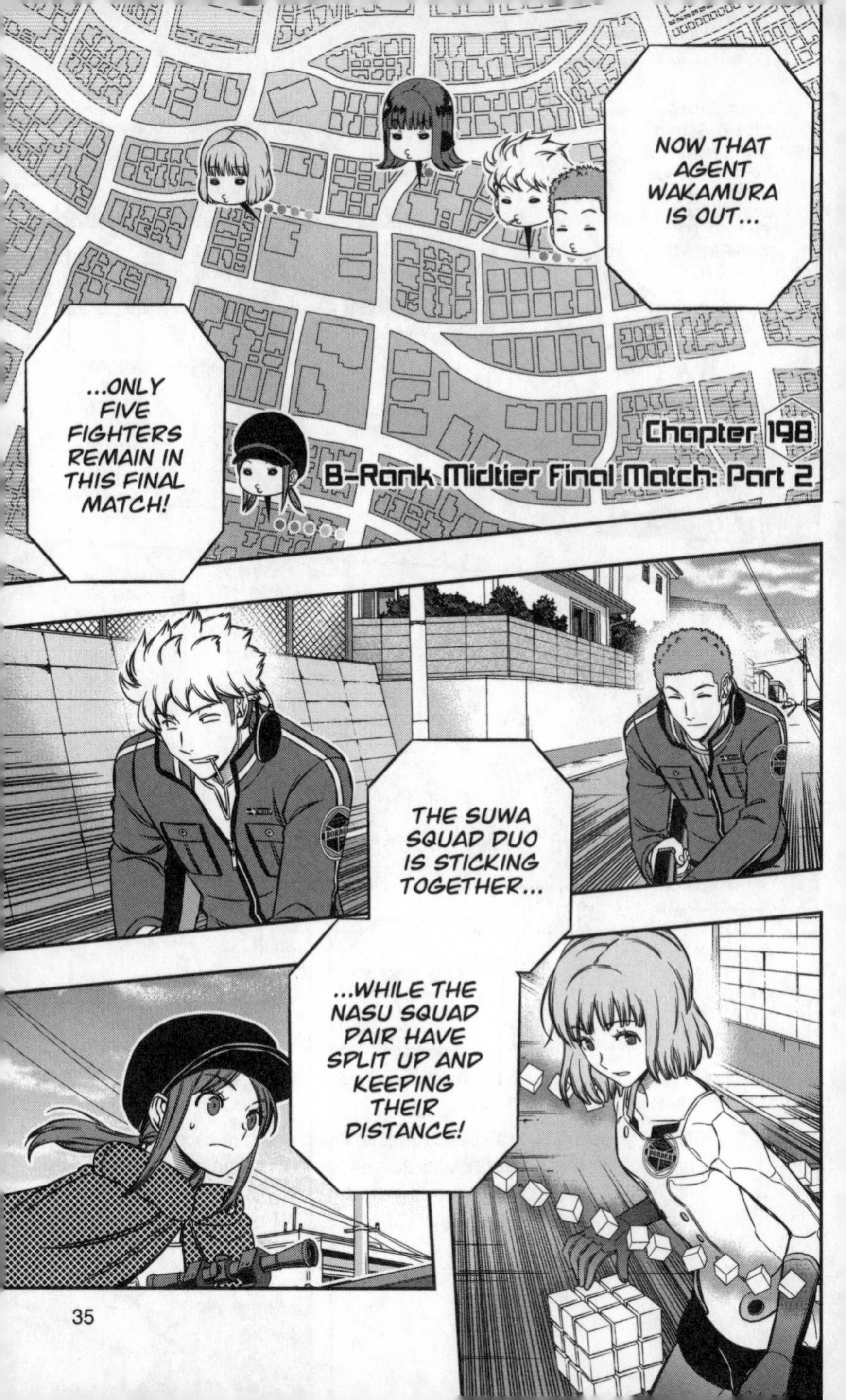
NOW THAT AGENT WAKAMURA IS OUT...
...ONLY FIVE FIGHTERS REMAIN IN THIS FINAL MATCH!
Chapter 198
B-Rank Midtier Final Match: Part 2
THE SUWA SQUAD DUO IS STICKING TOGETHER...
...WHILE THE NASU SQUAD PAIR HAVE SPLIT UP AND KEEPING THEIR DISTANCE!

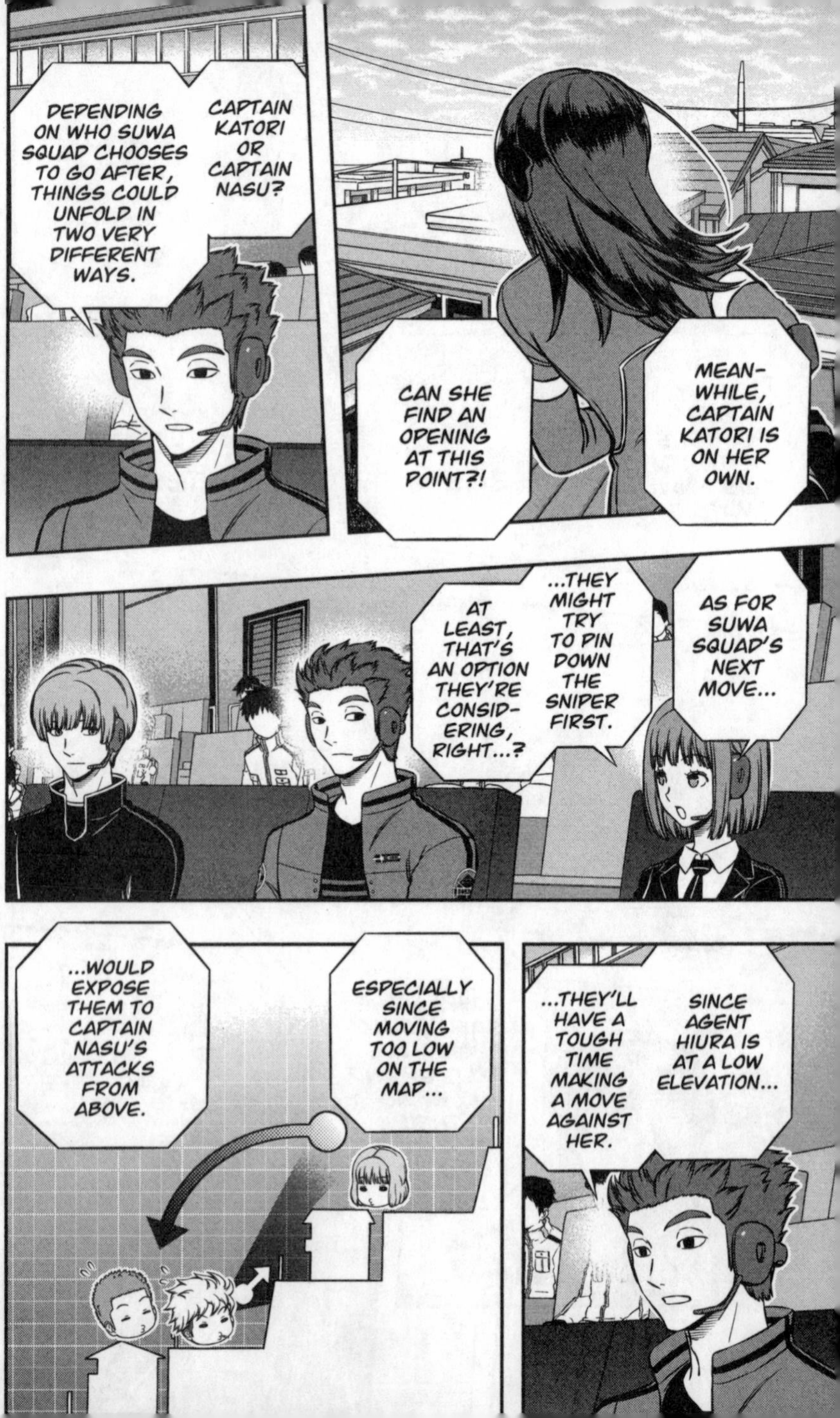
MEANWHILE, CAPTAIN KATORI IS ON HER OWN.
CAN SHE FIND AN OPENING AT THIS POINT?!
CAPTAIN KATORI OR CAPTAIN NASU?
DEPENDING ON WHO SUWA SQUAD CHOOSES TO GO AFTER, THINGS COULD UNFOLD IN TWO VERY DIFFERENT WAYS.
AS FOR SUWA SQUAD'S NEXT MOVE...
...THEY MIGHT TRY TO PIN DOWN THE SNIPER FIRST.
AT LEAST, THAT'S AN OPTION THEY'RE CONSIDERING, RIGHT...?
SINCE AGENT HIURA IS AT A LOW ELEVATION...
...THEY'LL HAVE A TOUGH TIME MAKING A MOVE AGAINST HER.
ESPECIALLY SINCE MOVING TOO LOW ON THE MAP...
...WOULD EXPOSE THEM TO CAPTAIN NASU'S ATTACKS FROM ABOVE.

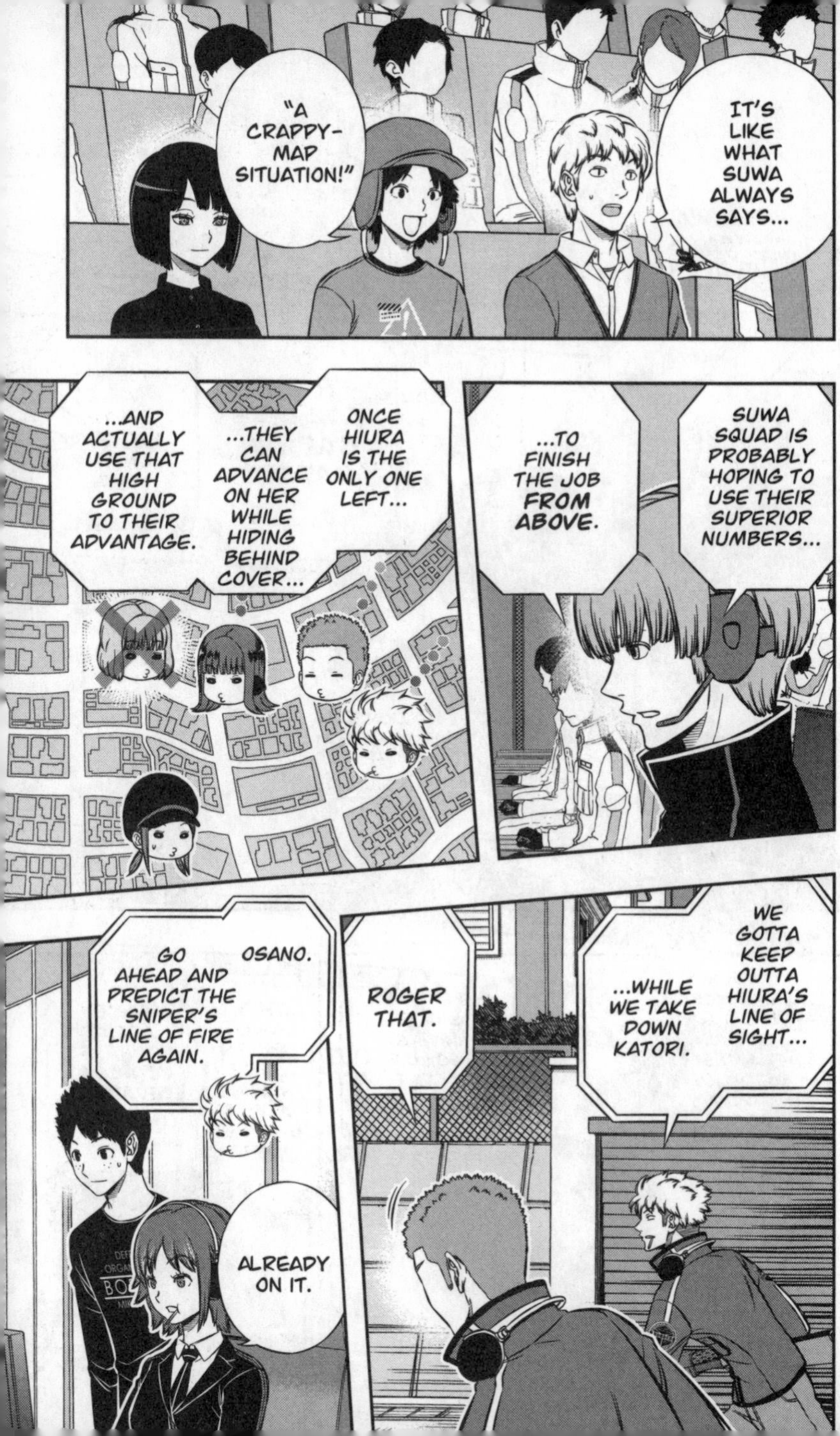
IT'S LIKE WHAT SUWA ALWAYS SAYS...
"A CRAPPY-MAP SITUATION!"
SUWA SQUAD IS PROBABLY HOPING TO USE THEIR SUPERIOR NUMBERS...
...TO FINISH THE JOB FROM ABOVE.
ONCE HIURA IS THE ONLY ONE LEFT...
...THEY CAN ADVANCE ON HER WHILE HIDING BEHIND COVER...
...AND ACTUALLY USE THAT HIGH GROUND TO THEIR ADVANTAGE.
WE GOTTA KEEP OUTTA HIURA'S LINE OF SIGHT...
...WHILE WE TAKE DOWN KATORI.
ROGER THAT.
OSANO.
GO AHEAD AND PREDICT THE SNIPER'S LINE OF FIRE AGAIN.
ALREADY ON IT.

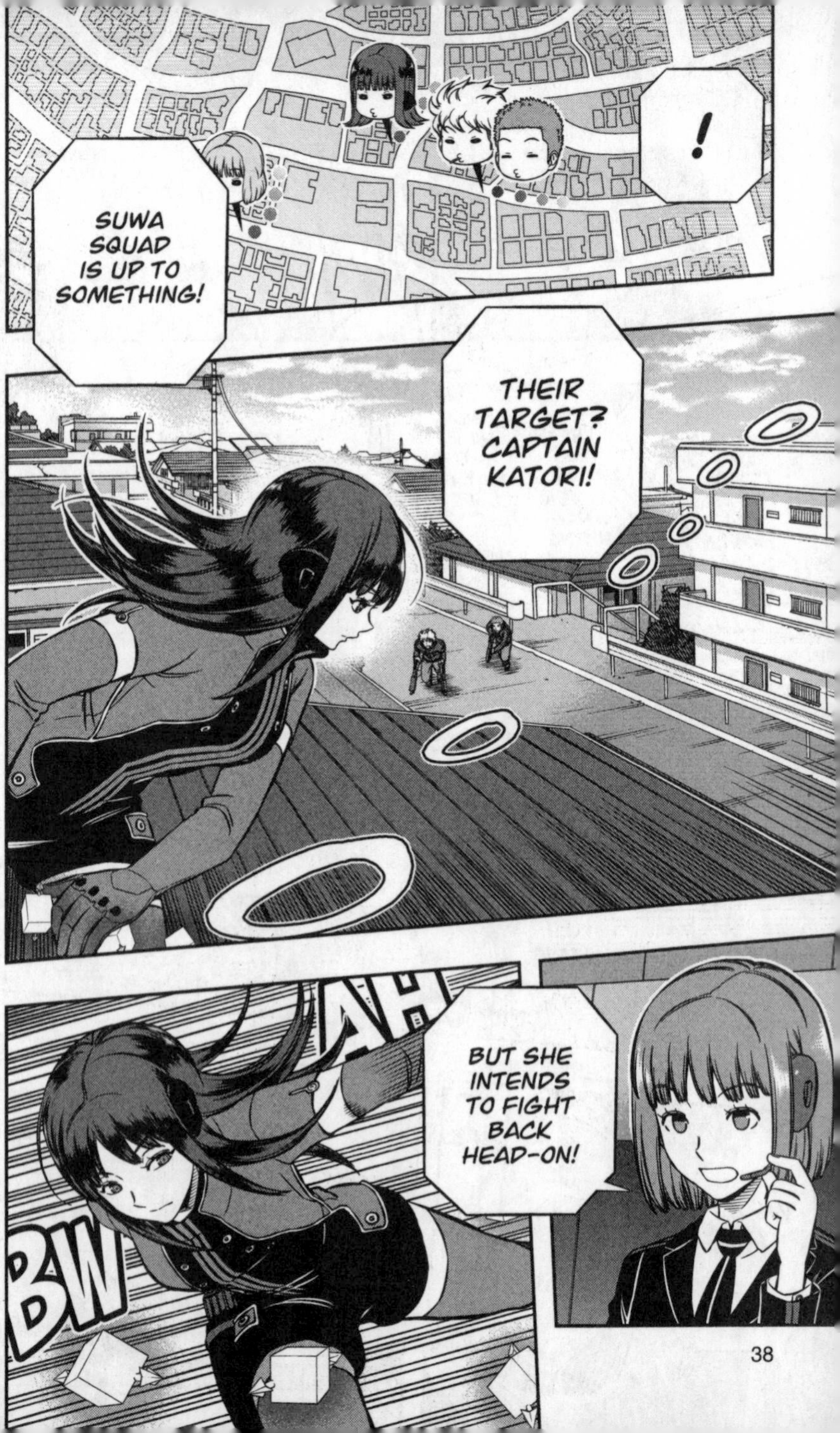
!
SUWA SQUAD IS UP TO SOMETHING!
THEIR TARGET? CAPTAIN KATORI!
BUT SHE INTENDS TO FIGHT BACK HEAD-ON!
BWAH

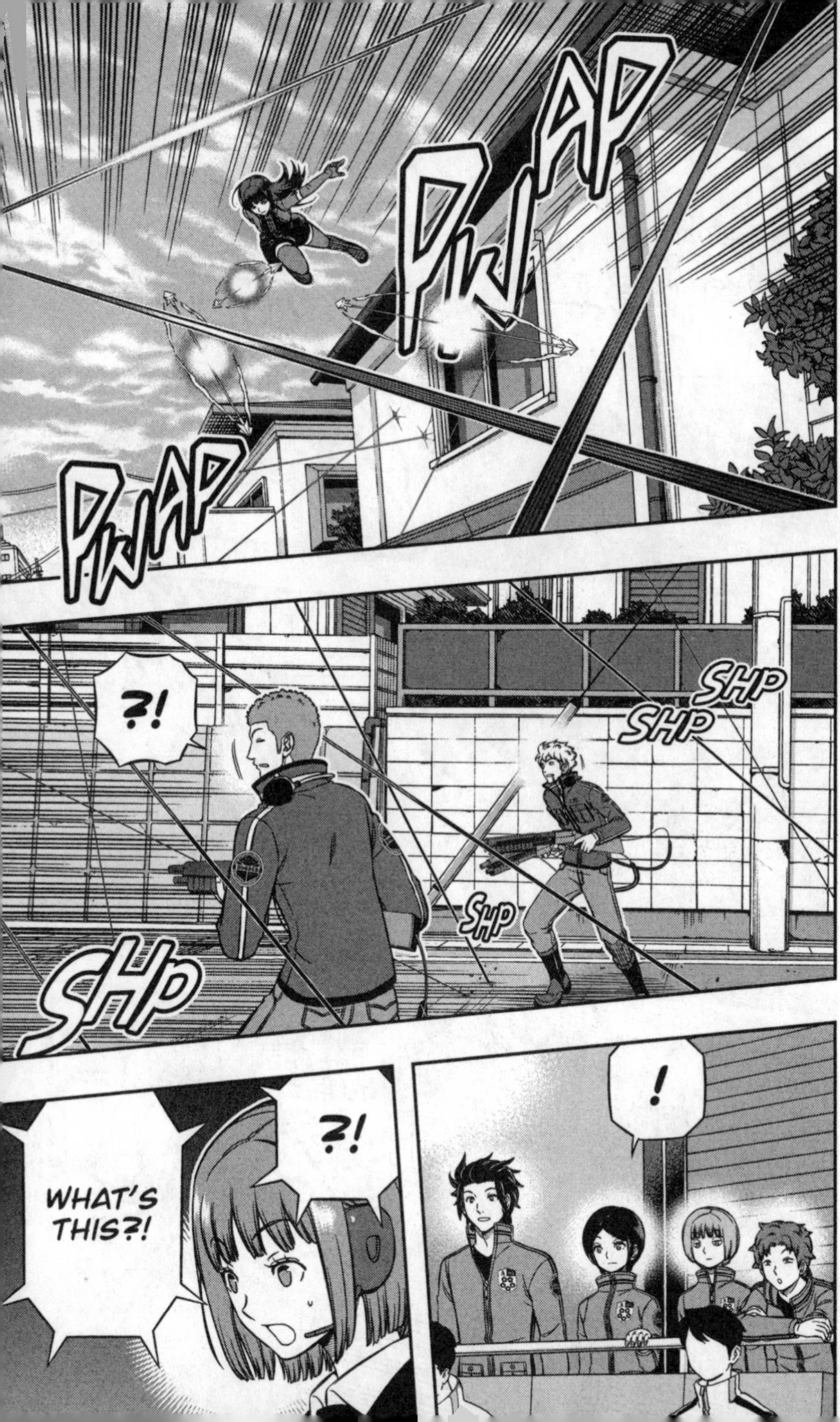
PWAP
PWAP
SHP
SHP
?!
SHP
SHP
!
?!
WHAT'S THIS?!

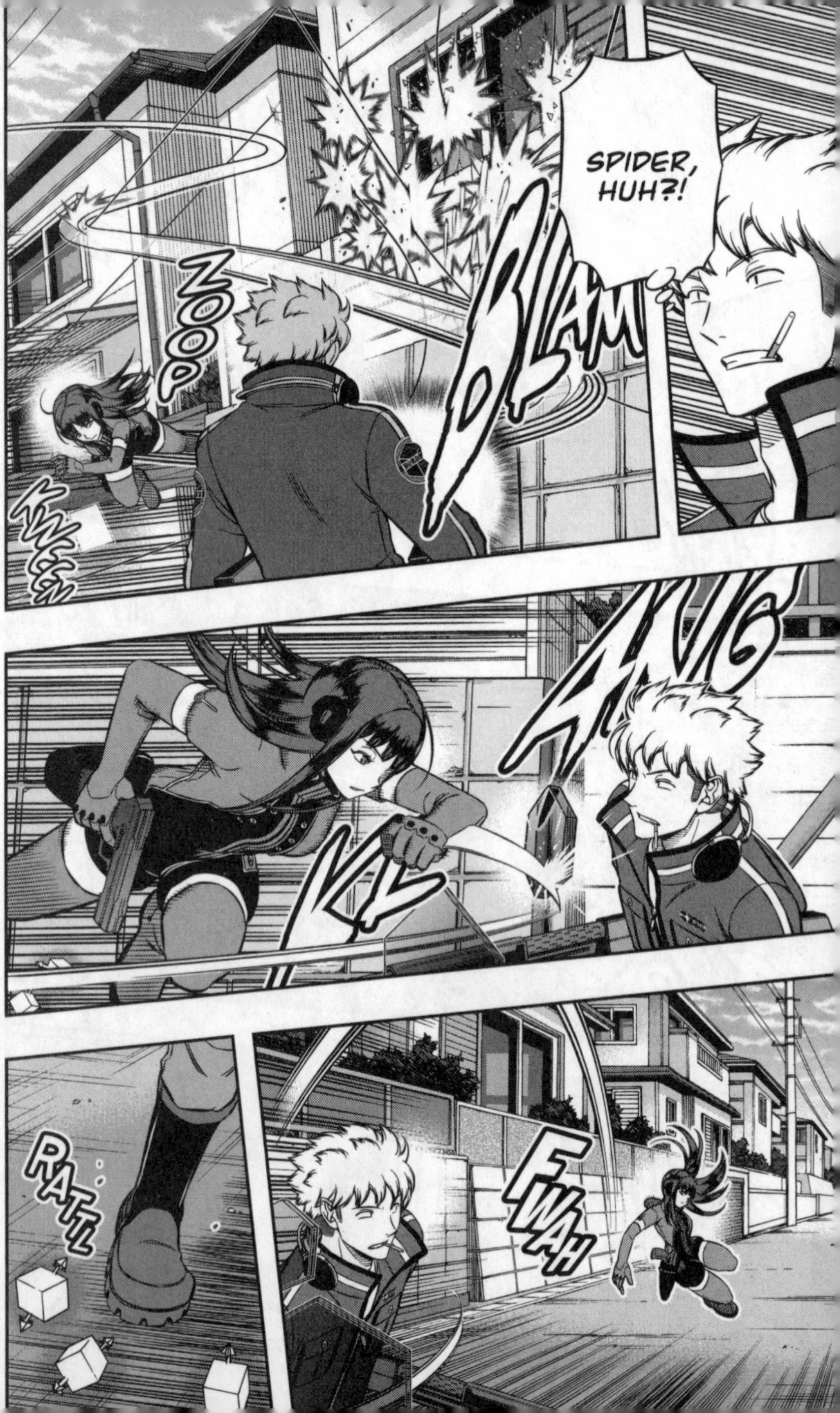
SPIDER, HUH?!
BLAM
ZOOP
KWEEN
RATTL
FWAH

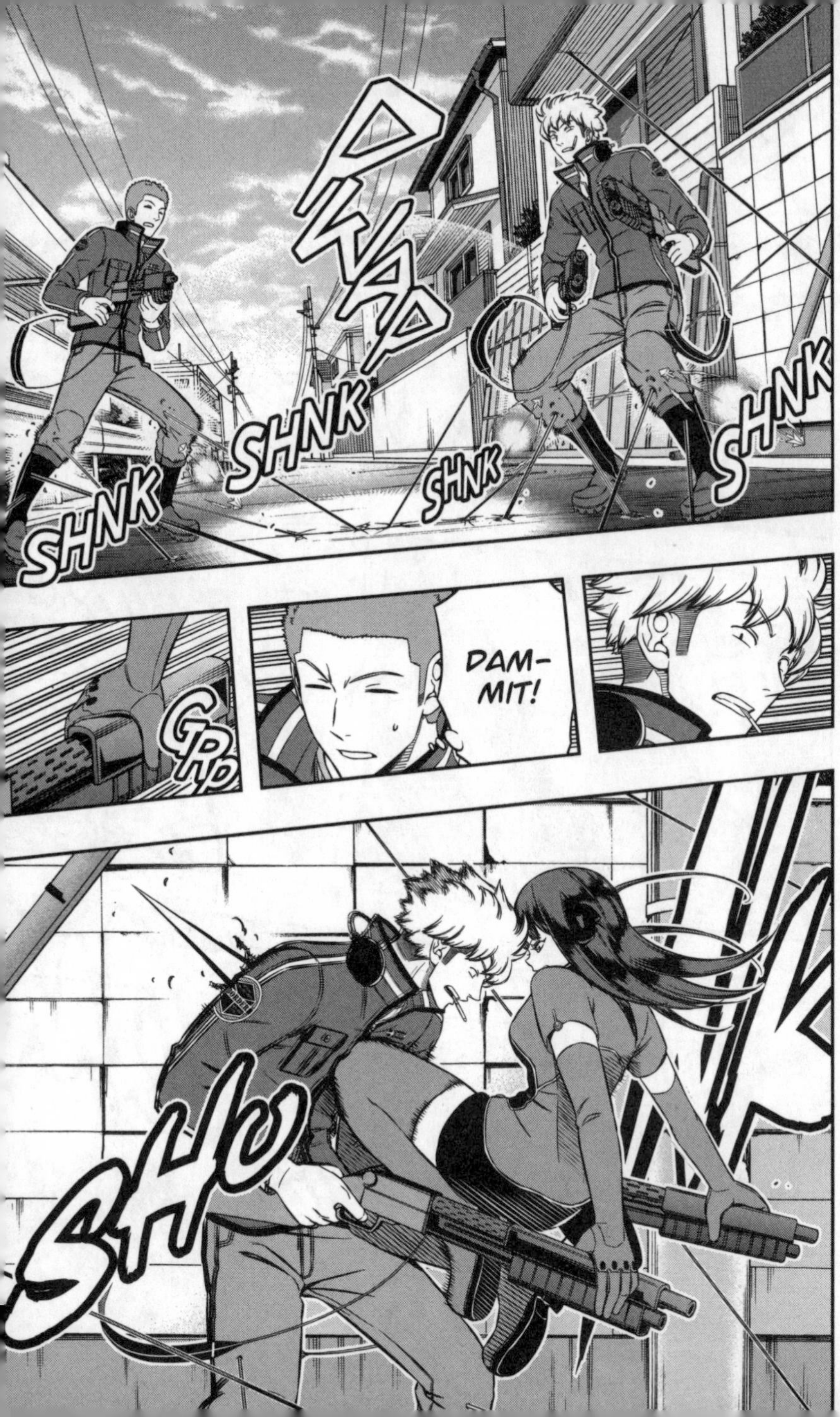
DKWAP
SHNK
SHNK
SHNK
SHNK
DAM-
MIT!
GRP
SHK

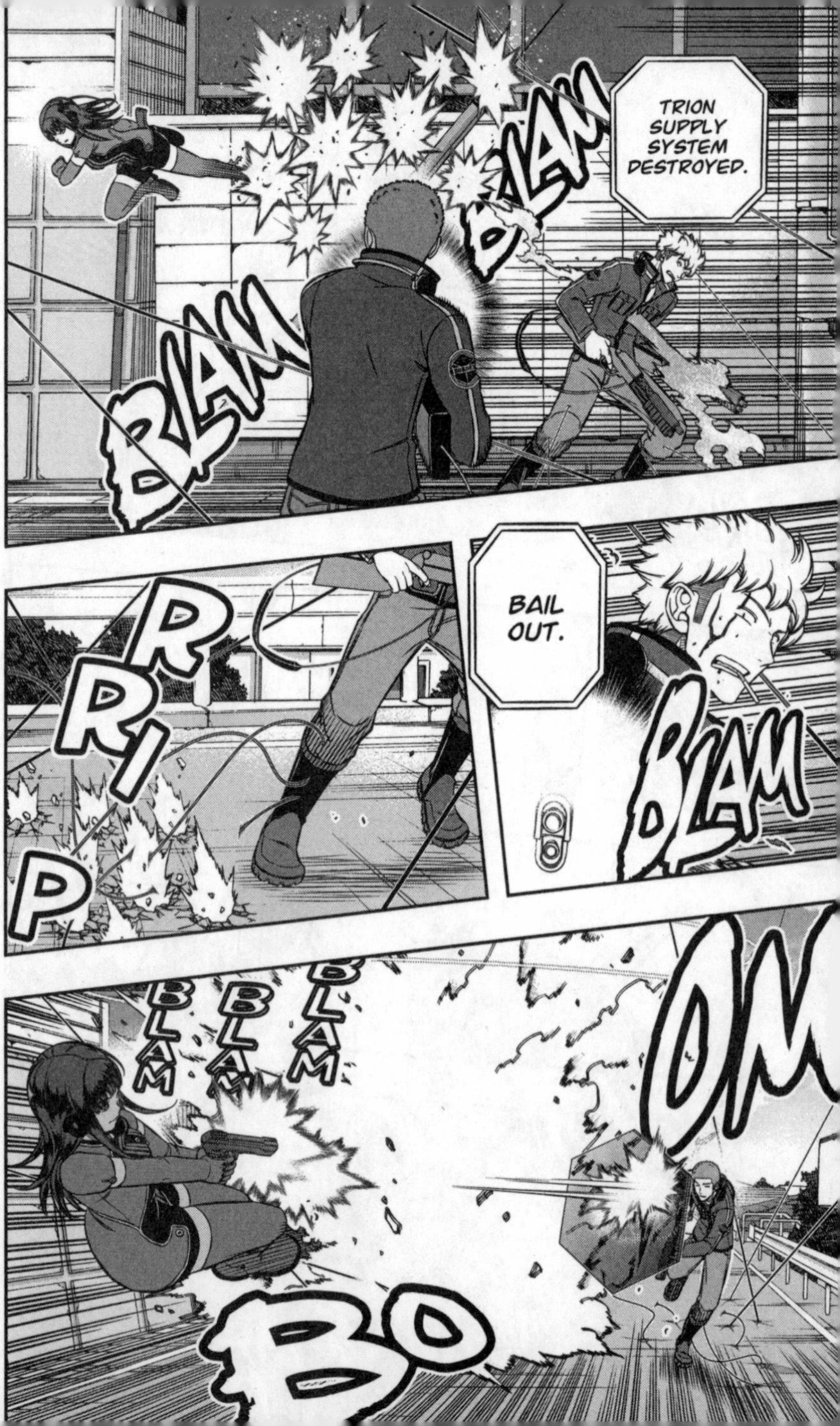
BLAM
BLAM
TRION SUPPLY SYSTEM DESTROYED.
BAIL OUT.
BLAM
RRIP
OM
BO
BLAM
BLAM
BLAM

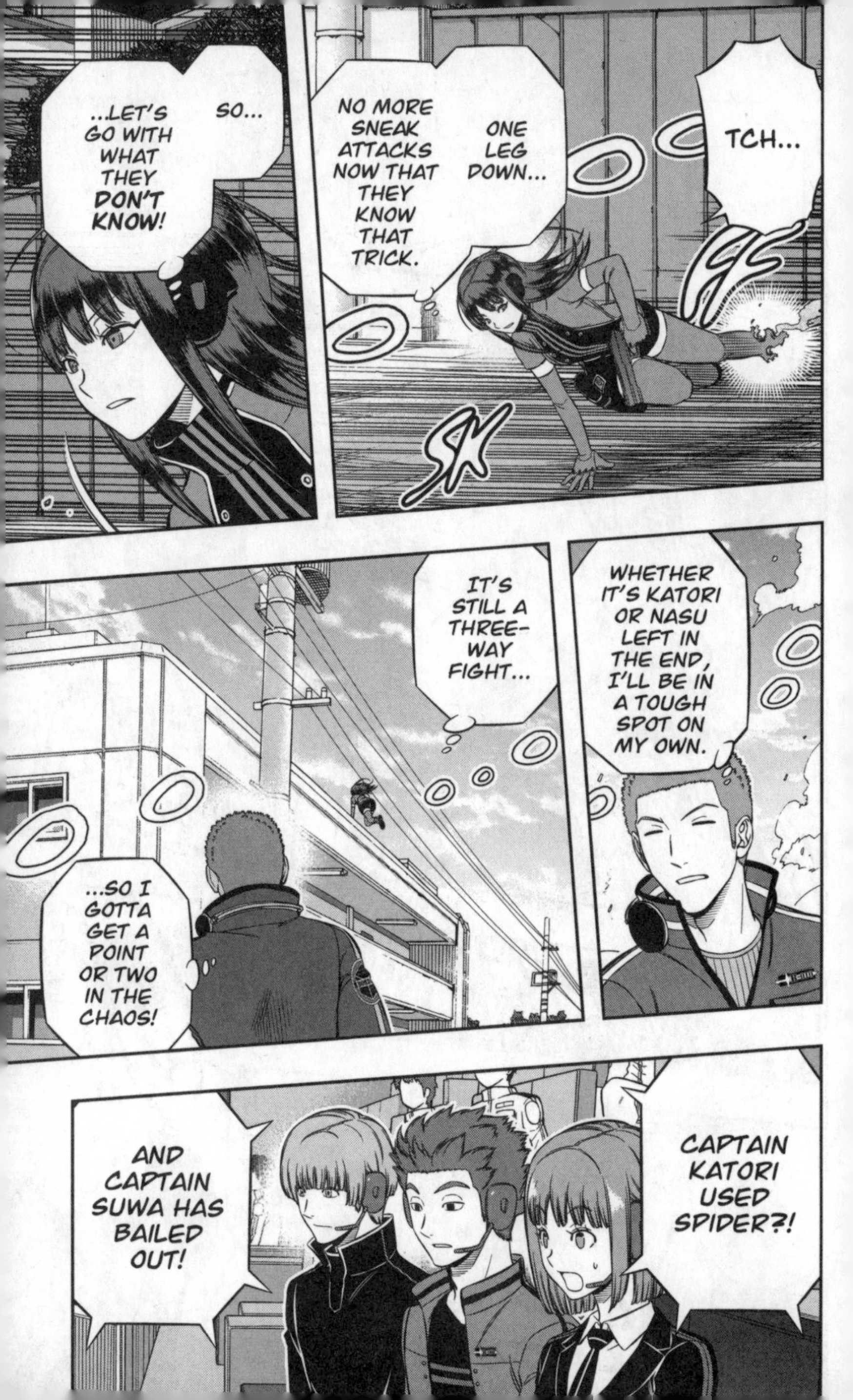
TCH...
ONE LEG DOWN...
NO MORE SNEAK ATTACKS NOW THAT THEY KNOW THAT TRICK.
SK
SO...
...LET'S GO WITH WHAT THEY DON'T KNOW!
WHETHER IT'S KATORI OR NASU LEFT IN THE END, I'LL BE IN A TOUGH SPOT ON MY OWN.
IT'S STILL A THREE-WAY FIGHT...
...SO I GOTTA GET A POINT OR TWO IN THE CHAOS!
CAPTAIN KATORI USED SPIDER?!
AND CAPTAIN SUWA HAS BAILED OUT!

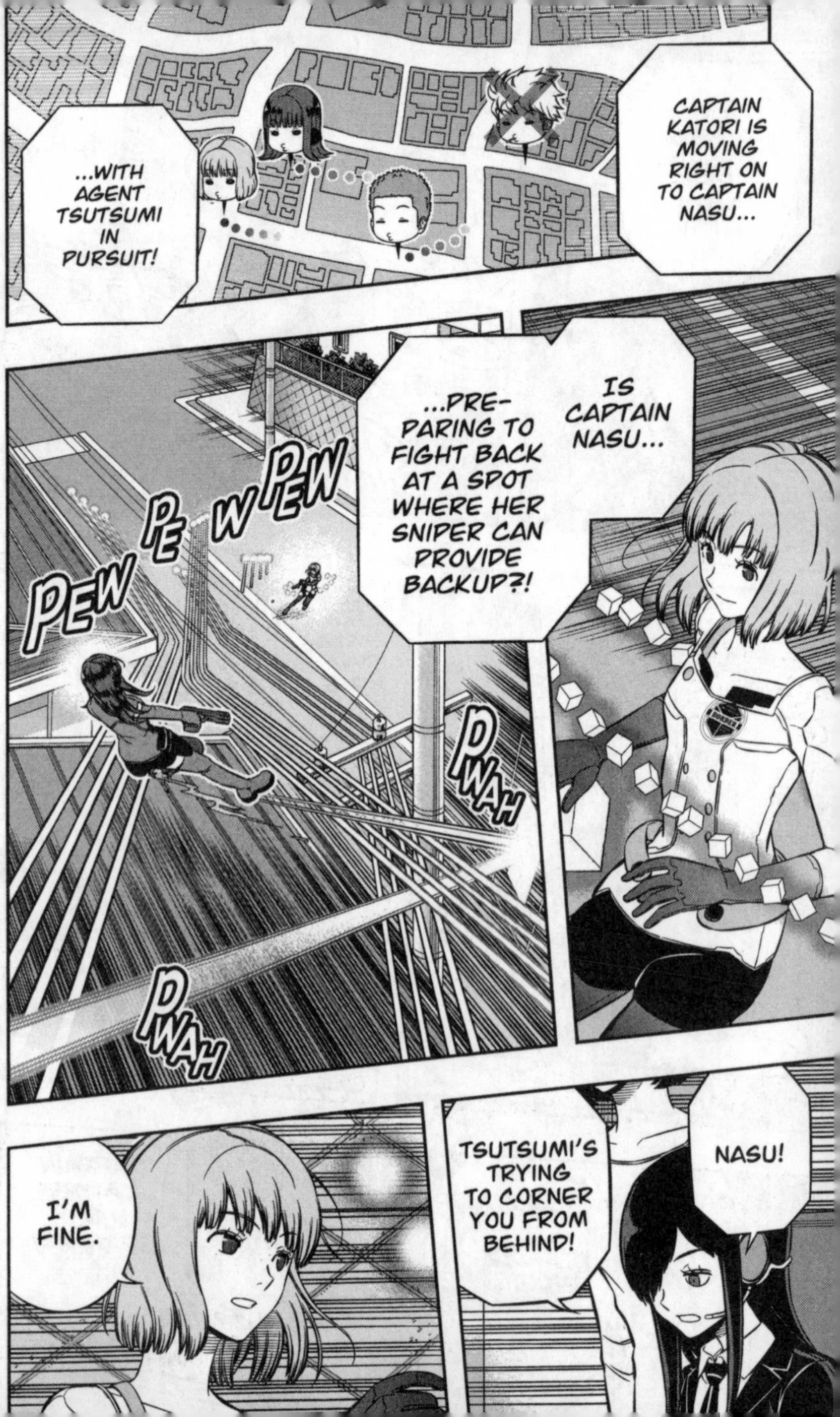
CAPTAIN KATORI IS MOVING RIGHT ON TO CAPTAIN NASU...
...WITH AGENT TSUTSUMI IN PURSUIT!
IS CAPTAIN NASU...
...PRE-PARING TO FIGHT BACK AT A SPOT WHERE HER SNIPER CAN PROVIDE BACKUP?!
PEW PEW PEW
PEW
PWAH
PWAH
NASU!
TSUTSUMI'S TRYING TO CORNER YOU FROM BEHIND!
I'M FINE.

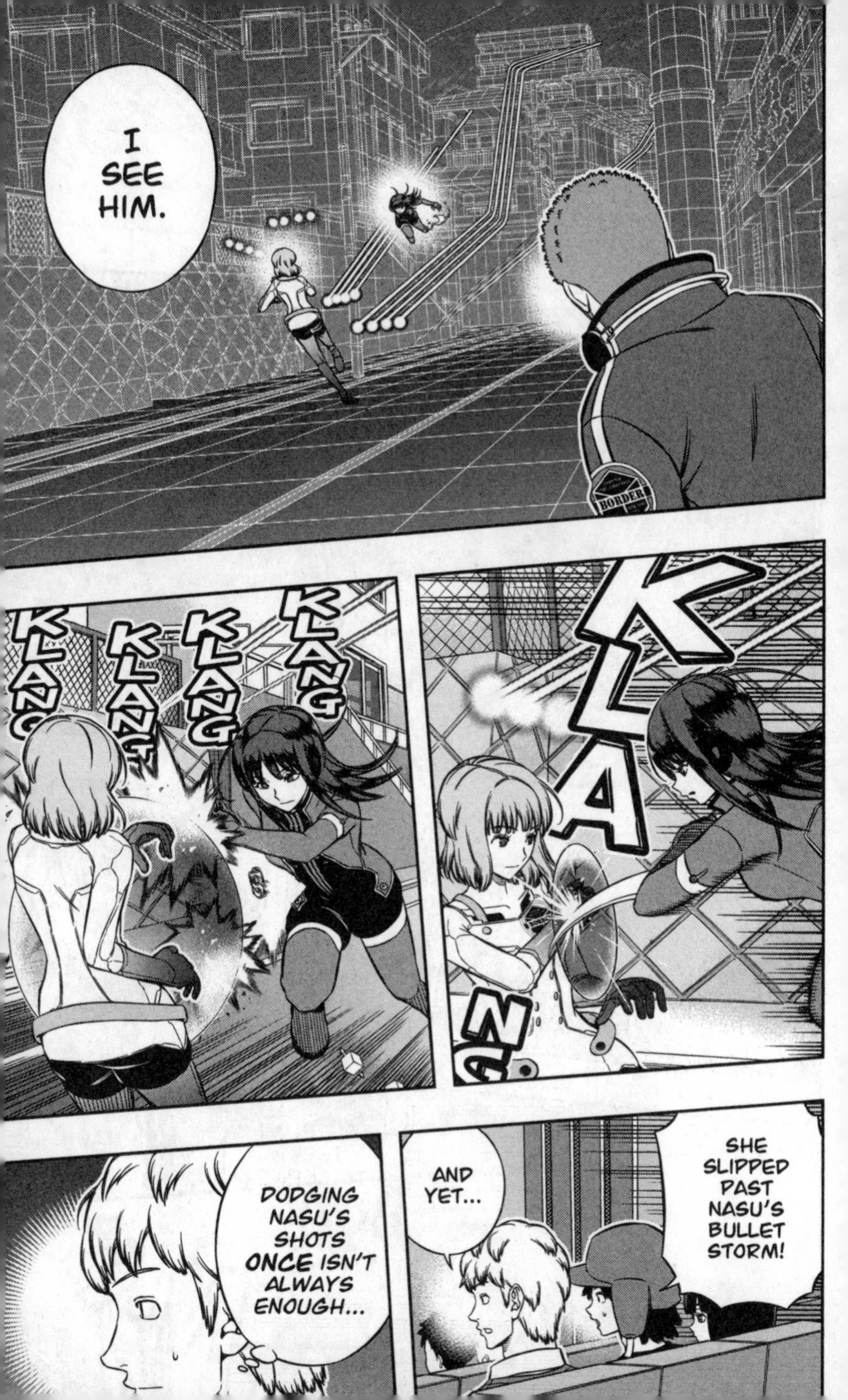

I SEE HIM.
KLANG
KLANG
KLANG
KLANG
KLANG
SHE SLIPPED PAST NASU'S BULLET STORM!
AND YET...
DODGING NASU'S SHOTS ONCE ISN'T ALWAYS ENOUGH...

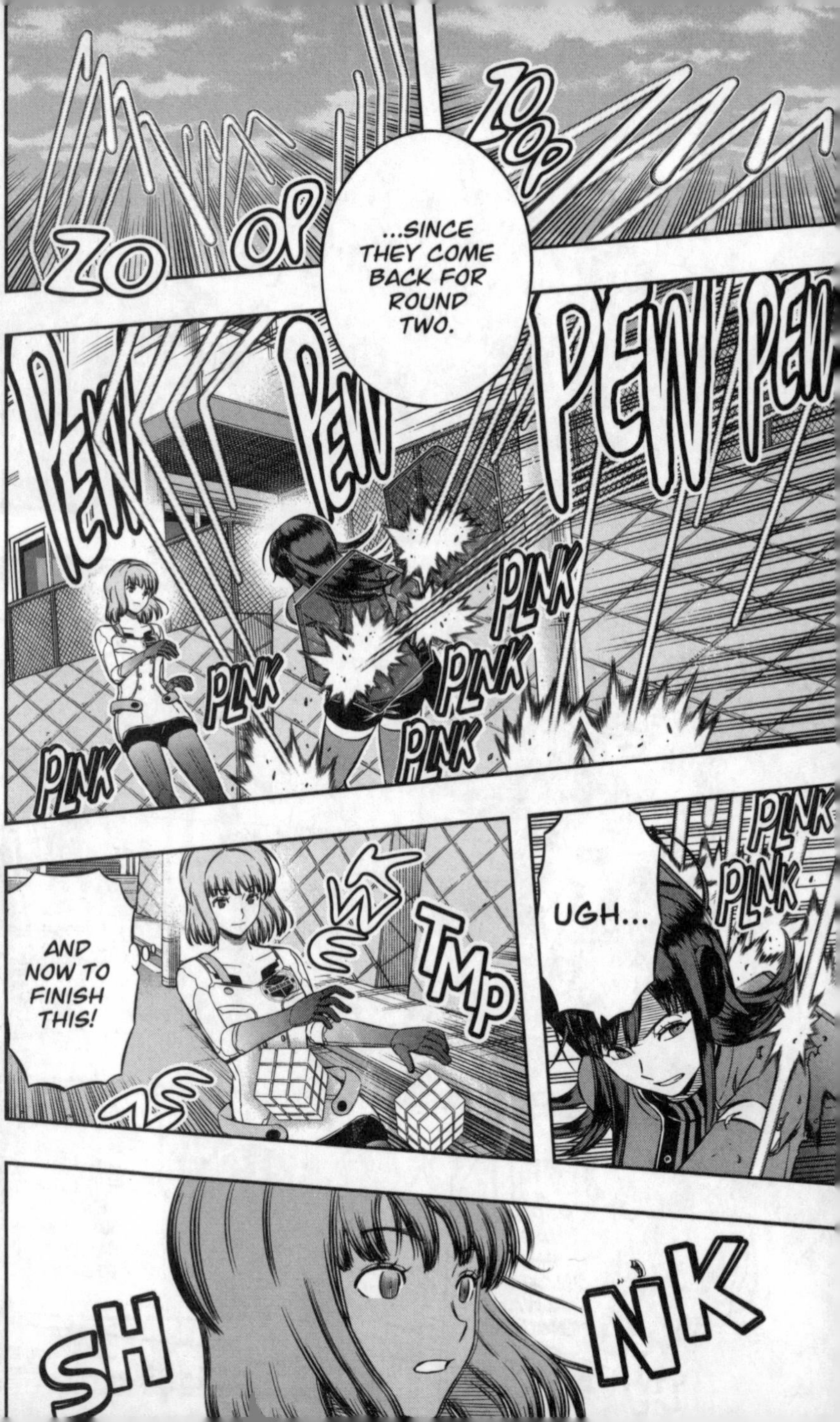
ZOOP
ZO OP
...SINCE THEY COME BACK FOR ROUND TWO.
PEW PEW
PEW PEW
PLINK
PLINK
PLINK
PLINK
PLINK
PLINK
PLINK
UGH...
AND NOW TO FINISH THIS!
TMP
SH NK

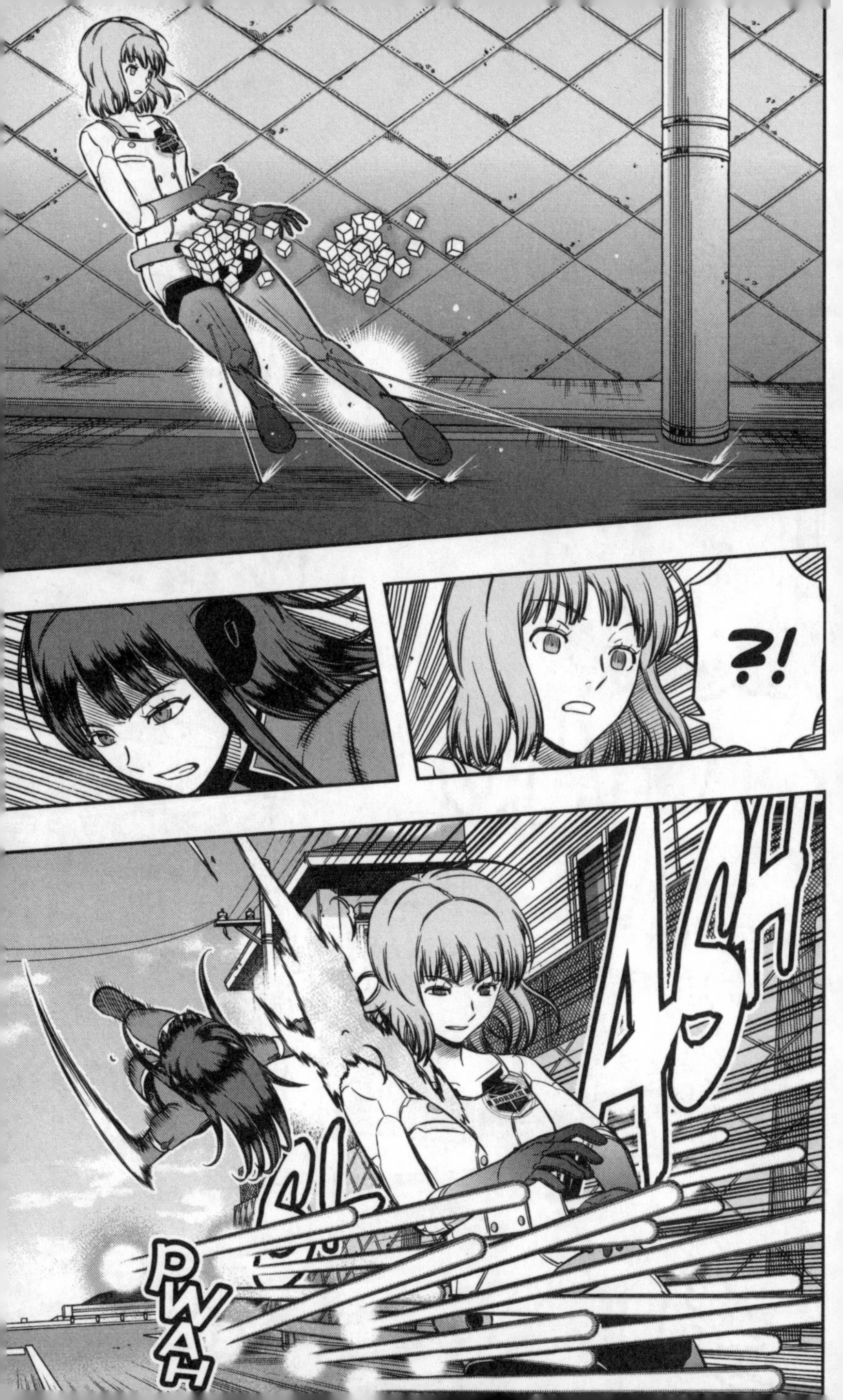
?!
PWAH

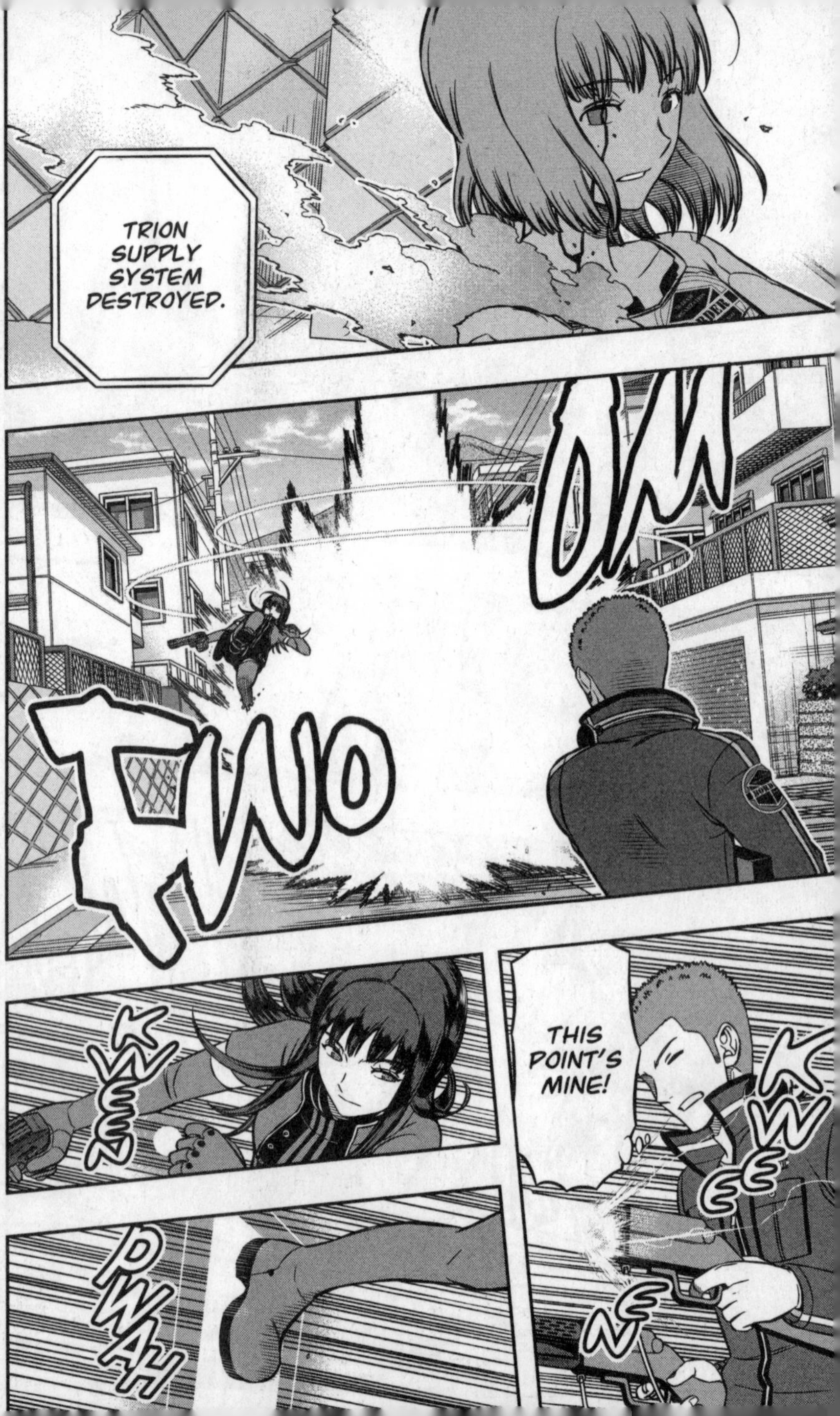
TRION SUPPLY SYSTEM DESTROYED.
FWOOM
THIS POINT'S MINE!
KWEE
KWEEZ
EEN
PWAH

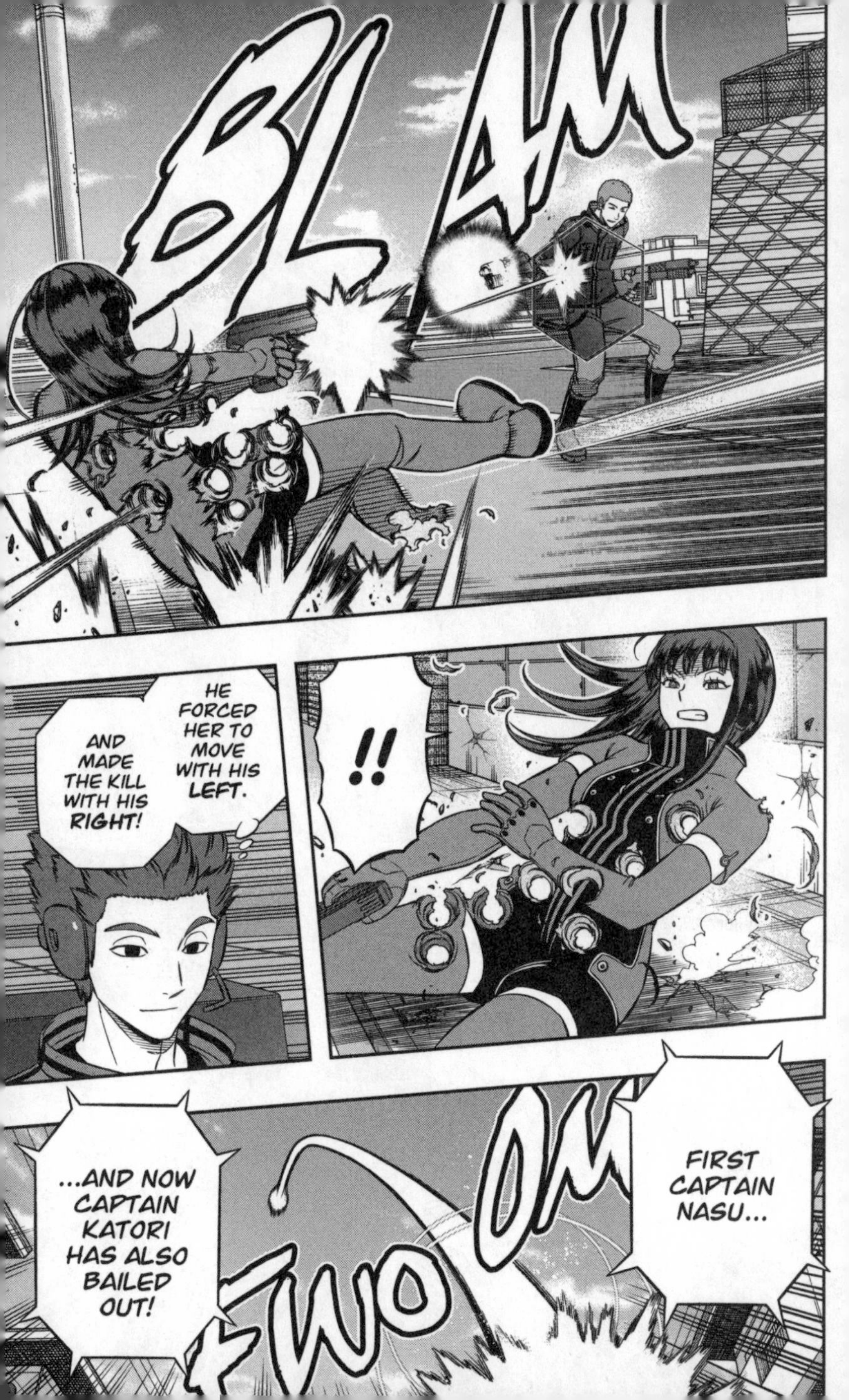
BLAM
!!
HE FORCED HER TO MOVE WITH HIS LEFT.
AND MADE THE KILL WITH HIS RIGHT!
FIRST CAPTAIN NASU...
FWOOM
...AND NOW CAPTAIN KATORI HAS ALSO BAILED OUT!

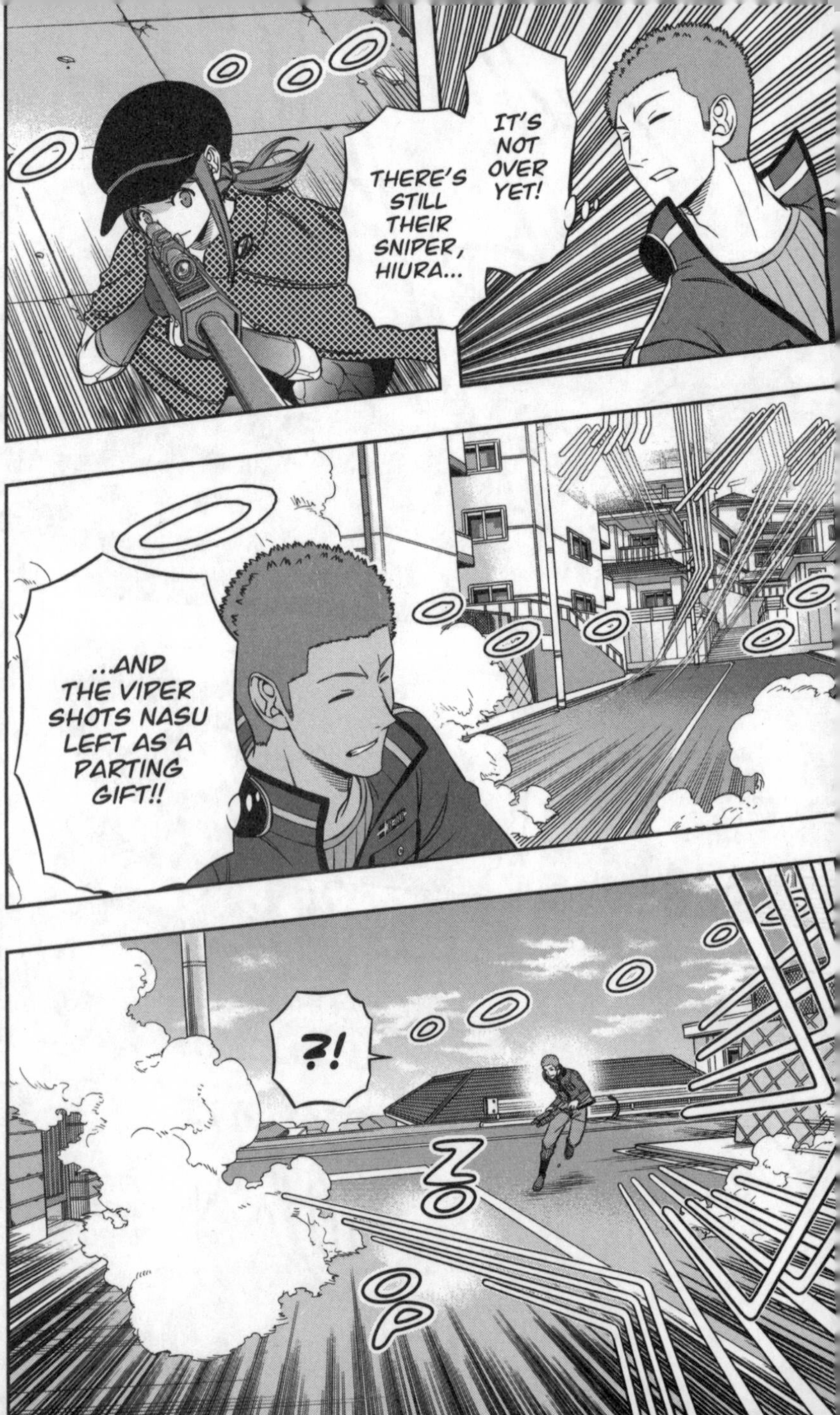
IT'S NOT OVER YET!
THERE'S STILL THEIR SNIPER, HIURA...
...AND THE VIPER SHOTS NASU LEFT AS A PARTING GIFT!!
?!
ZOOP

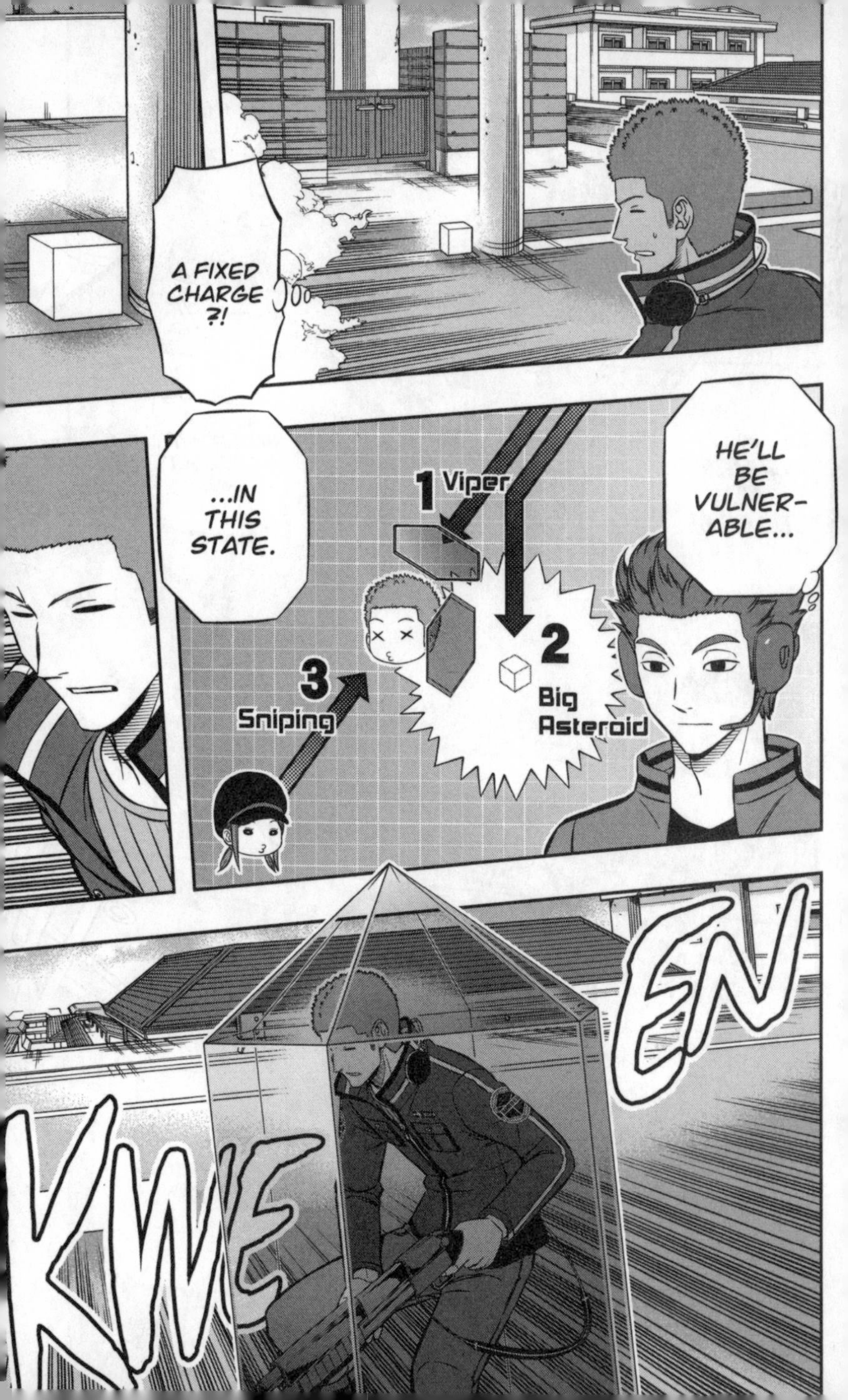
A FIXED CHARGE ?!
HE'LL BE VULNER-ABLE...
1 Viper
2 Big Asteroid
3 Sniping
...IN THIS STATE.
KWE EN

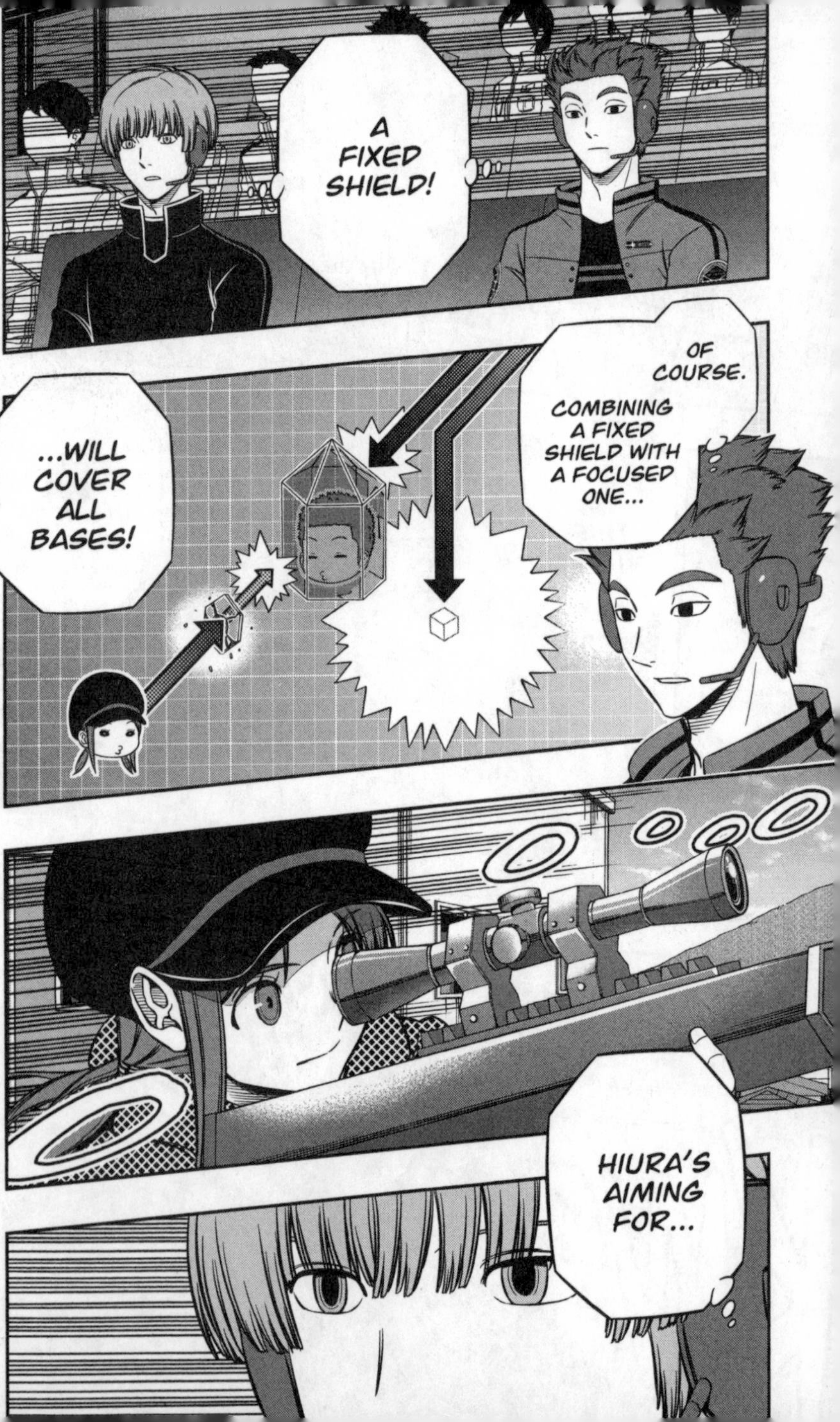
A FIXED SHIELD!
OF COURSE.
COMBINING A FIXED SHIELD WITH A FOCUSED ONE...
...WILL COVER ALL BASES!
HIURA'S AIMING FOR...

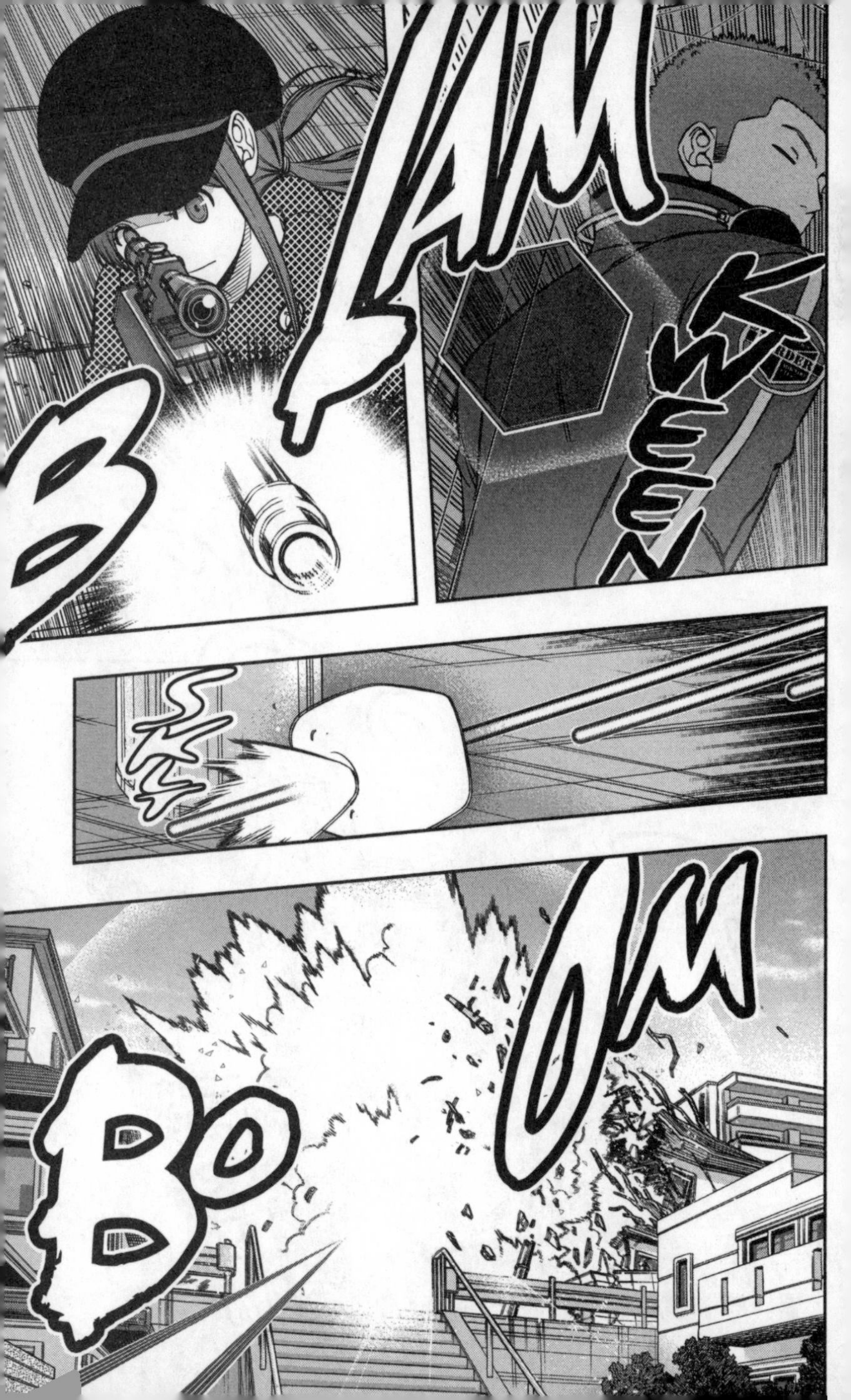
KWEEN
BLAM
BOOM

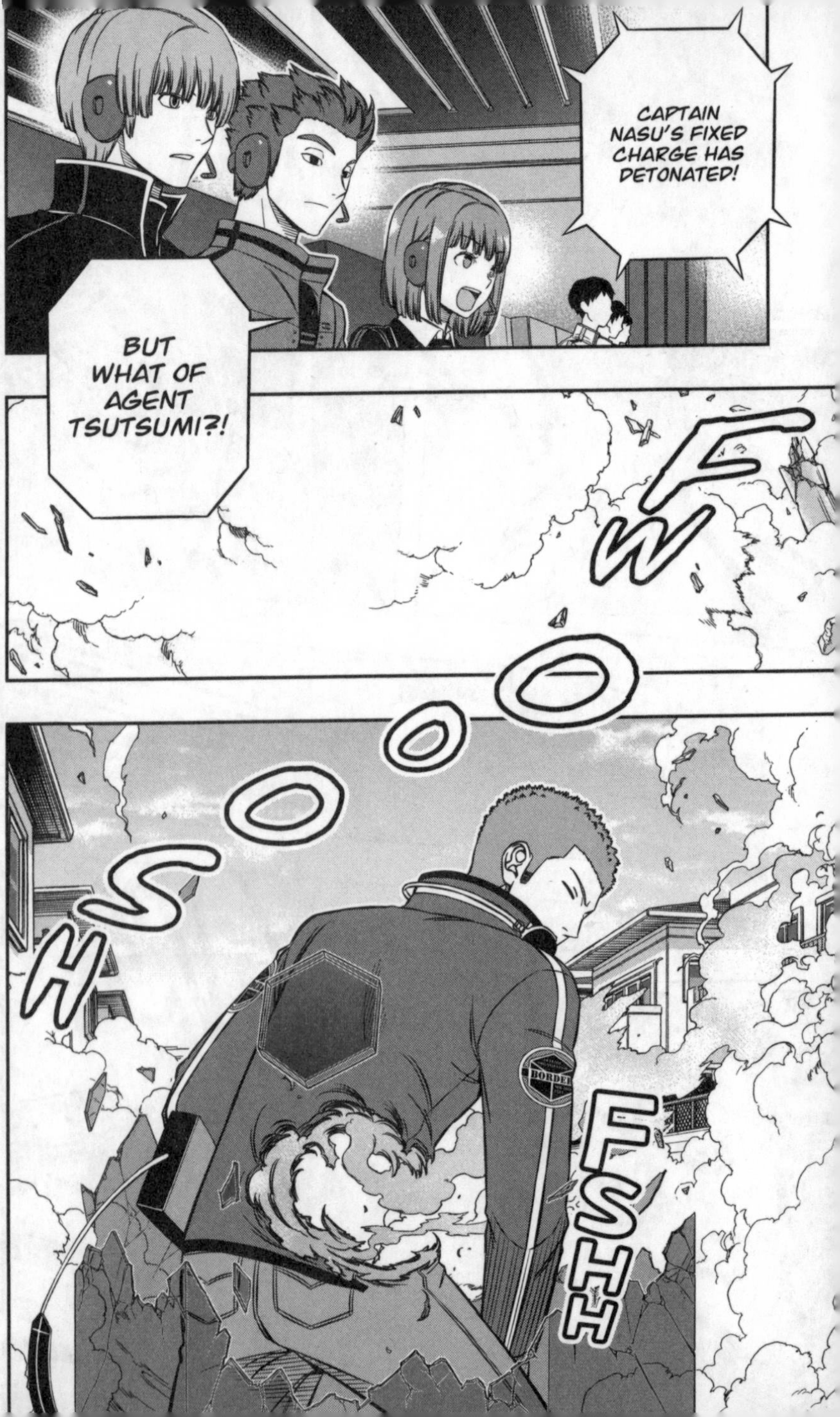
CAPTAIN NASU'S FIXED CHARGE HAS DETONATED!
BUT WHAT OF AGENT TSUTSUMI?!
FWOOOSH
FSHH

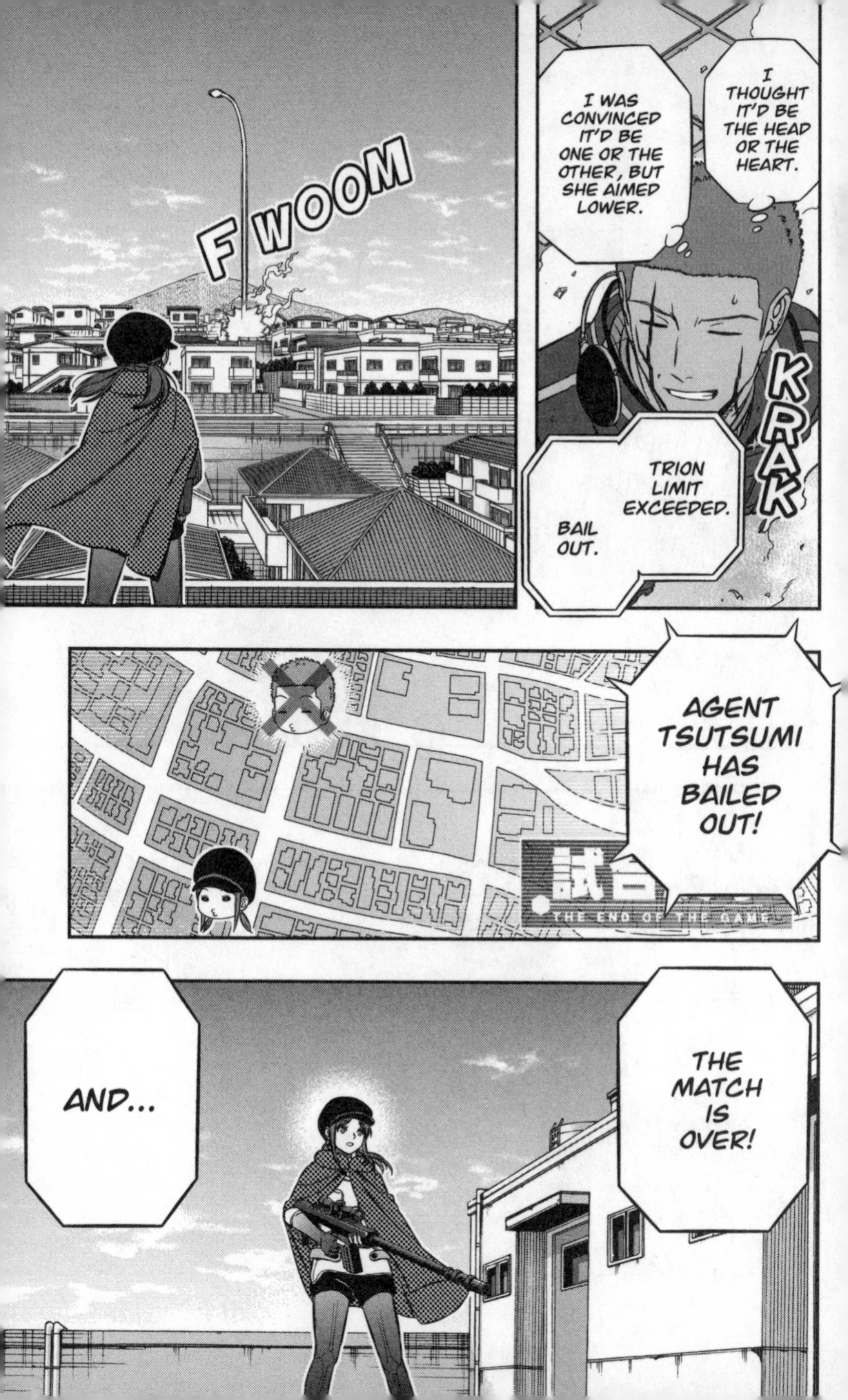
I THOUGHT IT'D BE THE HEAD OR THE HEART.
I WAS CONVINCED IT'D BE ONE OR THE OTHER, BUT SHE AIMED LOWER.
KRAK
TRION LIMIT EXCEEDED.
BAIL OUT.
FWOOM
AGENT TSUTSUMI HAS BAILED OUT!
試合
THE END OF THE GAME
THE MATCH IS OVER!
AND...

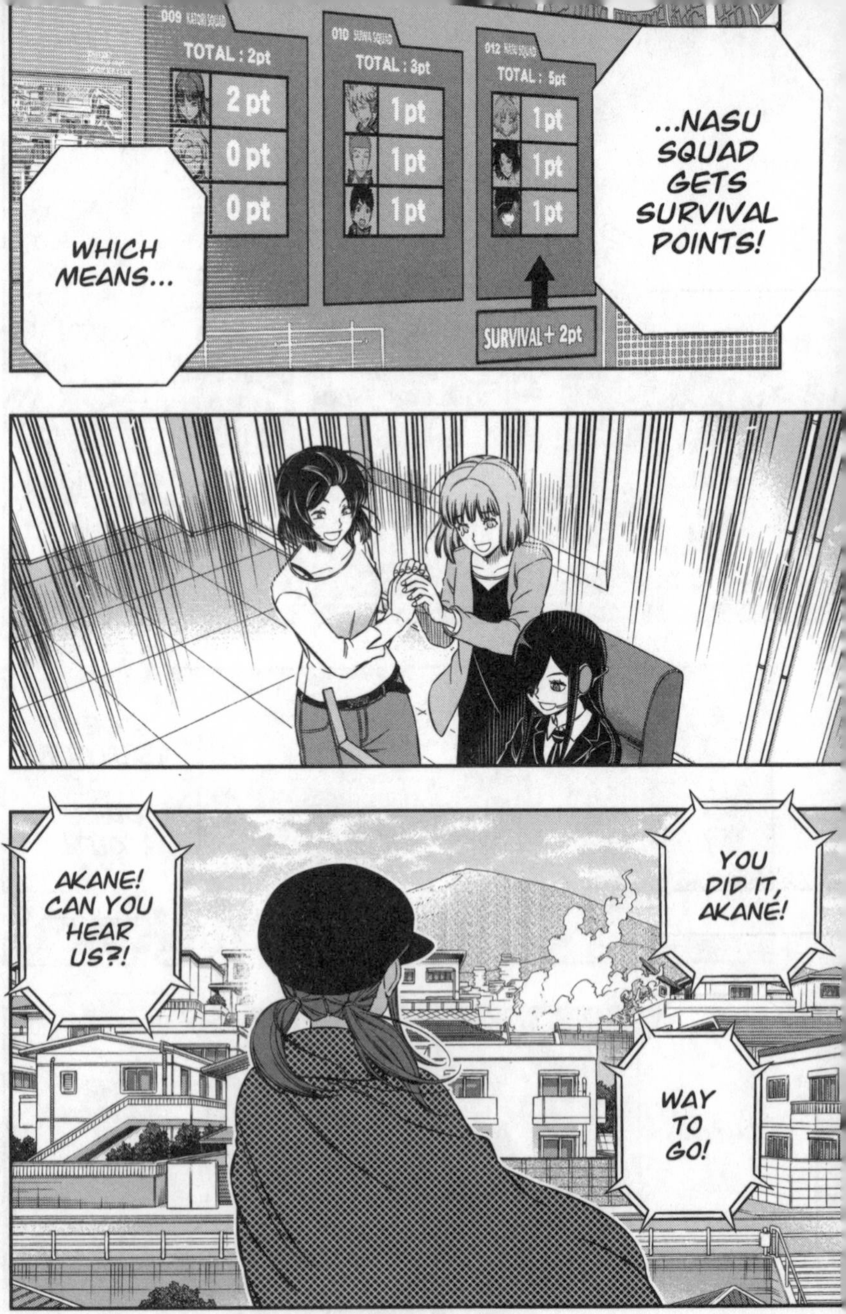
WHICH MEANS...
...NASU SQUAD GETS SURVIVAL POINTS!
012 NASU SQUAD
TOTAL : 5pt
1pt
1pt
1pt
SURVIVAL + 2pt
010 SUWA SQUAD
TOTAL : 3pt
1pt
1pt
1pt
009 KATORI SQUAD
TOTAL : 2pt
2 pt
0 pt
0 pt
YOU DID IT, AKANE!
AKANE! CAN YOU HEAR US?!
WAY TO GO!

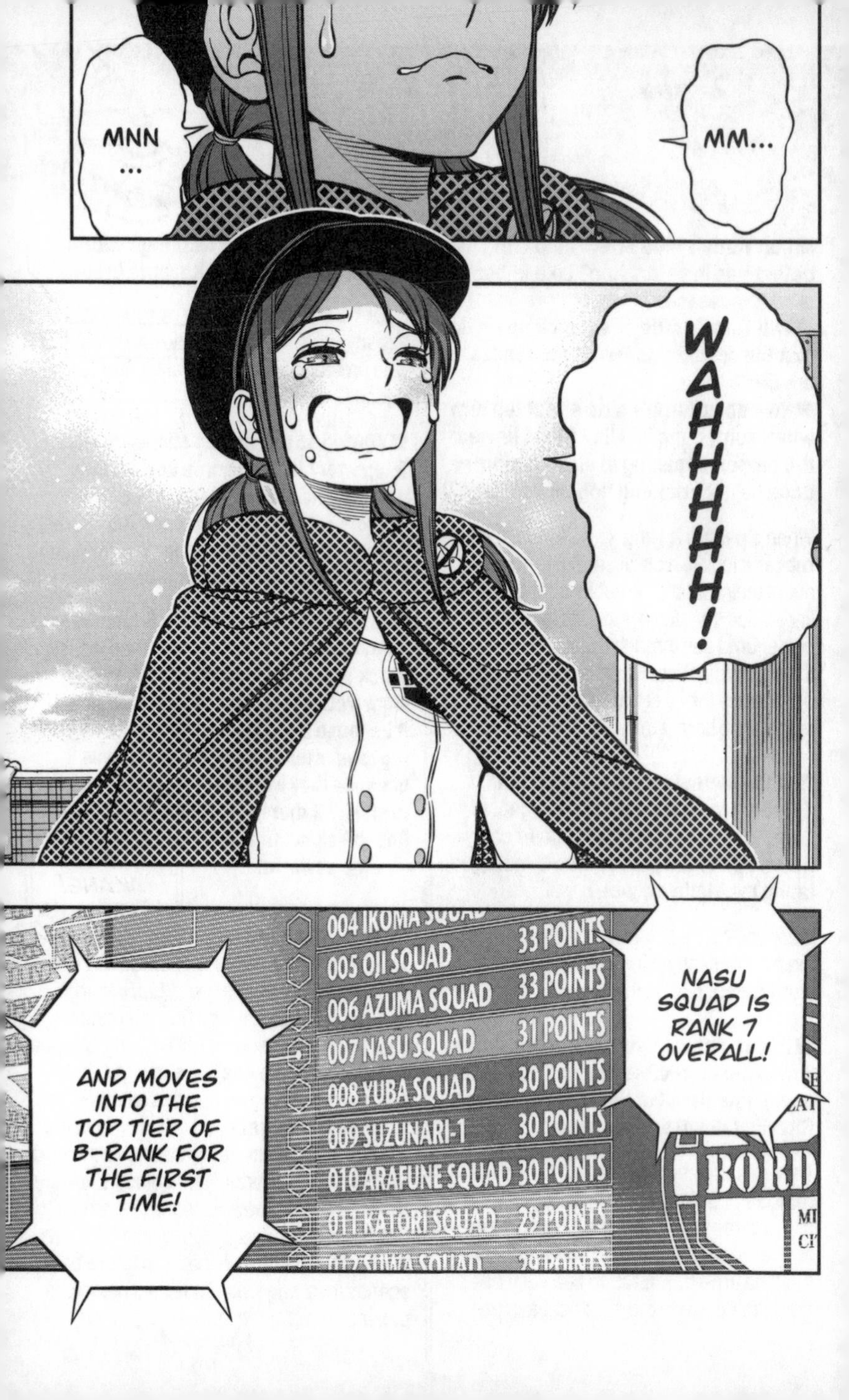
MM...
MNN ...
WAHHHHHH!
NASU SQUAD IS RANK 7 OVERALL!
004 IKOMA SQUAD 33 POINTS
005 OJI SQUAD 33 POINTS
006 AZUMA SQUAD 33 POINTS
007 NASU SQUAD 31 POINTS
008 YUBA SQUAD 30 POINTS
009 SUZUNARI-1 30 POINTS
010 ARAFUNE SQUAD 30 POINTS
011 KATORI SQUAD 29 POINTS
AND MOVES INTO THE TOP TIER OF B-RANK FOR THE FIRST TIME!

Q&A: Part 18
The questions have
been piling up.

■Can Yuma's side effect help him detect lies in writing too? Like in books or text messages?

■Will Yuma's side effect pick up on lies that the speaker doesn't even realize are lies?

■How does Yuma's side effect tell him when something is a lie? (Does he hear the person speaking in slow motion, or does he get prickling tingles like Kage?)

When a person is lying, Yuma's side effect makes it look like black smoke is pouring out of their mouth. The subtle changes in the liar's voice transform into a visual cue that helps Yuma see through the lie. So no, I don't think his side effect would work if the person didn't know they were lying or if he were reading the lie in a text.

■At the start of round 7, Kage used Scorpion to swing across a big gap. Is Scorpion really strong enough to carry the weight of the person who's manipulating the blade's shape?

Weapons made of Trion are superstrong, even for non-attacking purposes. Definitely sturdy enough to do the job.

■The engineers who created the round 7 map are incredible. Do they replicate every little detail of the areas of Mikado City right down to the wiring?

They're using technology that scans the real-life buildings and components of the city and replicates them all in the virtual space. For that night map, the engineers took the time and effort to faithfully upgrade the data on the electrical system.

■Are there any other siblings within Border other than the Kazama brothers?

In terms of characters who've appeared already, there's Tsukimi's little sister and Zoe's little brother, both of whom are in Yoshizato Squad (C-Rank).

■Why do so few agents choose to wield Teleporter? Is there some downside to using it, like not being able to use one's Triggers within a certain range immediately after, or one's body freezing up? If not, that seems like an overpowered Trigger.

Also, why didn't Arashiyama Squad wear goggles during the scramble for the Black Trigger? Concealing their lines of sight would've been a big advantage. Is it because that was their first time using Teleporter in a real battle? Or was it because they were purposely getting Toma to shoot? If there's no downside beside the line-of-sight thing, then I think Teleporter is way too powerful.

Ah, you're a Teleporter diehard. Thank you for the question(s). Given Izumi's shock when Arashiyama used Teleporter in volume 4, it's safe-ish to assume that was his first time using it. Kako Squad—the first Teleporter users—had a reason for not wearing goggles (which could hide one's line of sight), but if Arashiyama had worn goggles after his first use of Teleporter revealed the trick, I bet that would've made him really strong. I also tend to think that Teleporter is ridiculously powerful, but there are downsides, and learning to use it properly takes a high level of skill. I'm hoping to elaborate on that with future battle scenes involving Kako Squad, so please be patient.

Chapter 199 B-Rank War's End

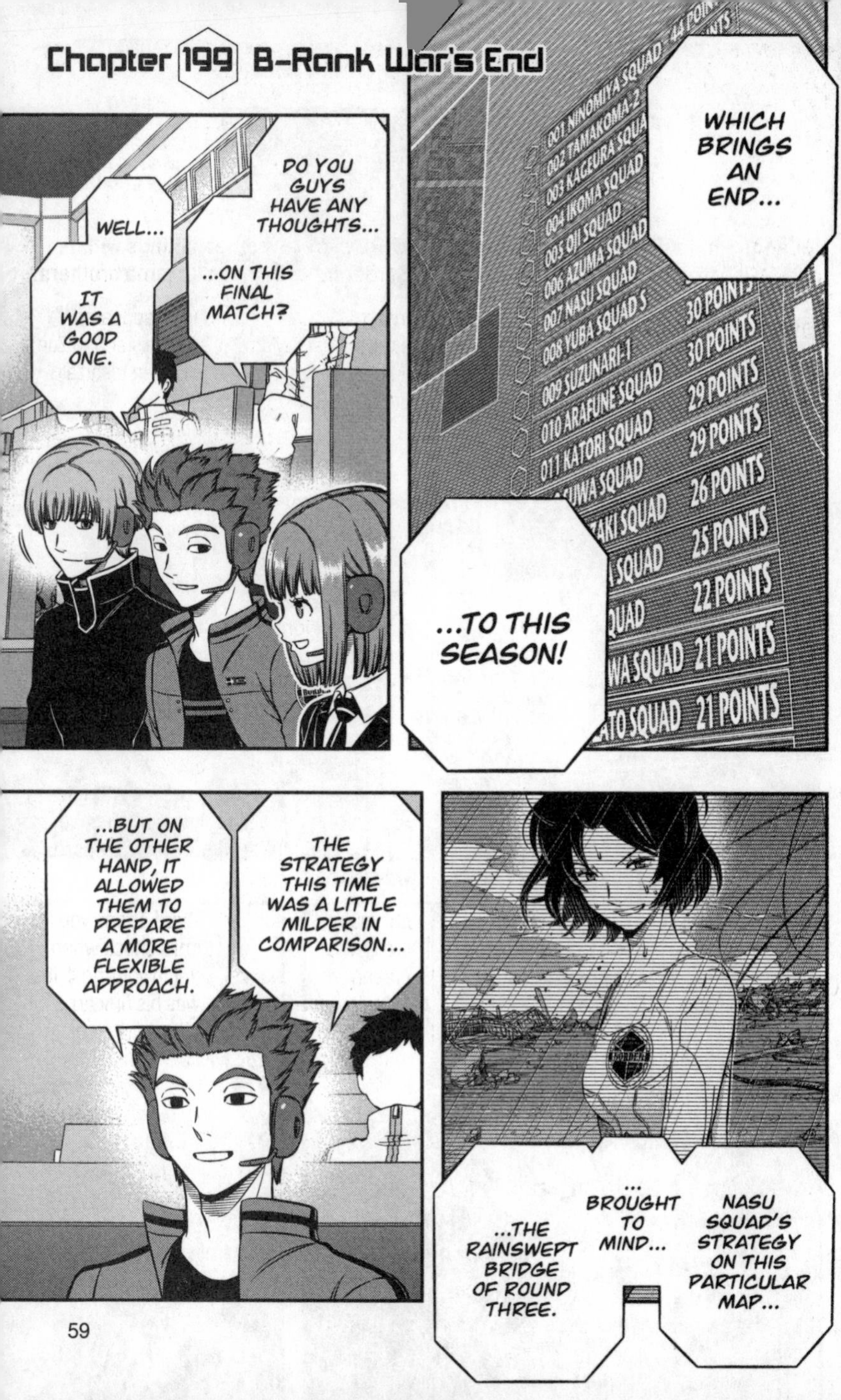
WHICH BRINGS AN END...
...TO THIS SEASON!
001 NINOMIYA SQUAD
002 TAMAKOMA-2
003 KAGEURA SQUAD
004 IKOMA SQUAD
005 OJI SQUAD
006 AZUMA SQUAD
007 NASU SQUAD
008 YUBA SQUAD
009 SUZUNARI-1
010 ARAFUNE SQUAD
011 KATORI SQUAD
DO YOU GUYS HAVE ANY THOUGHTS...
...ON THIS FINAL MATCH?
WELL...
IT WAS A GOOD ONE.
NASU SQUAD'S STRATEGY ON THIS PARTICULAR MAP...
...BROUGHT TO MIND...
...THE RAINSWEPT BRIDGE OF ROUND THREE.
THE STRATEGY THIS TIME WAS A LITTLE MILDER IN COMPARISON...
...BUT ON THE OTHER HAND, IT ALLOWED THEM TO PREPARE A MORE FLEXIBLE APPROACH.

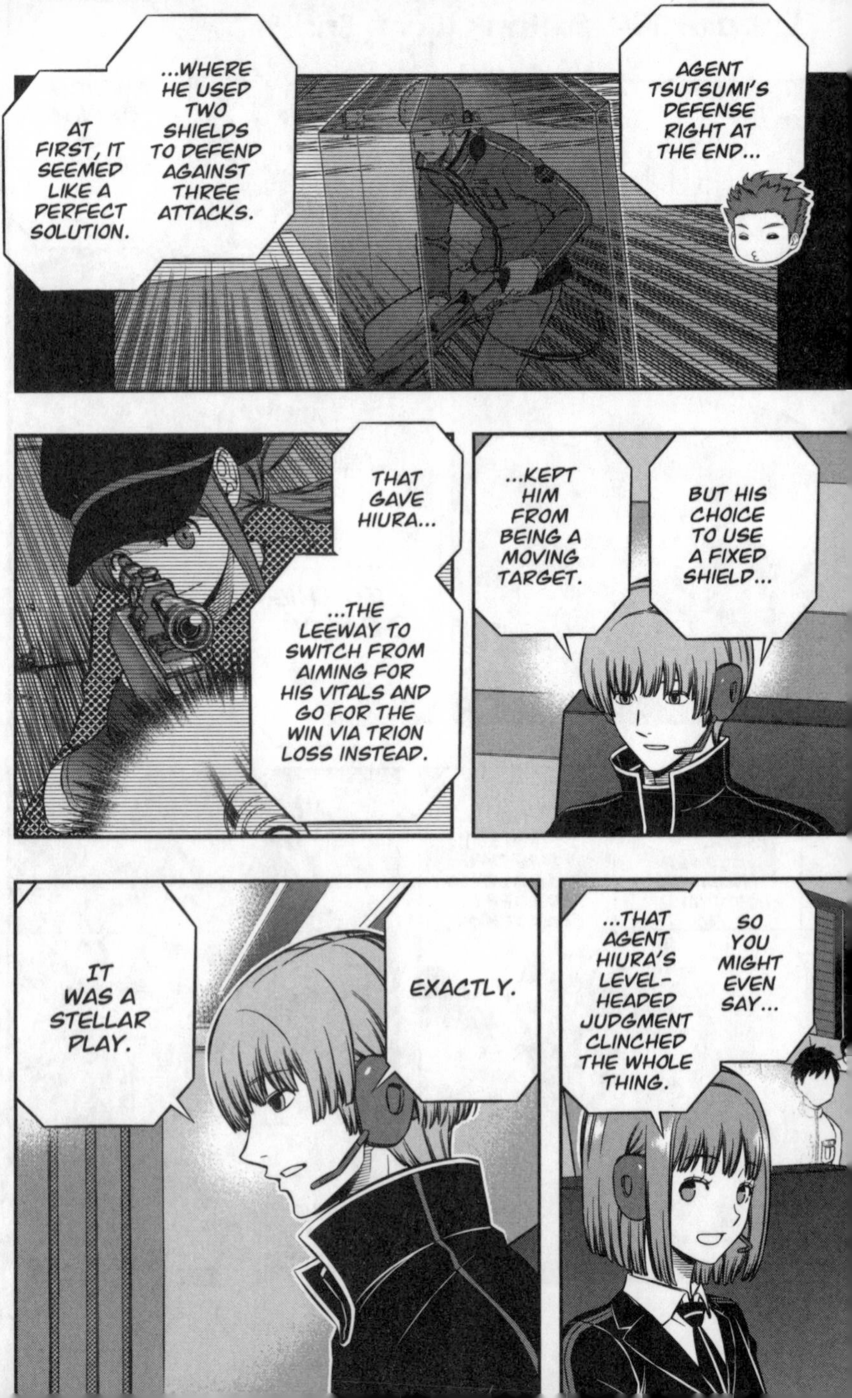
AGENT TSUTSUMI'S DEFENSE RIGHT AT THE END...
...WHERE HE USED TWO SHIELDS TO DEFEND AGAINST THREE ATTACKS.
AT FIRST, IT SEEMED LIKE A PERFECT SOLUTION.
BUT HIS CHOICE TO USE A FIXED SHIELD...
...KEPT HIM FROM BEING A MOVING TARGET.
THAT GAVE HIURA...
...THE LEEWAY TO SWITCH FROM AIMING FOR HIS VITALS AND GO FOR THE WIN VIA TRION LOSS INSTEAD.
SO YOU MIGHT EVEN SAY...
...THAT AGENT HIURA'S LEVEL-HEADED JUDGMENT CLINCHED THE WHOLE THING.
EXACTLY.
IT WAS A STELLAR PLAY.

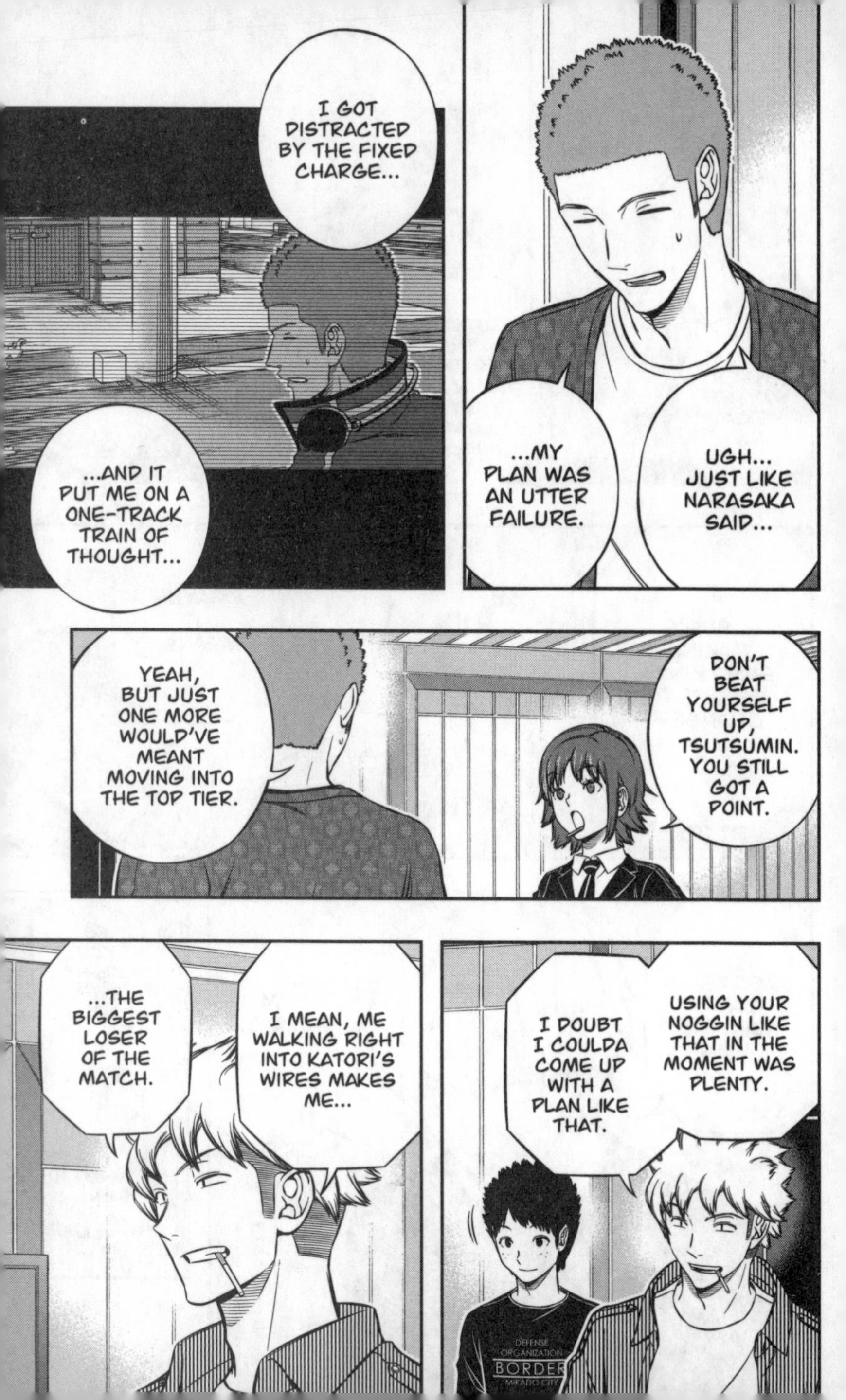
UGH... JUST LIKE NARASAKA SAID...
...MY PLAN WAS AN UTTER FAILURE.
I GOT DISTRACTED BY THE FIXED CHARGE...
...AND IT PUT ME ON A ONE-TRACK TRAIN OF THOUGHT...
DON'T BEAT YOURSELF UP, TSUTSUMIN. YOU STILL GOT A POINT.
YEAH, BUT JUST ONE MORE WOULD'VE MEANT MOVING INTO THE TOP TIER.
USING YOUR NOGGIN LIKE THAT IN THE MOMENT WAS PLENTY.
I DOUBT I COULDA COME UP WITH A PLAN LIKE THAT.
DEFENSE ORGANIZATION BORDER MIKADO CITY
I MEAN, ME WALKING RIGHT INTO KATORI'S WIRES MAKES ME...
...THE BIGGEST LOSER OF THE MATCH.

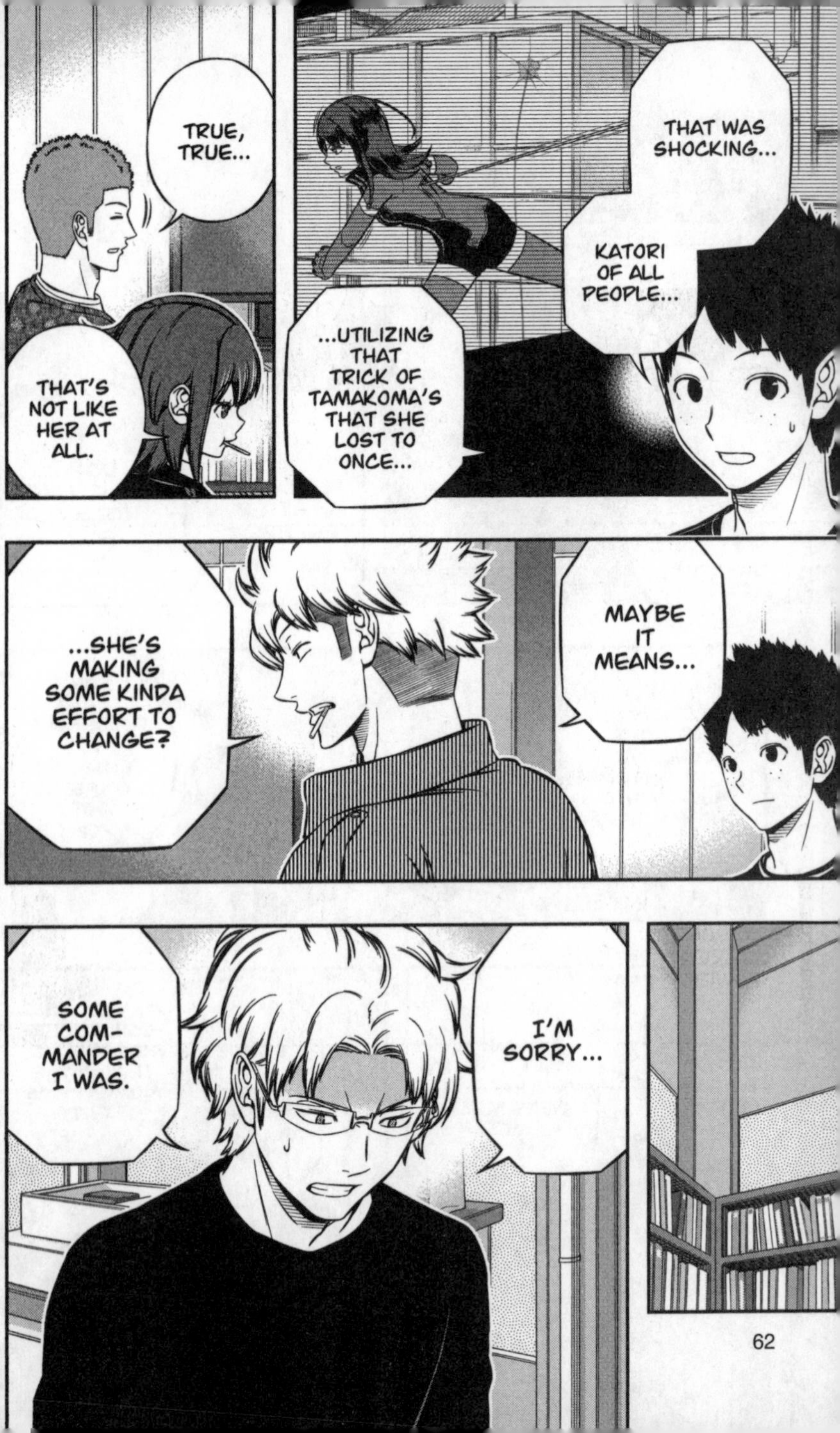
THAT WAS SHOCKING...
KATORI OF ALL PEOPLE...
...UTILIZING THAT TRICK OF TAMAKOMA'S THAT SHE LOST TO ONCE...
TRUE, TRUE...
THAT'S NOT LIKE HER AT ALL.
MAYBE IT MEANS...
...SHE'S MAKING SOME KINDA EFFORT TO CHANGE?
I'M SORRY...
SOME COM-MANDER I WAS.

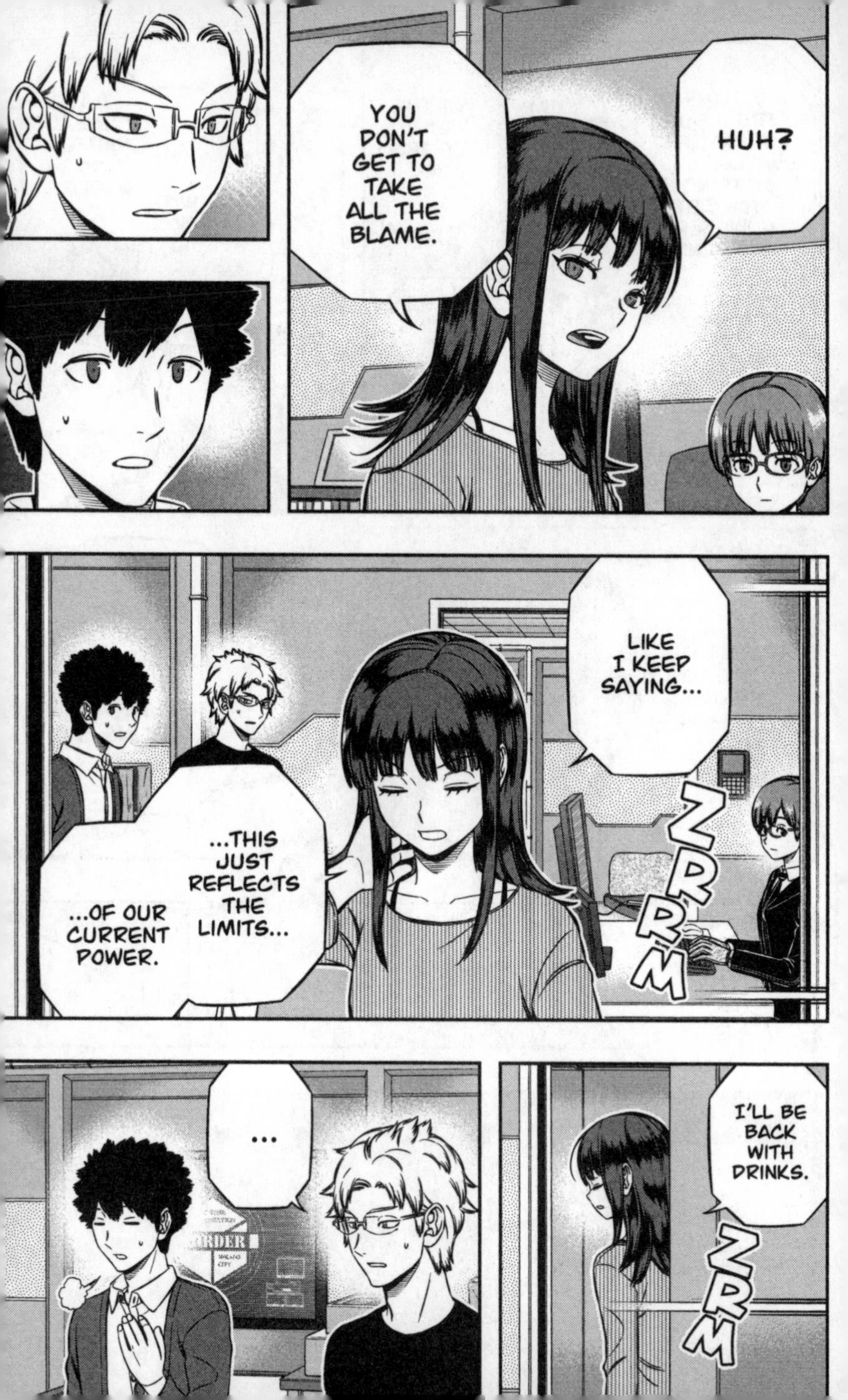
HUH?
YOU DON'T GET TO TAKE ALL THE BLAME.
LIKE I KEEP SAYING...
ZRRM
...THIS JUST REFLECTS THE LIMITS...
...OF OUR CURRENT POWER.
I'LL BE BACK WITH DRINKS.
ZRM
...

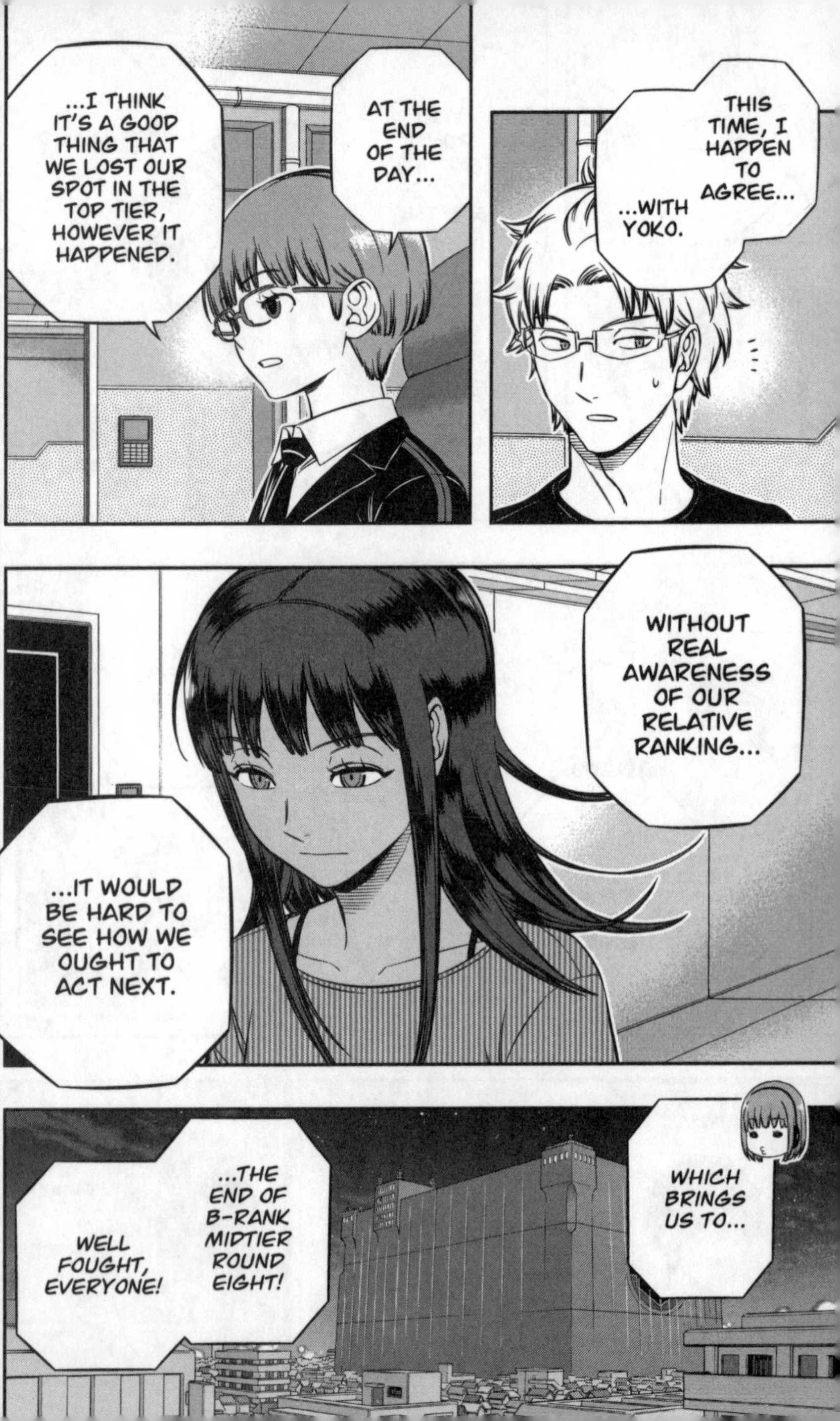
THIS TIME, I HAPPEN TO AGREE...
...WITH YOKO.
AT THE END OF THE DAY...
...I THINK IT'S A GOOD THING THAT WE LOST OUR SPOT IN THE TOP TIER, HOWEVER IT HAPPENED.
WITHOUT REAL AWARENESS OF OUR RELATIVE RANKING...
...IT WOULD BE HARD TO SEE HOW WE OUGHT TO ACT NEXT.
WHICH BRINGS US TO...
...THE END OF B-RANK MIDTIER ROUND EIGHT!
WELL FOUGHT, EVERYONE!

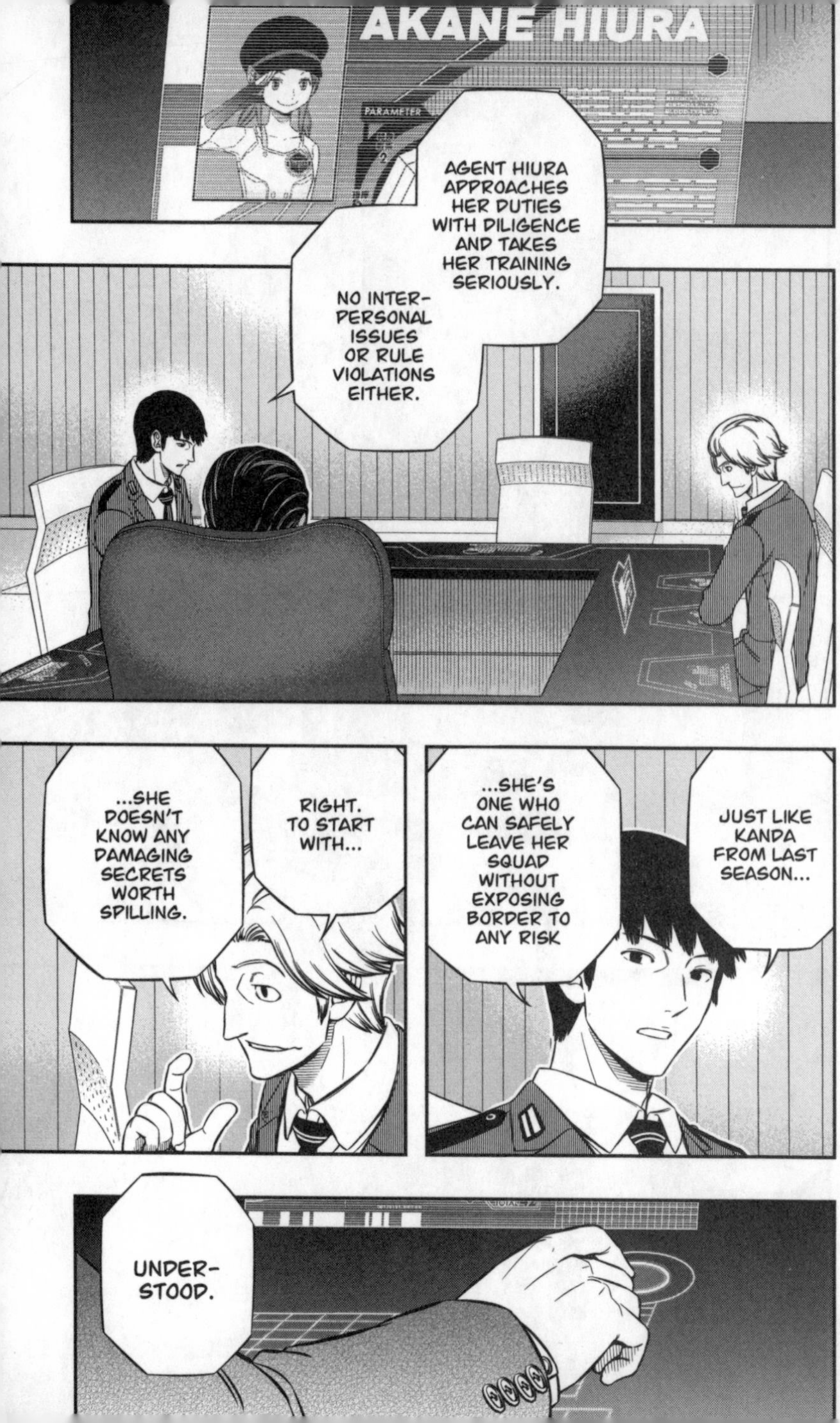
AKANE HIURA
PARAMETER
AGENT HIURA APPROACHES HER DUTIES WITH DILIGENCE AND TAKES HER TRAINING SERIOUSLY.
NO INTER-PERSONAL ISSUES OR RULE VIOLATIONS EITHER.
JUST LIKE KANDA FROM LAST SEASON...
...SHE'S ONE WHO CAN SAFELY LEAVE HER SQUAD WITHOUT EXPOSING BORDER TO ANY RISK
RIGHT. TO START WITH...
...SHE DOESN'T KNOW ANY DAMAGING SECRETS WORTH SPILLING.
UNDER-STOOD.

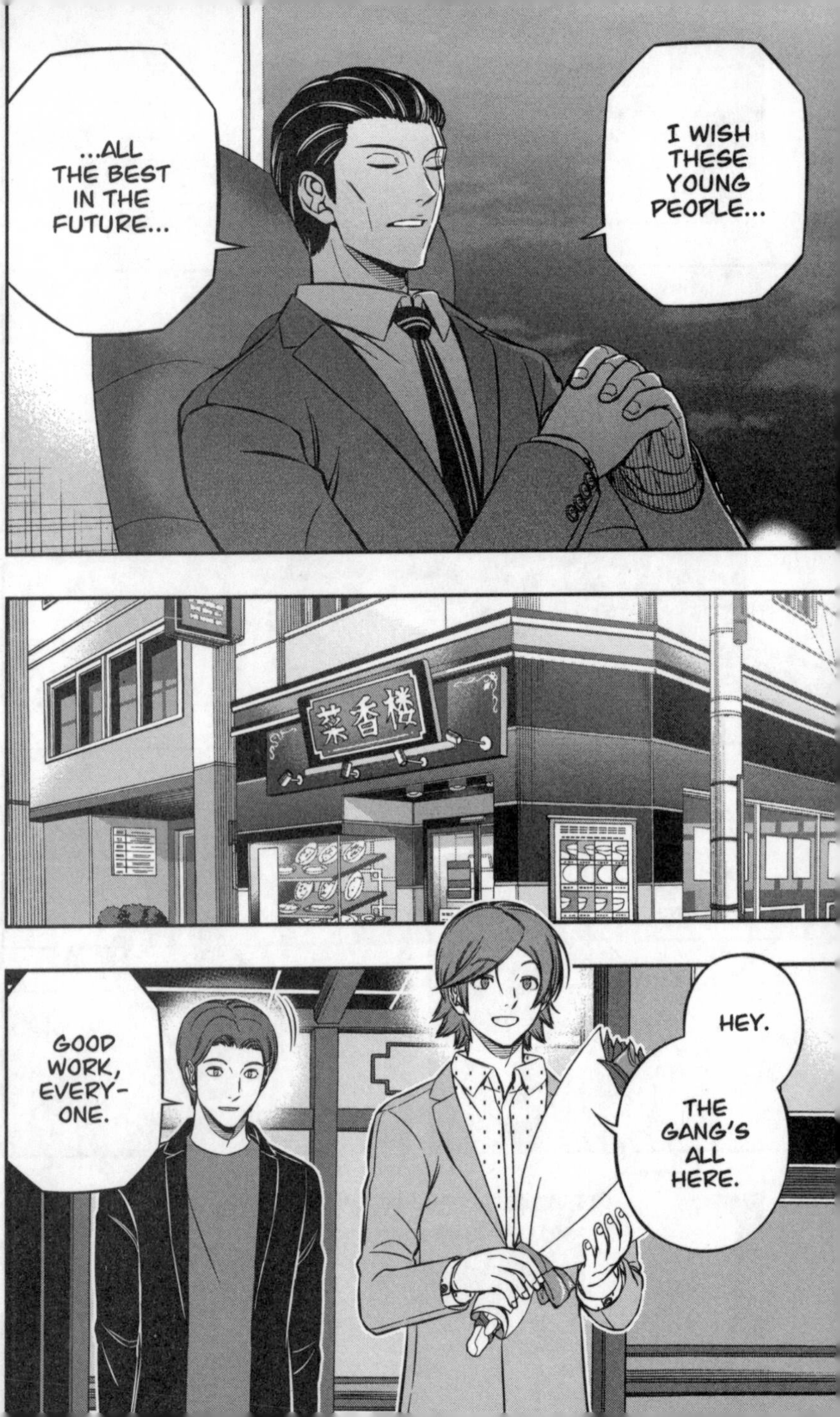
I WISH THESE YOUNG PEOPLE...
...ALL THE BEST IN THE FUTURE...
菜香楼
HEY.
THE GANG'S ALL HERE.
GOOD WORK, EVERY-ONE.

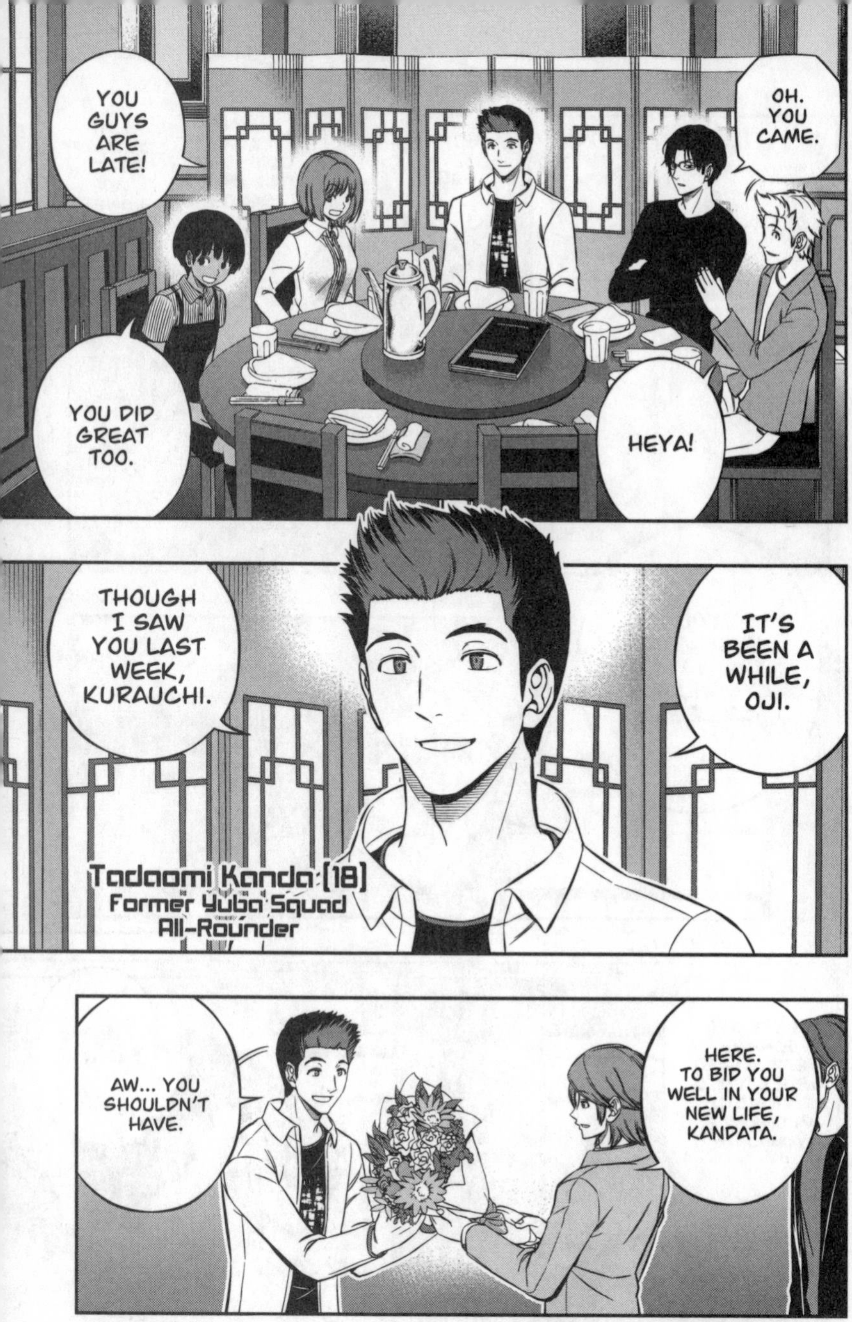
OH. YOU CAME.
YOU GUYS ARE LATE!
HEYA!
YOU DID GREAT TOO.
IT'S BEEN A WHILE, OJI.
THOUGH I SAW YOU LAST WEEK, KURAUCHI.
Tadaomi Kanda [18]
Former Yuba Squad All-Rounder
HERE. TO BID YOU WELL IN YOUR NEW LIFE, KANDATA.
AW... YOU SHOULDN'T HAVE.

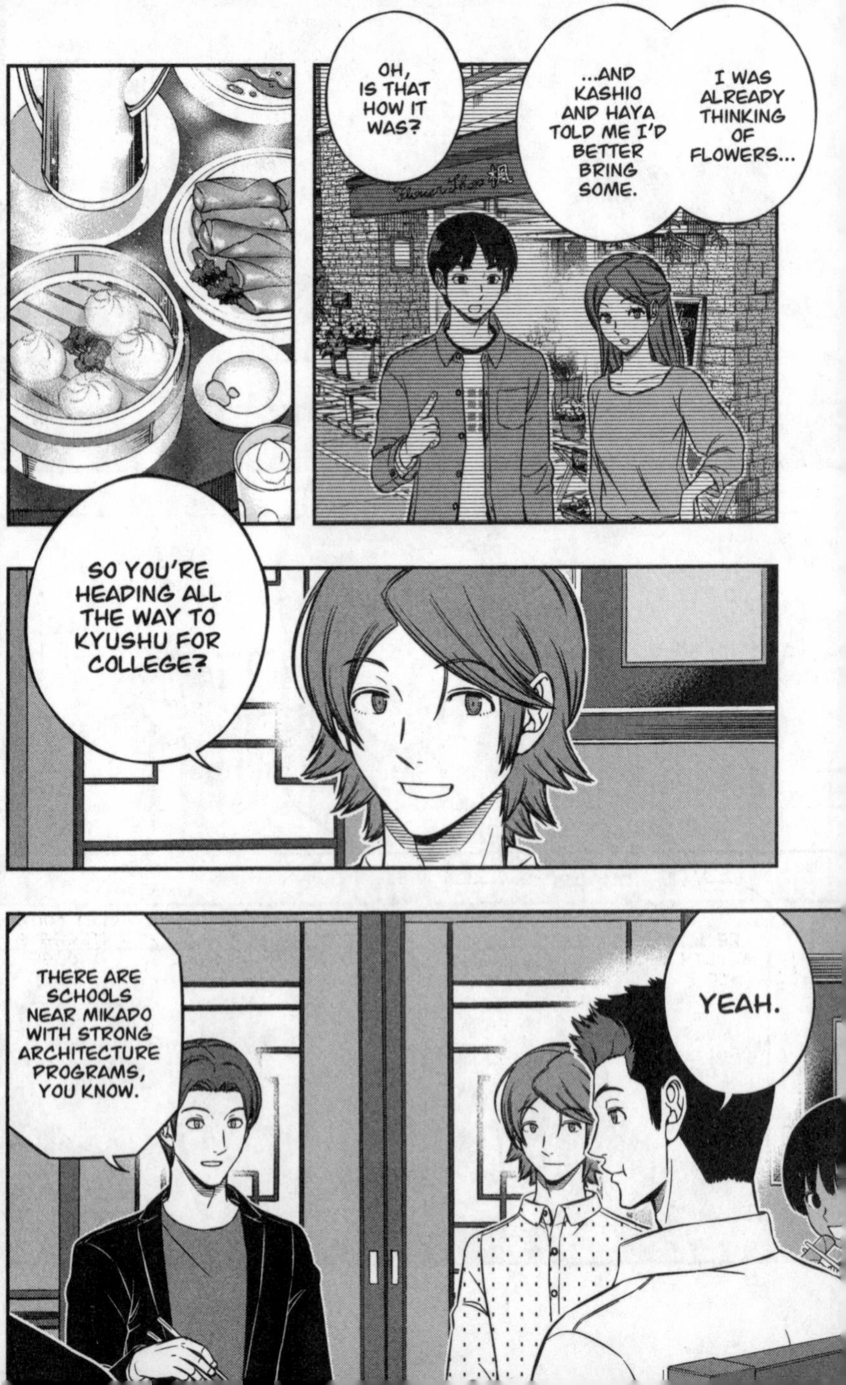
I WAS ALREADY THINKING OF FLOWERS...
...AND KASHIO AND HAYA TOLD ME I'D BETTER BRING SOME.
OH, IS THAT HOW IT WAS?
SO YOU'RE HEADING ALL THE WAY TO KYUSHU FOR COLLEGE?
YEAH.
THERE ARE SCHOOLS NEAR MIKADO WITH STRONG ARCHITECTURE PROGRAMS, YOU KNOW.

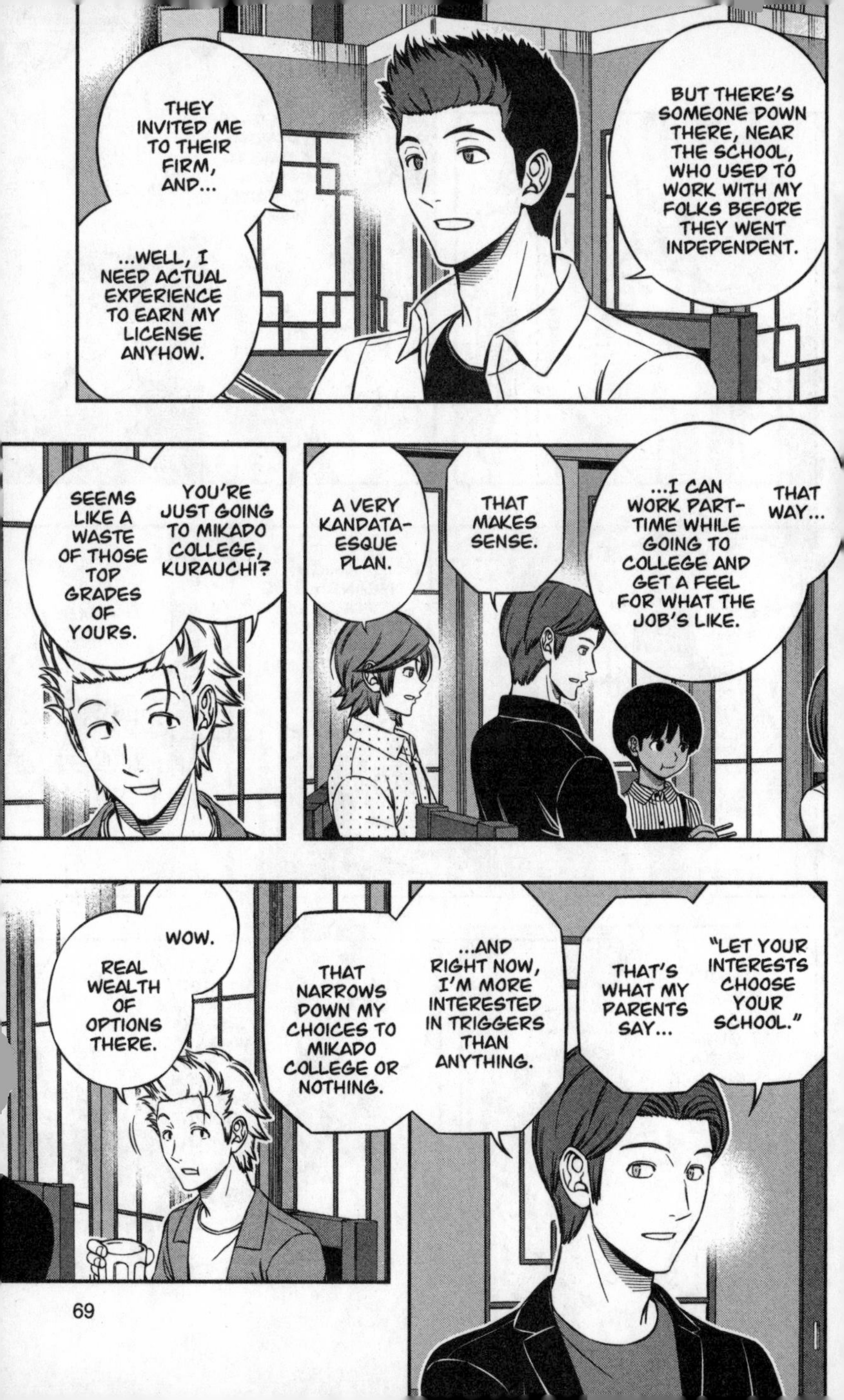
BUT THERE'S SOMEONE DOWN THERE, NEAR THE SCHOOL, WHO USED TO WORK WITH MY FOLKS BEFORE THEY WENT INDEPENDENT.
THEY INVITED ME TO THEIR FIRM, AND...
...WELL, I NEED ACTUAL EXPERIENCE TO EARN MY LICENSE ANYHOW.
THAT WAY...
...I CAN WORK PART-TIME WHILE GOING TO COLLEGE AND GET A FEEL FOR WHAT THE JOB'S LIKE.
THAT MAKES SENSE.
A VERY KANDATA-ESQUE PLAN.
YOU'RE JUST GOING TO MIKADO COLLEGE, KURAUCHI?
SEEMS LIKE A WASTE OF THOSE TOP GRADES OF YOURS.
"LET YOUR INTERESTS CHOOSE YOUR SCHOOL."
THAT'S WHAT MY PARENTS SAY...
...AND RIGHT NOW, I'M MORE INTERESTED IN TRIGGERS THAN ANYTHING.
THAT NARROWS DOWN MY CHOICES TO MIKADO COLLEGE OR NOTHING.
WOW.
REAL WEALTH OF OPTIONS THERE.

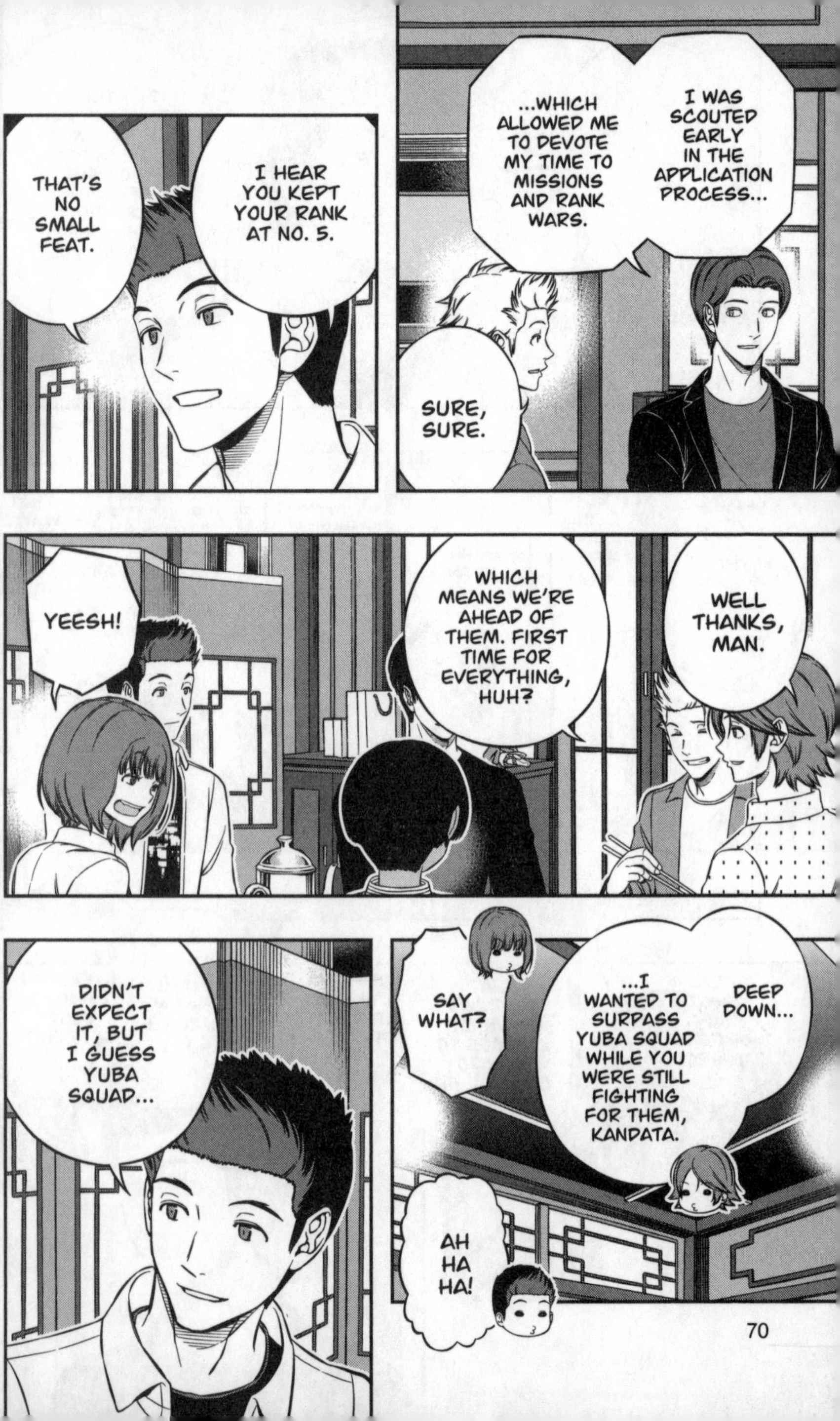
I WAS SCOUTED EARLY IN THE APPLICATION PROCESS...
...WHICH ALLOWED ME TO DEVOTE MY TIME TO MISSIONS AND RANK WARS.
SURE, SURE.
I HEAR YOU KEPT YOUR RANK AT NO. 5.
THAT'S NO SMALL FEAT.
WELL THANKS, MAN.
WHICH MEANS WE'RE AHEAD OF THEM. FIRST TIME FOR EVERYTHING, HUH?
YEESH!
DEEP DOWN...
...I WANTED TO SURPASS YUBA SQUAD WHILE YOU WERE STILL FIGHTING FOR THEM, KANDATA.
SAY WHAT?
AH HA HA!
DIDN'T EXPECT IT, BUT I GUESS YUBA SQUAD...

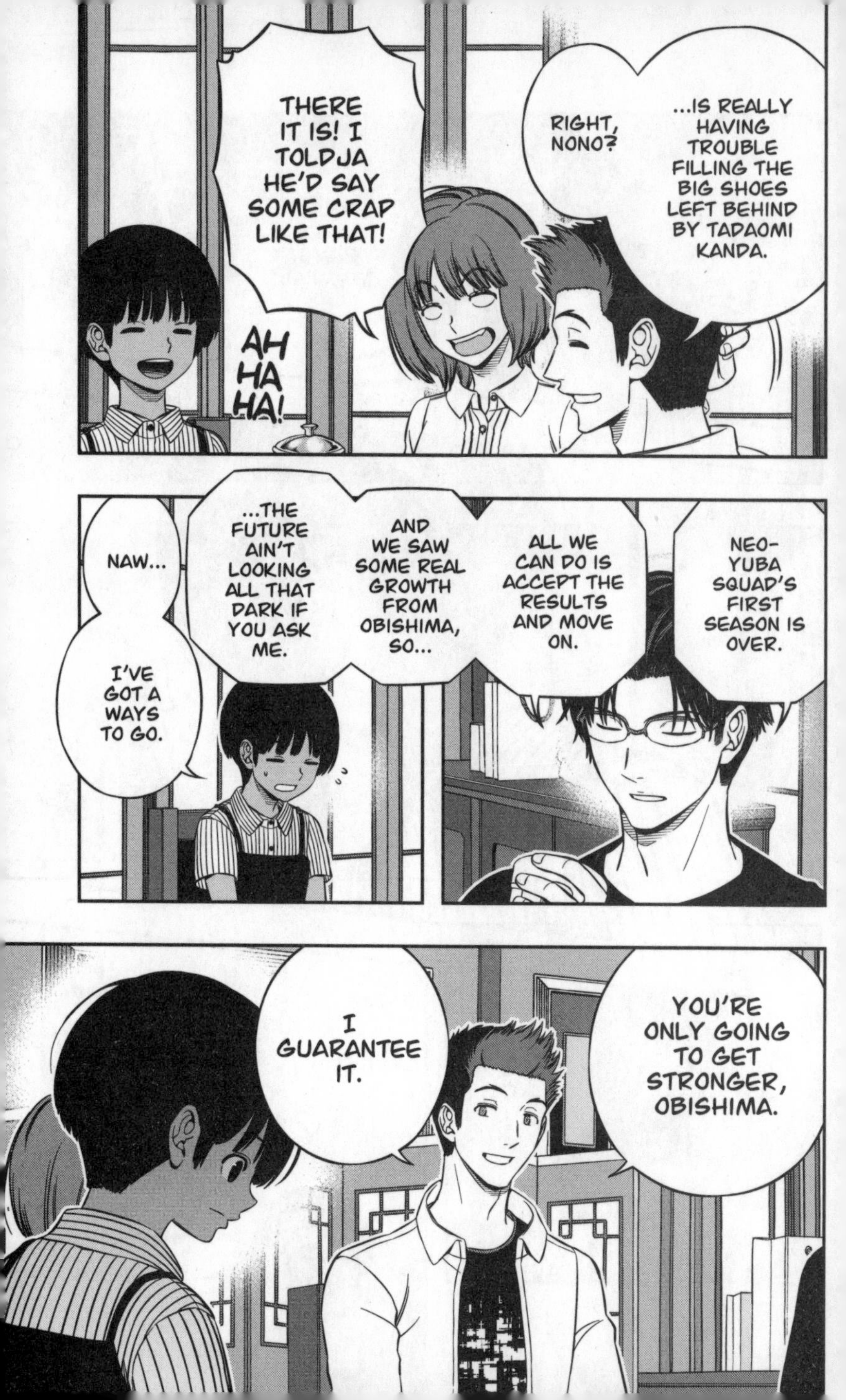
...IS REALLY HAVING TROUBLE FILLING THE BIG SHOES LEFT BEHIND BY TADAOMI KANDA.
RIGHT, NONO?
THERE IT IS! I TOLDJA HE'D SAY SOME CRAP LIKE THAT!
AH HA HA!
NEO-YUBA SQUAD'S FIRST SEASON IS OVER.
ALL WE CAN DO IS ACCEPT THE RESULTS AND MOVE ON.
AND WE SAW SOME REAL GROWTH FROM OBISHIMA, SO...
...THE FUTURE AIN'T LOOKING ALL THAT DARK IF YOU ASK ME.
NAW...
I'VE GOT A WAYS TO GO.
YOU'RE ONLY GOING TO GET STRONGER, OBISHIMA.
I GUARANTEE IT.

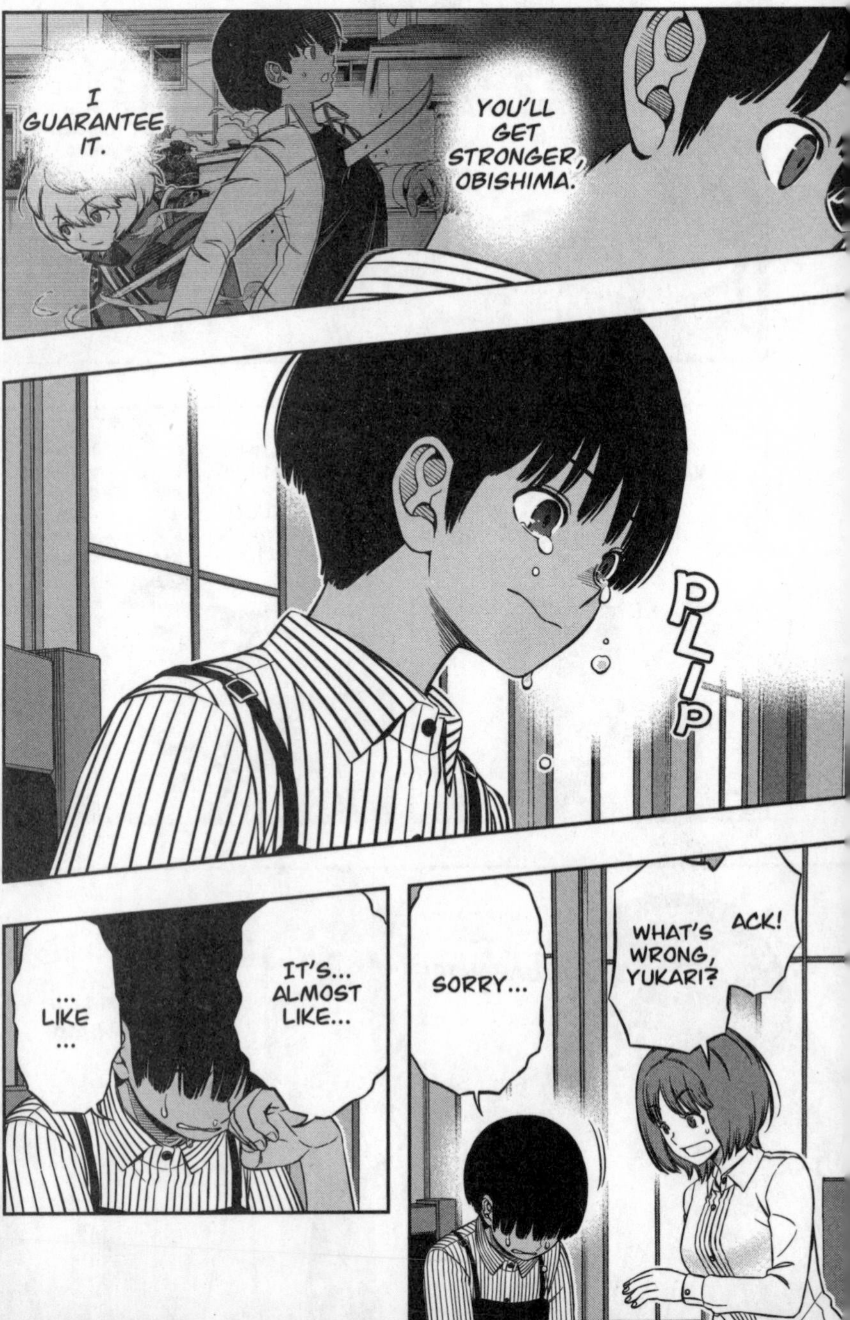
YOU'LL GET STRONGER, OBISHIMA.
I GUARANTEE IT.
PLIP
ACK!
WHAT'S WRONG, YUKARI?
SORRY...
IT'S... ALMOST LIKE...
... LIKE ...

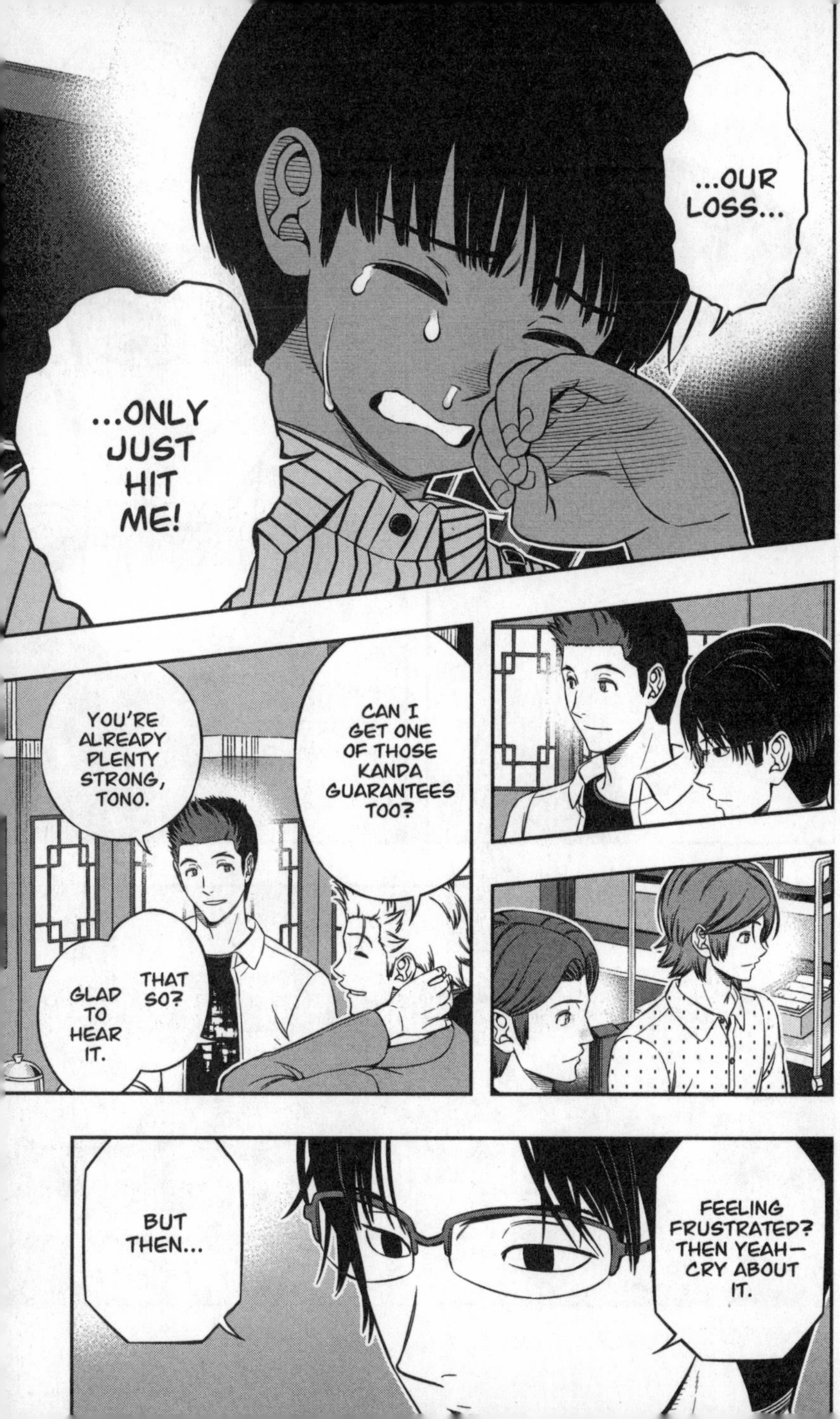

...OUR LOSS...
...ONLY JUST HIT ME!
CAN I GET ONE OF THOSE KANDA GUARANTEES TOO?
YOU'RE ALREADY PLENTY STRONG, TONO.
THAT SO?
GLAD TO HEAR IT.
FEELING FRUSTRATED? THEN YEAH—CRY ABOUT IT.
BUT THEN...

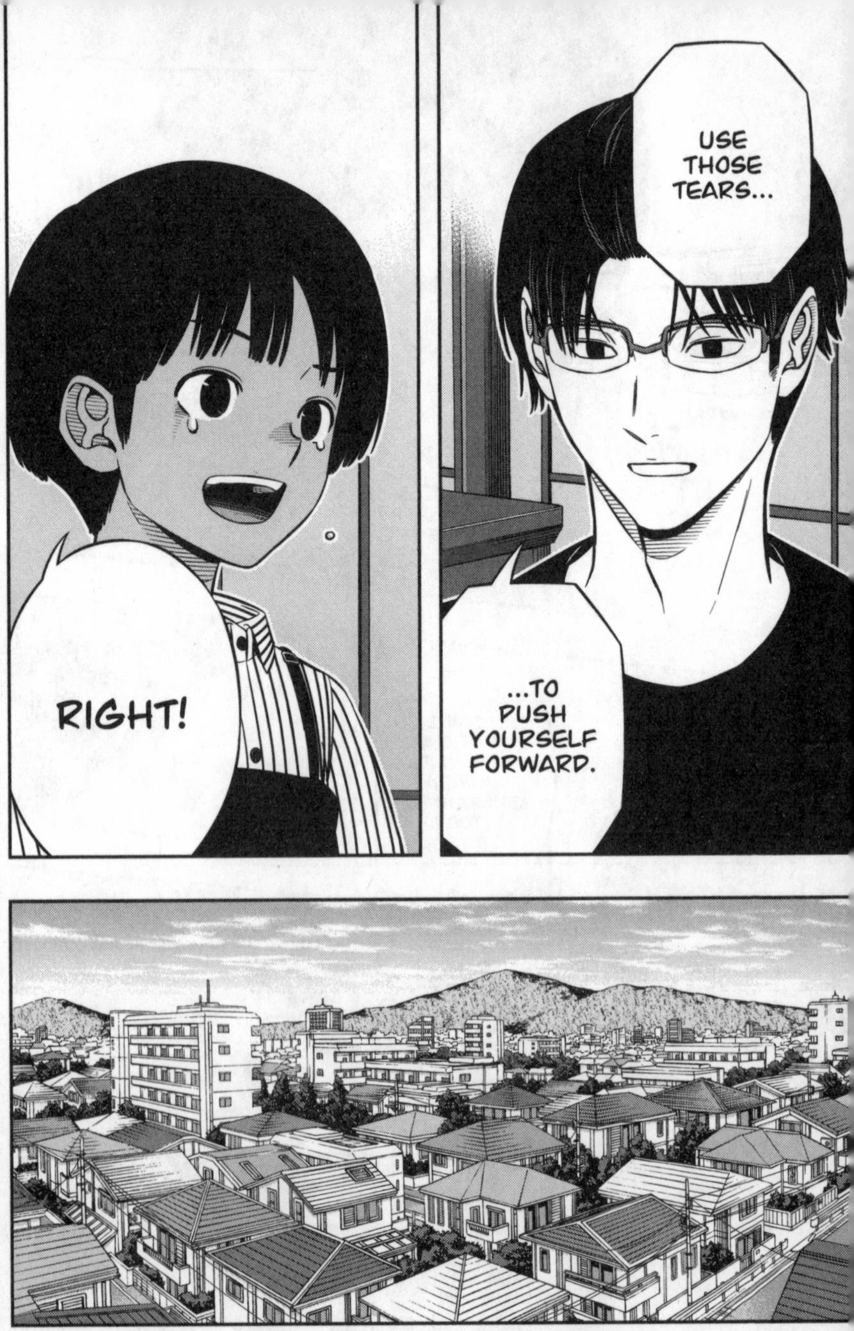
USE THOSE TEARS...
...TO PUSH YOURSELF FORWARD.
RIGHT!

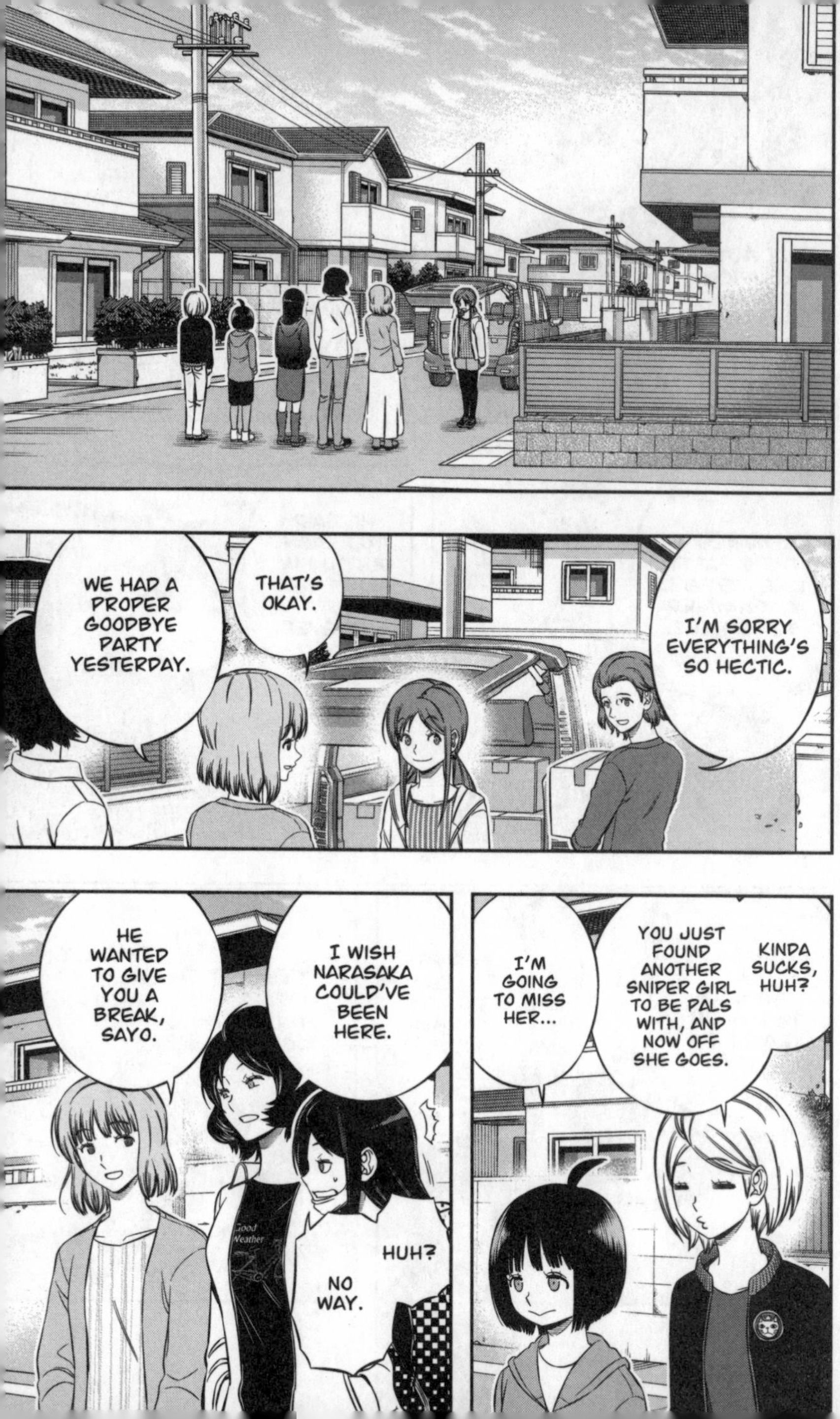
I'M SORRY EVERYTHING'S SO HECTIC.
THAT'S OKAY.
WE HAD A PROPER GOODBYE PARTY YESTERDAY.
KINDA SUCKS, HUH?
YOU JUST FOUND ANOTHER SNIPER GIRL TO BE PALS WITH, AND NOW OFF SHE GOES.
I'M GOING TO MISS HER...
I WISH NARASAKA COULD'VE BEEN HERE.
HE WANTED TO GIVE YOU A BREAK, SAYO.
HUH?
NO WAY.

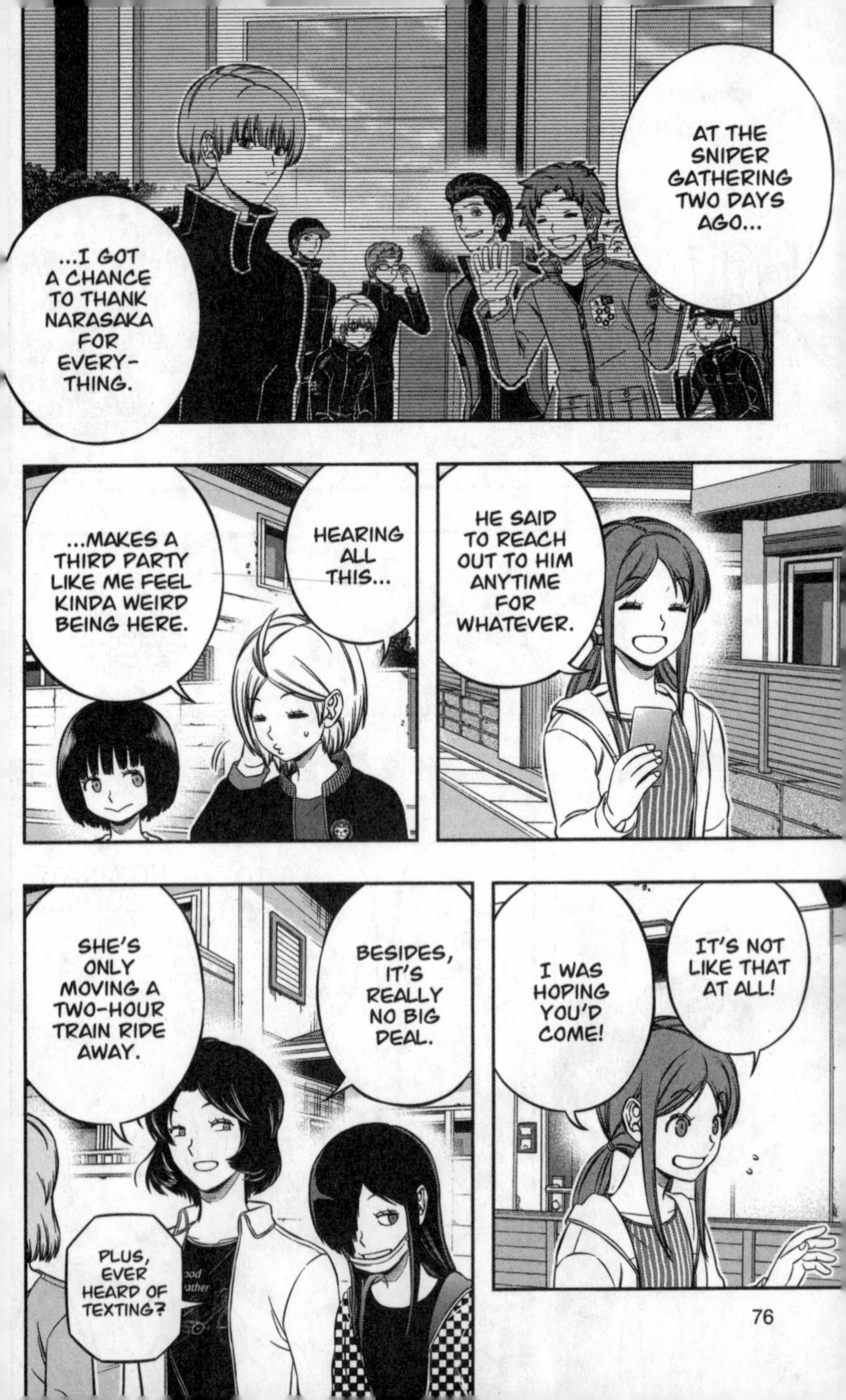
AT THE SNIPER GATHERING TWO DAYS AGO...
...I GOT A CHANCE TO THANK NARASAKA FOR EVERY-THING.
HE SAID TO REACH OUT TO HIM ANYTIME FOR WHATEVER.
HEARING ALL THIS...
...MAKES A THIRD PARTY LIKE ME FEEL KINDA WEIRD BEING HERE.
IT'S NOT LIKE THAT AT ALL!
I WAS HOPING YOU'D COME!
BESIDES, IT'S REALLY NO BIG DEAL.
SHE'S ONLY MOVING A TWO-HOUR TRAIN RIDE AWAY.
PLUS, EVER HEARD OF TEXTING?

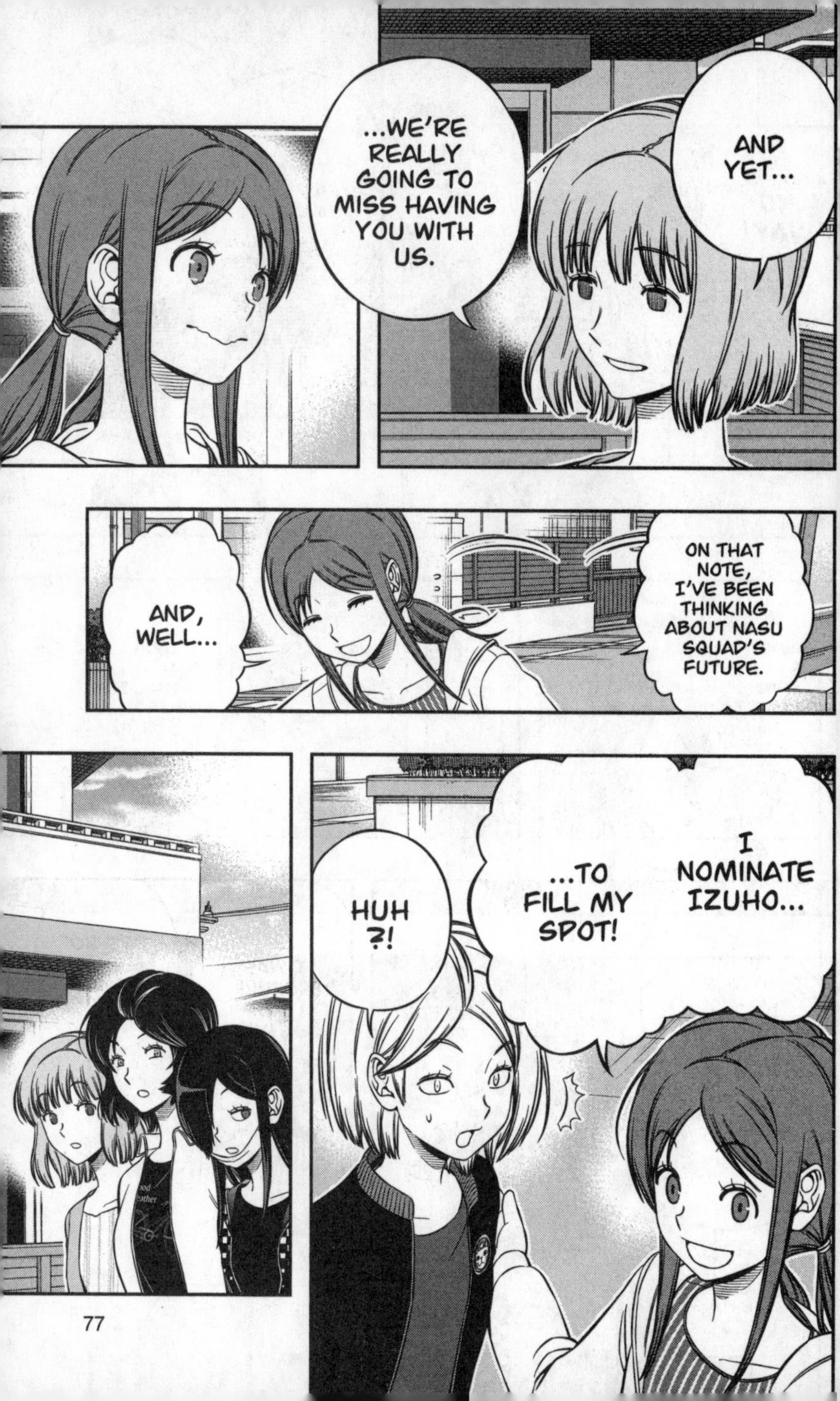
AND YET...
...WE'RE REALLY GOING TO MISS HAVING YOU WITH US.
ON THAT NOTE, I'VE BEEN THINKING ABOUT NASU SQUAD'S FUTURE.
AND, WELL...
I NOMINATE IZUHO...
...TO FILL MY SPOT!
HUH ?!

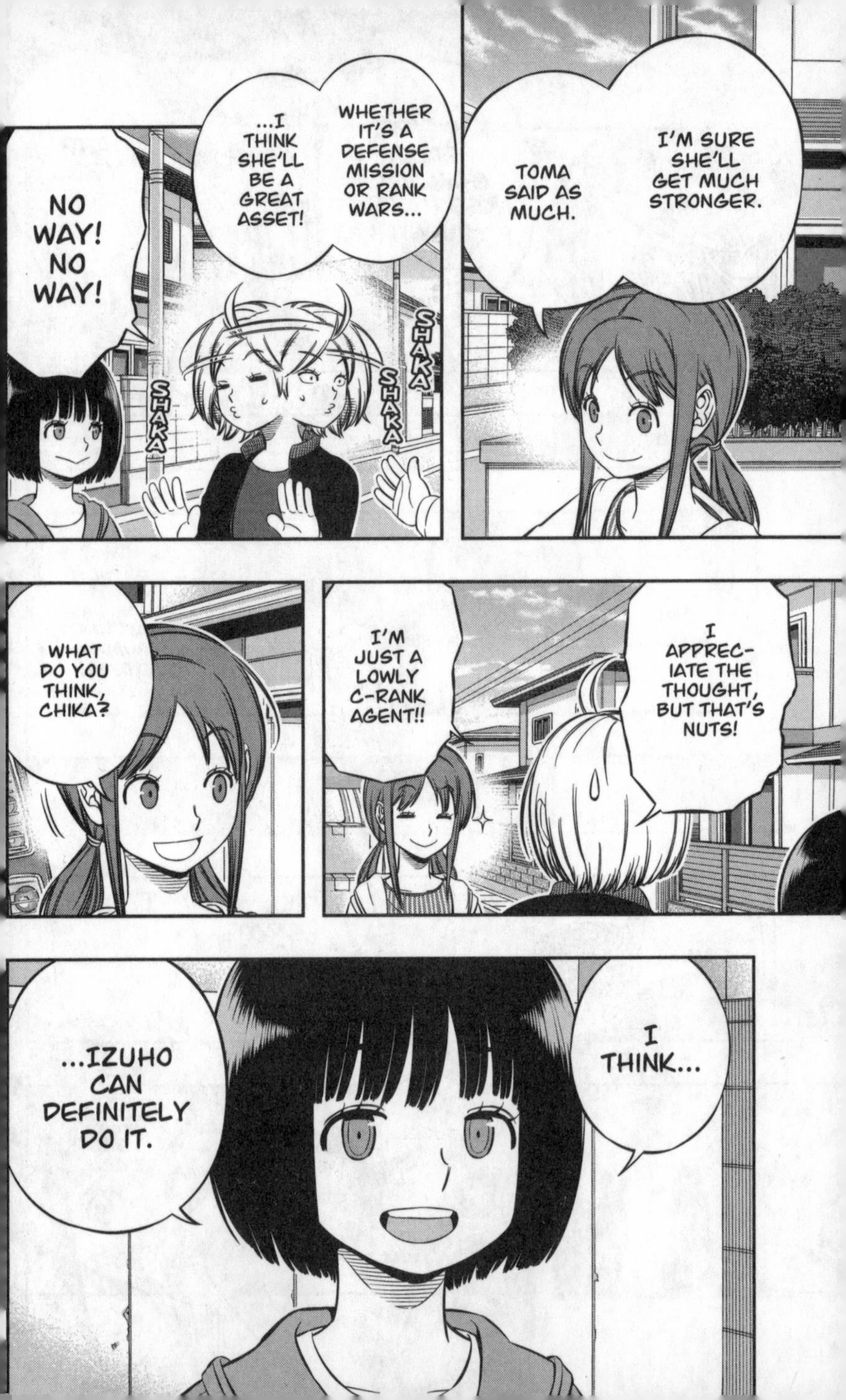
I'M SURE SHE'LL GET MUCH STRONGER.
TOMA SAID AS MUCH.
WHETHER IT'S A DEFENSE MISSION OR RANK WARS...
...I THINK SHE'LL BE A GREAT ASSET!
SHAKA
SHAKA
SHAKA
NO WAY! NO WAY!
I APPRECIATE THE THOUGHT, BUT THAT'S NUTS!
I'M JUST A LOWLY C-RANK AGENT!!
WHAT DO YOU THINK, CHIKA?
I THINK...
...IZUHO CAN DEFINITELY DO IT.

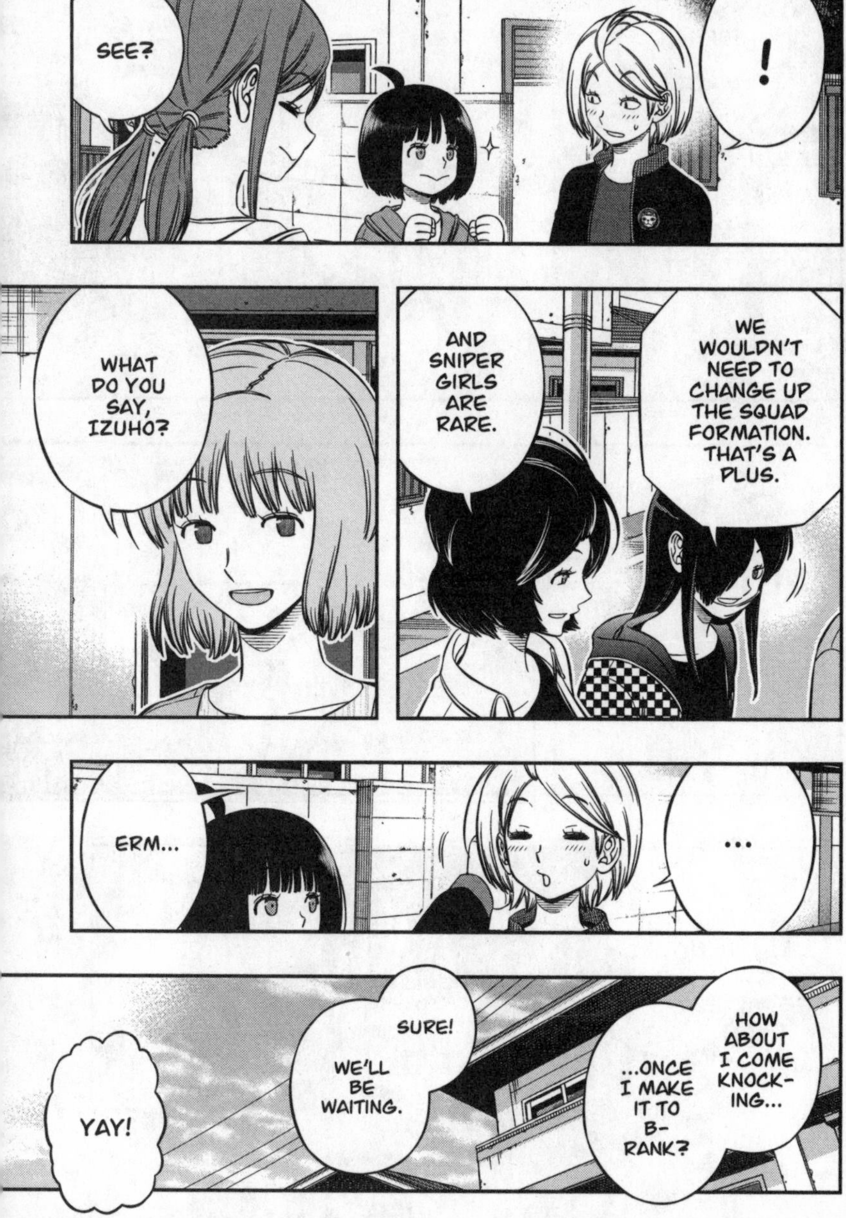
!
SEE?
WE WOULDN'T NEED TO CHANGE UP THE SQUAD FORMATION. THAT'S A PLUS.
AND SNIPER GIRLS ARE RARE.
WHAT DO YOU SAY, IZUHO?
...
ERM...
HOW ABOUT I COME KNOCK-ING...
...ONCE I MAKE IT TO B-RANK?
SURE!
WE'LL BE WAITING.
YAY!

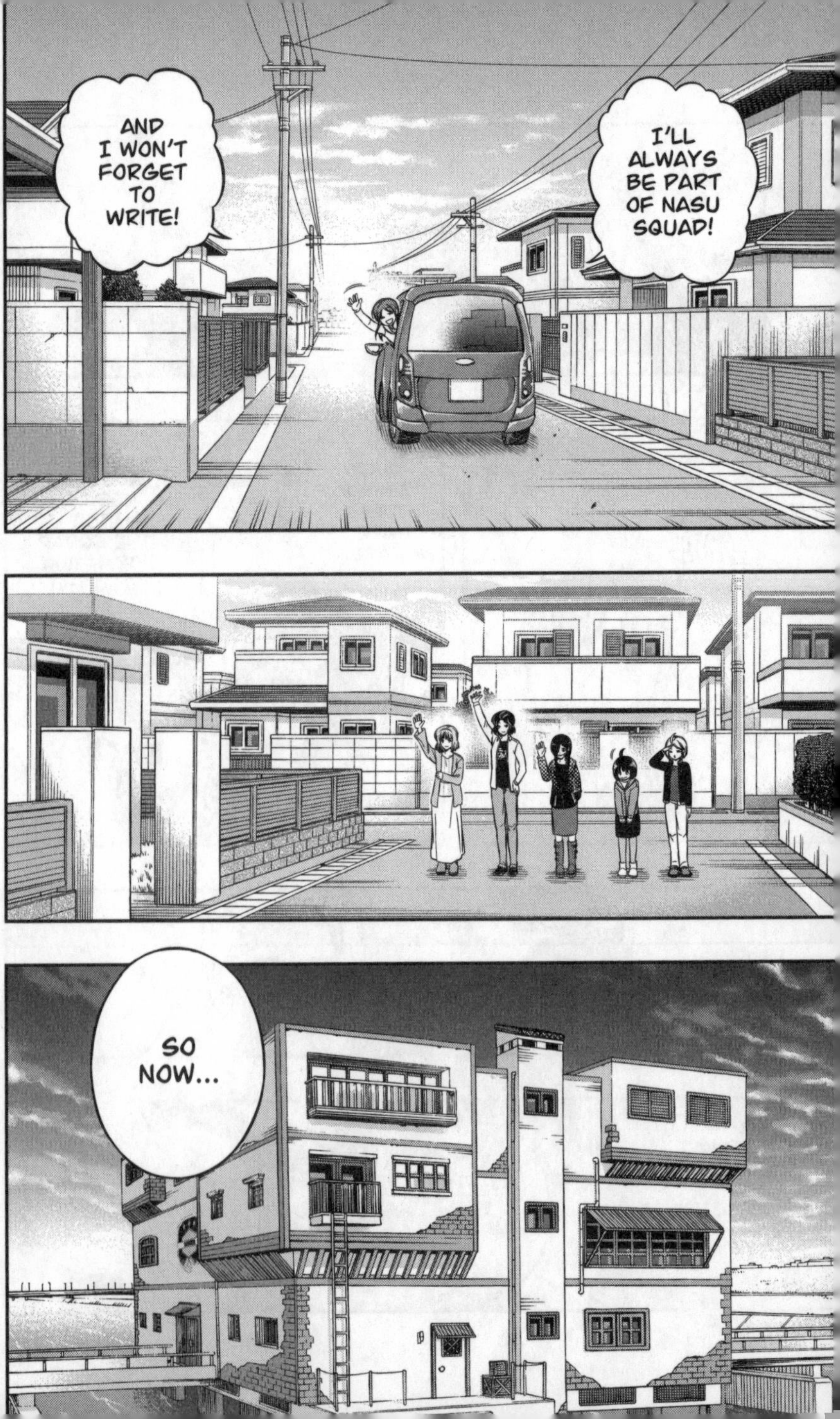
I'LL ALWAYS BE PART OF NASU SQUAD!
AND I WON'T FORGET TO WRITE!
SO NOW...

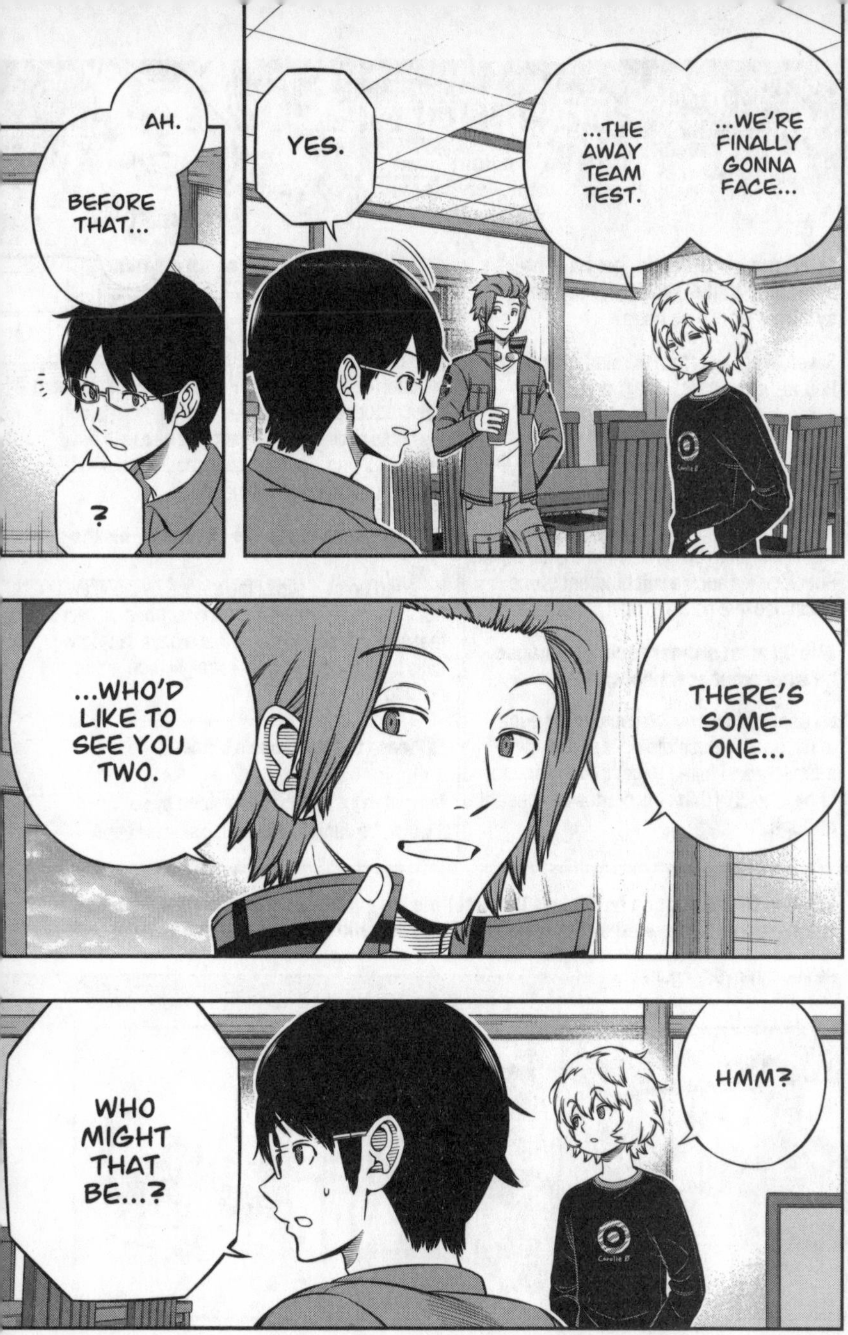
...WE'RE FINALLY GONNA FACE...
...THE AWAY TEAM TEST.
YES.
AH.
BEFORE THAT...
?
THERE'S SOME-ONE...
...WHO'D LIKE TO SEE YOU TWO.
HMM?
WHO MIGHT THAT BE...?

Q&A: Part 19
Questions I can't totally answer yet.

■Did Yuma's Black Trigger have no symbol initially? Which of the standard symbols would he have?

Seven altogether from the start, including Hound, Burst, Shield, Chain, and Echo.

■When the Escudo popped out of Murakami's body, did it feel heavy to him like a Lead Bullet? Or did it just impede his movement because of the bulk?

I think it's got to be lighter than a Lead Bullet. But since it's such a stiff hindrance, one could use that move to really annoy people.

■Is Oji at an ordinary school because he's not great at schoolwork?

Oji used to have much more of an edge to him, so it's possible he bungled the interview and failed to get into the school of his choice. I think his grades are decent enough.

■Can a Sniper Trigger shoot anything besides Asteroid or Lead Bullet?

Strictly speaking, a sniper's "bullets" aren't Asteroids, but sure—I bet they could make a special request to the engineers. However, the result would have reduced power, speed, and range, making the shots easier to block. It might be fun to have them shooting Viper shots, but nailing a far-off target would be pretty difficult.

■Who came up with the "Torimaru" nickname?

It started up as a slip of the tongue by Tachikawa, but it seems as though Konami jumped all over that and spread it around. These days, Tachikawa calls him "Kyosuke" with a straight face, accepting no blame.

■Please tell us Hyuse's birthday.

Translated into a date understood by our world, it would be June 12. His zodiac sign is Lepus.

■When Oji mentioned how it was the first time his squad got ahead of Yuba Squad, Yuba's face was covered by the speech bubble! How did he react to that line from Oji?

He LOL'd, maybe? I guess.

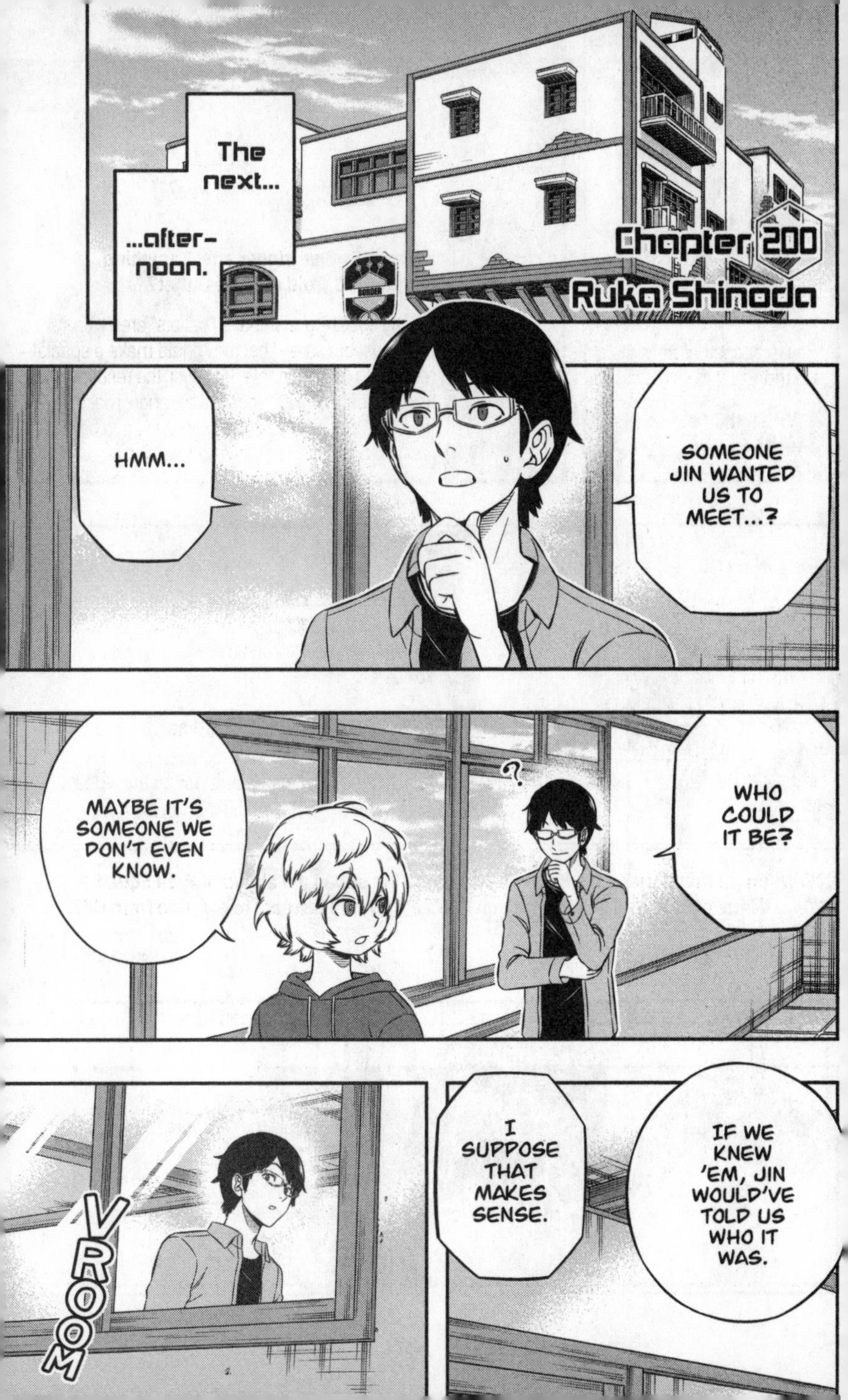
Chapter 200
Ruka Shinoda
The next...
...after-noon.
SOMEONE JIN WANTED US TO MEET...?
HMM...
WHO COULD IT BE?
MAYBE IT'S SOMEONE WE DON'T EVEN KNOW.
IF WE KNEW 'EM, JIN WOULD'VE TOLD US WHO IT WAS.
I SUPPOSE THAT MAKES SENSE.
VROOM

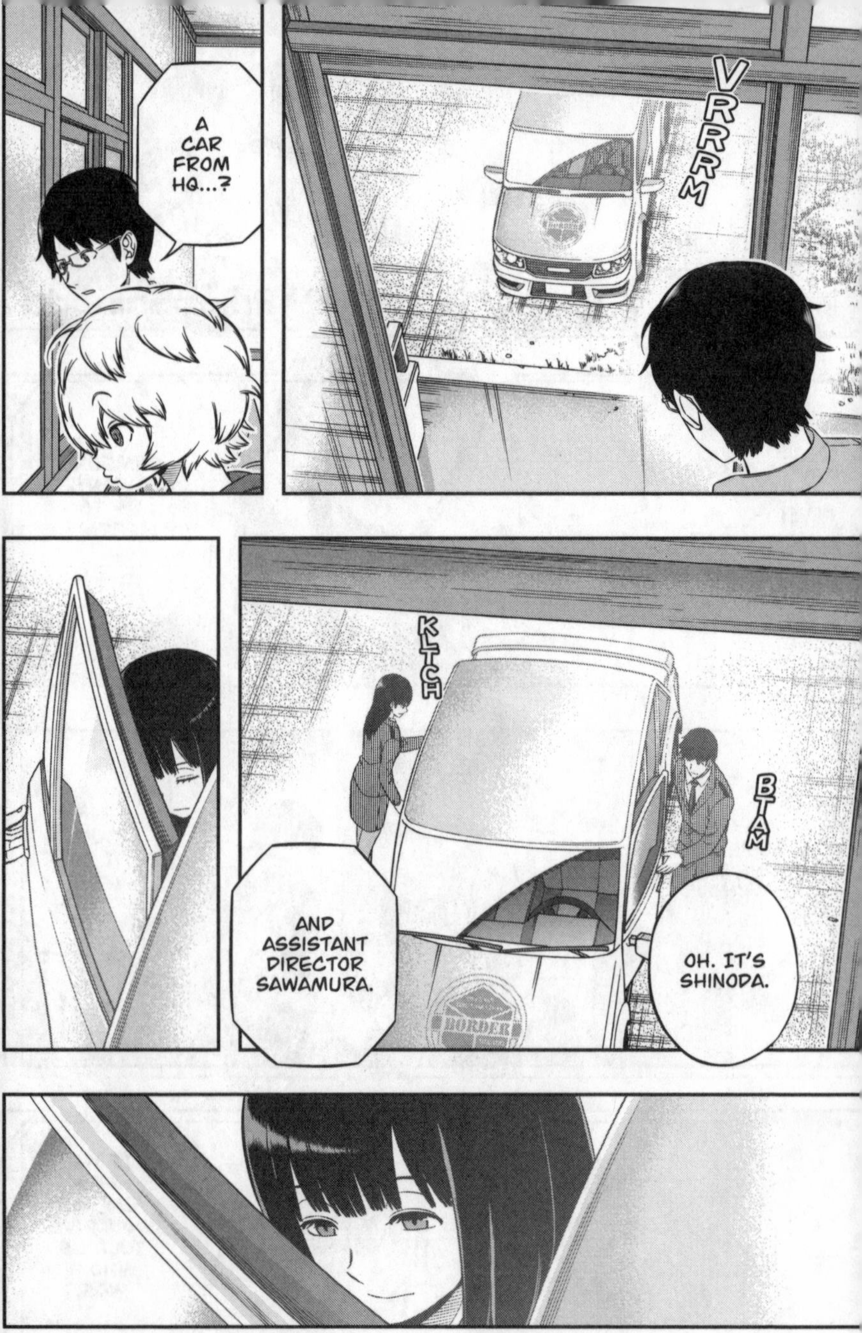
VRRRM
A CAR FROM HQ...?
KLTCH
BTAM
OH. IT'S SHINODA.
AND ASSISTANT DIRECTOR SAWAMURA.
BORDER

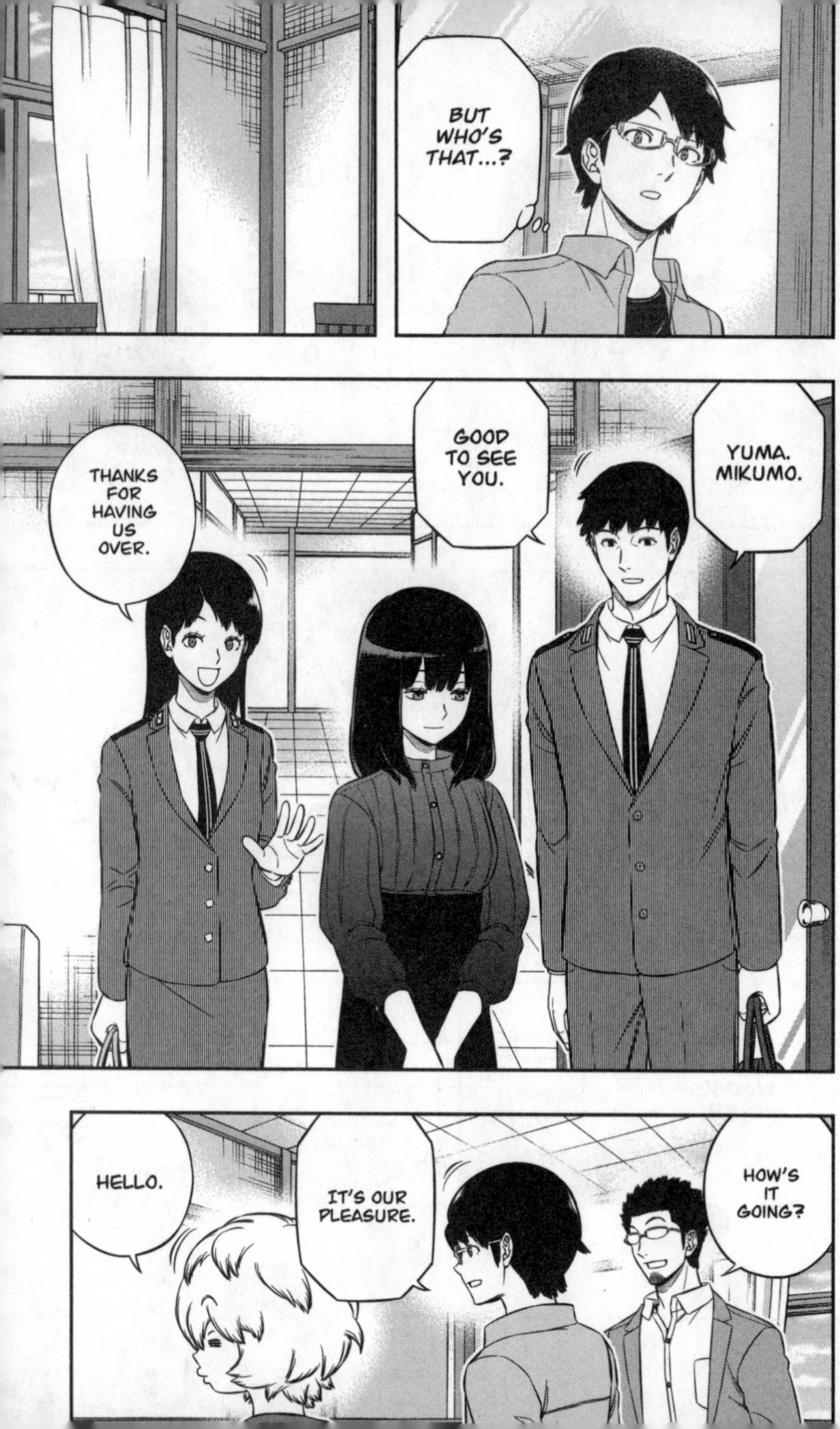
BUT WHO'S THAT...?
YUMA. MIKUMO.
GOOD TO SEE YOU.
THANKS FOR HAVING US OVER.
HOW'S IT GOING?
IT'S OUR PLEASURE.
HELLO.

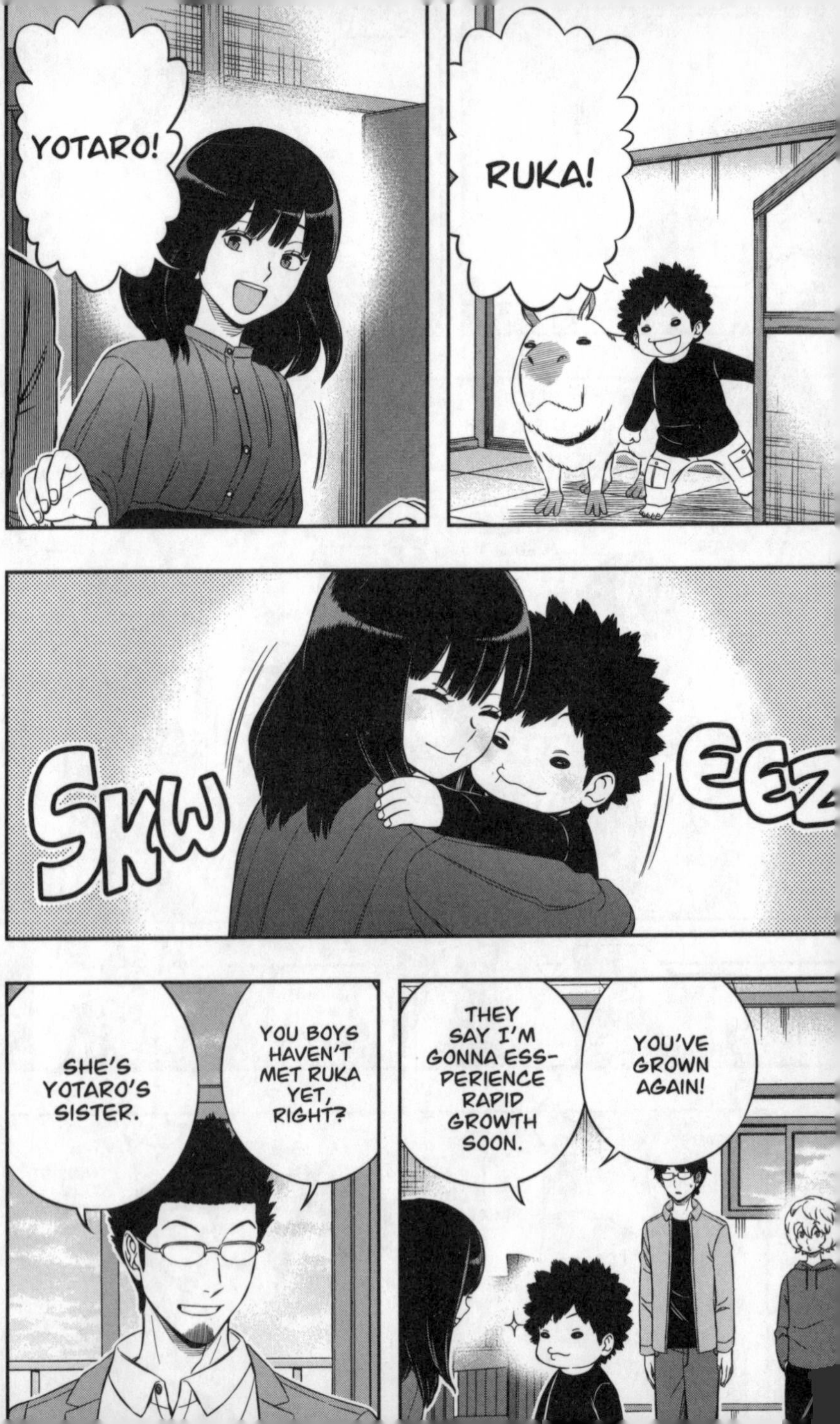
RUKA!
YOTARO!
SKW
EEZ
YOU'VE GROWN AGAIN!
THEY SAY I'M GONNA ESS-PERIENCE RAPID GROWTH SOON.
YOU BOYS HAVEN'T MET RUKA YET, RIGHT?
SHE'S YOTARO'S SISTER.

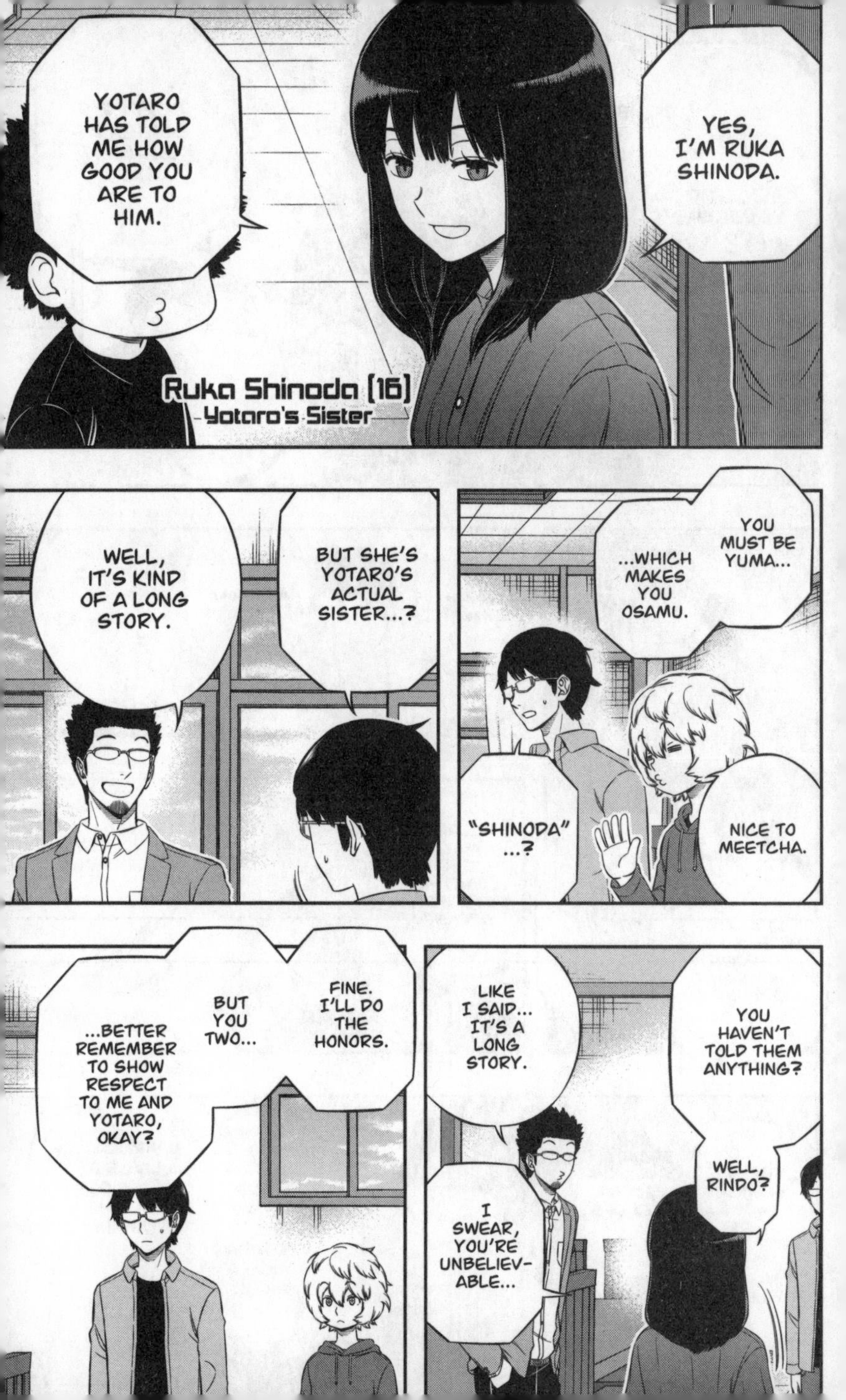
YES, I'M RUKA SHINODA.
YOTARO HAS TOLD ME HOW GOOD YOU ARE TO HIM.
Ruka Shinoda (16)
Yotaro's Sister
YOU MUST BE YUMA...
...WHICH MAKES YOU OSAMU.
NICE TO MEETCHA.
"SHINODA" ...?
BUT SHE'S YOTARO'S ACTUAL SISTER...?
WELL, IT'S KIND OF A LONG STORY.
YOU HAVEN'T TOLD THEM ANYTHING?
WELL, RINDO?
LIKE I SAID... IT'S A LONG STORY.
I SWEAR, YOU'RE UNBELIEV-ABLE...
FINE. I'LL DO THE HONORS.
BUT YOU TWO...
...BETTER REMEMBER TO SHOW RESPECT TO ME AND YOTARO, OKAY?

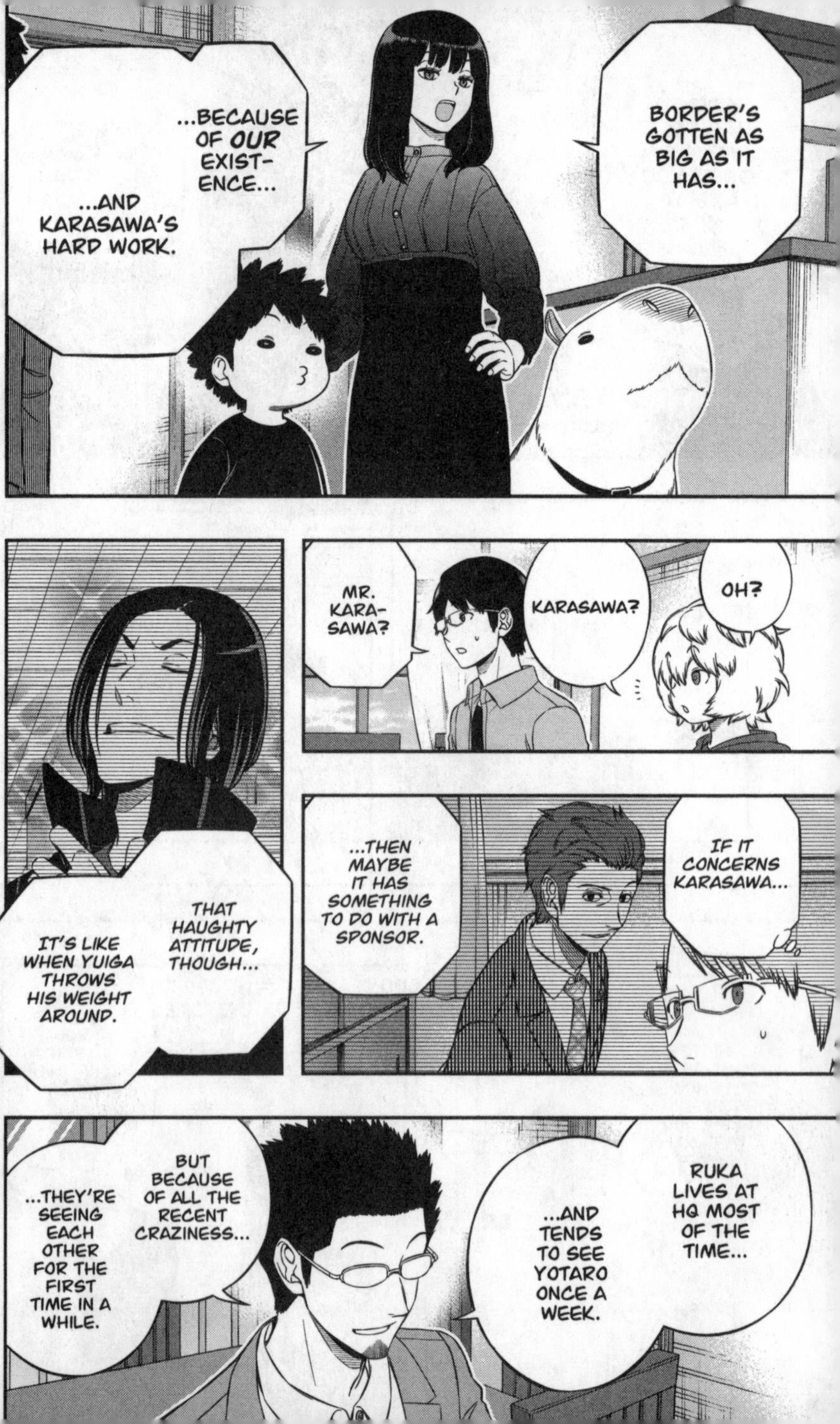
BORDER'S GOTTEN AS BIG AS IT HAS...
...BECAUSE OF *OUR* EXISTENCE...
...AND KARASAWA'S HARD WORK.
OH?
KARASAWA?
MR. KARA-SAWA?
IF IT CONCERNS KARASAWA...
...THEN MAYBE IT HAS SOMETHING TO DO WITH A SPONSOR.
THAT HAUGHTY ATTITUDE, THOUGH...
IT'S LIKE WHEN YUIGA THROWS HIS WEIGHT AROUND.
RUKA LIVES AT HQ MOST OF THE TIME...
...AND TENDS TO SEE YOTARO ONCE A WEEK.
BUT BECAUSE OF ALL THE RECENT CRAZINESS...
...THEY'RE SEEING EACH OTHER FOR THE FIRST TIME IN A WHILE.

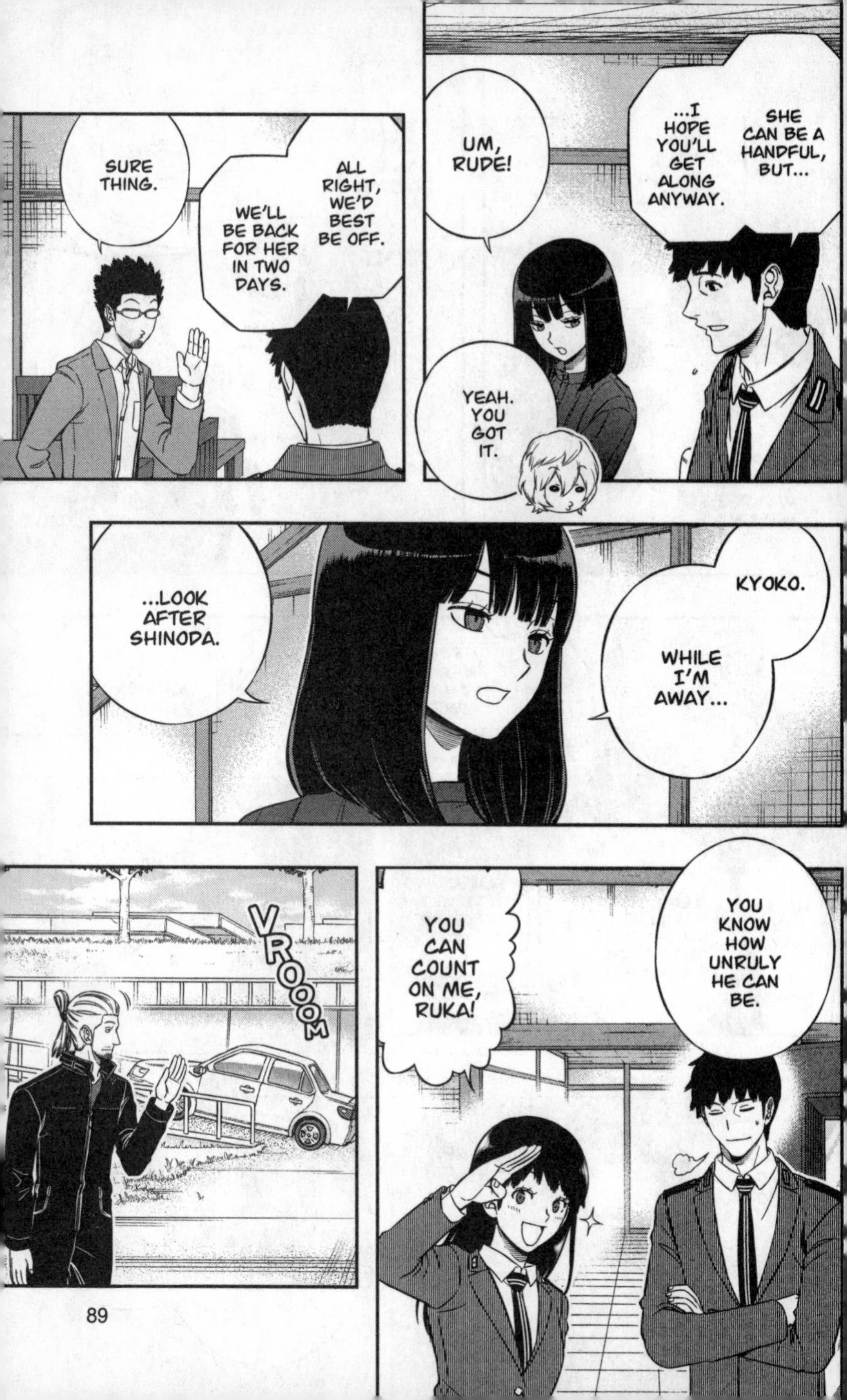
SHE CAN BE A HANDFUL, BUT...
...I HOPE YOU'LL GET ALONG ANYWAY.
UM, RUDE!
YEAH. YOU GOT IT.
ALL RIGHT, WE'D BEST BE OFF.
WE'LL BE BACK FOR HER IN TWO DAYS.
SURE THING.
KYOKO.
WHILE I'M AWAY...
...LOOK AFTER SHINODA.
YOU KNOW HOW UNRULY HE CAN BE.
YOU CAN COUNT ON ME, RUKA!
VROOOM

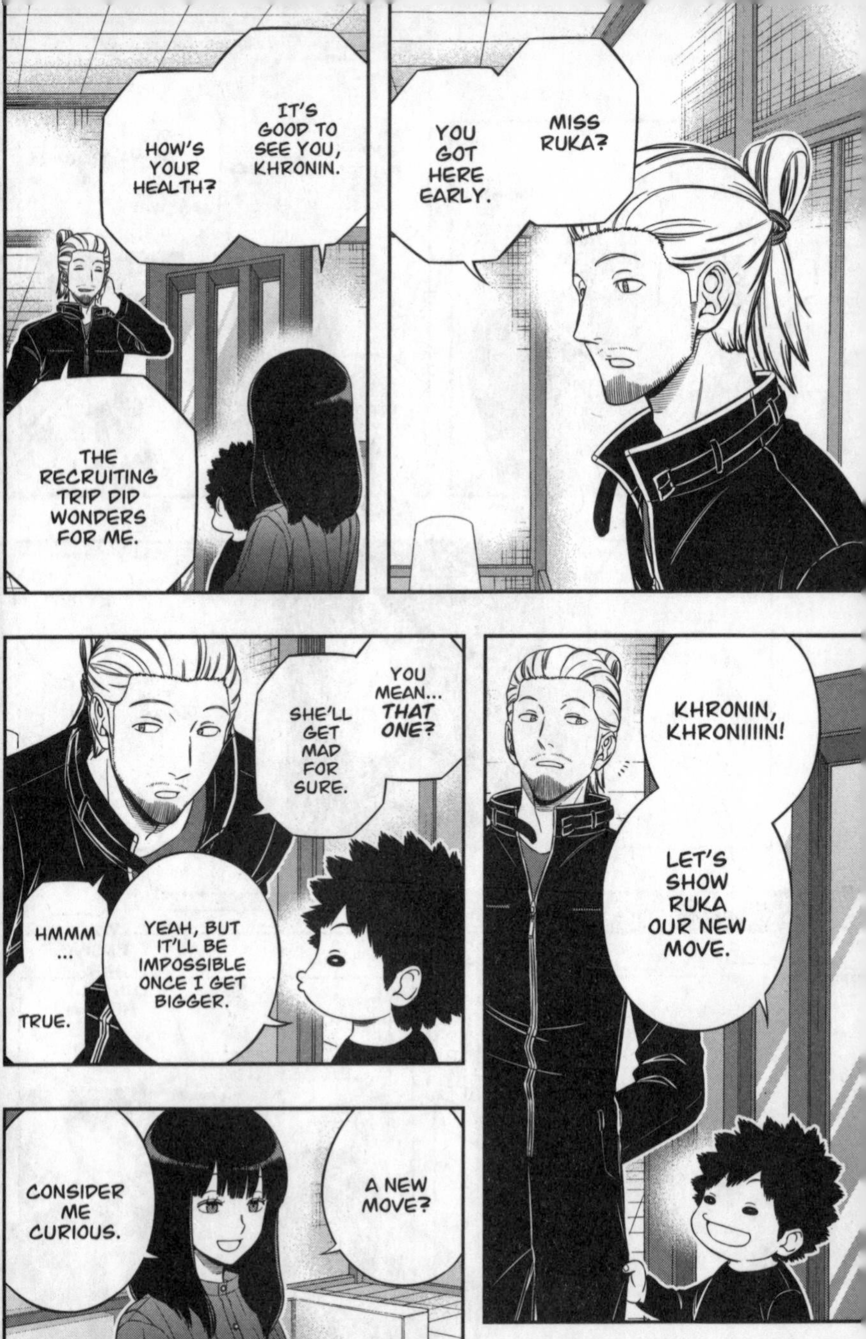
MISS RUKA?
YOU GOT HERE EARLY.
IT'S GOOD TO SEE YOU, KHRONIN.
HOW'S YOUR HEALTH?
THE RECRUITING TRIP DID WONDERS FOR ME.
KHRONIN, KHRONIIIIN!
LET'S SHOW RUKA OUR NEW MOVE.
YOU MEAN... THAT ONE?
SHE'LL GET MAD FOR SURE.
YEAH, BUT IT'LL BE IMPOSSIBLE ONCE I GET BIGGER.
HMMM ...
TRUE.
A NEW MOVE?
CONSIDER ME CURIOUS.

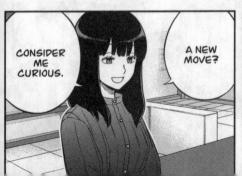

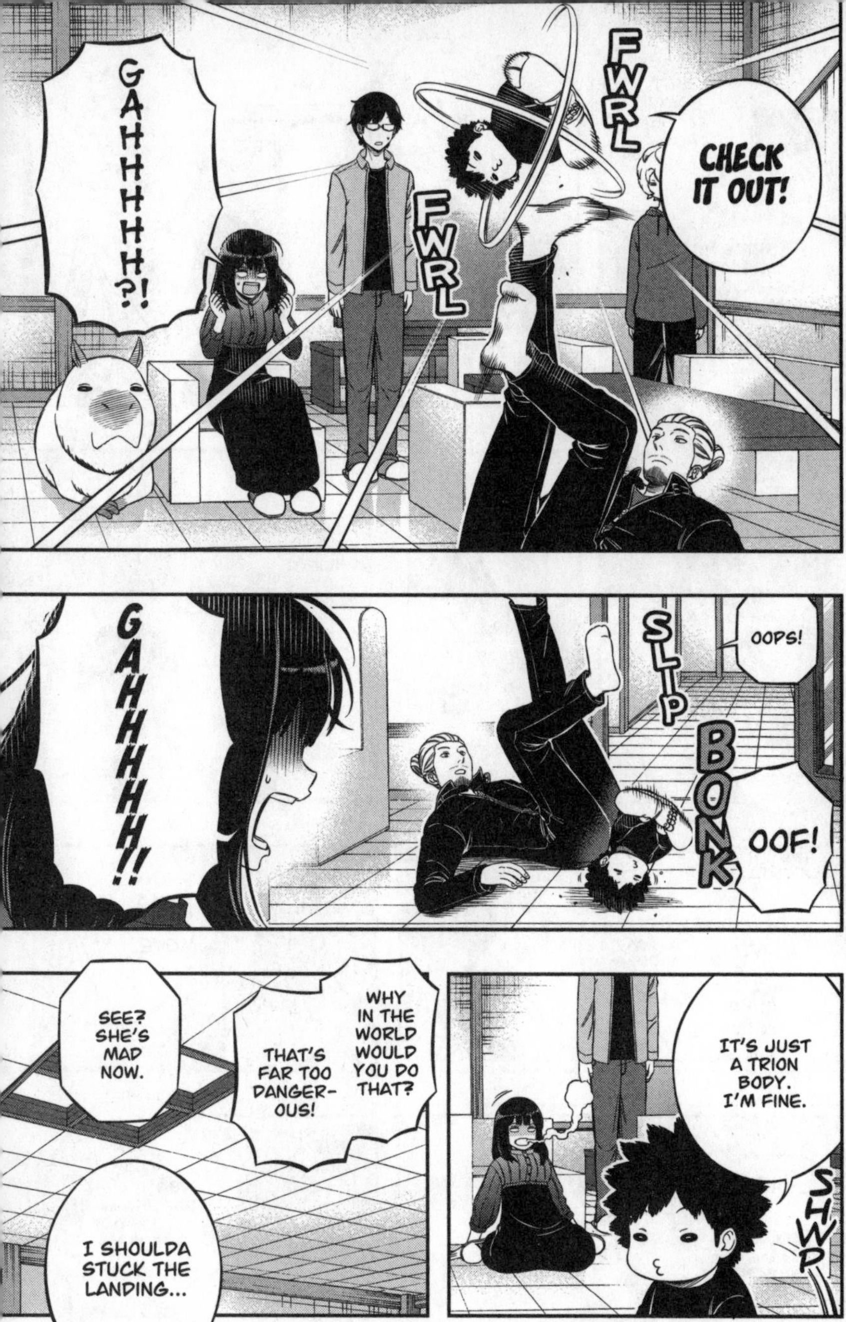
CHECK IT OUT!
FWRL
FWRL
GAHHHHHH?!
OOPS!
SLIP
BONK
OOF!
GAHHHHHH!!
IT'S JUST A TRION BODY. I'M FINE.
SHWP
WHY IN THE WORLD WOULD YOU DO THAT?
THAT'S FAR TOO DANGER-OUS!
SEE? SHE'S MAD NOW.
I SHOULDA STUCK THE LANDING...

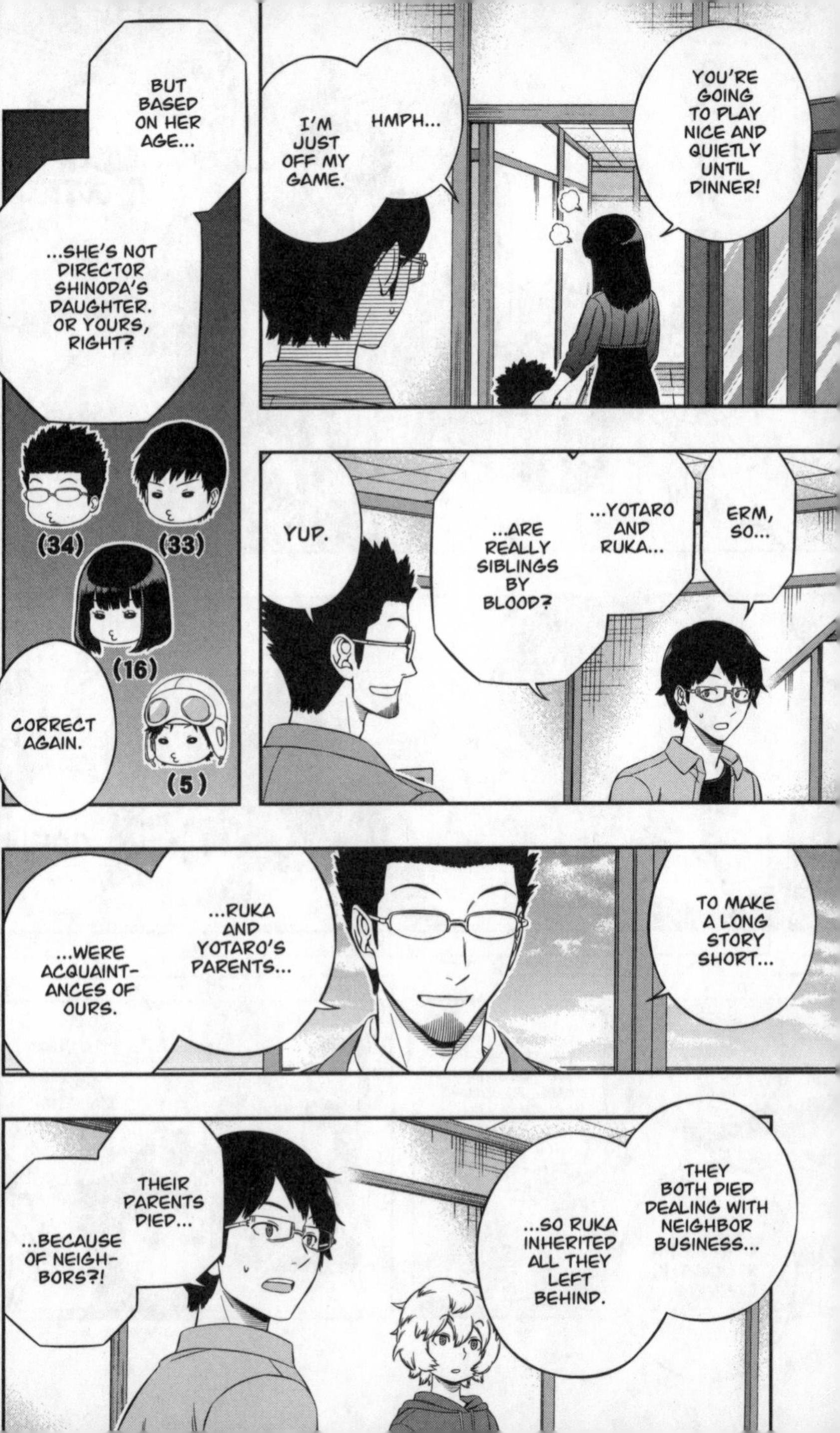
YOU'RE GOING TO PLAY NICE AND QUIETLY UNTIL DINNER!
HMPH...
I'M JUST OFF MY GAME.
ERM, SO...
...YOTARO AND RUKA...
...ARE REALLY SIBLINGS BY BLOOD?
YUP.
BUT BASED ON HER AGE...
...SHE'S NOT DIRECTOR SHINODA'S DAUGHTER. OR YOURS, RIGHT?
(33)
(34)
(16)
(5)
CORRECT AGAIN.
TO MAKE A LONG STORY SHORT...
...RUKA AND YOTARO'S PARENTS...
...WERE ACQUAINT-ANCES OF OURS.
THEY BOTH DIED DEALING WITH NEIGHBOR BUSINESS...
...SO RUKA INHERITED ALL THEY LEFT BEHIND.
THEIR PARENTS DIED...
...BECAUSE OF NEIGH-BORS?!

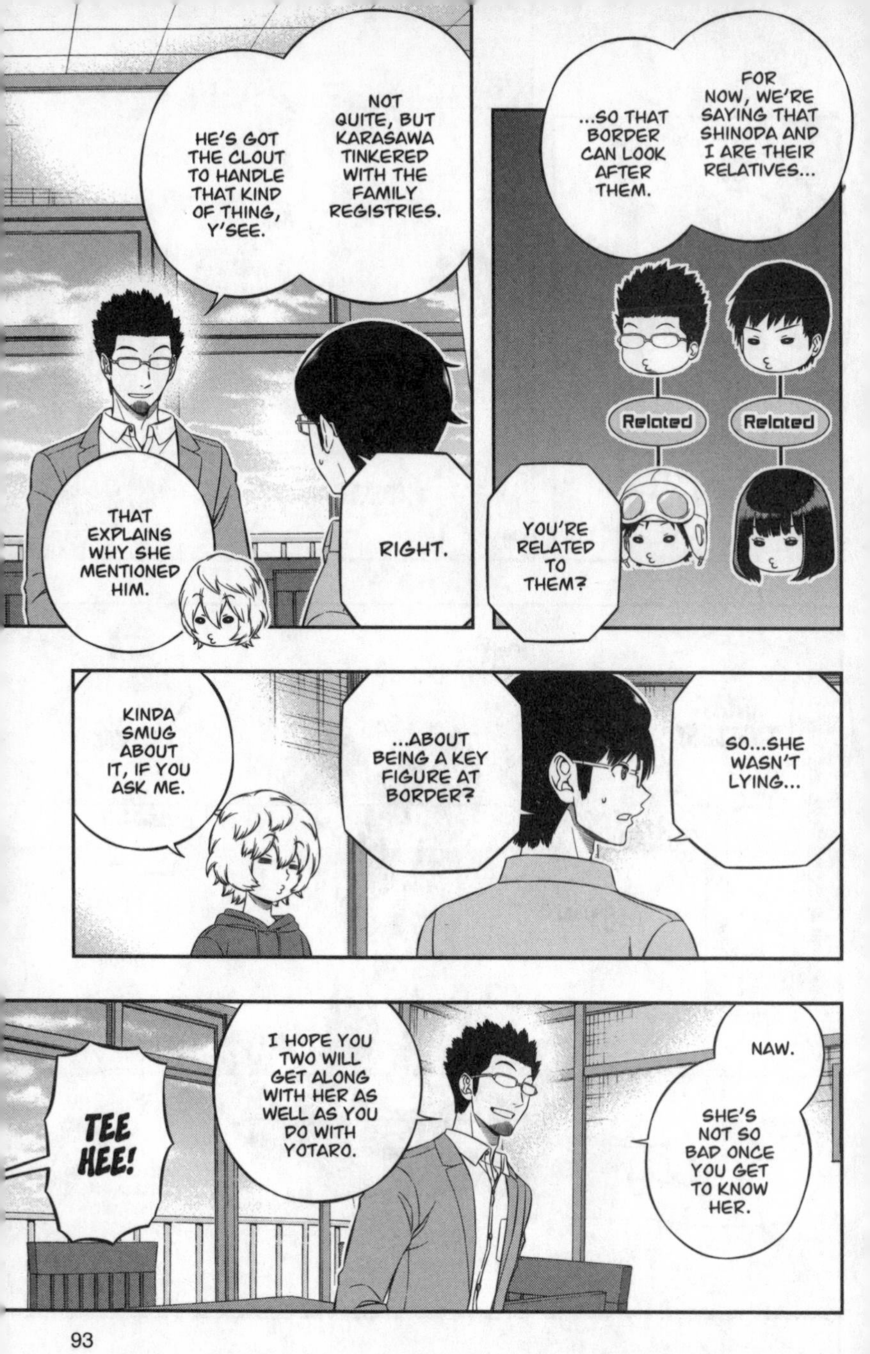
FOR NOW, WE'RE SAYING THAT SHINODA AND I ARE THEIR RELATIVES...
...SO THAT BORDER CAN LOOK AFTER THEM.
Related
Related
YOU'RE RELATED TO THEM?
NOT QUITE, BUT KARASAWA TINKERED WITH THE FAMILY REGISTRIES.
HE'S GOT THE CLOUT TO HANDLE THAT KIND OF THING, Y'SEE.
RIGHT.
THAT EXPLAINS WHY SHE MENTIONED HIM.
SO...SHE WASN'T LYING...
...ABOUT BEING A KEY FIGURE AT BORDER?
KINDA SMUG ABOUT IT, IF YOU ASK ME.
NAW.
SHE'S NOT SO BAD ONCE YOU GET TO KNOW HER.
I HOPE YOU TWO WILL GET ALONG WITH HER AS WELL AS YOU DO WITH YOTARO.
TEE HEE!

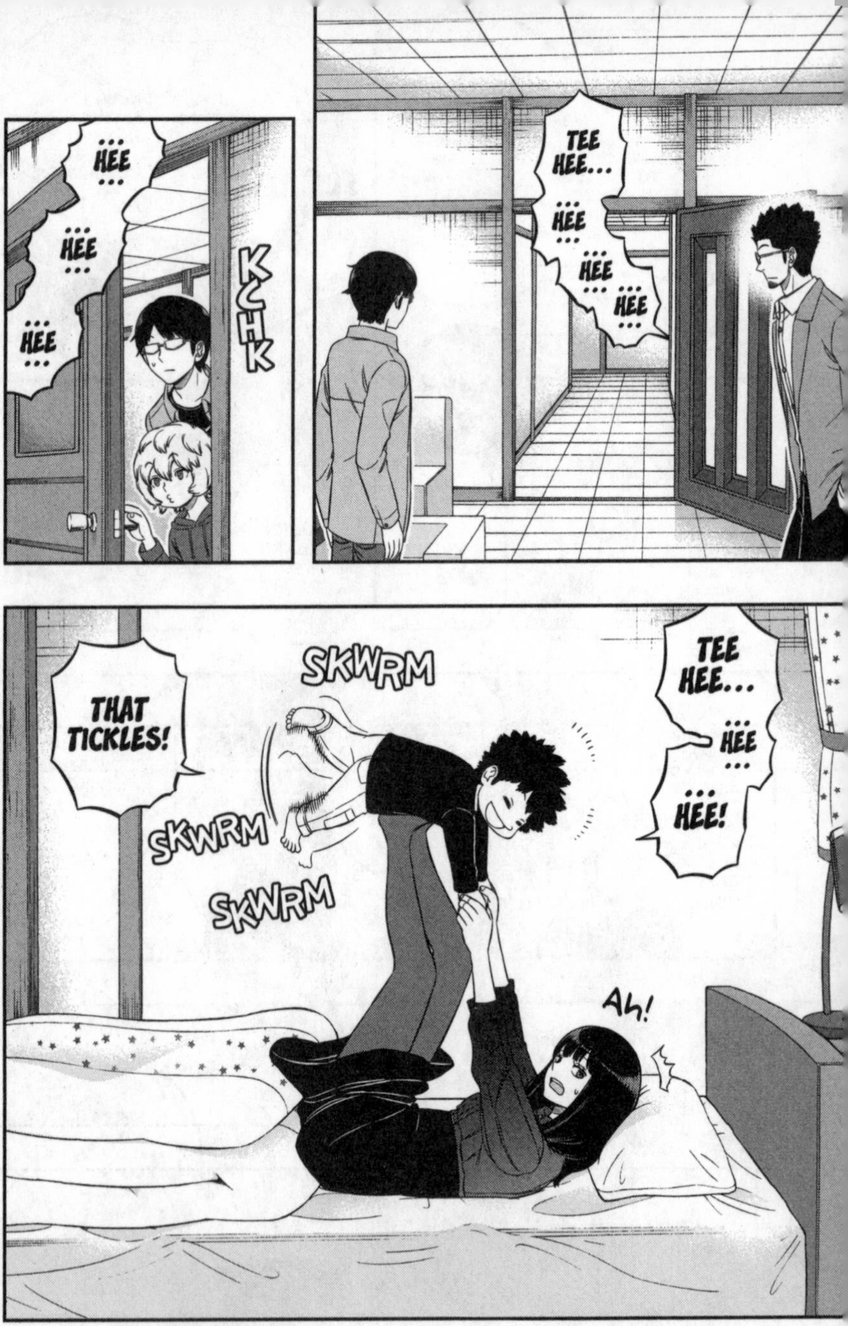
TEE HEE... ...HEE ...HEE ...HEE
...HEE... ...HEE... ...HEE...
KCHK
TEE HEE... ...HEE... ...HEE!
Ah!
SKWRM
THAT TICKLES!
SKWRM
SKWRM

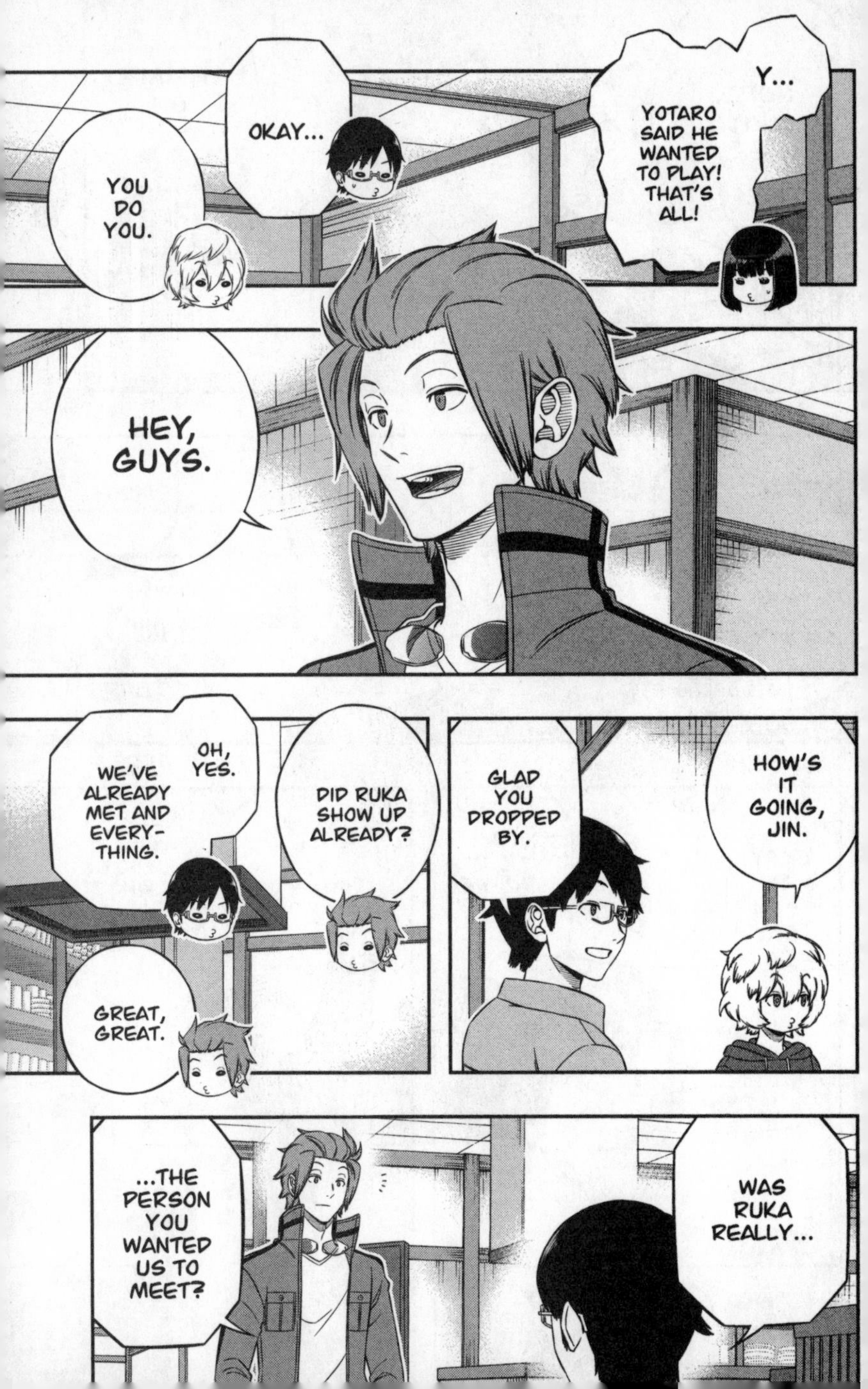
Y... YOTARO SAID HE WANTED TO PLAY! THAT'S ALL!
OKAY...
YOU DO YOU.
HEY, GUYS.
HOW'S IT GOING, JIN.
GLAD YOU DROPPED BY.
DID RUKA SHOW UP ALREADY?
OH, YES. WE'VE ALREADY MET AND EVERY-THING.
GREAT, GREAT.
WAS RUKA REALLY...
...THE PERSON YOU WANTED US TO MEET?

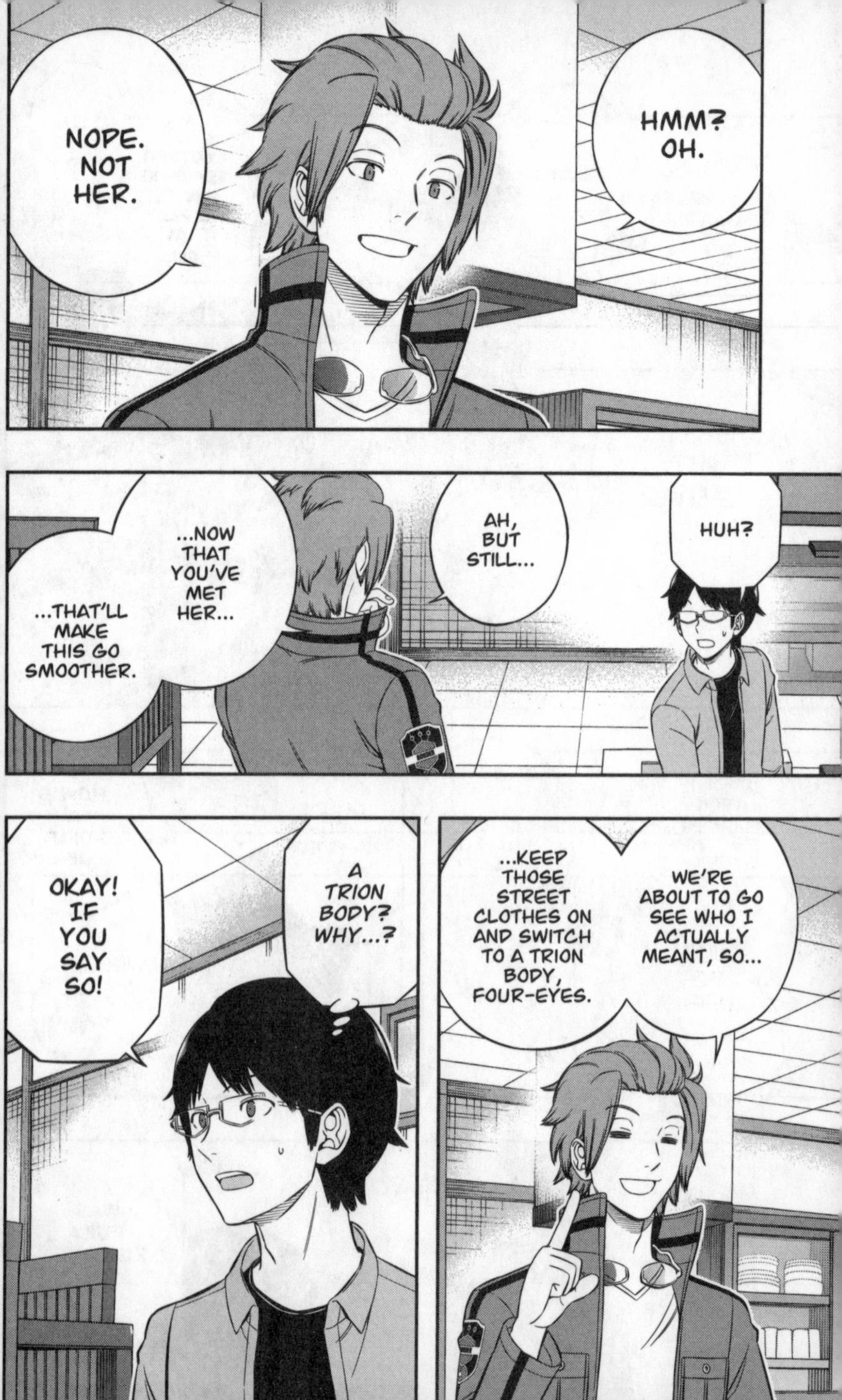
HMM? OH.
NOPE. NOT HER.
HUH?
AH, BUT STILL...
...NOW THAT YOU'VE MET HER...
...THAT'LL MAKE THIS GO SMOOTHER.
WE'RE ABOUT TO GO SEE WHO I ACTUALLY MEANT, SO...
...KEEP THOSE STREET CLOTHES ON AND SWITCH TO A TRION BODY, FOUR-EYES.
A TRION BODY? WHY...?
OKAY! IF YOU SAY SO!

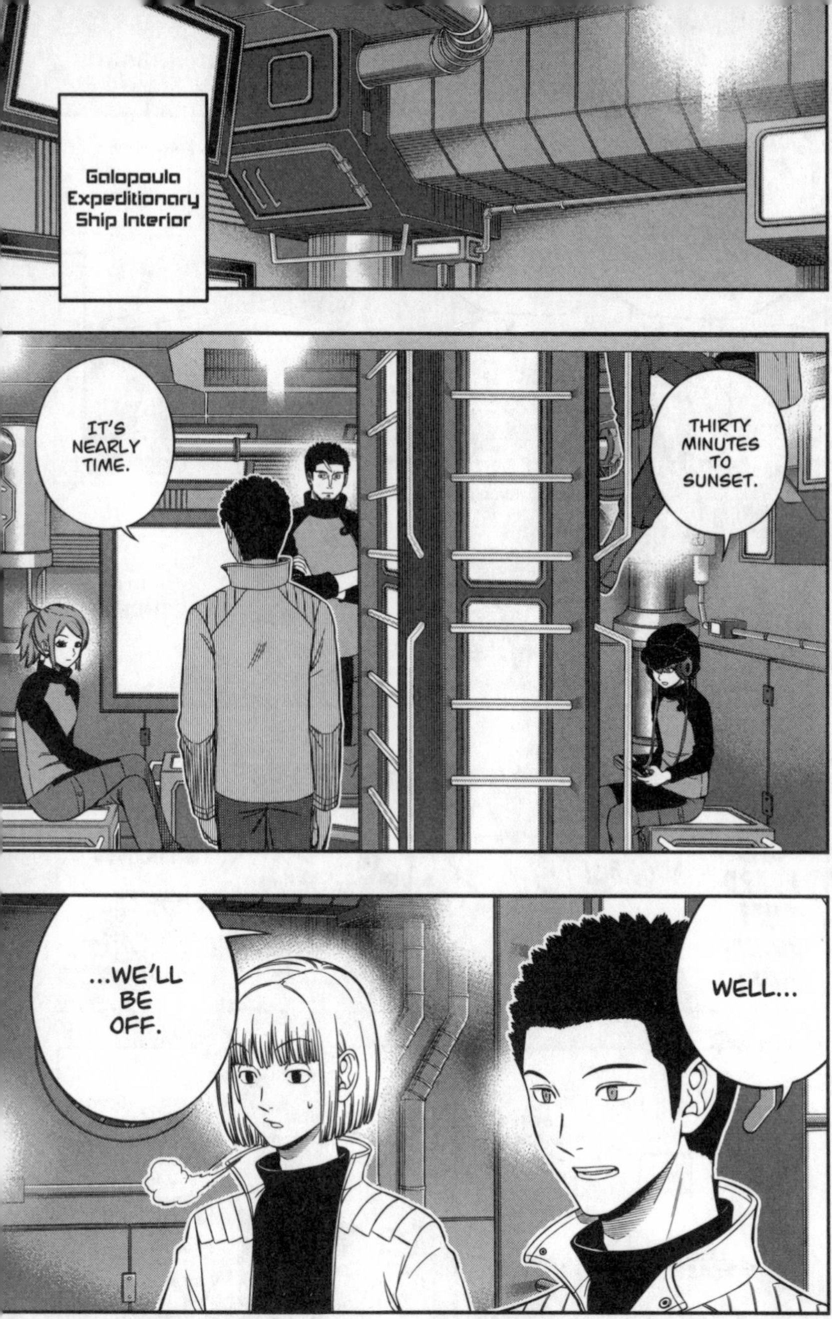
Galopoula Expeditionary Ship Interior
THIRTY MINUTES TO SUNSET.
IT'S NEARLY TIME.
WELL...
...WE'LL BE OFF.

Bonus: A Scene Cut for Page-Count and Pacing Reasons

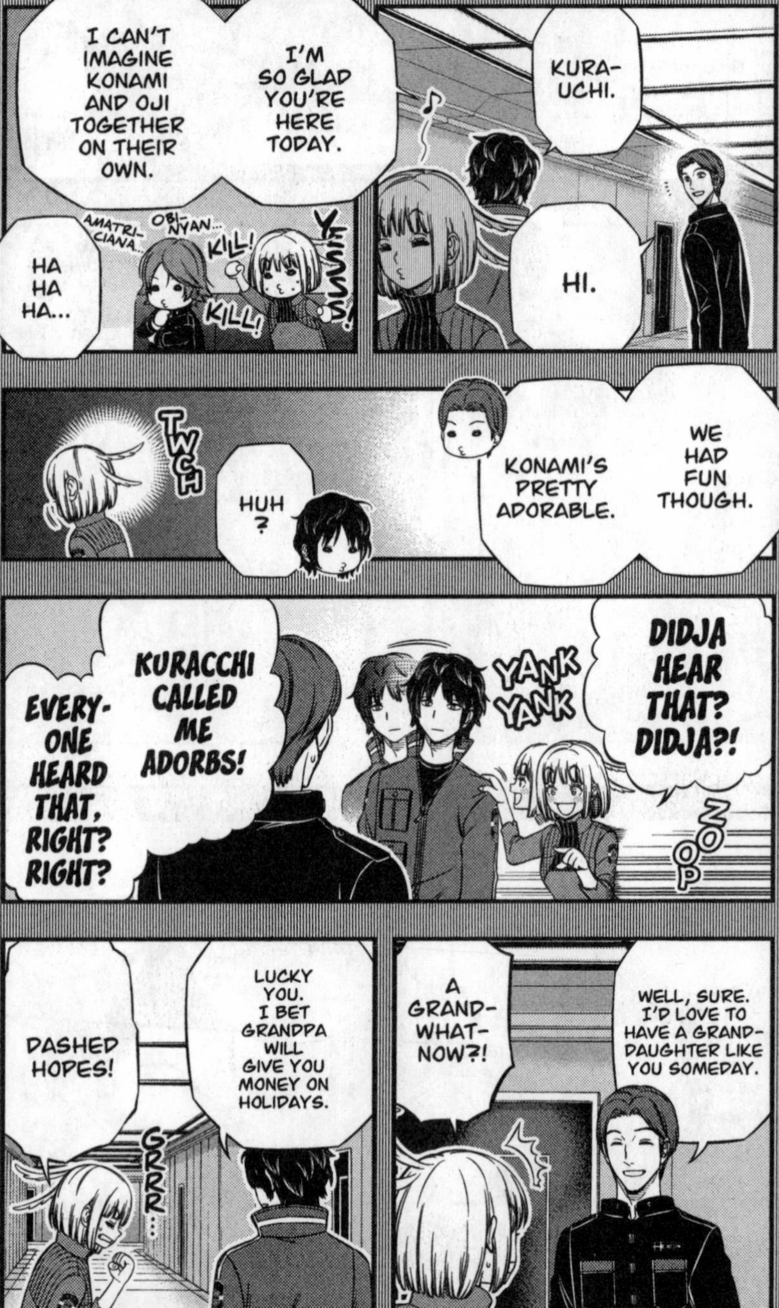
KURA-UCHI.
HI.
I'M SO GLAD YOU'RE HERE TODAY.
I CAN'T IMAGINE KONAMI AND OJI TOGETHER ON THEIR OWN.
YSSSSS!
OBI-NYAN...
KILL!
AMATRICIANA...
KILL!
HA HA HA...
WE HAD FUN THOUGH.
KONAMI'S PRETTY ADORABLE.
HUH?
TWCH
DIDJA HEAR THAT? DIDJA?!
ZOOP
YANK YANK
KURACCHI CALLED ME ADORBS!
EVERY-ONE HEARD THAT, RIGHT? RIGHT?
WELL, SURE. I'D LOVE TO HAVE A GRAND-DAUGHTER LIKE YOU SOMEDAY.
A GRAND-WHAT-NOW?!
LUCKY YOU. I BET GRANDPA WILL GIVE YOU MONEY ON HOLIDAYS.
GRRR...
DASHED HOPES!

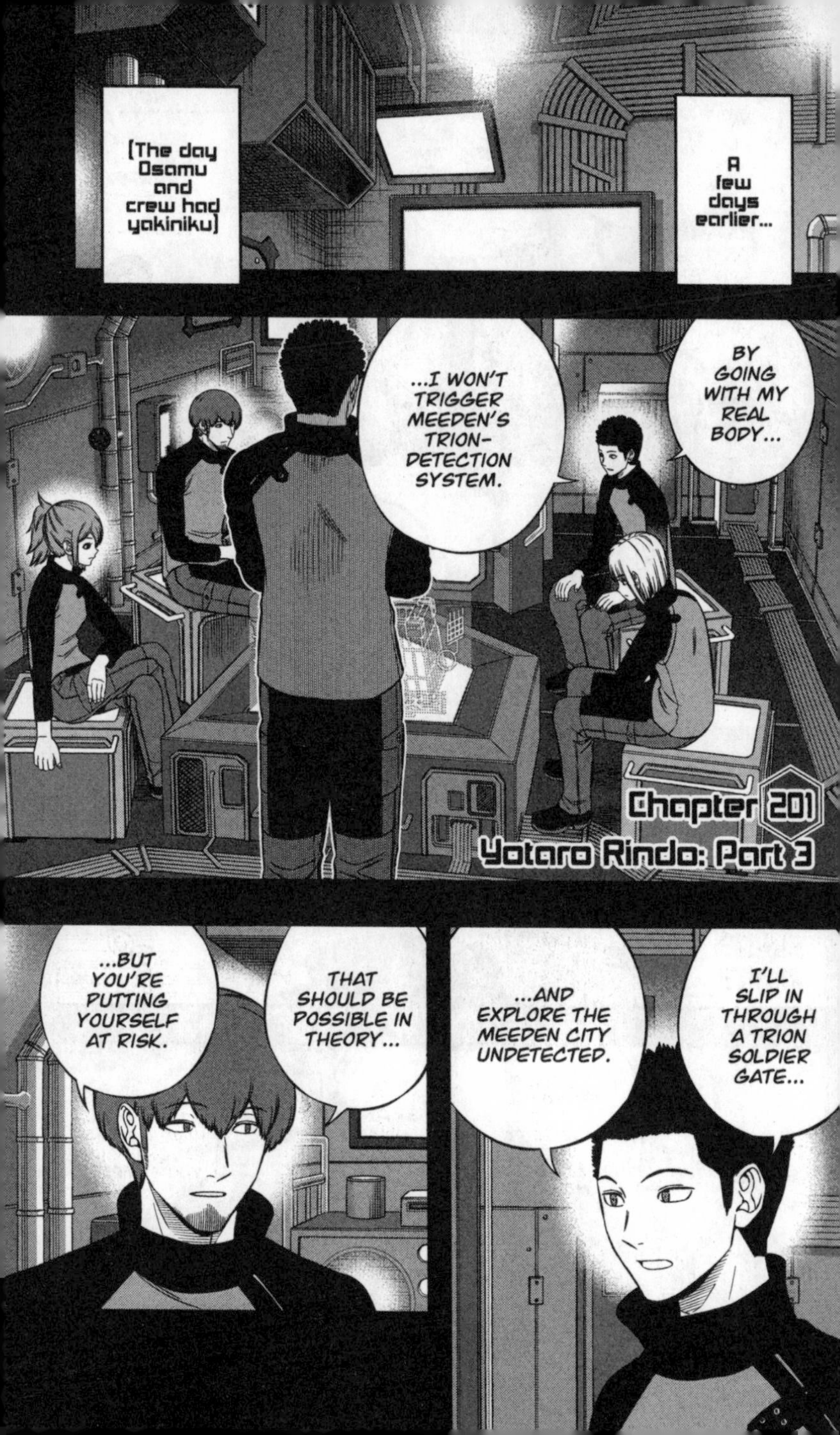
A few days earlier...
(The day Osamu and crew had yakiniku)
BY GOING WITH MY REAL BODY...
...I WON'T TRIGGER MEEDEN'S TRION-DETECTION SYSTEM.
Chapter 201
Yotaro Rindo: Part 3
I'LL SLIP IN THROUGH A TRION SOLDIER GATE...
...AND EXPLORE THE MEEDEN CITY UNDETECTED.
THAT SHOULD BE POSSIBLE IN THEORY...
...BUT YOU'RE PUTTING YOURSELF AT RISK.

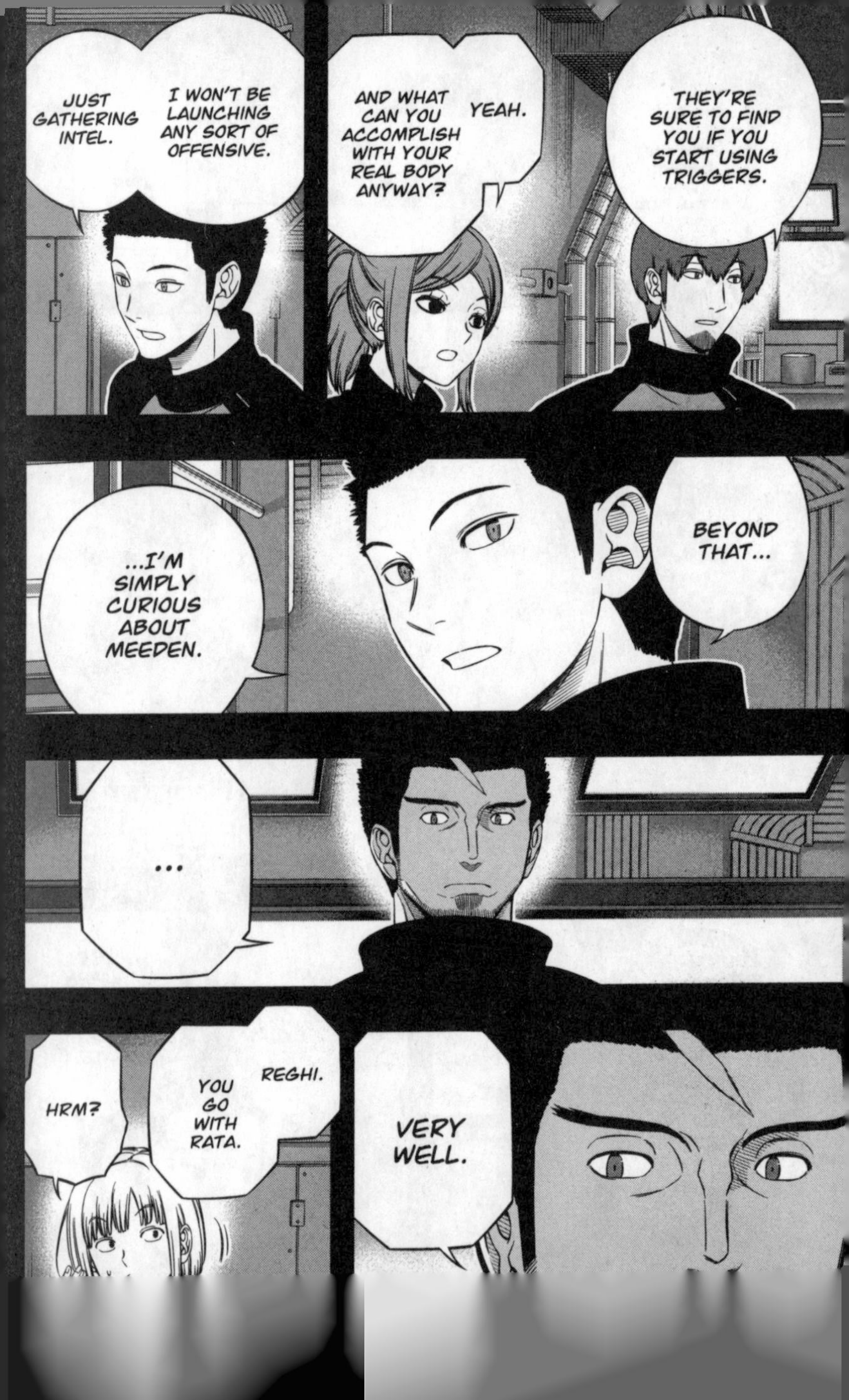
THEY'RE SURE TO FIND YOU IF YOU START USING TRIGGERS.
YEAH.
AND WHAT CAN YOU ACCOMPLISH WITH YOUR REAL BODY ANYWAY?
I WON'T BE LAUNCHING ANY SORT OF OFFENSIVE.
JUST GATHERING INTEL.
BEYOND THAT...
...I'M SIMPLY CURIOUS ABOUT MEEDEN.
...
VERY WELL.
REGHI.
YOU GO WITH RATA.
HRM?

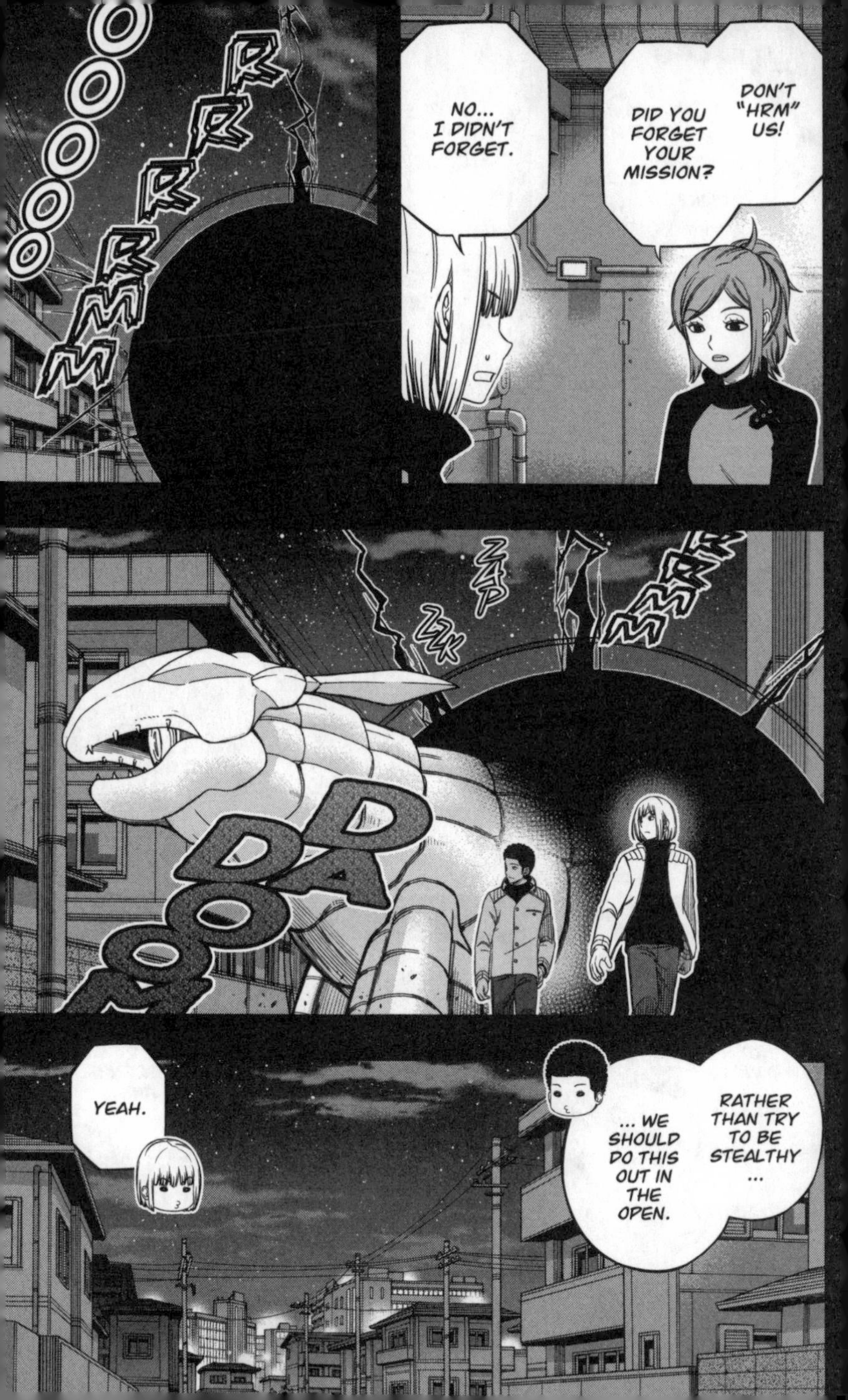
DON'T "HRM" US!
DID YOU FORGET YOUR MISSION?
NO... I DIDN'T FORGET.
RRRRMM
OOOOO
RRMM
ZZAP
ZZK
DADOOM
RATHER THAN TRY TO BE STEALTHY ...
... WE SHOULD DO THIS OUT IN THE OPEN.
YEAH.

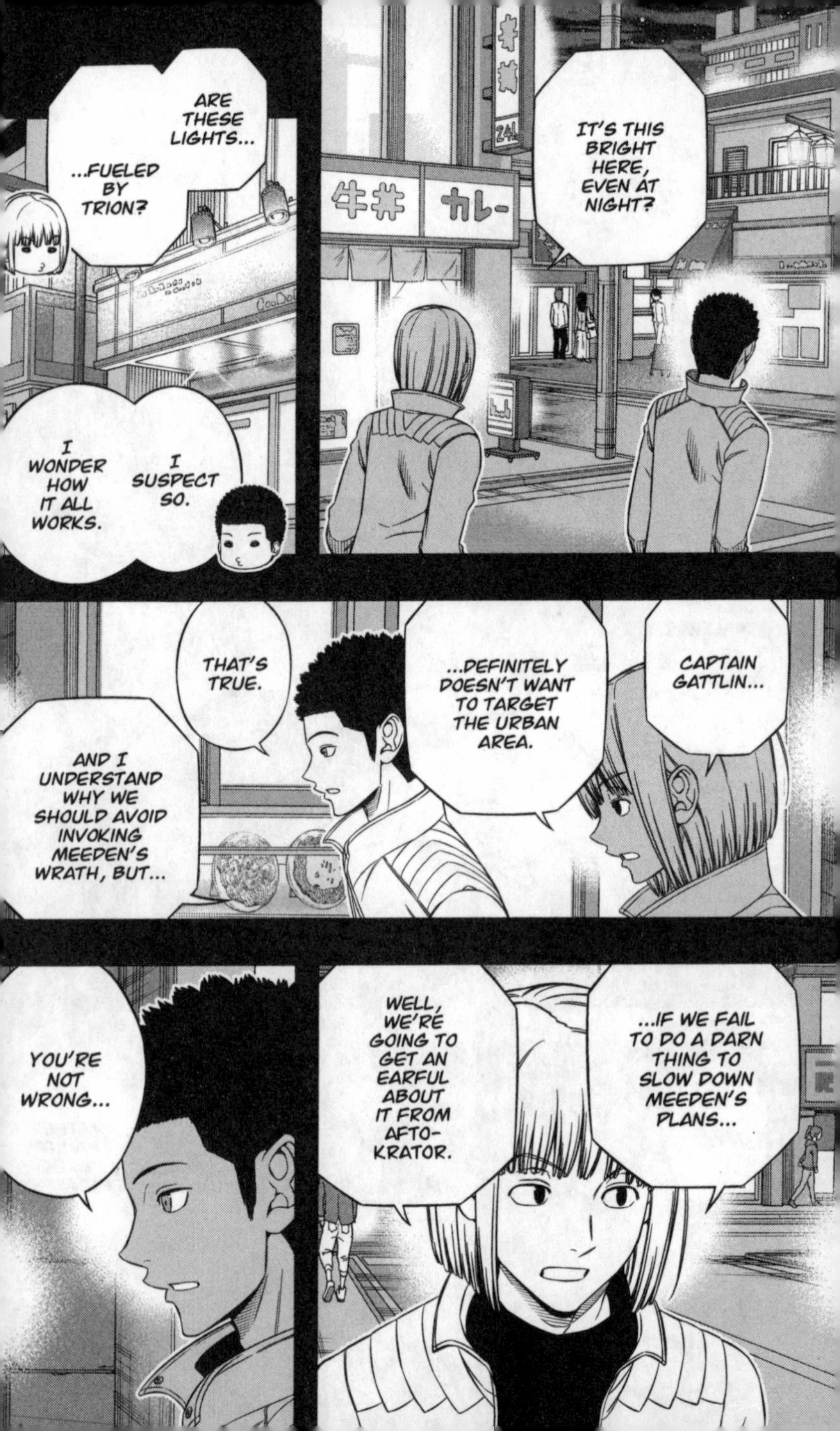
IT'S THIS BRIGHT HERE, EVEN AT NIGHT?
ARE THESE LIGHTS...
...FUELED BY TRION?
I SUSPECT SO.
I WONDER HOW IT ALL WORKS.
CAPTAIN GATTLIN...
...DEFINITELY DOESN'T WANT TO TARGET THE URBAN AREA.
THAT'S TRUE.
AND I UNDERSTAND WHY WE SHOULD AVOID INVOKING MEEDEN'S WRATH, BUT...
...IF WE FAIL TO DO A DARN THING TO SLOW DOWN MEEDEN'S PLANS...
WELL, WE'RE GOING TO GET AN EARFUL ABOUT IT FROM AFTO-KRATOR.
YOU'RE NOT WRONG...

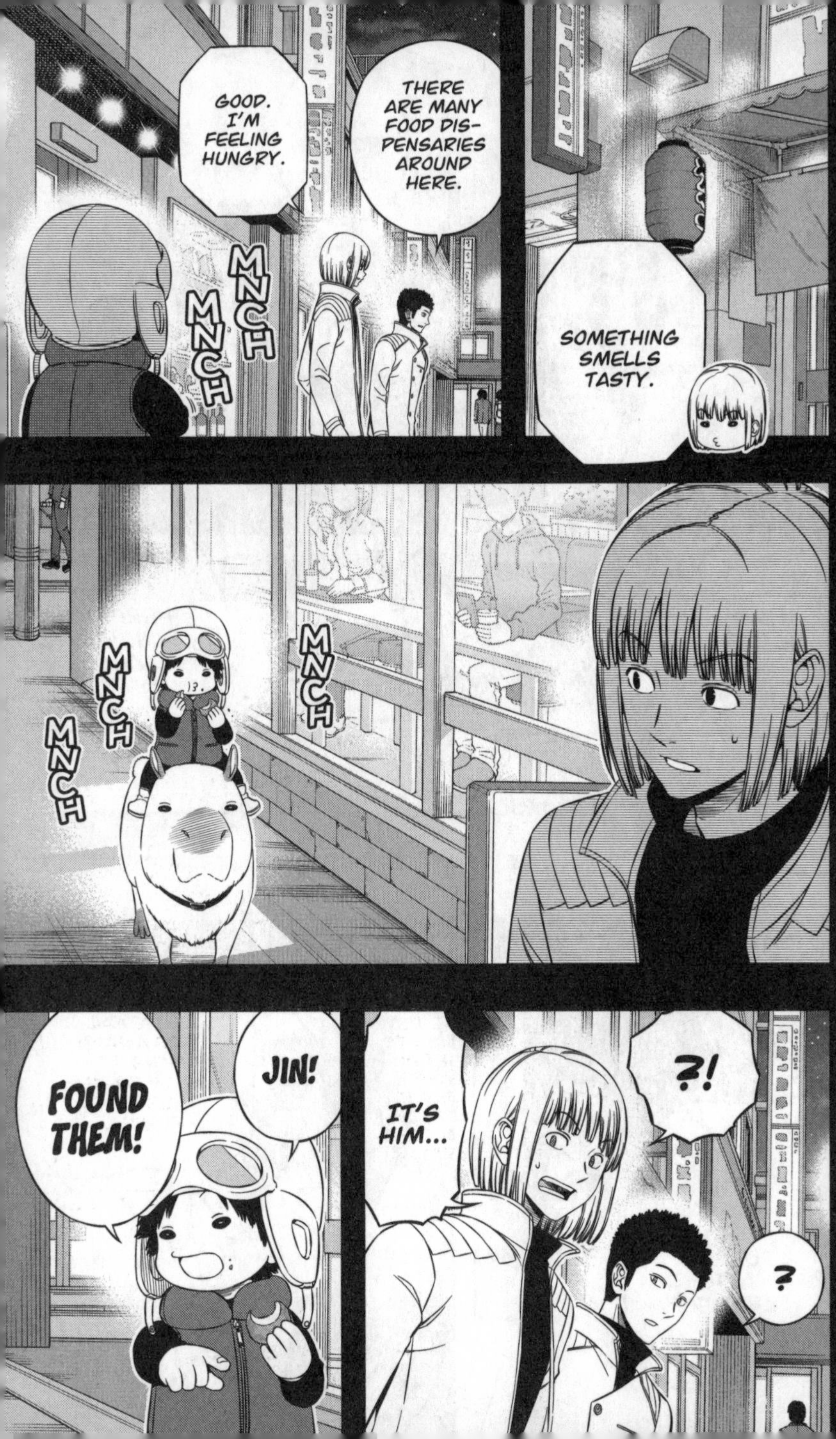
SOMETHING SMELLS TASTY.
THERE ARE MANY FOOD DISPENSARIES AROUND HERE.
GOOD. I'M FEELING HUNGRY.
MNCH
MNCH
MNCH
MNCH
MNCH
?!
IT'S HIM...
?
JIN!
FOUND THEM!

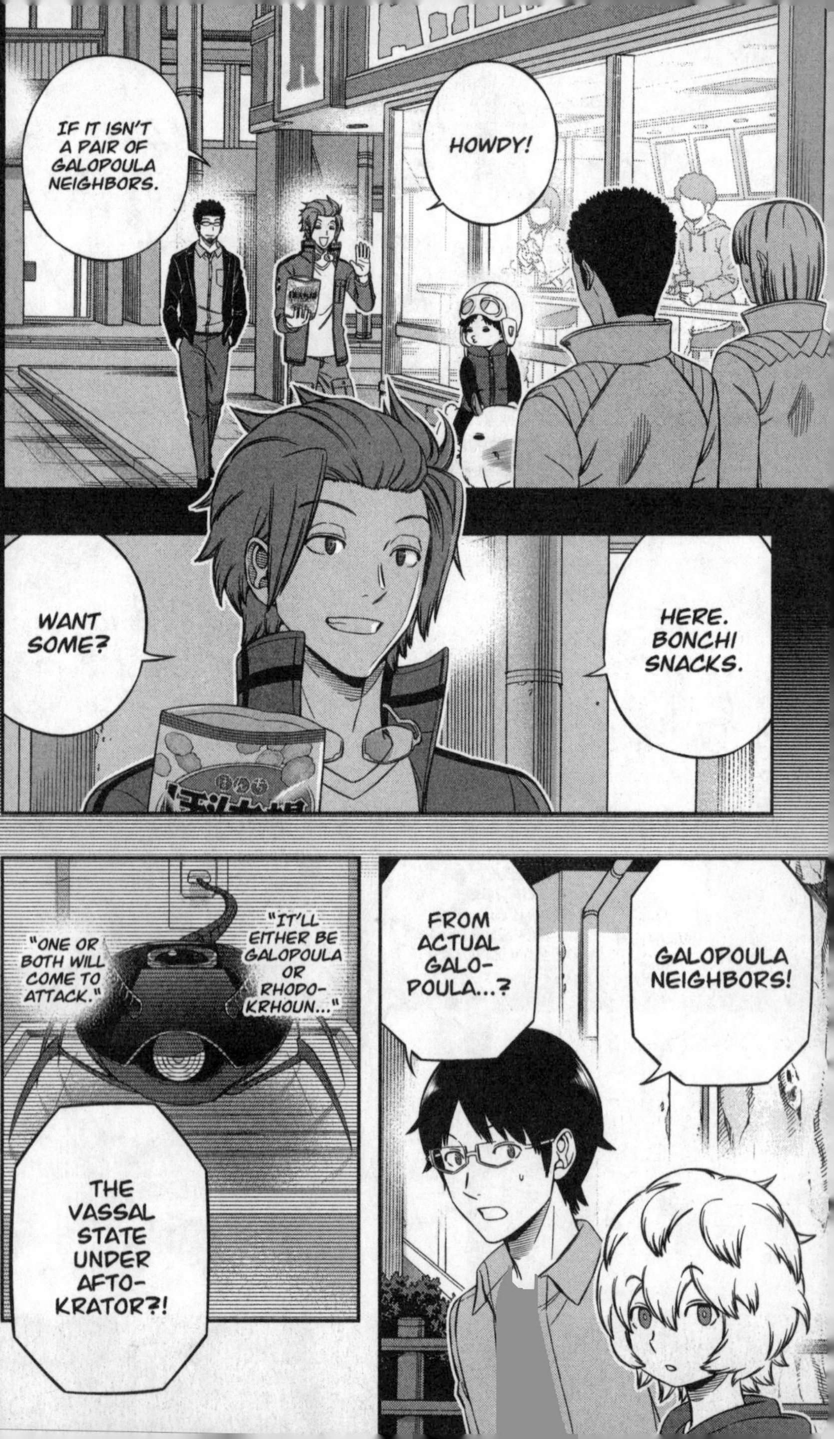
HOWDY!
IF IT ISN'T A PAIR OF GALOPOULA NEIGHBORS.
HERE. BONCHI SNACKS.
WANT SOME?
GALOPOULA NEIGHBORS!
FROM ACTUAL GALO-POULA...?
"IT'LL EITHER BE GALOPOULA OR RHODO-KRHOUN..."
"ONE OR BOTH WILL COME TO ATTACK."
THE VASSAL STATE UNDER AFTO-KRATOR?!

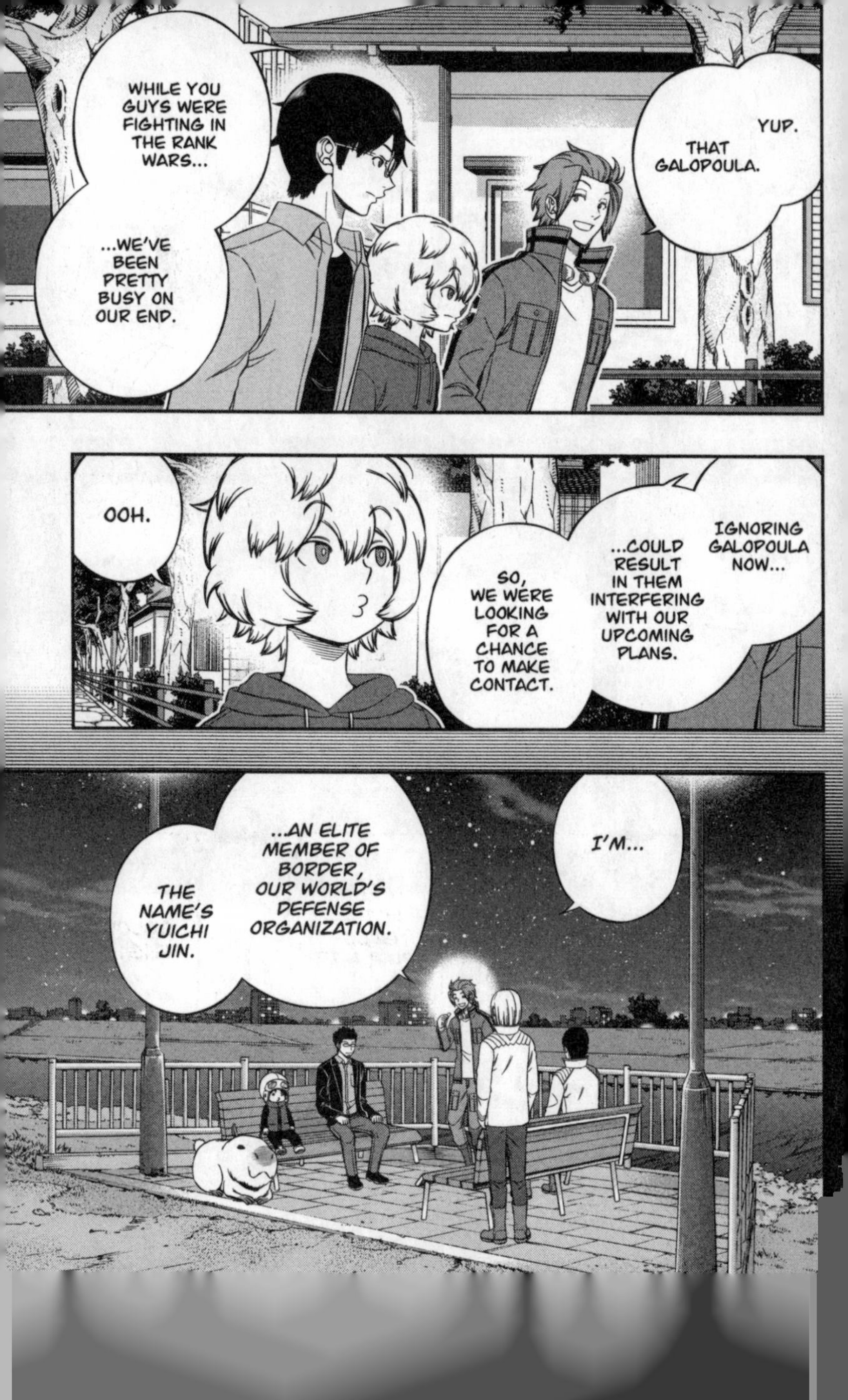
YUP. THAT GALOPOULA.
WHILE YOU GUYS WERE FIGHTING IN THE RANK WARS...
...WE'VE BEEN PRETTY BUSY ON OUR END.
IGNORING GALOPOULA NOW...
...COULD RESULT IN THEM INTERFERING WITH OUR UPCOMING PLANS.
SO, WE WERE LOOKING FOR A CHANCE TO MAKE CONTACT.
OOH.
I'M...
...AN ELITE MEMBER OF BORDER, OUR WORLD'S DEFENSE ORGANIZATION.
THE NAME'S YUICHI JIN.

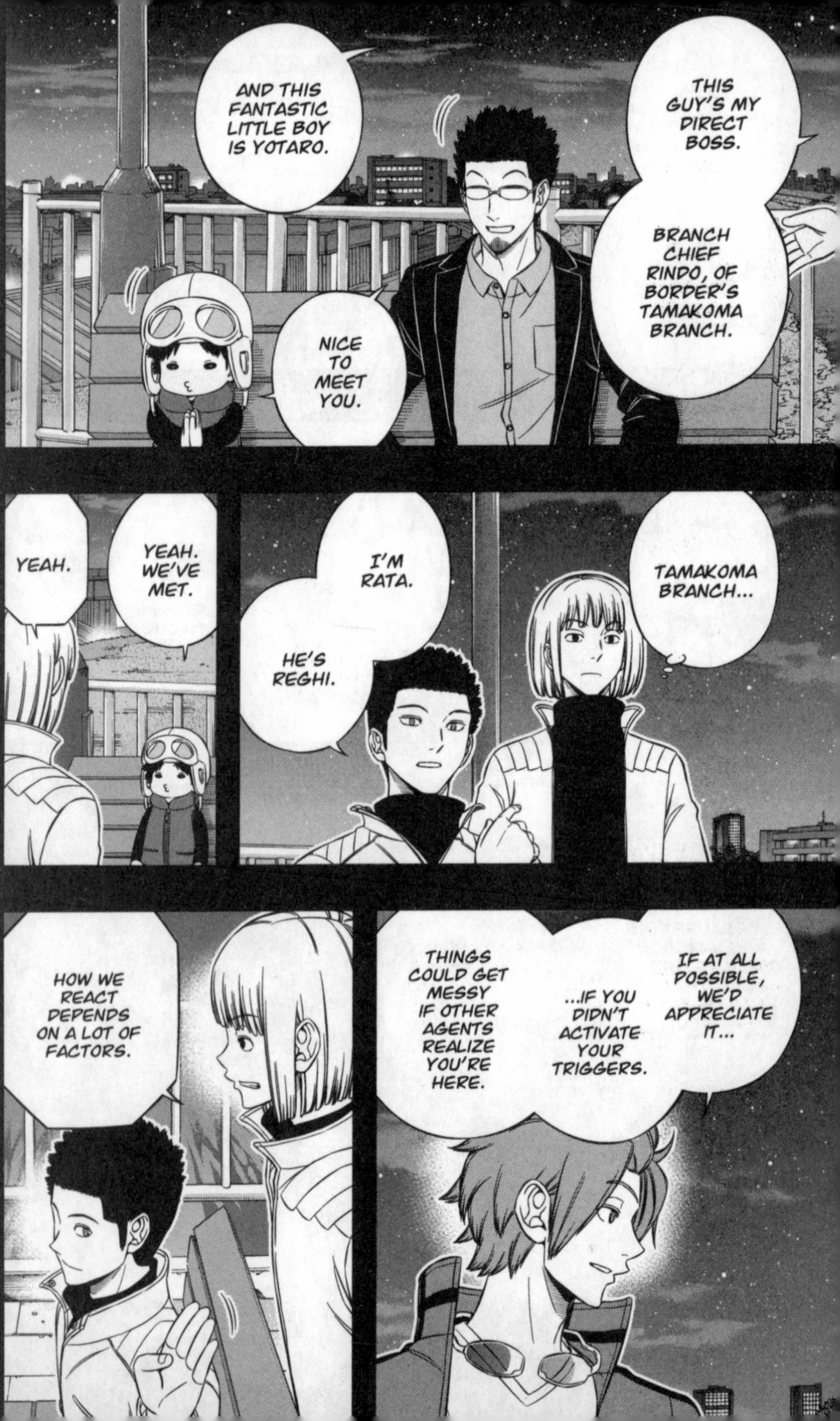
THIS GUY'S MY DIRECT BOSS.
BRANCH CHIEF RINDO, OF BORDER'S TAMAKOMA BRANCH.
AND THIS FANTASTIC LITTLE BOY IS YOTARO.
NICE TO MEET YOU.
TAMAKOMA BRANCH...
I'M RATA.
HE'S REGHI.
YEAH. WE'VE MET.
YEAH.
IF AT ALL POSSIBLE, WE'D APPRECIATE IT...
...IF YOU DIDN'T ACTIVATE YOUR TRIGGERS.
THINGS COULD GET MESSY IF OTHER AGENTS REALIZE YOU'RE HERE.
HOW WE REACT DEPENDS ON A LOT OF FACTORS.

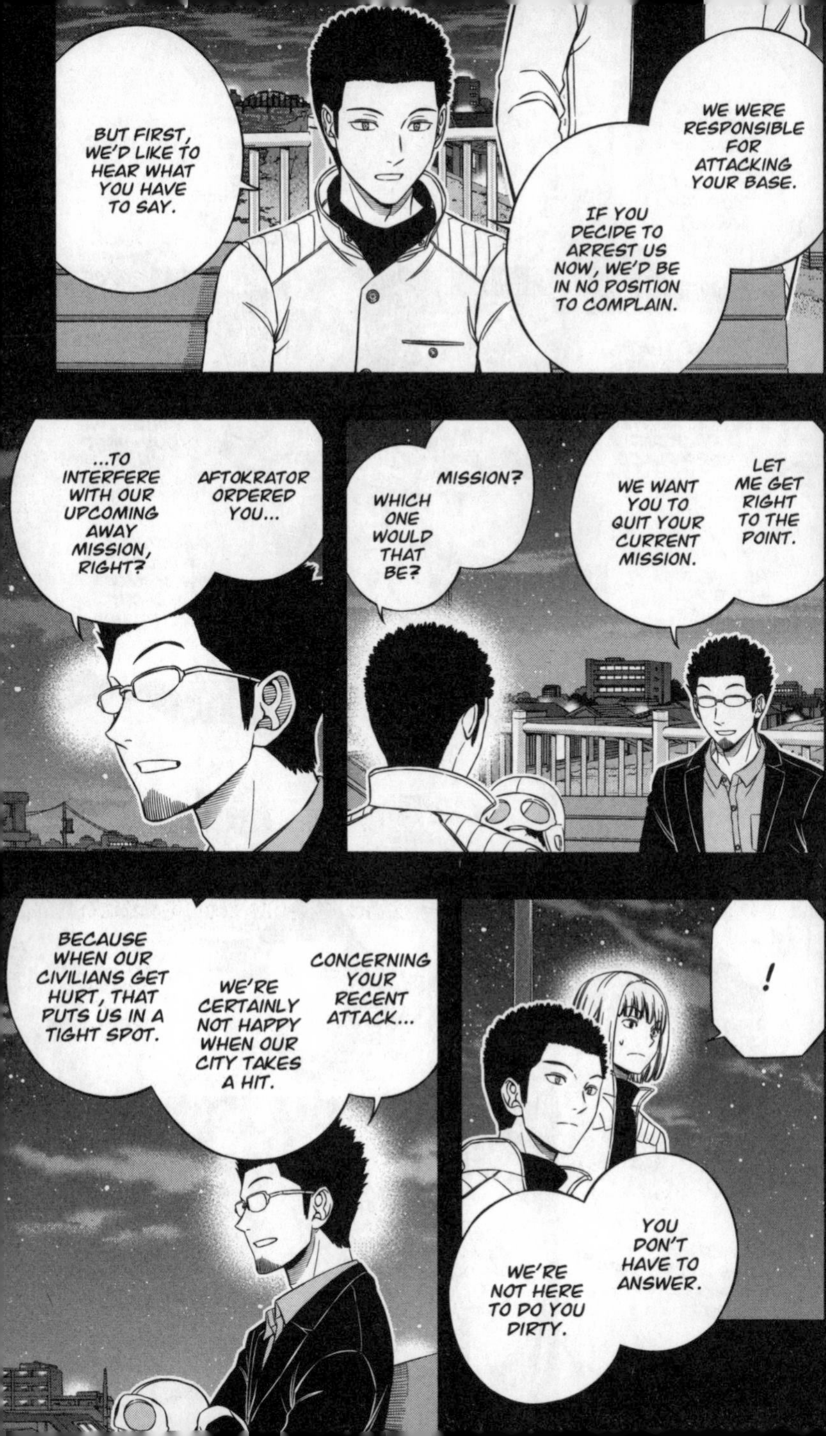
WE WERE RESPONSIBLE FOR ATTACKING YOUR BASE.
IF YOU DECIDE TO ARREST US NOW, WE'D BE IN NO POSITION TO COMPLAIN.
BUT FIRST, WE'D LIKE TO HEAR WHAT YOU HAVE TO SAY.
LET ME GET RIGHT TO THE POINT.
WE WANT YOU TO QUIT YOUR CURRENT MISSION.
MISSION?
WHICH ONE WOULD THAT BE?
AFTOKRATOR ORDERED YOU...
...TO INTERFERE WITH OUR UPCOMING AWAY MISSION, RIGHT?
!
YOU DON'T HAVE TO ANSWER.
WE'RE NOT HERE TO DO YOU DIRTY.
CONCERNING YOUR RECENT ATTACK...
WE'RE CERTAINLY NOT HAPPY WHEN OUR CITY TAKES A HIT.
BECAUSE WHEN OUR CIVILIANS GET HURT, THAT PUTS US IN A TIGHT SPOT.

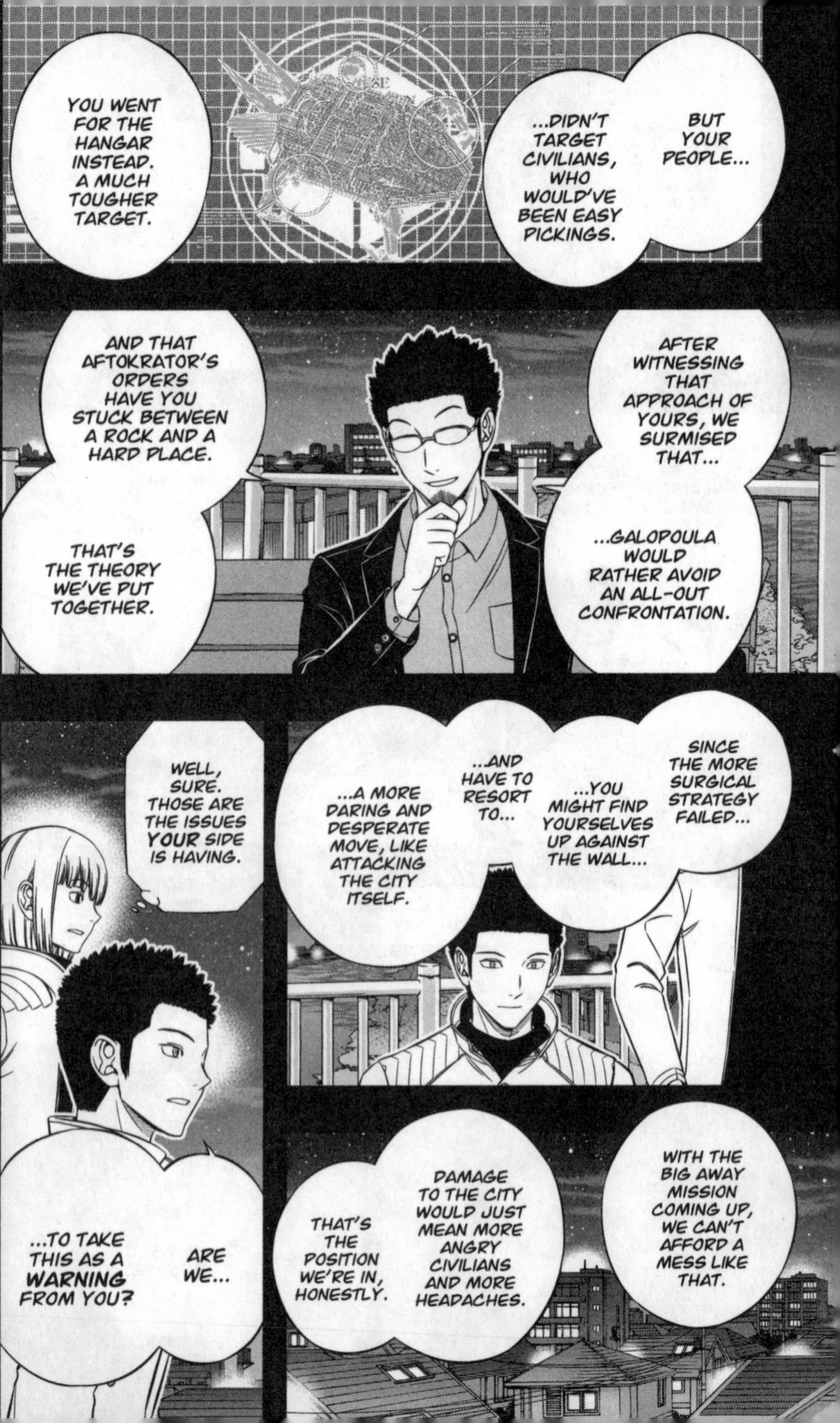
BUT YOUR PEOPLE...
...DIDN'T TARGET CIVILIANS, WHO WOULD'VE BEEN EASY PICKINGS.
YOU WENT FOR THE HANGAR INSTEAD. A MUCH TOUGHER TARGET.
AFTER WITNESSING THAT APPROACH OF YOURS, WE SURMISED THAT...
...GALOPOULA WOULD RATHER AVOID AN ALL-OUT CONFRONTATION.
AND THAT AFTOKRATOR'S ORDERS HAVE YOU STUCK BETWEEN A ROCK AND A HARD PLACE.
THAT'S THE THEORY WE'VE PUT TOGETHER.
SINCE THE MORE SURGICAL STRATEGY FAILED...
...YOU MIGHT FIND YOURSELVES UP AGAINST THE WALL...
...AND HAVE TO RESORT TO...
...A MORE DARING AND DESPERATE MOVE, LIKE ATTACKING THE CITY ITSELF.
WITH THE BIG AWAY MISSION COMING UP, WE CAN'T AFFORD A MESS LIKE THAT.
DAMAGE TO THE CITY WOULD JUST MEAN MORE ANGRY CIVILIANS AND MORE HEADACHES.
THAT'S THE POSITION WE'RE IN, HONESTLY.
WELL, SURE. THOSE ARE THE ISSUES YOUR SIDE IS HAVING.
ARE WE...
...TO TAKE THIS AS A WARNING FROM YOU?

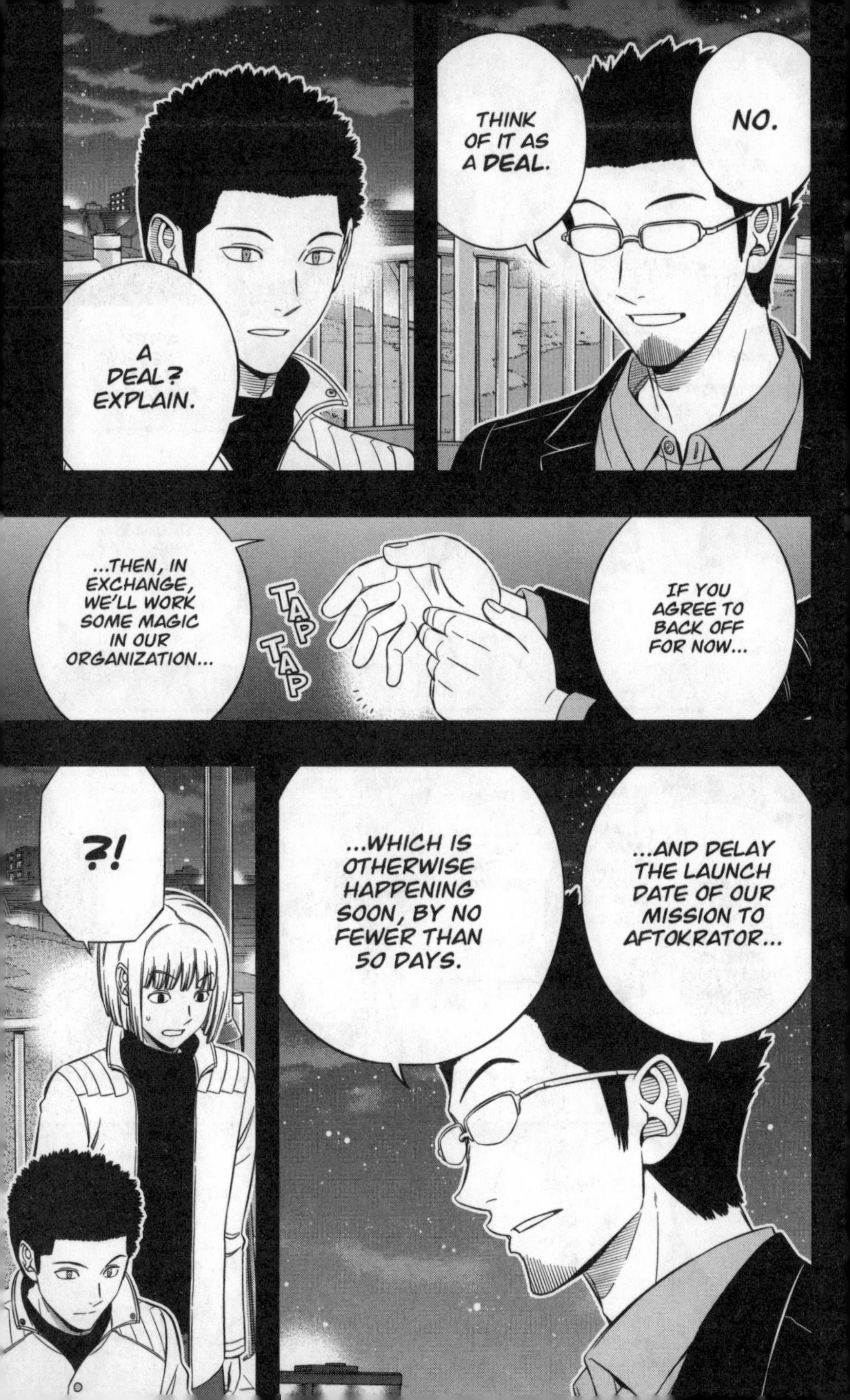
NO.
THINK OF IT AS A DEAL.
A DEAL? EXPLAIN.
IF YOU AGREE TO BACK OFF FOR NOW...
TAP TAP
...THEN, IN EXCHANGE, WE'LL WORK SOME MAGIC IN OUR ORGANIZATION...
...AND DELAY THE LAUNCH DATE OF OUR MISSION TO AFTOKRATOR...
...WHICH IS OTHERWISE HAPPENING SOON, BY NO FEWER THAN 50 DAYS.
?!

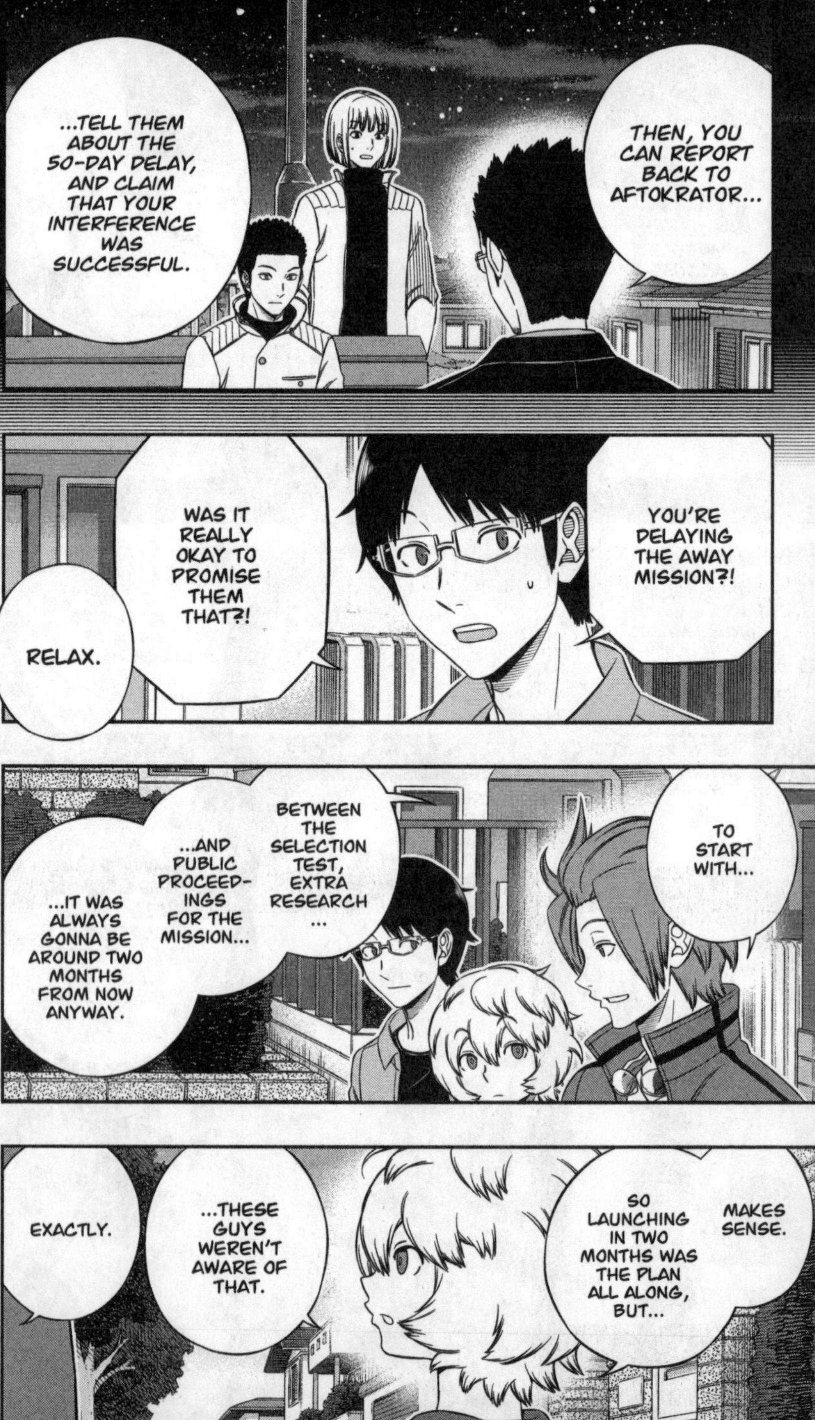
THEN, YOU CAN REPORT BACK TO AFTOKRATOR...
...TELL THEM ABOUT THE 50-DAY DELAY, AND CLAIM THAT YOUR INTERFERENCE WAS SUCCESSFUL.
YOU'RE DELAYING THE AWAY MISSION?!
WAS IT REALLY OKAY TO PROMISE THEM THAT?!
RELAX.
TO START WITH...
BETWEEN THE SELECTION TEST, EXTRA RESEARCH ...
...AND PUBLIC PROCEED-INGS FOR THE MISSION...
...IT WAS ALWAYS GONNA BE AROUND TWO MONTHS FROM NOW ANYWAY.
MAKES SENSE.
SO LAUNCHING IN TWO MONTHS WAS THE PLAN ALL ALONG, BUT...
...THESE GUYS WEREN'T AWARE OF THAT.
EXACTLY.

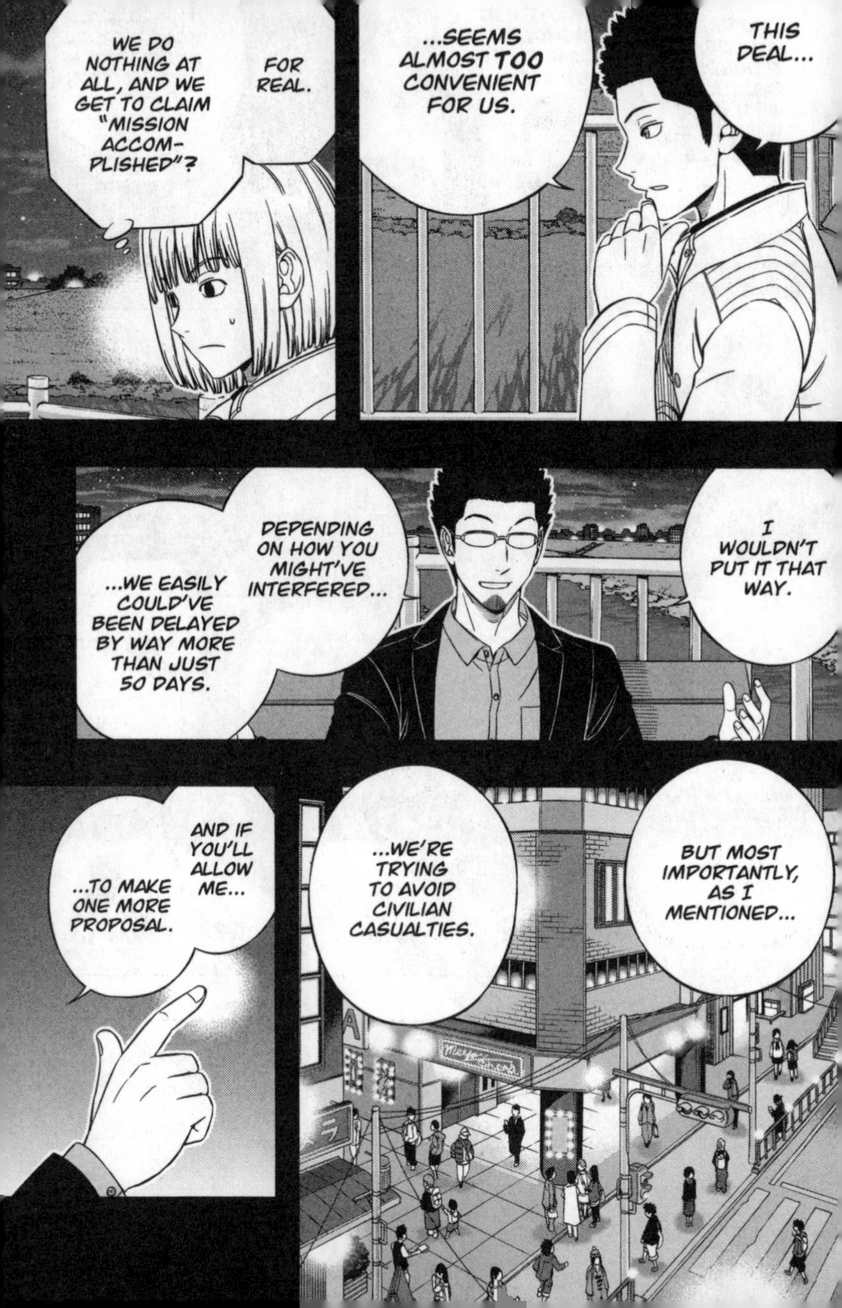
THIS DEAL...
...SEEMS ALMOST TOO CONVENIENT FOR US.
FOR REAL.
WE DO NOTHING AT ALL, AND WE GET TO CLAIM "MISSION ACCOMPLISHED"?
I WOULDN'T PUT IT THAT WAY.
DEPENDING ON HOW YOU MIGHT'VE INTERFERED...
...WE EASILY COULD'VE BEEN DELAYED BY WAY MORE THAN JUST 50 DAYS.
BUT MOST IMPORTANTLY, AS I MENTIONED...
...WE'RE TRYING TO AVOID CIVILIAN CASUALTIES.
AND IF YOU'LL ALLOW ME...
...TO MAKE ONE MORE PROPOSAL.

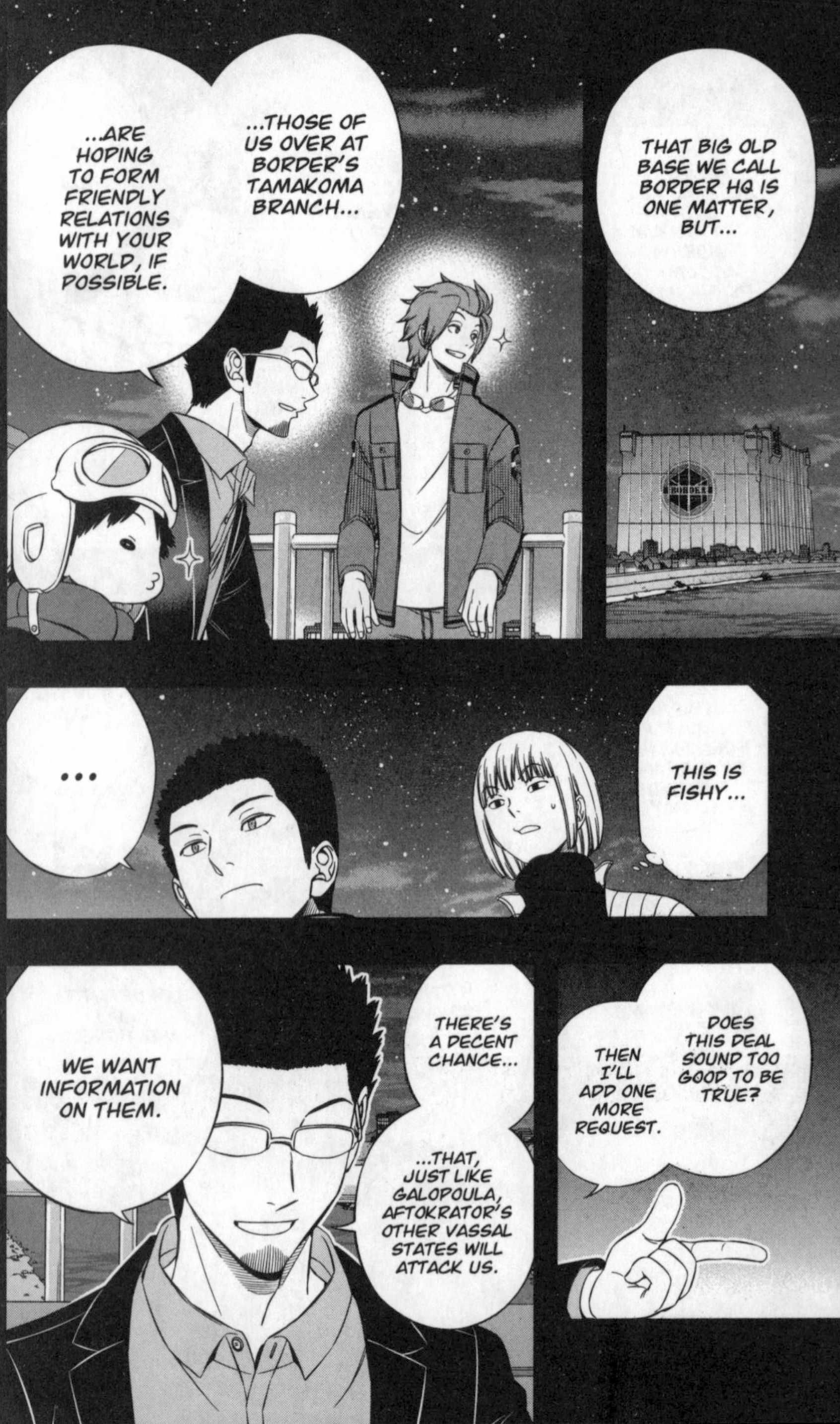
THAT BIG OLD BASE WE CALL BORDER HQ IS ONE MATTER, BUT...
...THOSE OF US OVER AT BORDER'S TAMAKOMA BRANCH...
...ARE HOPING TO FORM FRIENDLY RELATIONS WITH YOUR WORLD, IF POSSIBLE.
THIS IS FISHY...
...
DOES THIS DEAL SOUND TOO GOOD TO BE TRUE?
THEN I'LL ADD ONE MORE REQUEST.
THERE'S A DECENT CHANCE...
...THAT, JUST LIKE GALOPOULA, AFTOKRATOR'S OTHER VASSAL STATES WILL ATTACK US.
WE WANT INFORMATION ON THEM.

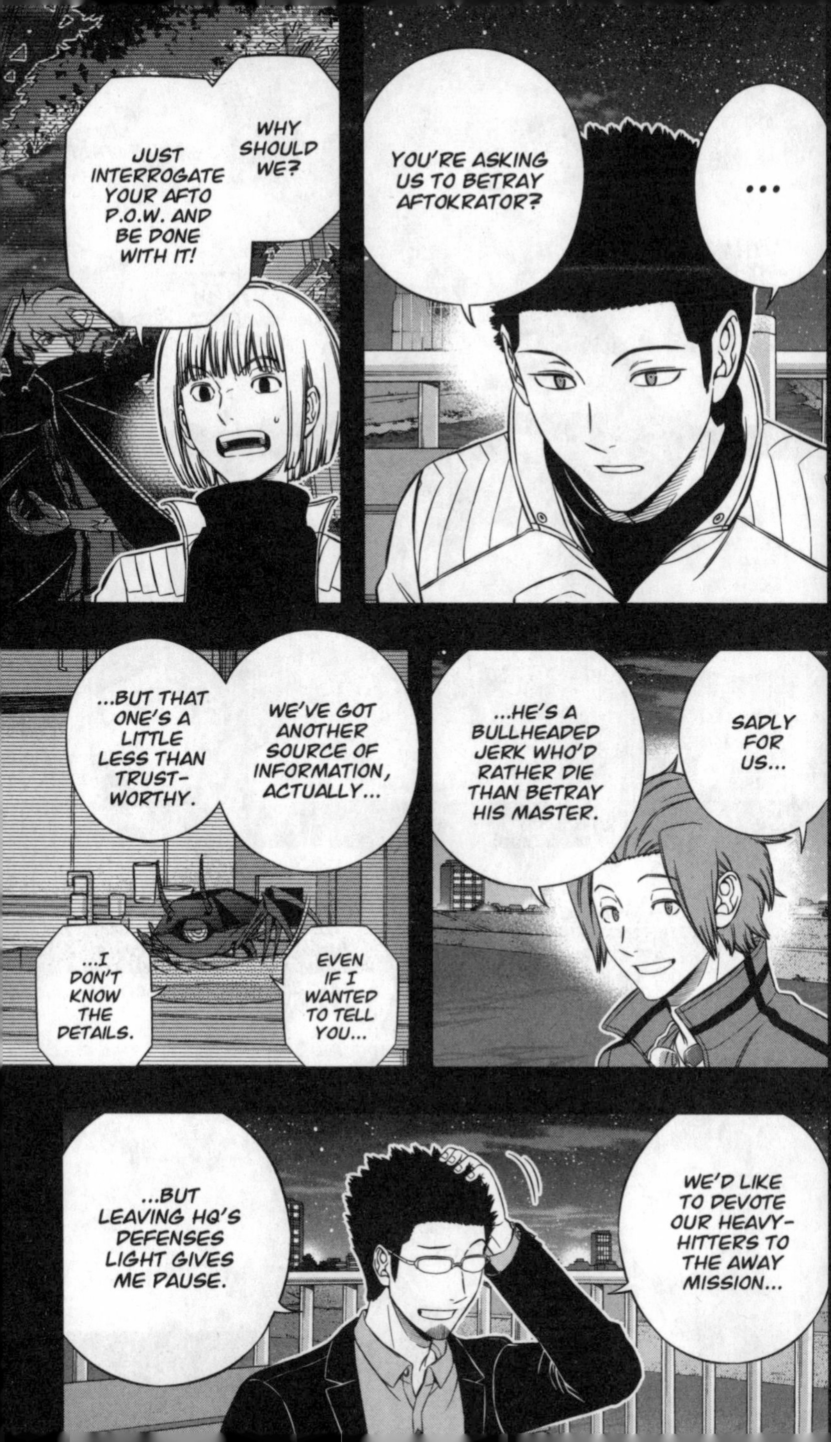
...
YOU'RE ASKING US TO BETRAY AFTOKRATOR?
WHY SHOULD WE?
JUST INTERROGATE YOUR AFTO P.O.W. AND BE DONE WITH IT!
SADLY FOR US...
...HE'S A BULLHEADED JERK WHO'D RATHER DIE THAN BETRAY HIS MASTER.
WE'VE GOT ANOTHER SOURCE OF INFORMATION, ACTUALLY...
...BUT THAT ONE'S A LITTLE LESS THAN TRUST-WORTHY.
EVEN IF I WANTED TO TELL YOU...
...I DON'T KNOW THE DETAILS.
WE'D LIKE TO DEVOTE OUR HEAVY-HITTERS TO THE AWAY MISSION...
...BUT LEAVING HQ'S DEFENSES LIGHT GIVES ME PAUSE.

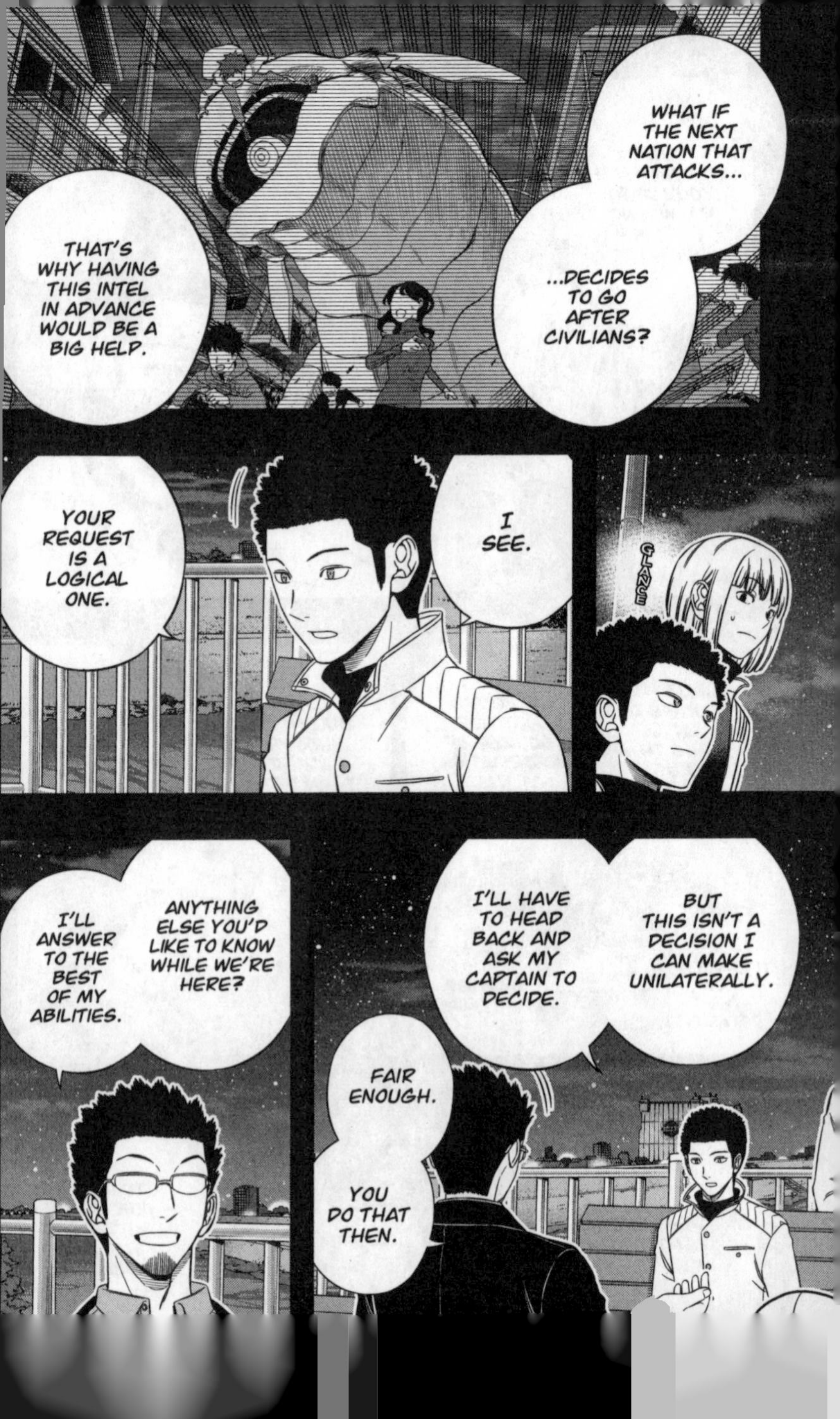
WHAT IF THE NEXT NATION THAT ATTACKS...
...DECIDES TO GO AFTER CIVILIANS?
THAT'S WHY HAVING THIS INTEL IN ADVANCE WOULD BE A BIG HELP.
GLANCE
I SEE.
YOUR REQUEST IS A LOGICAL ONE.
BUT THIS ISN'T A DECISION I CAN MAKE UNILATERALLY.
I'LL HAVE TO HEAD BACK AND ASK MY CAPTAIN TO DECIDE.
FAIR ENOUGH.
YOU DO THAT THEN.
ANYTHING ELSE YOU'D LIKE TO KNOW WHILE WE'RE HERE?
I'LL ANSWER TO THE BEST OF MY ABILITIES.

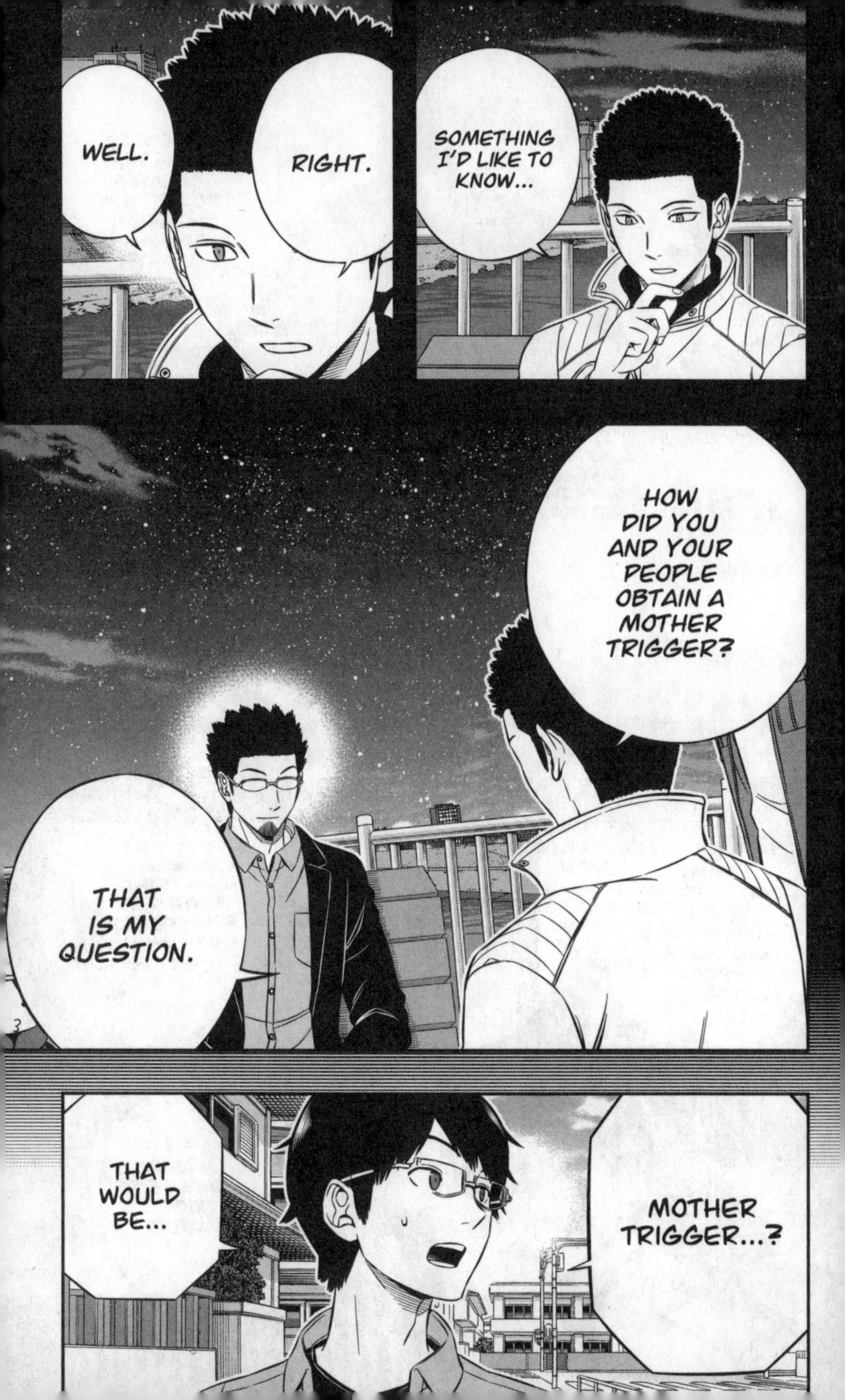
SOMETHING I'D LIKE TO KNOW...
RIGHT.
WELL.
HOW DID YOU AND YOUR PEOPLE OBTAIN A MOTHER TRIGGER?
THAT IS MY QUESTION.
MOTHER TRIGGER...?
THAT WOULD BE...

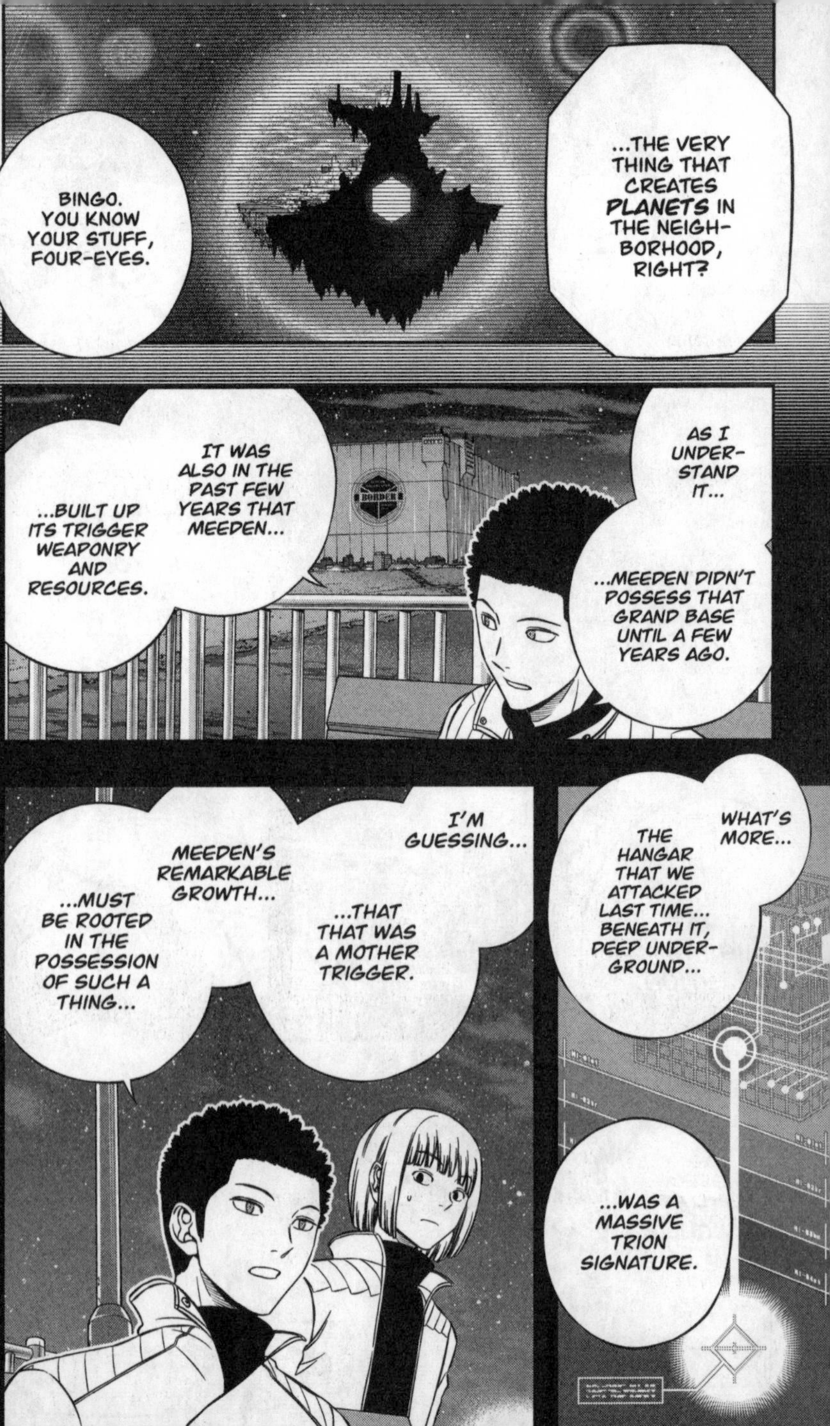
...THE VERY THING THAT CREATES PLANETS IN THE NEIGHBORHOOD, RIGHT?
BINGO. YOU KNOW YOUR STUFF, FOUR-EYES.
AS I UNDERSTAND IT...
...MEEDEN DIDN'T POSSESS THAT GRAND BASE UNTIL A FEW YEARS AGO.
IT WAS ALSO IN THE PAST FEW YEARS THAT MEEDEN...
...BUILT UP ITS TRIGGER WEAPONRY AND RESOURCES.
WHAT'S MORE...
THE HANGAR THAT WE ATTACKED LAST TIME... BENEATH IT, DEEP UNDERGROUND...
...WAS A MASSIVE TRION SIGNATURE.
I'M GUESSING...
...THAT THAT WAS A MOTHER TRIGGER.
MEEDEN'S REMARKABLE GROWTH...
...MUST BE ROOTED IN THE POSSESSION OF SUCH A THING...

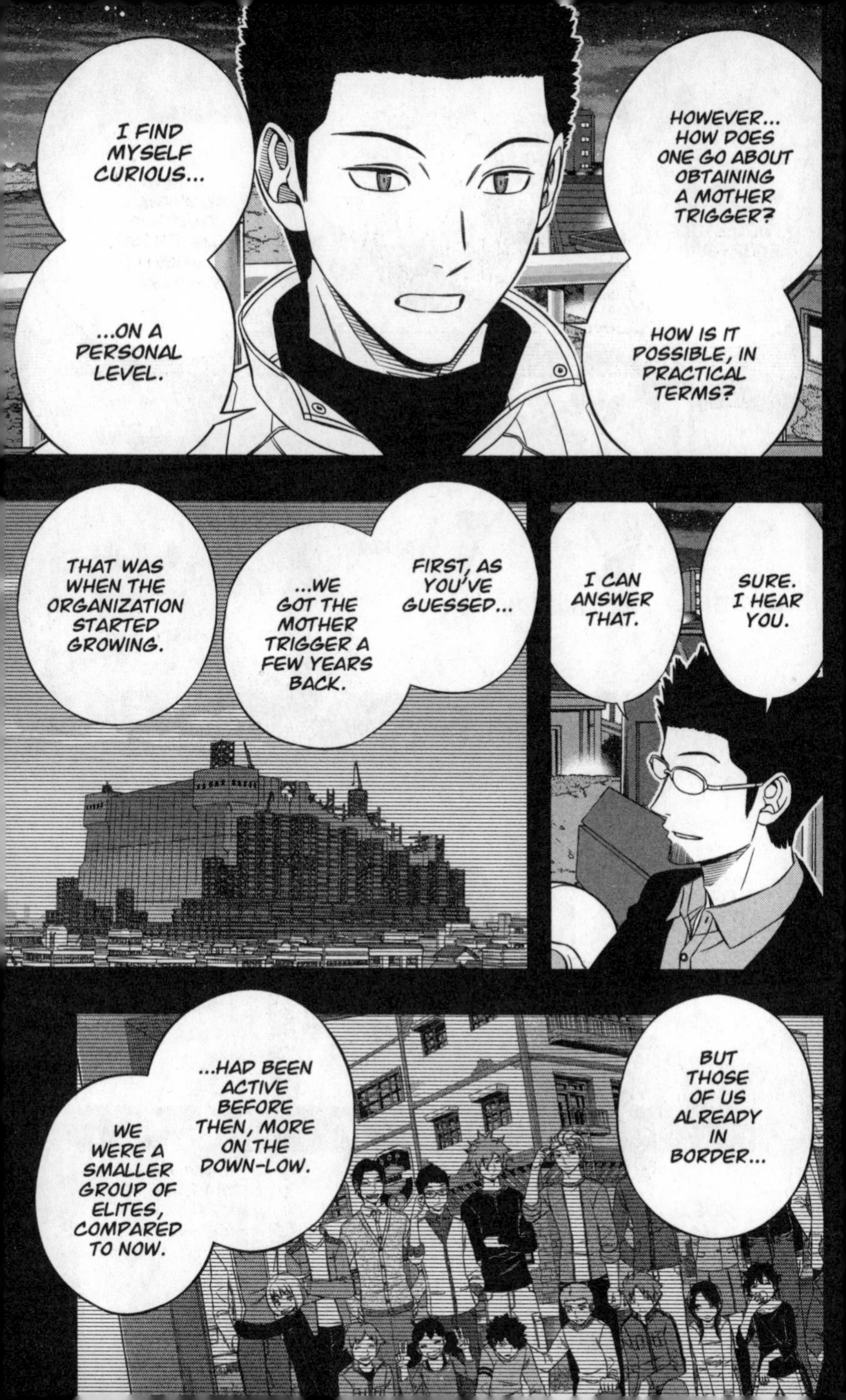

I FIND MYSELF CURIOUS...
...ON A PERSONAL LEVEL.
HOWEVER... HOW DOES ONE GO ABOUT OBTAINING A MOTHER TRIGGER?
HOW IS IT POSSIBLE, IN PRACTICAL TERMS?
SURE. I HEAR YOU.
I CAN ANSWER THAT.
FIRST, AS YOU'VE GUESSED...
...WE GOT THE MOTHER TRIGGER A FEW YEARS BACK.
THAT WAS WHEN THE ORGANIZATION STARTED GROWING.
BUT THOSE OF US ALREADY IN BORDER...
...HAD BEEN ACTIVE BEFORE THEN, MORE ON THE DOWN-LOW.
WE WERE A SMALLER GROUP OF ELITES, COMPARED TO NOW.

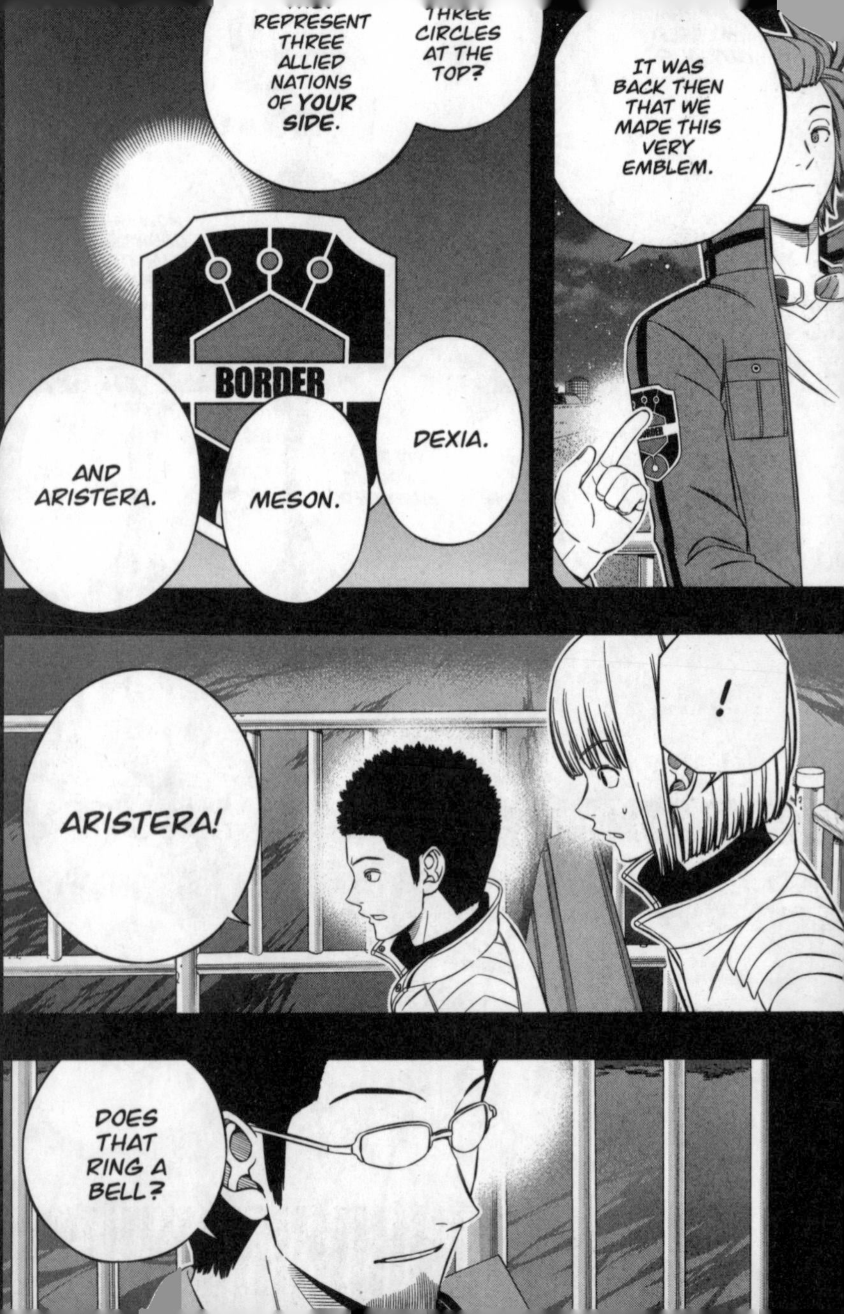

IT WAS BACK THEN THAT WE MADE THIS VERY EMBLEM.
CIRCLES AT THE TOP?
REPRESENT THREE ALLIED NATIONS OF YOUR SIDE.
BORDER
DEXIA.
MESON.
AND ARISTERA.
!
ARISTERA!
DOES THAT RING A BELL?

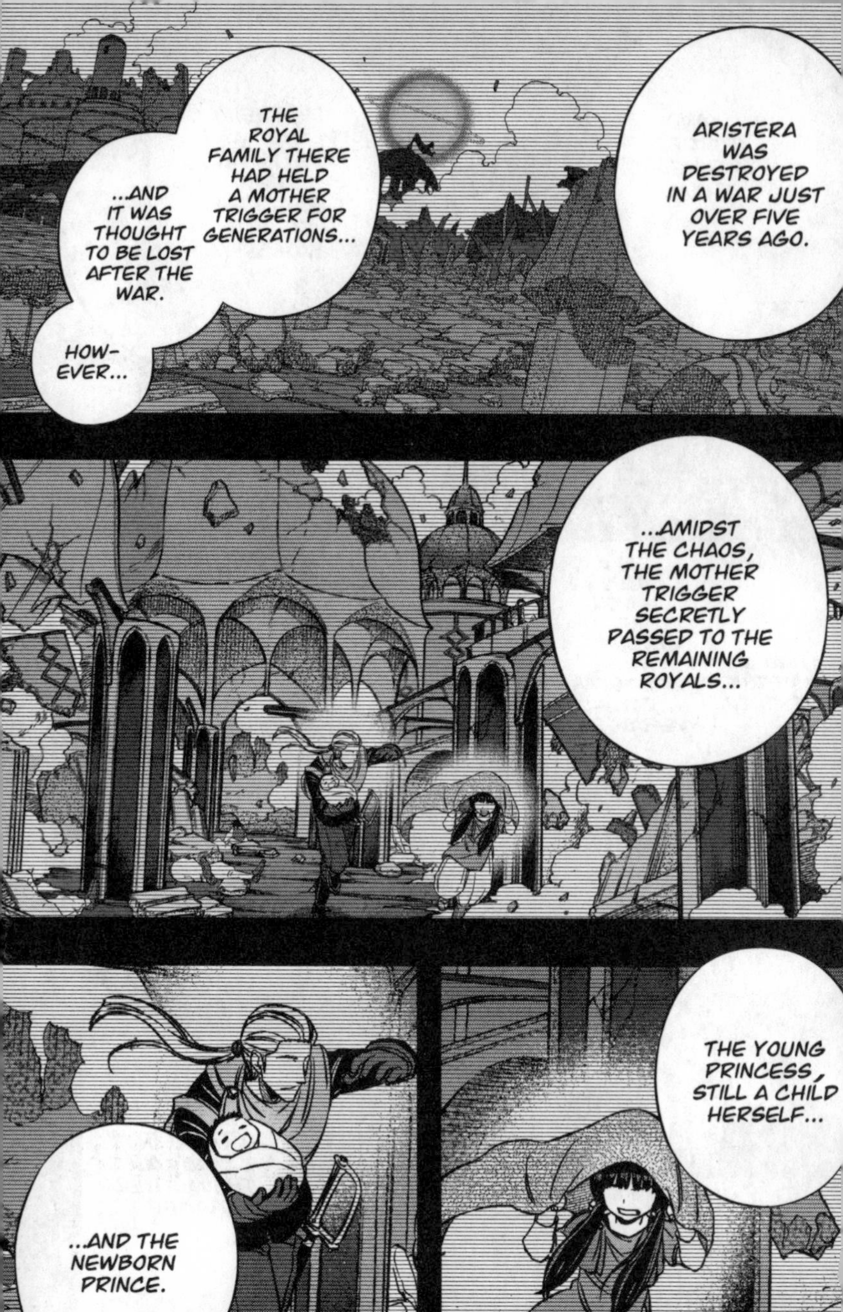
ARISTERA WAS DESTROYED IN A WAR JUST OVER FIVE YEARS AGO.
THE ROYAL FAMILY THERE HAD HELD A MOTHER TRIGGER FOR GENERATIONS...
...AND IT WAS THOUGHT TO BE LOST AFTER THE WAR.
HOW-EVER...
...AMIDST THE CHAOS, THE MOTHER TRIGGER SECRETLY PASSED TO THE REMAINING ROYALS...
THE YOUNG PRINCESS, STILL A CHILD HERSELF...
...AND THE NEWBORN PRINCE.

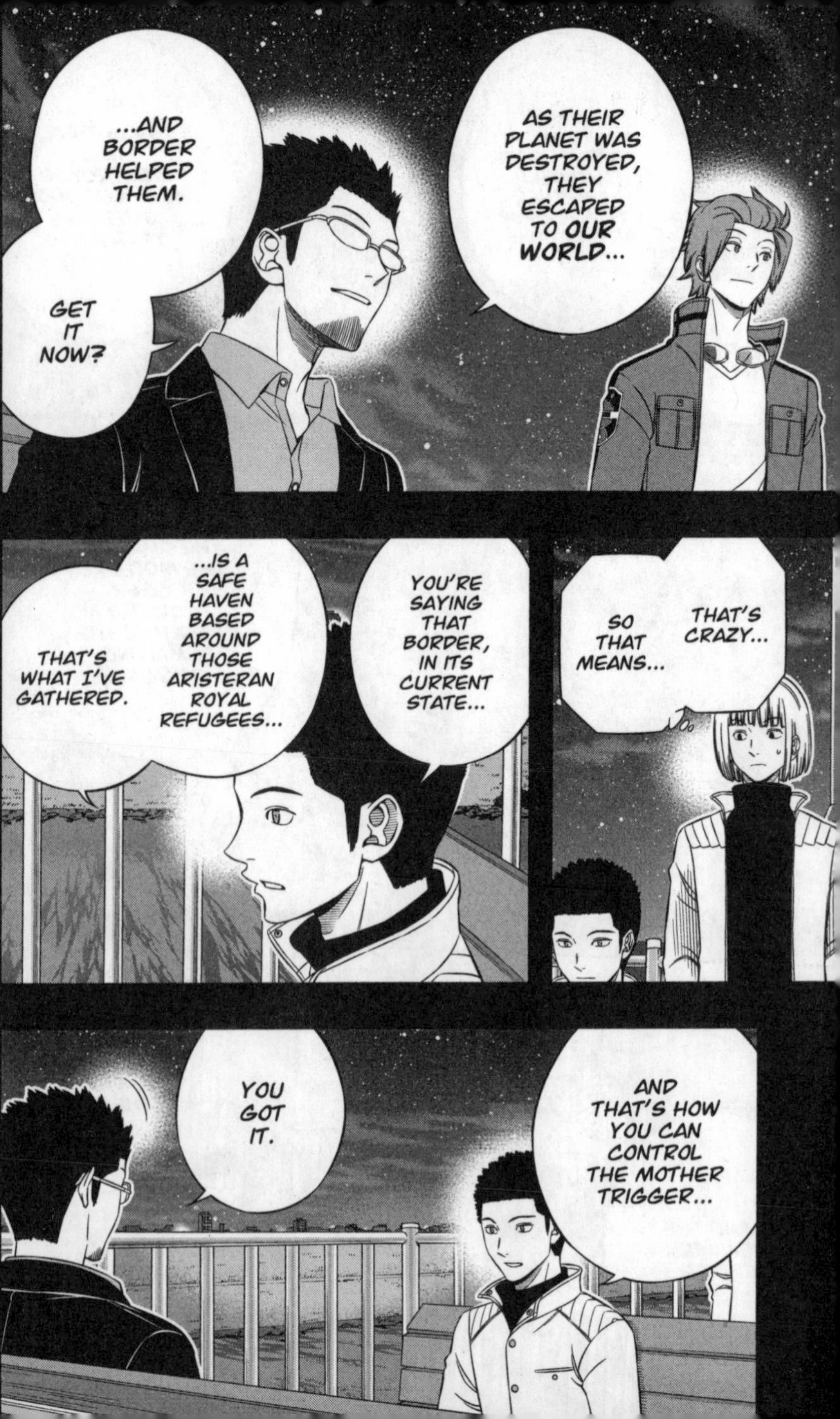
AS THEIR PLANET WAS DESTROYED, THEY ESCAPED TO OUR WORLD...
...AND BORDER HELPED THEM.
GET IT NOW?
THAT'S CRAZY...
SO THAT MEANS...
YOU'RE SAYING THAT BORDER, IN ITS CURRENT STATE...
...IS A SAFE HAVEN BASED AROUND THOSE ARISTERAN ROYAL REFUGEES...
THAT'S WHAT I'VE GATHERED.
AND THAT'S HOW YOU CAN CONTROL THE MOTHER TRIGGER...
YOU GOT IT.

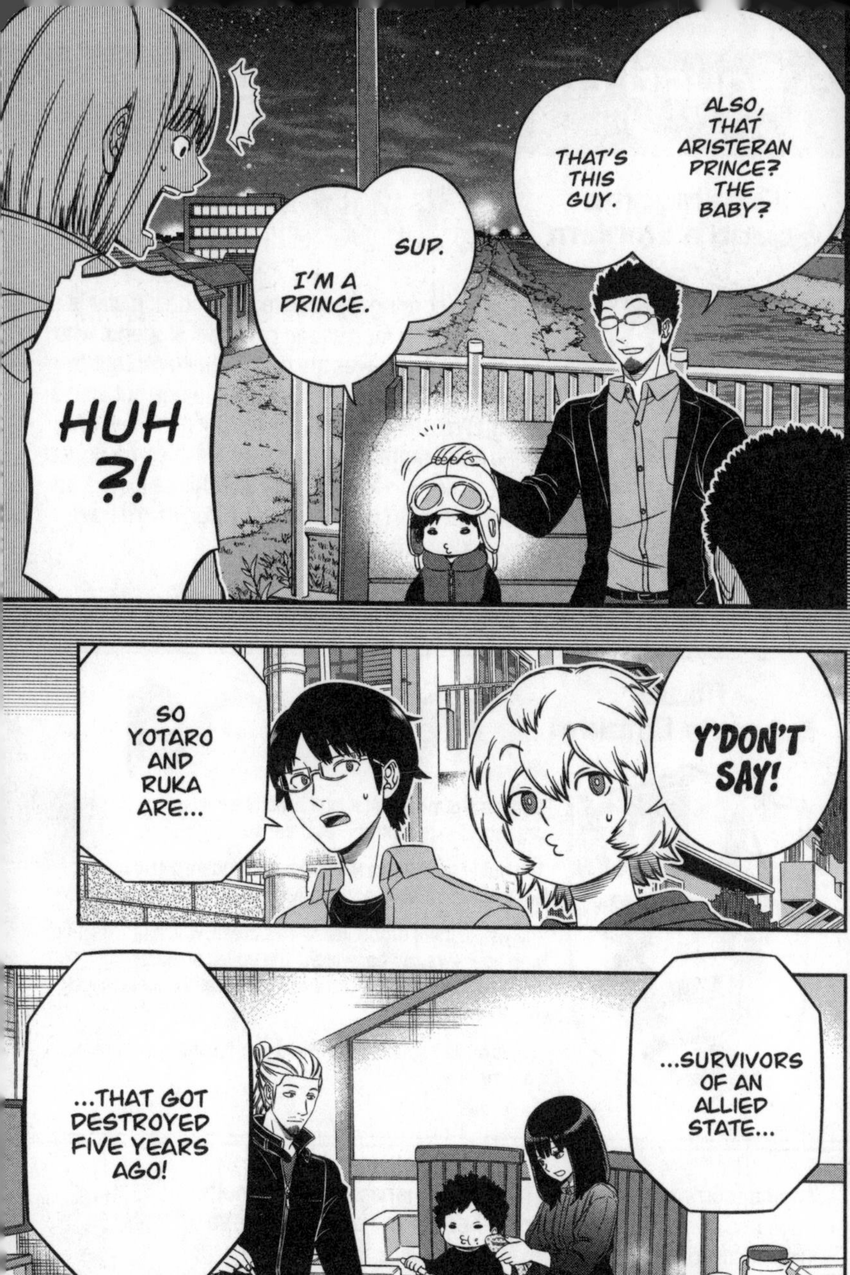
ALSO, THAT ARISTERAN PRINCE? THE BABY?
THAT'S THIS GUY.
SUP.
I'M A PRINCE.
HUH ?!
Y'DON'T SAY!
SO YOTARO AND RUKA ARE...
...SURVIVORS OF AN ALLIED STATE...
...THAT GOT DESTROYED FIVE YEARS AGO!

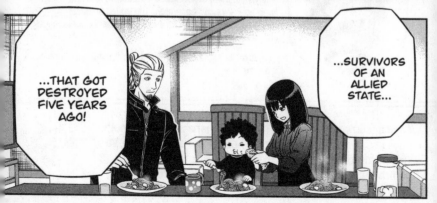

Squad Emblem Commentary: Part 3

Arashiyama Squad's Emblem

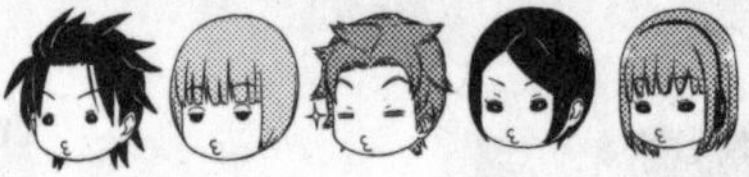

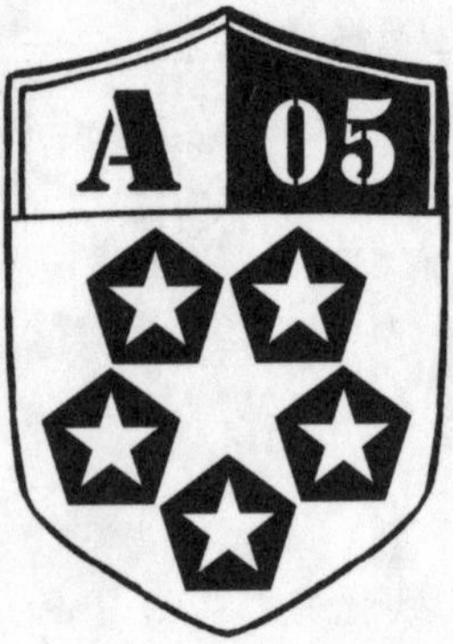
A
05

Five stars coming together to form one big star is a fitting emblem for a squad of model students who do lots of PR. This was the first A-Rank emblem to show up in the story, so it's a simple one but also a design I'm really fond of. One might think that one of the stars represents Zaki, but...Arashiyama Squad didn't make it to A-Rank until after Kitora joined, so no, it's not Zaki. I wonder what design they'd have used if Kitora had never joined?

Miwa Squad's Emblem

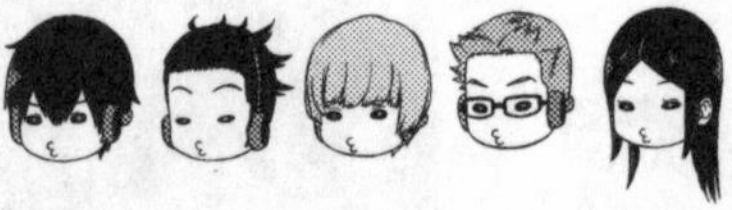

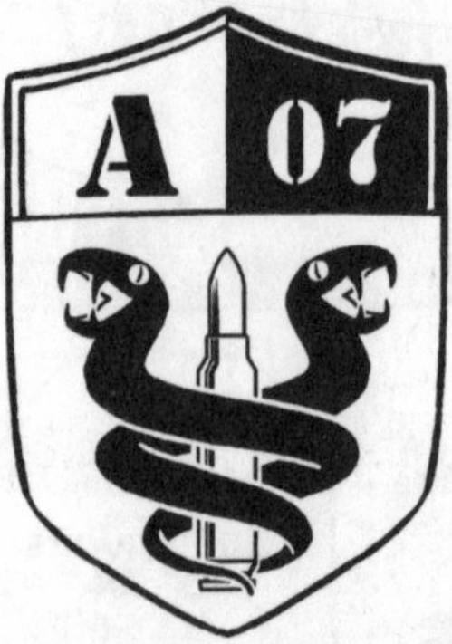
A
07

Snakes around a bullet isn't exactly a stellar look for an organization that promotes defense.

The bullet represents Narasaka and Kodera, while the two snakes are for Miwa and Yoneya, I guess?

The whole thing embodies Miwa's creed, which is, "Neighbors won't get away on our watch." The coiled snakes might also represent the squad's tactics of using Lead Bullets to lock the enemy down.

This is all just speculation, mind you. It barely qualifies as commentary.

Another command tossed at me by my manager means another page about emblems. I designed these ones really early on, so I've mostly forgotten what the concepts were. Still, the visuals communicate the right vibes, and isn't that good enough?

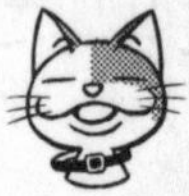

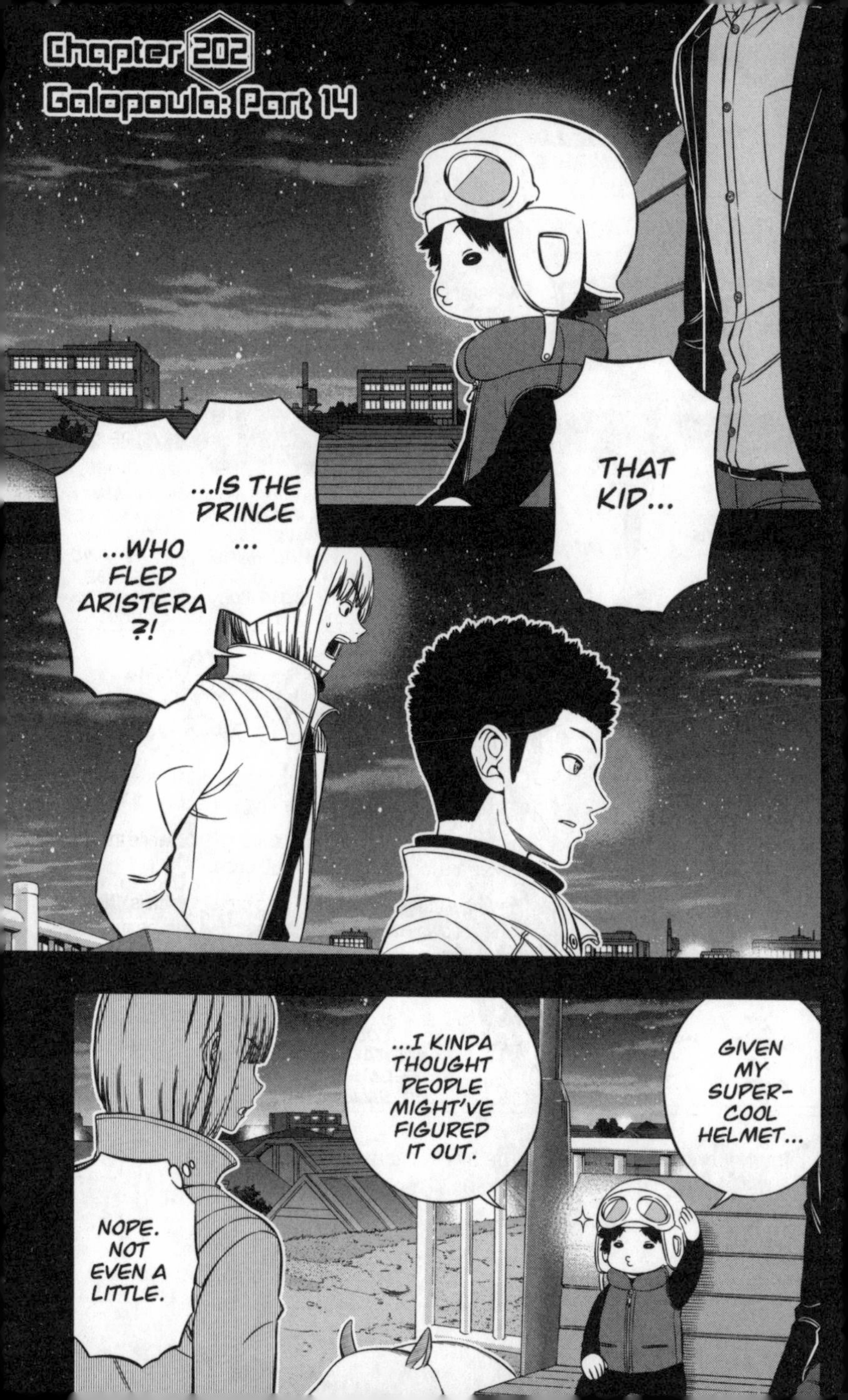
Chapter 202
Galopoula: Part 14
THAT KID...
...IS THE PRINCE...
...WHO FLED ARISTERA?!
GIVEN MY SUPER-COOL HELMET...
...I KINDA THOUGHT PEOPLE MIGHT'VE FIGURED IT OUT.
NOPE. NOT EVEN A LITTLE.

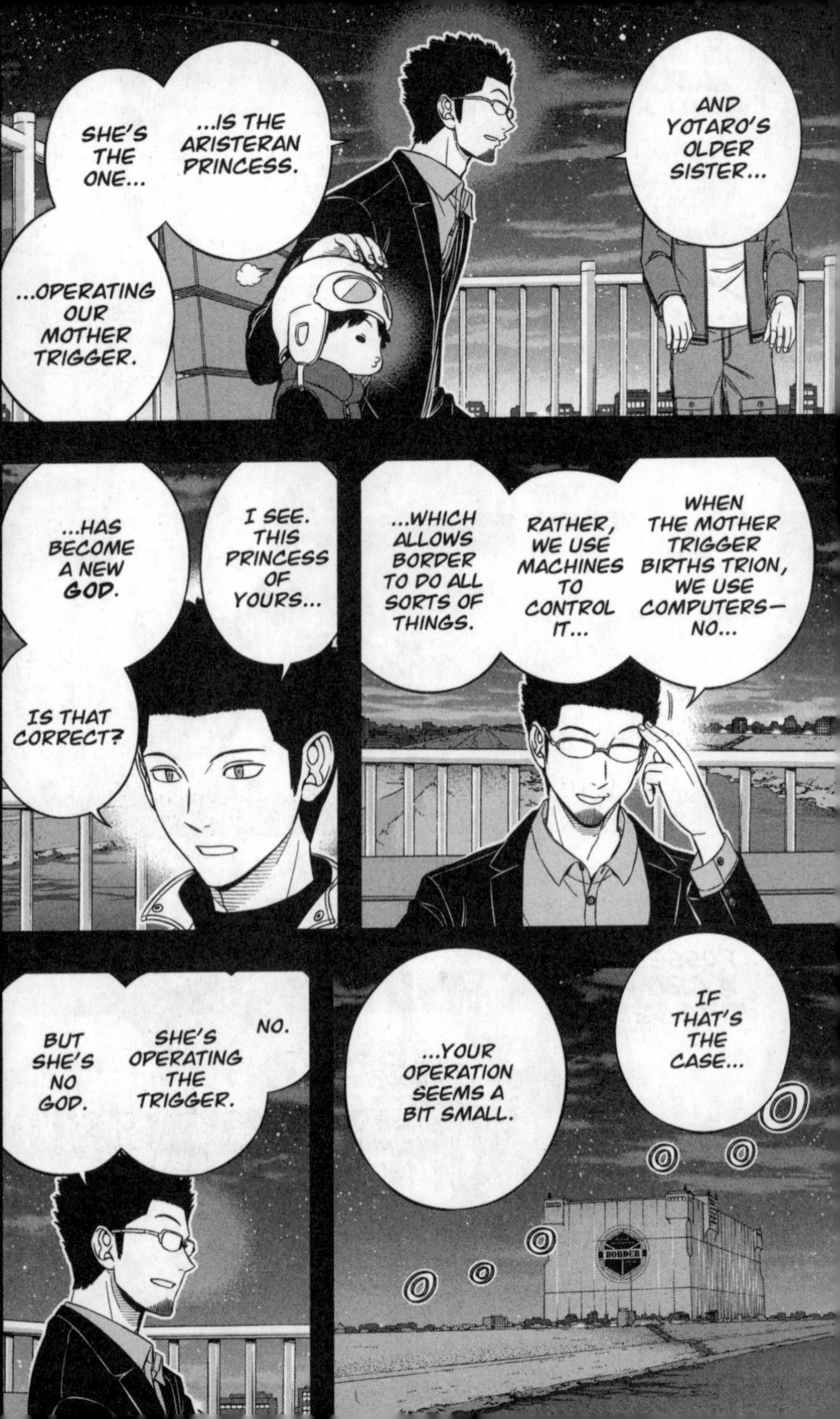
AND YOTARO'S OLDER SISTER...
...IS THE ARISTERAN PRINCESS.
SHE'S THE ONE...
...OPERATING OUR MOTHER TRIGGER.
WHEN THE MOTHER TRIGGER BIRTHS TRION, WE USE COMPUTERS— NO...
RATHER, WE USE MACHINES TO CONTROL IT...
...WHICH ALLOWS BORDER TO DO ALL SORTS OF THINGS.
I SEE. THIS PRINCESS OF YOURS...
...HAS BECOME A NEW **GOD**.
IS THAT CORRECT?
IF THAT'S THE CASE...
...YOUR OPERATION SEEMS A BIT SMALL.
NO.
SHE'S OPERATING THE TRIGGER.
BUT SHE'S NO GOD.

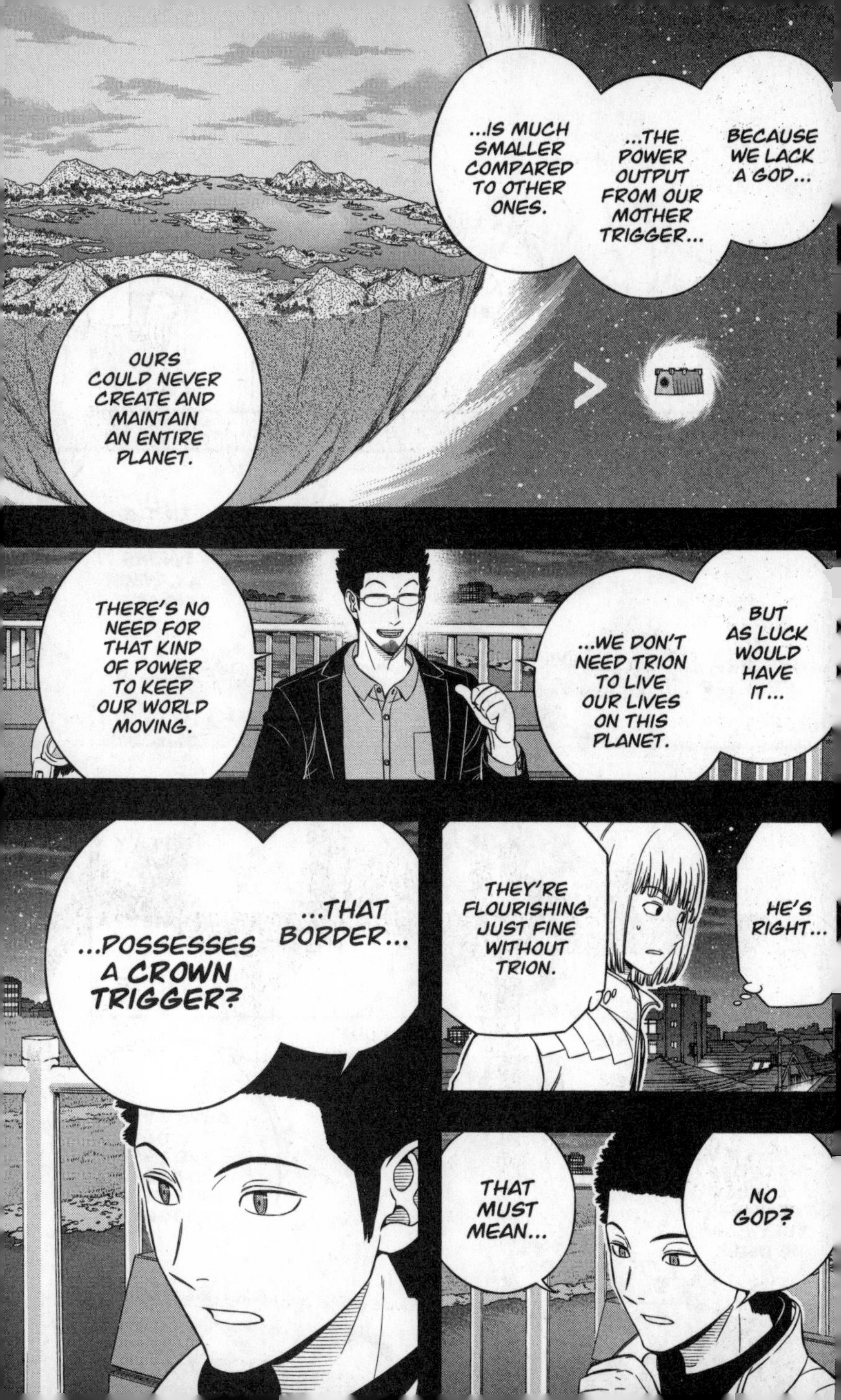
BECAUSE WE LACK A GOD...
...THE POWER OUTPUT FROM OUR MOTHER TRIGGER...
...IS MUCH SMALLER COMPARED TO OTHER ONES.
OURS COULD NEVER CREATE AND MAINTAIN AN ENTIRE PLANET.
BUT AS LUCK WOULD HAVE IT...
...WE DON'T NEED TRION TO LIVE OUR LIVES ON THIS PLANET.
THERE'S NO NEED FOR THAT KIND OF POWER TO KEEP OUR WORLD MOVING.
HE'S RIGHT...
THEY'RE FLOURISHING JUST FINE WITHOUT TRION.
NO GOD?
THAT MUST MEAN...
...THAT BORDER...
...POSSESSES A CROWN TRIGGER?

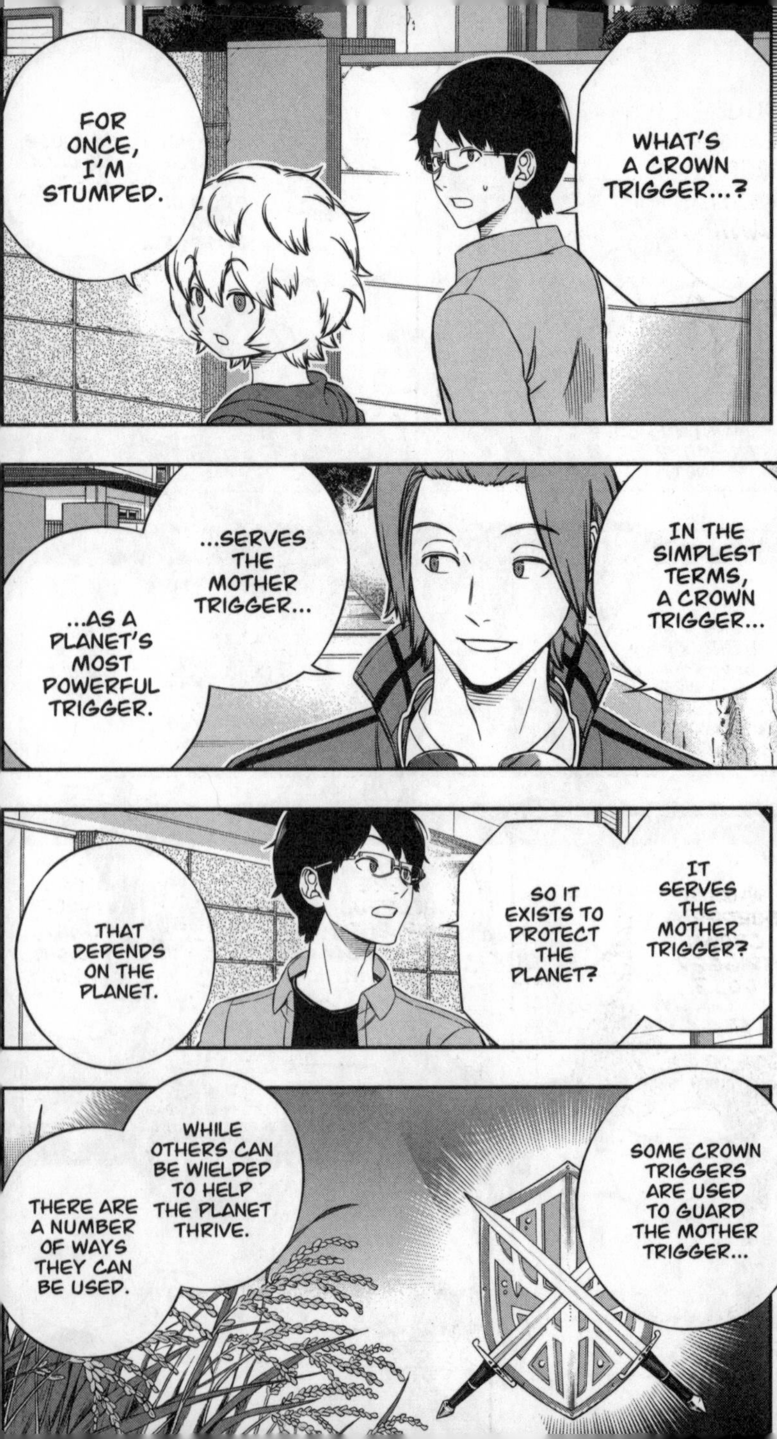
WHAT'S A CROWN TRIGGER...?
FOR ONCE, I'M STUMPED.
IN THE SIMPLEST TERMS, A CROWN TRIGGER...
...SERVES THE MOTHER TRIGGER...
...AS A PLANET'S MOST POWERFUL TRIGGER.
IT SERVES THE MOTHER TRIGGER?
SO IT EXISTS TO PROTECT THE PLANET?
THAT DEPENDS ON THE PLANET.
SOME CROWN TRIGGERS ARE USED TO GUARD THE MOTHER TRIGGER...
WHILE OTHERS CAN BE WIELDED TO HELP THE PLANET THRIVE.
THERE ARE A NUMBER OF WAYS THEY CAN BE USED.

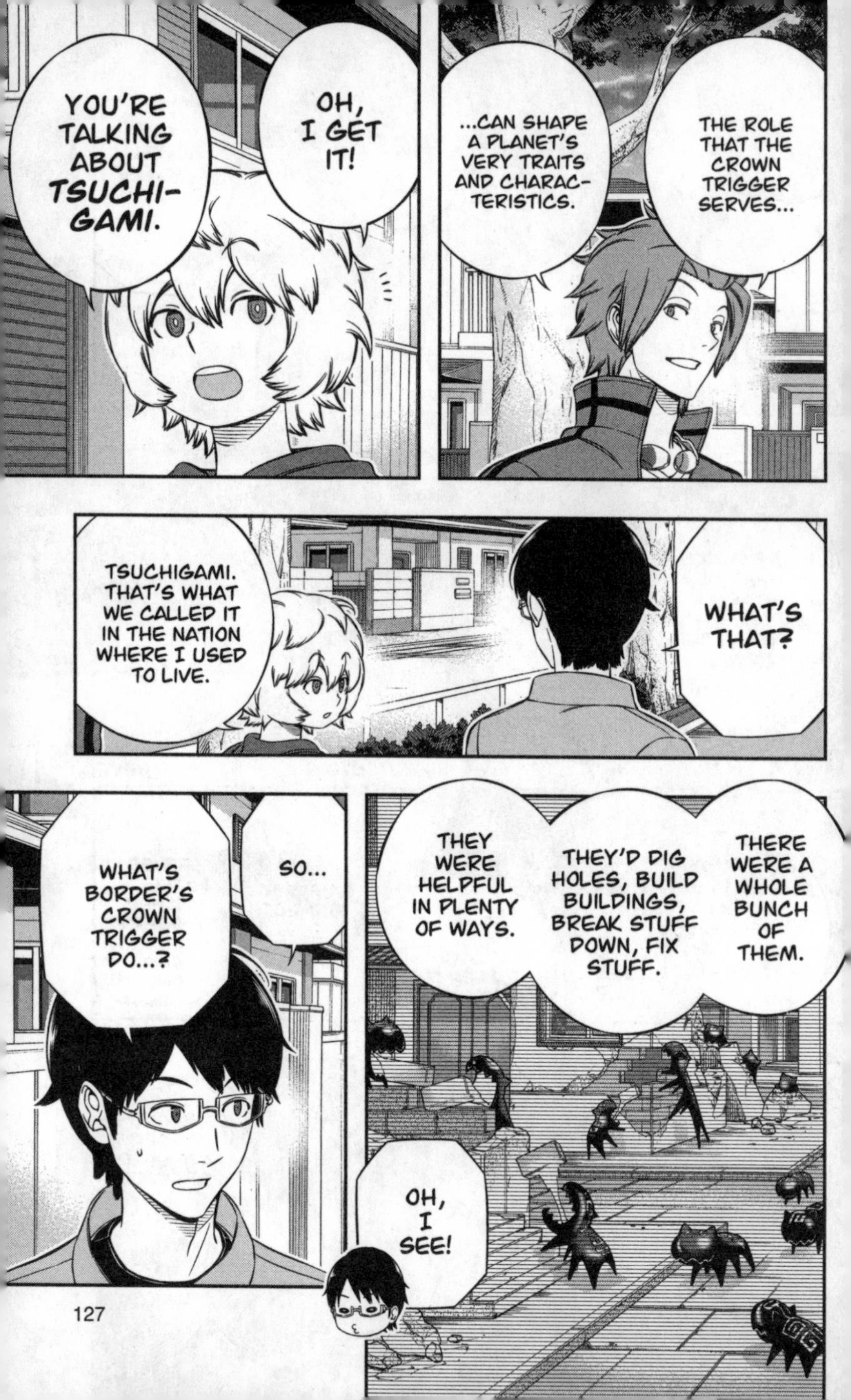
THE ROLE THAT THE CROWN TRIGGER SERVES...
...CAN SHAPE A PLANET'S VERY TRAITS AND CHARAC-TERISTICS.
OH, I GET IT!
YOU'RE TALKING ABOUT TSUCHI-GAMI.
WHAT'S THAT?
TSUCHIGAMI. THAT'S WHAT WE CALLED IT IN THE NATION WHERE I USED TO LIVE.
THERE WERE A WHOLE BUNCH OF THEM.
THEY'D DIG HOLES, BUILD BUILDINGS, BREAK STUFF DOWN, FIX STUFF.
THEY WERE HELPFUL IN PLENTY OF WAYS.
OH, I SEE!
SO...
WHAT'S BORDER'S CROWN TRIGGER DO...?

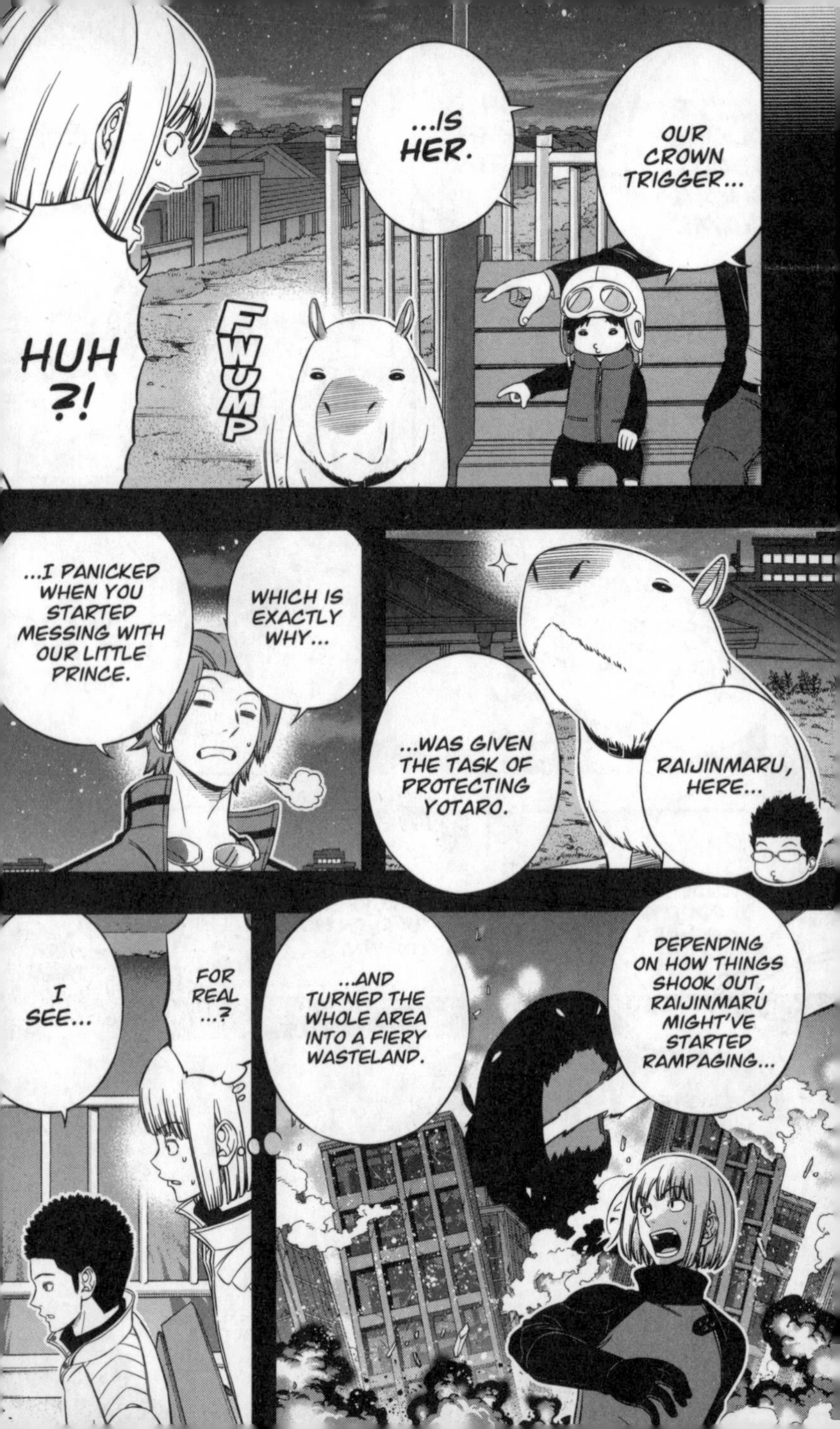
OUR CROWN TRIGGER...
...IS HER.
FWUMP
HUH?!
RAIJINMARU, HERE...
...WAS GIVEN THE TASK OF PROTECTING YOTARO.
WHICH IS EXACTLY WHY...
...I PANICKED WHEN YOU STARTED MESSING WITH OUR LITTLE PRINCE.
DEPENDING ON HOW THINGS SHOOK OUT, RAIJINMARU MIGHT'VE STARTED RAMPAGING...
...AND TURNED THE WHOLE AREA INTO A FIERY WASTELAND.
FOR REAL ...?
I SEE...

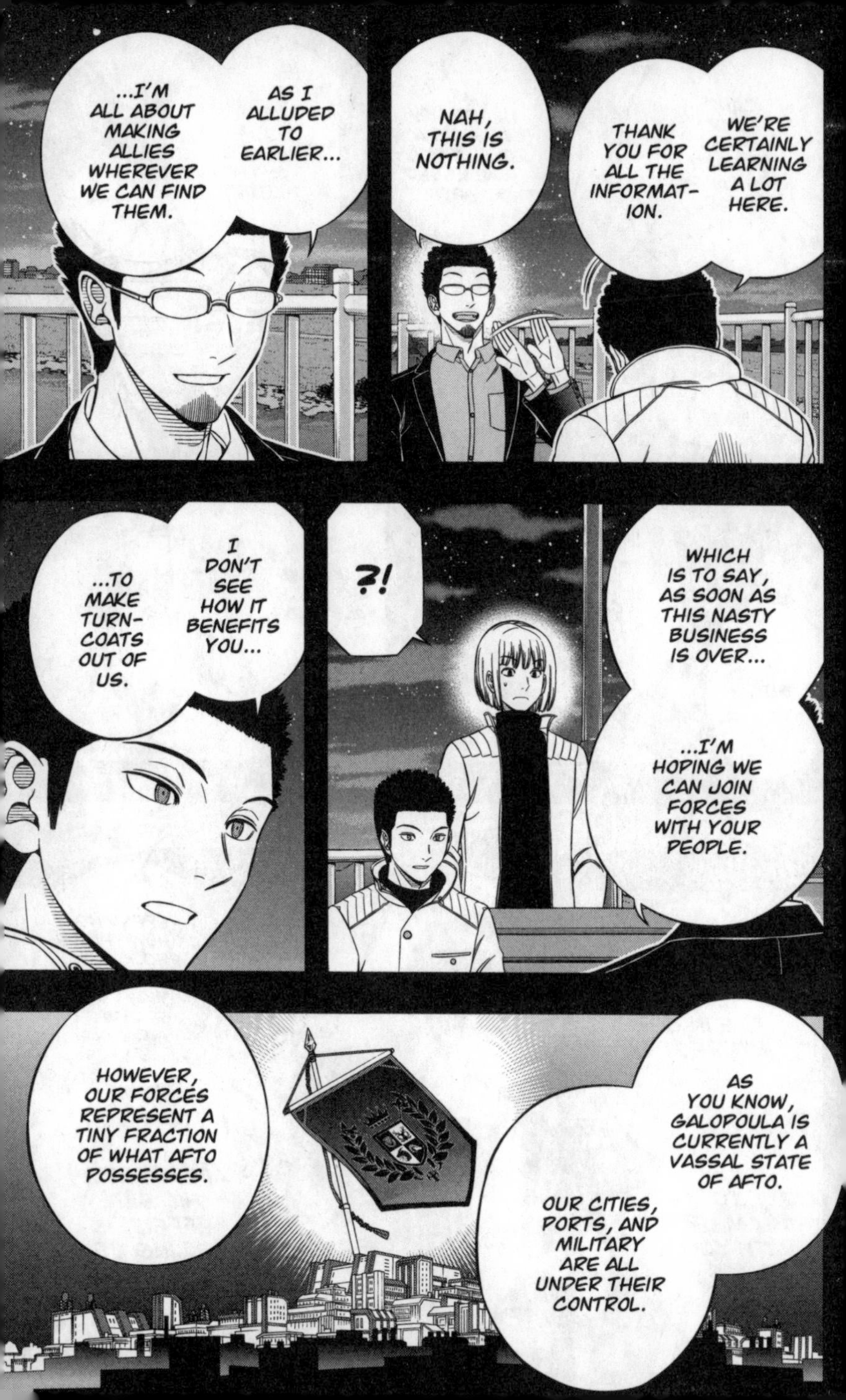
WE'RE CERTAINLY LEARNING A LOT HERE.
THANK YOU FOR ALL THE INFORMAT-ION.
NAH, THIS IS NOTHING.
AS I ALLUDED TO EARLIER...
...I'M ALL ABOUT MAKING ALLIES WHEREVER WE CAN FIND THEM.
WHICH IS TO SAY, AS SOON AS THIS NASTY BUSINESS IS OVER...
...I'M HOPING WE CAN JOIN FORCES WITH YOUR PEOPLE.
?!
I DON'T SEE HOW IT BENEFITS YOU...
...TO MAKE TURN-COATS OUT OF US.
AS YOU KNOW, GALOPOULA IS CURRENTLY A VASSAL STATE OF AFTO.
OUR CITIES, PORTS, AND MILITARY ARE ALL UNDER THEIR CONTROL.
HOWEVER, OUR FORCES REPRESENT A TINY FRACTION OF WHAT AFTO POSSESSES.

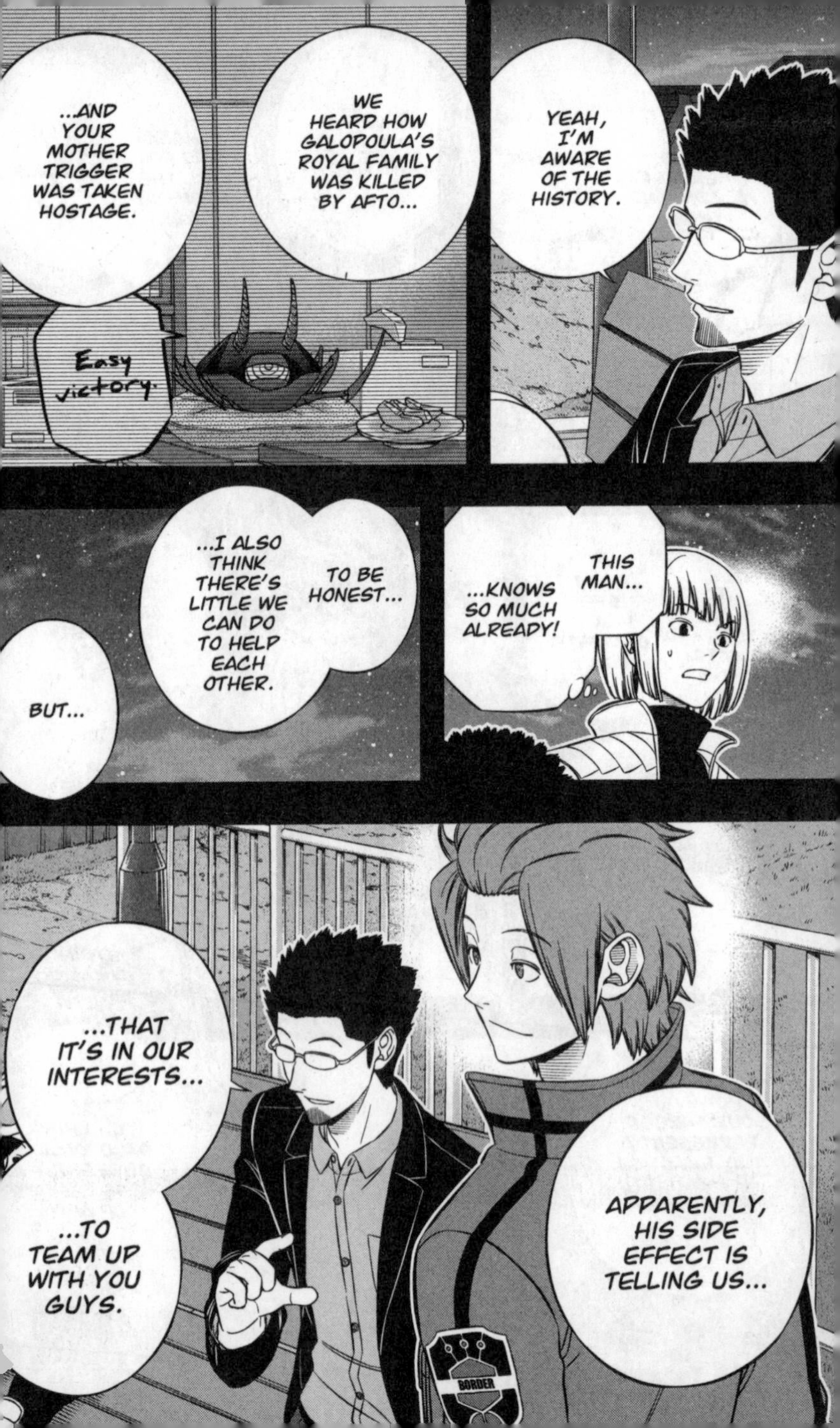
YEAH, I'M AWARE OF THE HISTORY.
WE HEARD HOW GALOPOULA'S ROYAL FAMILY WAS KILLED BY AFTO...
...AND YOUR MOTHER TRIGGER WAS TAKEN HOSTAGE.
Easy victory.
THIS MAN...
...KNOWS SO MUCH ALREADY!
TO BE HONEST...
...I ALSO THINK THERE'S LITTLE WE CAN DO TO HELP EACH OTHER.
BUT...
APPARENTLY, HIS SIDE EFFECT IS TELLING US...
...THAT IT'S IN OUR INTERESTS...
...TO TEAM UP WITH YOU GUYS.
BORDER

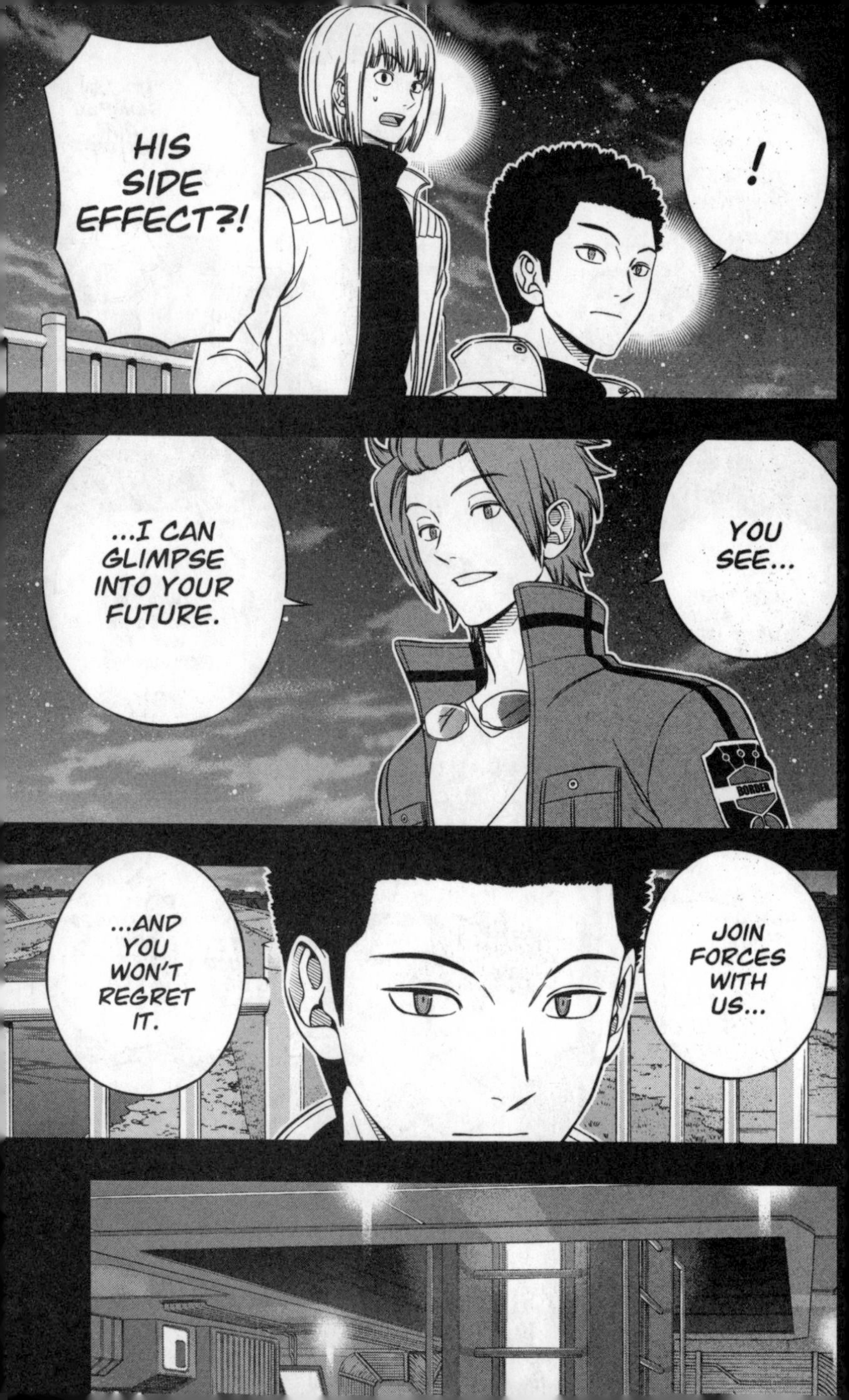
!
HIS SIDE EFFECT?!
YOU SEE...
...I CAN GLIMPSE INTO YOUR FUTURE.
JOIN FORCES WITH US...
...AND YOU WON'T REGRET IT.

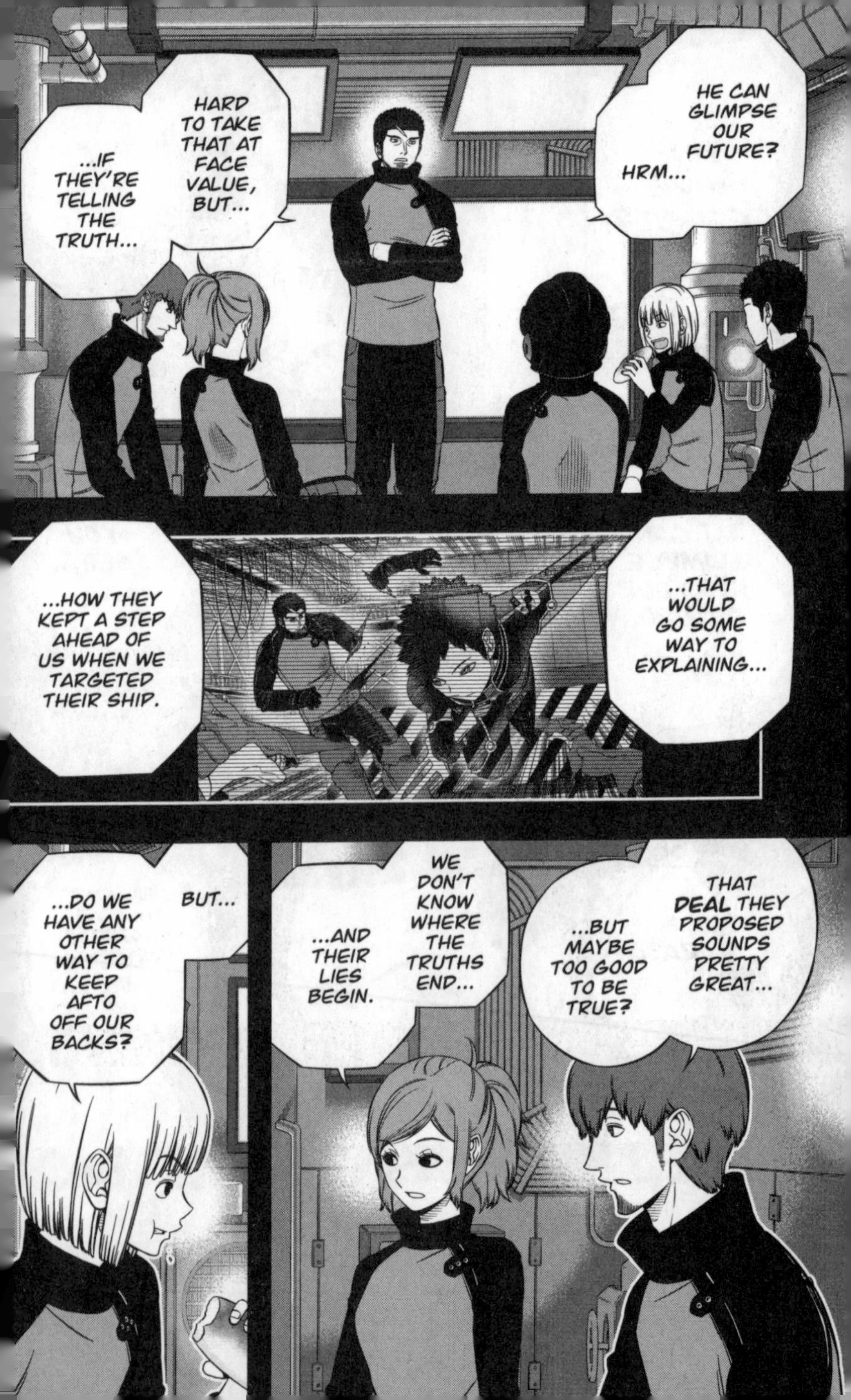
HE CAN GLIMPSE OUR FUTURE?
HRM...
HARD TO TAKE THAT AT FACE VALUE, BUT...
...IF THEY'RE TELLING THE TRUTH...
...THAT WOULD GO SOME WAY TO EXPLAINING...
...HOW THEY KEPT A STEP AHEAD OF US WHEN WE TARGETED THEIR SHIP.
THAT **DEAL** THEY PROPOSED SOUNDS PRETTY GREAT...
...BUT MAYBE TOO GOOD TO BE TRUE?
WE DON'T KNOW WHERE THE TRUTHS END...
...AND THEIR LIES BEGIN.
BUT...
...DO WE HAVE ANY OTHER WAY TO KEEP AFTO OFF OUR BACKS?

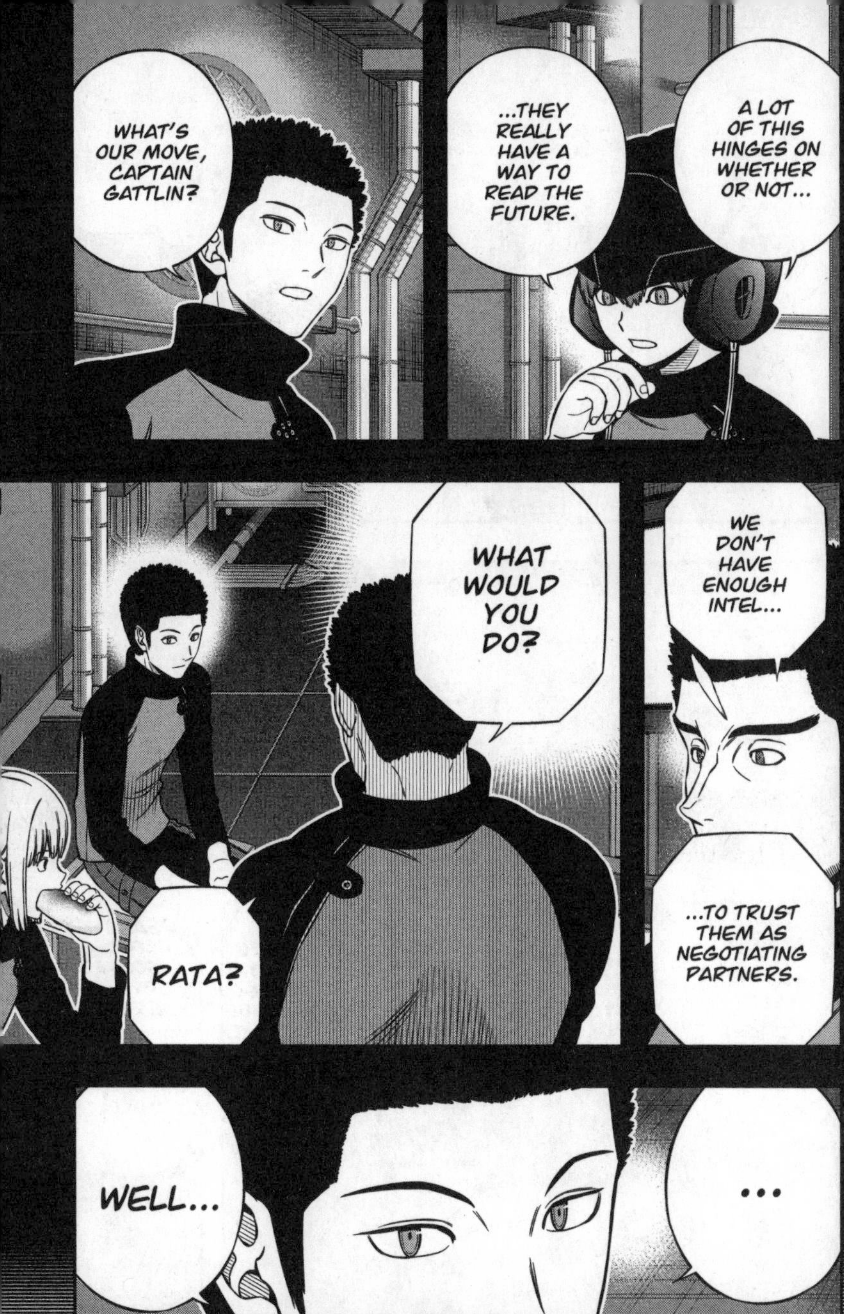
A LOT OF THIS HINGES ON WHETHER OR NOT...
...THEY REALLY HAVE A WAY TO READ THE FUTURE.
WHAT'S OUR MOVE, CAPTAIN GATTLIN?
WE DON'T HAVE ENOUGH INTEL...
...TO TRUST THEM AS NEGOTIATING PARTNERS.
WHAT WOULD YOU DO?
RATA?
...
WELL...

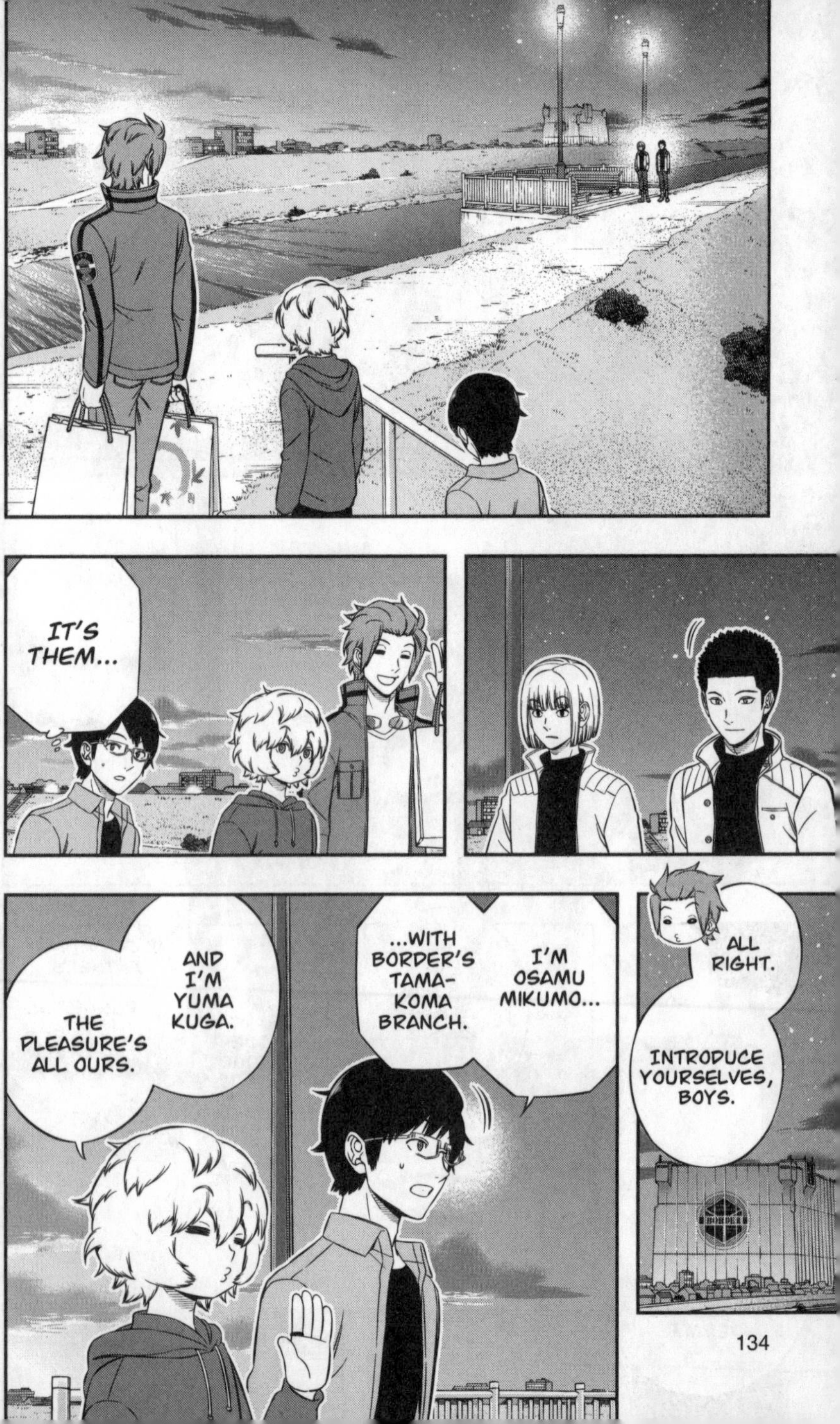
IT'S THEM...
ALL RIGHT.
INTRODUCE YOURSELVES, BOYS.
I'M OSAMU MIKUMO...
...WITH BORDER'S TAMA-KOMA BRANCH.
AND I'M YUMA KUGA.
THE PLEASURE'S ALL OURS.

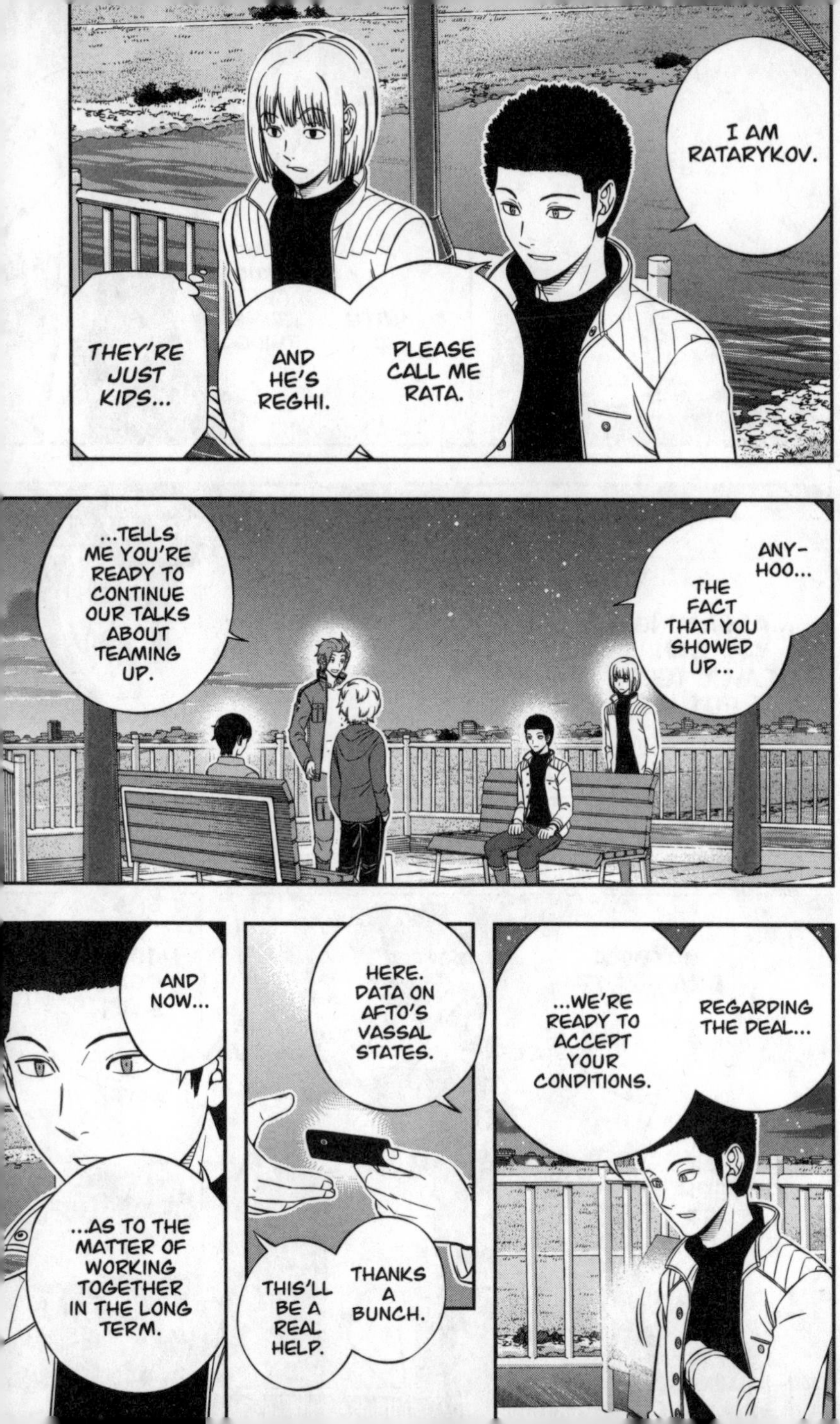
I AM RATARYKOV.
PLEASE CALL ME RATA.
AND HE'S REGHI.
THEY'RE JUST KIDS...
ANY-HOO... THE FACT THAT YOU SHOWED UP...
...TELLS ME YOU'RE READY TO CONTINUE OUR TALKS ABOUT TEAMING UP.
REGARDING THE DEAL...
...WE'RE READY TO ACCEPT YOUR CONDITIONS.
HERE. DATA ON AFTO'S VASSAL STATES.
THANKS A BUNCH.
THIS'LL BE A REAL HELP.
AND NOW...
...AS TO THE MATTER OF WORKING TOGETHER IN THE LONG TERM.

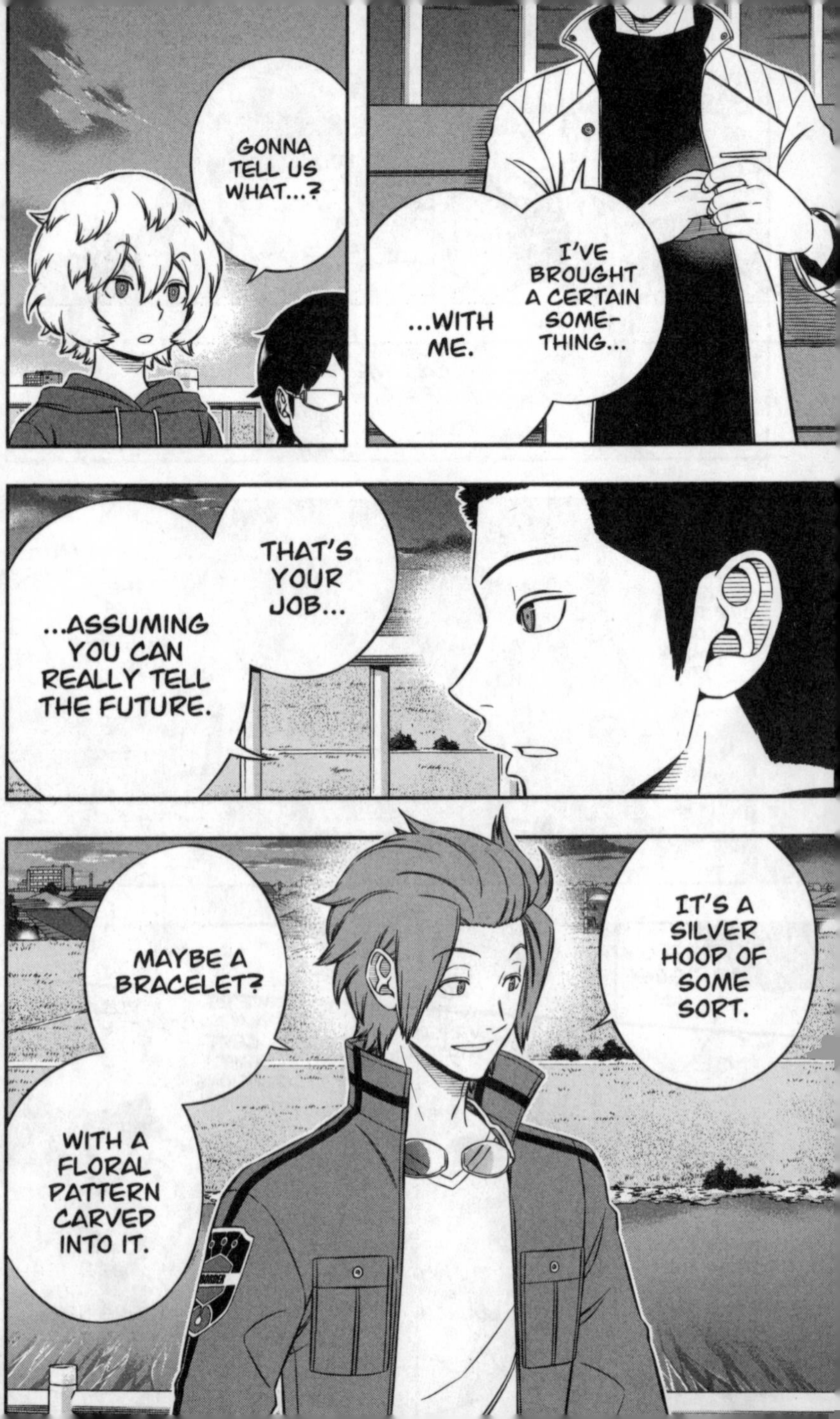
I'VE BROUGHT A CERTAIN SOME-THING...
...WITH ME.
GONNA TELL US WHAT...?
THAT'S YOUR JOB...
...ASSUMING YOU CAN REALLY TELL THE FUTURE.
IT'S A SILVER HOOP OF SOME SORT.
MAYBE A BRACELET?
WITH A FLORAL PATTERN CARVED INTO IT.

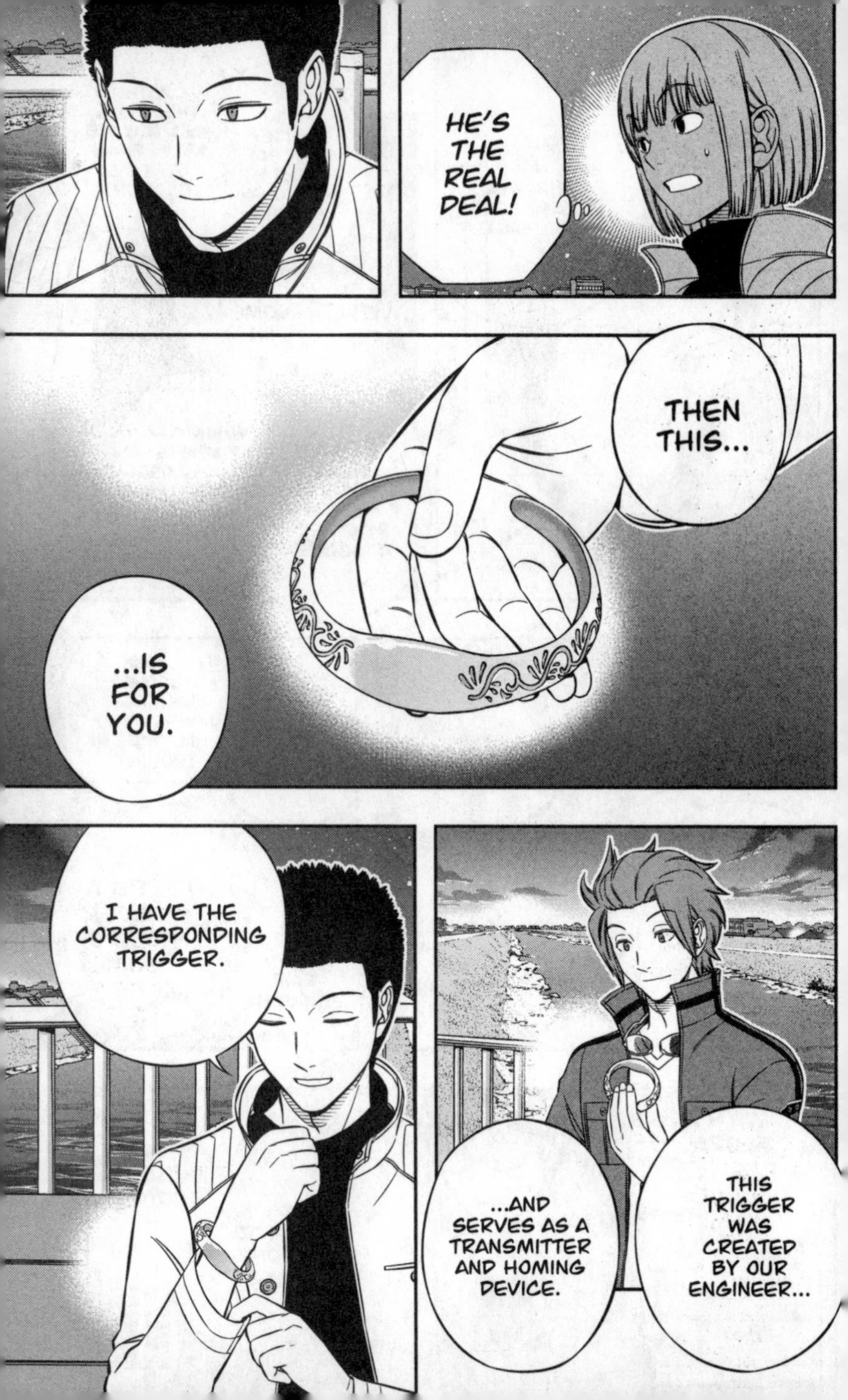
HE'S THE REAL DEAL!
THEN THIS...
...IS FOR YOU.
THIS TRIGGER WAS CREATED BY OUR ENGINEER...
...AND SERVES AS A TRANSMITTER AND HOMING DEVICE.
I HAVE THE CORRESPONDING TRIGGER.

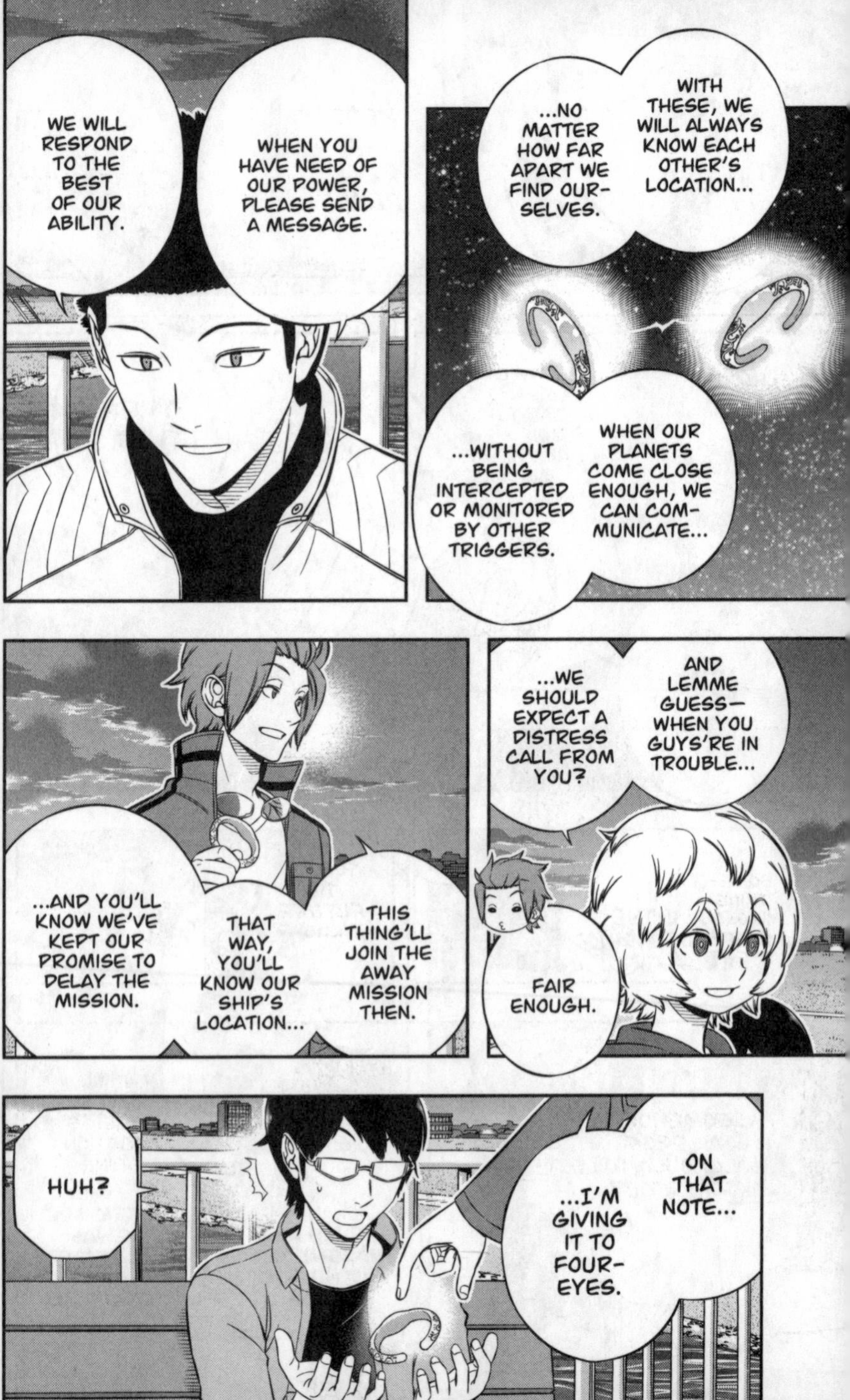
WITH THESE, WE WILL ALWAYS KNOW EACH OTHER'S LOCATION...
...NO MATTER HOW FAR APART WE FIND OURSELVES.
WHEN OUR PLANETS COME CLOSE ENOUGH, WE CAN COMMUNICATE...
...WITHOUT BEING INTERCEPTED OR MONITORED BY OTHER TRIGGERS.
WHEN YOU HAVE NEED OF OUR POWER, PLEASE SEND A MESSAGE.
WE WILL RESPOND TO THE BEST OF OUR ABILITY.
AND LEMME GUESS—WHEN YOU GUYS'RE IN TROUBLE...
...WE SHOULD EXPECT A DISTRESS CALL FROM YOU?
FAIR ENOUGH.
THIS THING'LL JOIN THE AWAY MISSION THEN.
THAT WAY, YOU'LL KNOW OUR SHIP'S LOCATION...
...AND YOU'LL KNOW WE'VE KEPT OUR PROMISE TO DELAY THE MISSION.
ON THAT NOTE...
...I'M GIVING IT TO FOUR-EYES.
HUH?

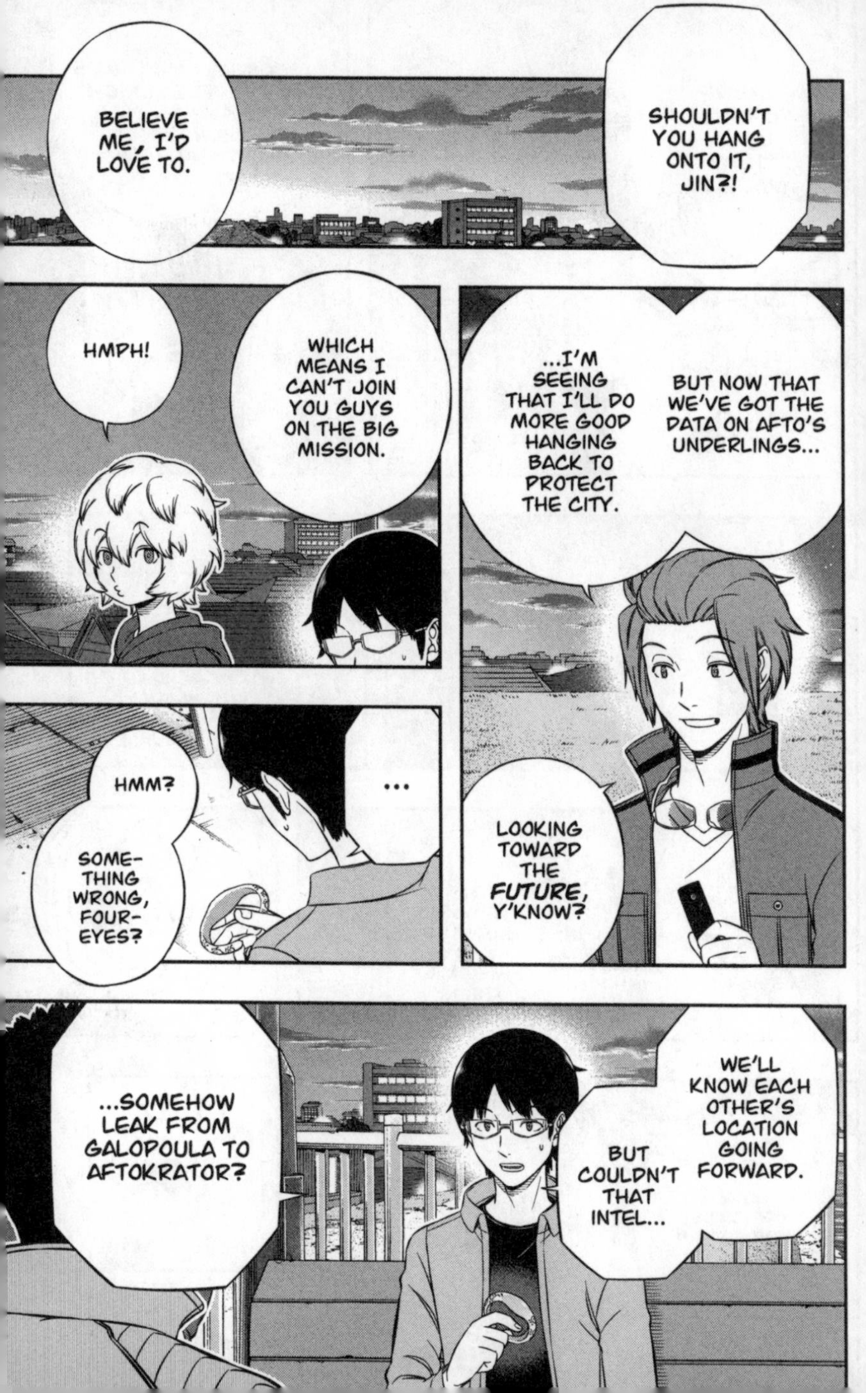
SHOULDN'T YOU HANG ONTO IT, JIN?!
BELIEVE ME, I'D LOVE TO.
BUT NOW THAT WE'VE GOT THE DATA ON AFTO'S UNDERLINGS...
...I'M SEEING THAT I'LL DO MORE GOOD HANGING BACK TO PROTECT THE CITY.
LOOKING TOWARD THE *FUTURE*, Y'KNOW?
WHICH MEANS I CAN'T JOIN YOU GUYS ON THE BIG MISSION.
HMPH!
...
HMM?
SOME-THING WRONG, FOUR-EYES?
WE'LL KNOW EACH OTHER'S LOCATION GOING FORWARD.
BUT COULDN'T THAT INTEL...
...SOMEHOW LEAK FROM GALOPOULA TO AFTOKRATOR?

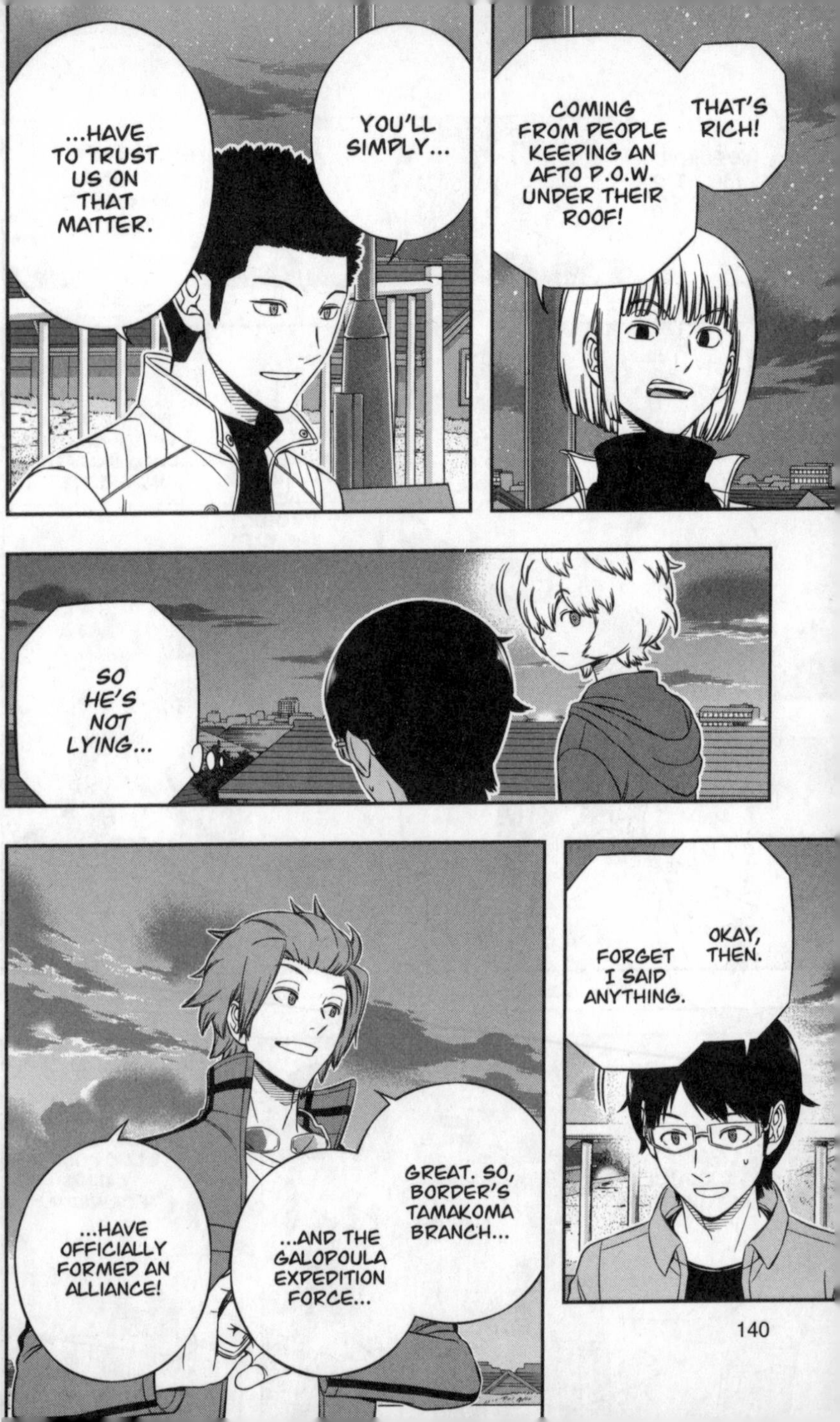
THAT'S RICH!
COMING FROM PEOPLE KEEPING AN AFTO P.O.W. UNDER THEIR ROOF!
YOU'LL SIMPLY...
...HAVE TO TRUST US ON THAT MATTER.
SO HE'S NOT LYING...
OKAY, THEN.
FORGET I SAID ANYTHING.
GREAT. SO, BORDER'S TAMAKOMA BRANCH...
...AND THE GALOPOULA EXPEDITION FORCE...
...HAVE OFFICIALLY FORMED AN ALLIANCE!

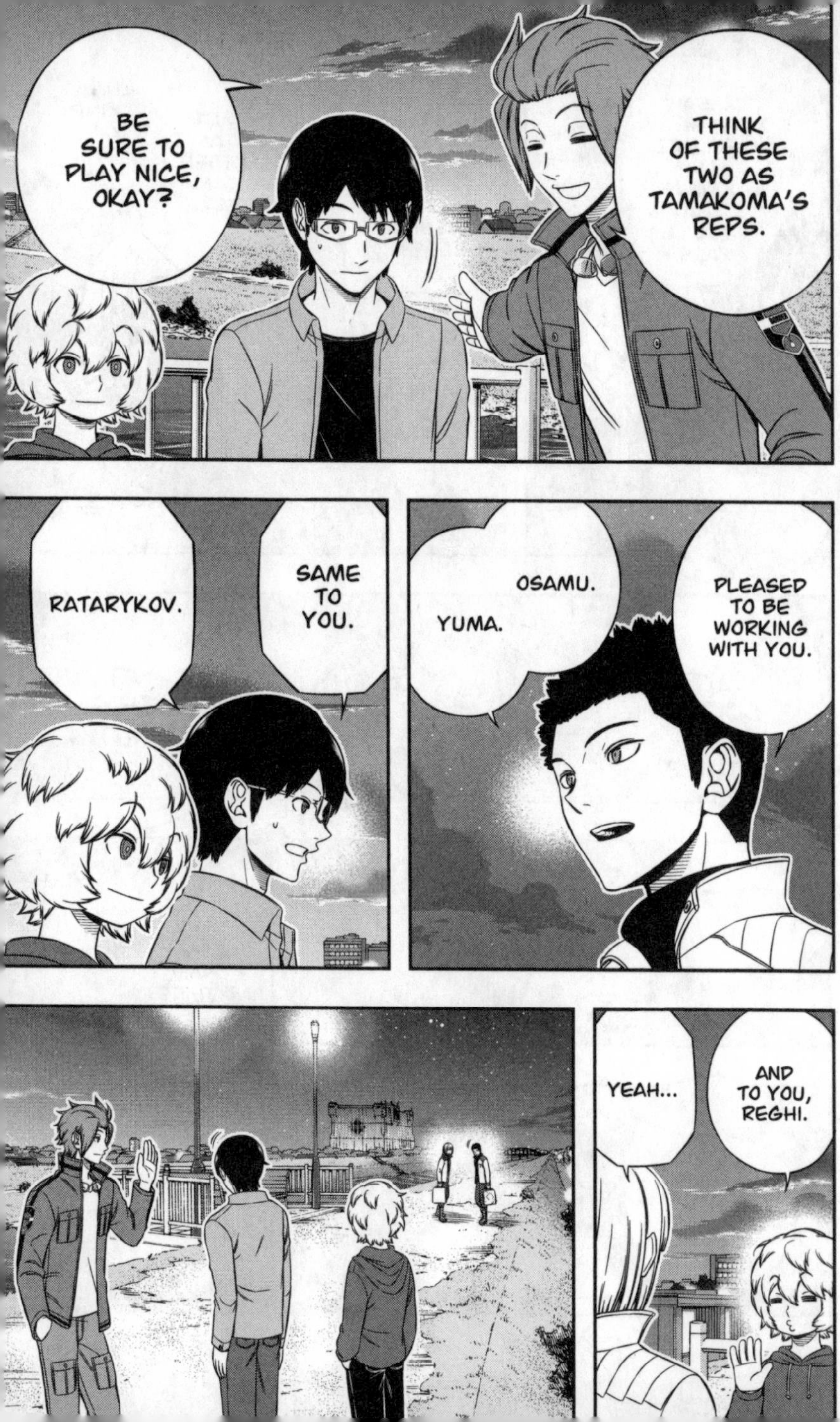
THINK OF THESE TWO AS TAMAKOMA'S REPS.
BE SURE TO PLAY NICE, OKAY?
PLEASED TO BE WORKING WITH YOU.
OSAMU. YUMA.
SAME TO YOU.
RATARYKOV.
AND TO YOU, REGHI.
YEAH...

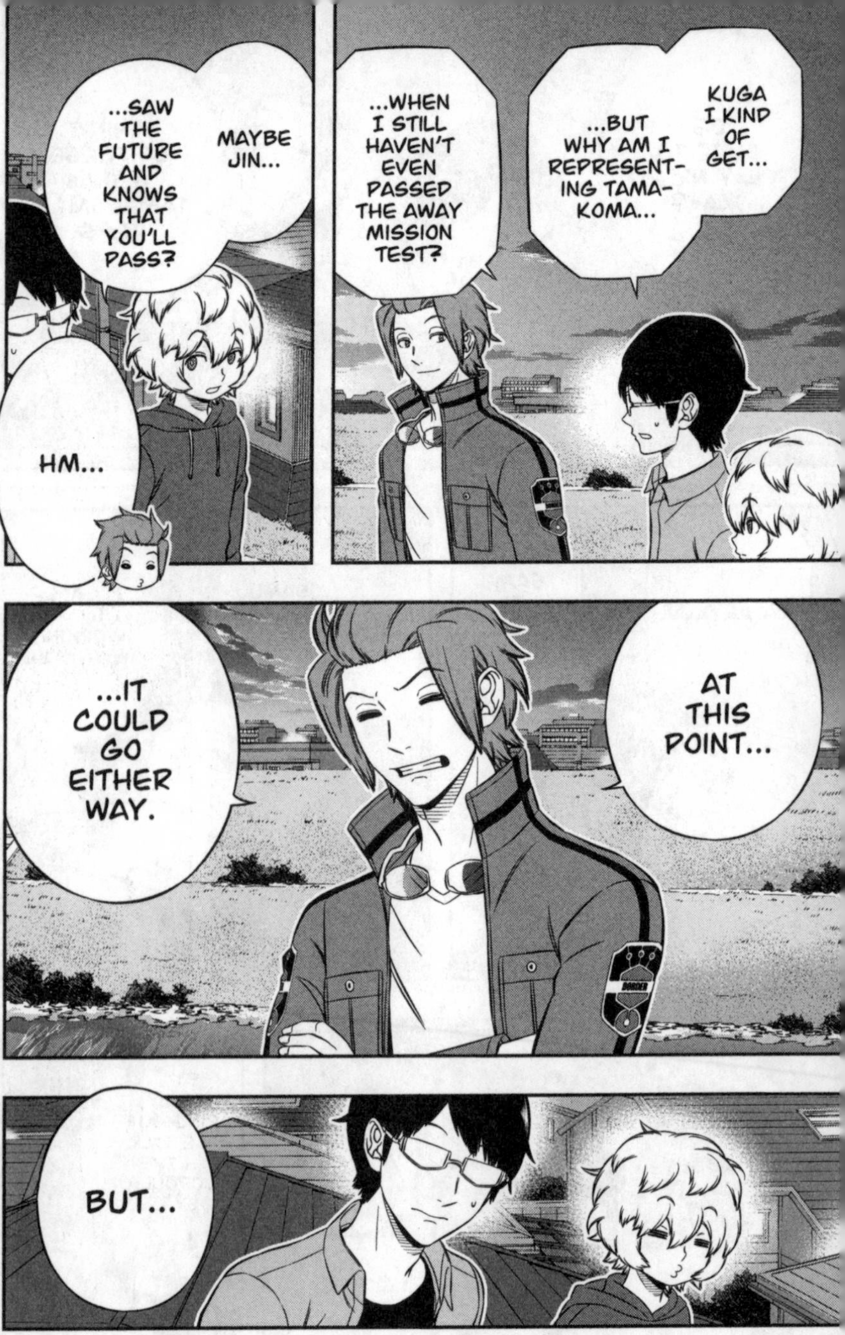
KUGA I KIND OF GET...
...BUT WHY AM I REPRESENT-ING TAMA-KOMA...
...WHEN I STILL HAVEN'T EVEN PASSED THE AWAY MISSION TEST?
MAYBE JIN...
...SAW THE FUTURE AND KNOWS THAT YOU'LL PASS?
HM...
AT THIS POINT...
...IT COULD GO EITHER WAY.
BUT...

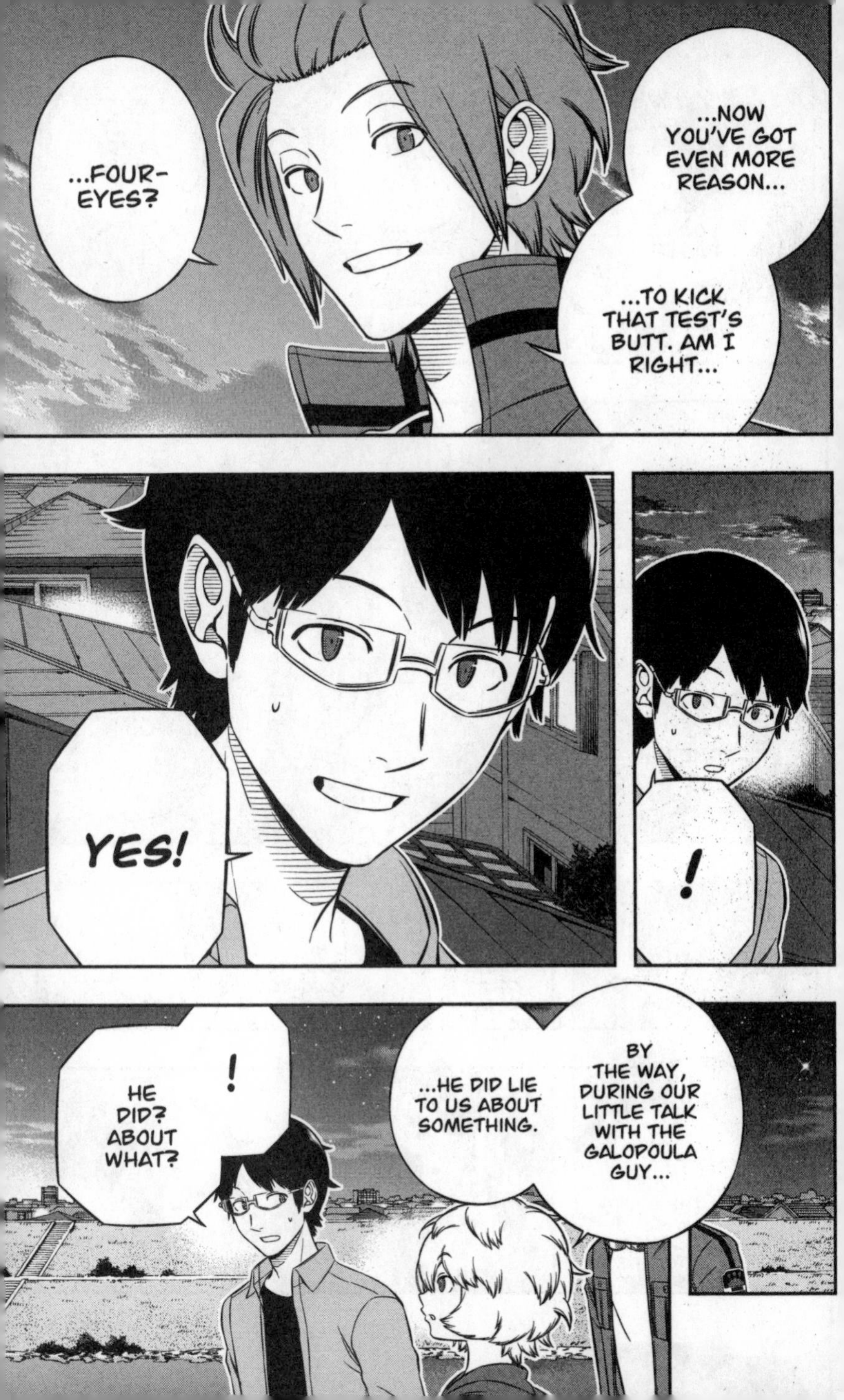
...NOW YOU'VE GOT EVEN MORE REASON...
...TO KICK THAT TEST'S BUTT. AM I RIGHT...
...FOUR-EYES?
!
YES!
BY THE WAY, DURING OUR LITTLE TALK WITH THE GALOPOULA GUY...
...HE DID LIE TO US ABOUT SOMETHING.
!
HE DID? ABOUT WHAT?

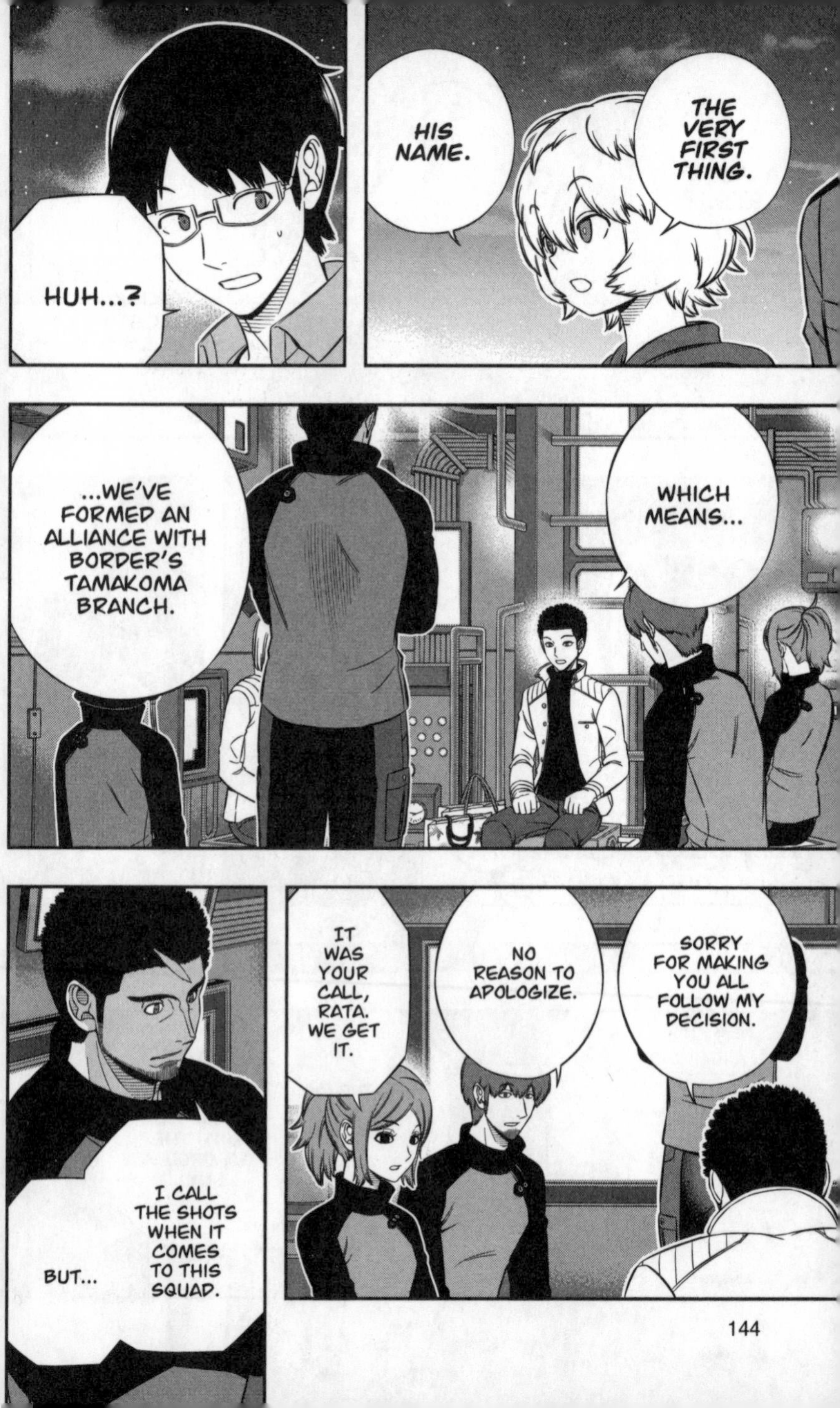
THE VERY FIRST THING.
HIS NAME.
HUH...?
WHICH MEANS...
...WE'VE FORMED AN ALLIANCE WITH BORDER'S TAMAKOMA BRANCH.
SORRY FOR MAKING YOU ALL FOLLOW MY DECISION.
NO REASON TO APOLOGIZE.
IT WAS YOUR CALL, RATA. WE GET IT.
I CALL THE SHOTS WHEN IT COMES TO THIS SQUAD.
BUT...

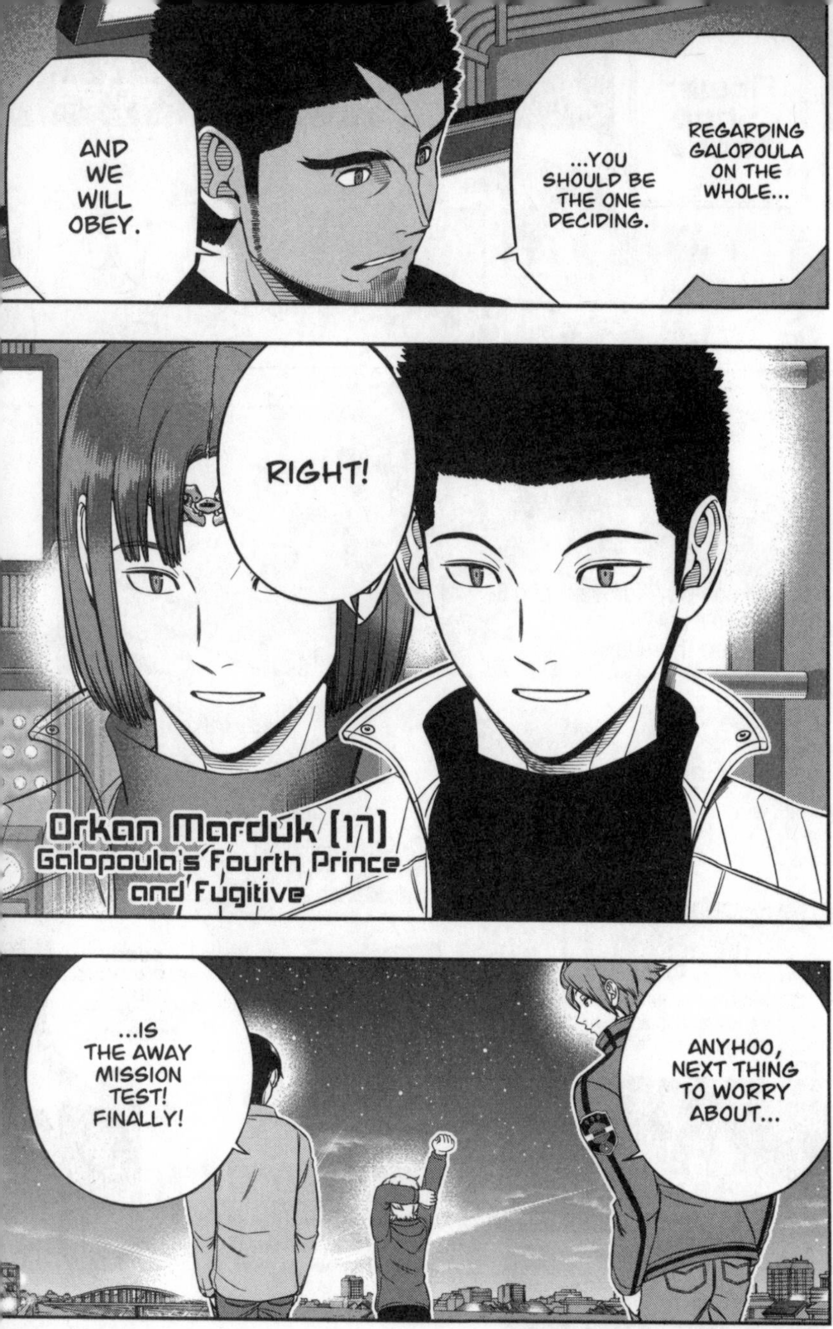
REGARDING GALOPOULA ON THE WHOLE...
...YOU SHOULD BE THE ONE DECIDING.
AND WE WILL OBEY.
RIGHT!
Orkan Marduk (17)
Galopoula's Fourth Prince and Fugitive
ANYHOO, NEXT THING TO WORRY ABOUT...
...IS THE AWAY MISSION TEST! FINALLY!

Mikado Revealed

Flower Shop Kaede

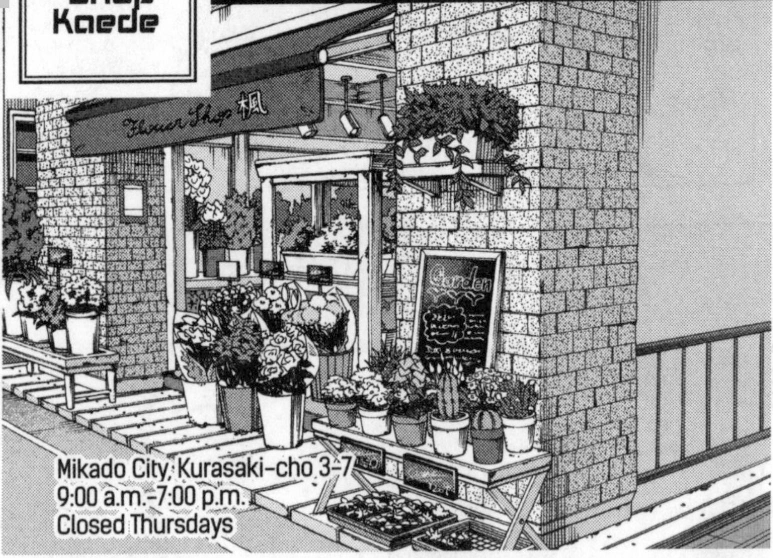
Flower Shop 楓
Garden

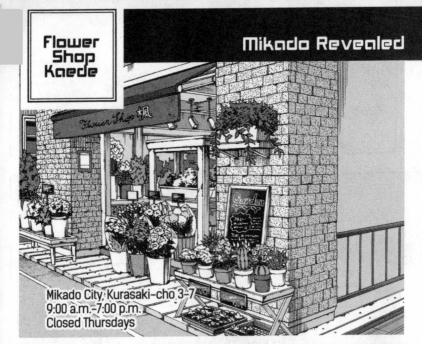

Mikado City, Kurasaki-cho 3-7
9:00 a.m.-7:00 p.m.
Closed Thursdays

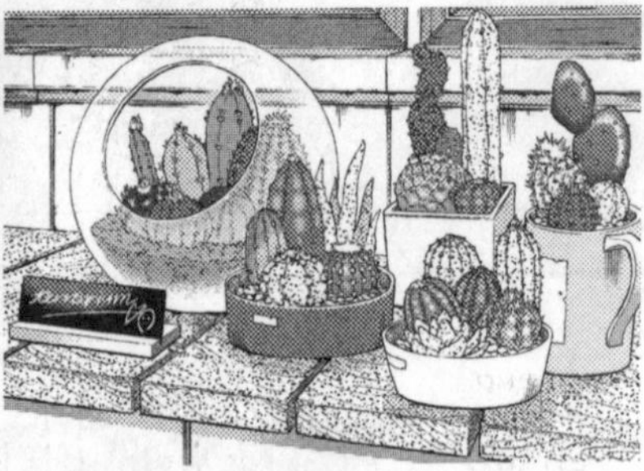

↑ Terrariums and potted plants are popular offerings. They've even got cacti and mosses.

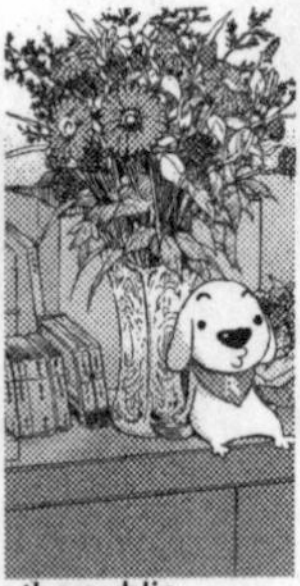

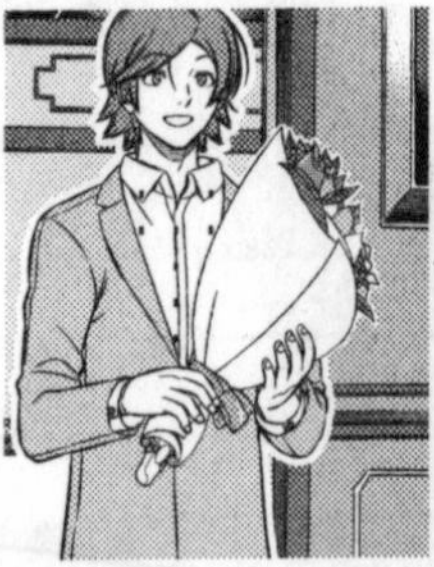

↑ Conveniently located near the public hospital and the shopping district, for all your celebratory and visiting-a-sick-person needs.

A Flowery Street Corner

This flower shop opened on a corner in Kurasaki-cho six years ago.

In the wake of the first Neighbor attack, demand for decorative plants rose. The sales boom allowed Flower Shop Kaede to open a second branch in Hayanuma 1-chome two years ago.

This is the flower shop shown behind Kashio and Haya. I bet that Mario (Ikoma Squad's operator) and the green-thumbed Netsuki do plenty of shopping here.

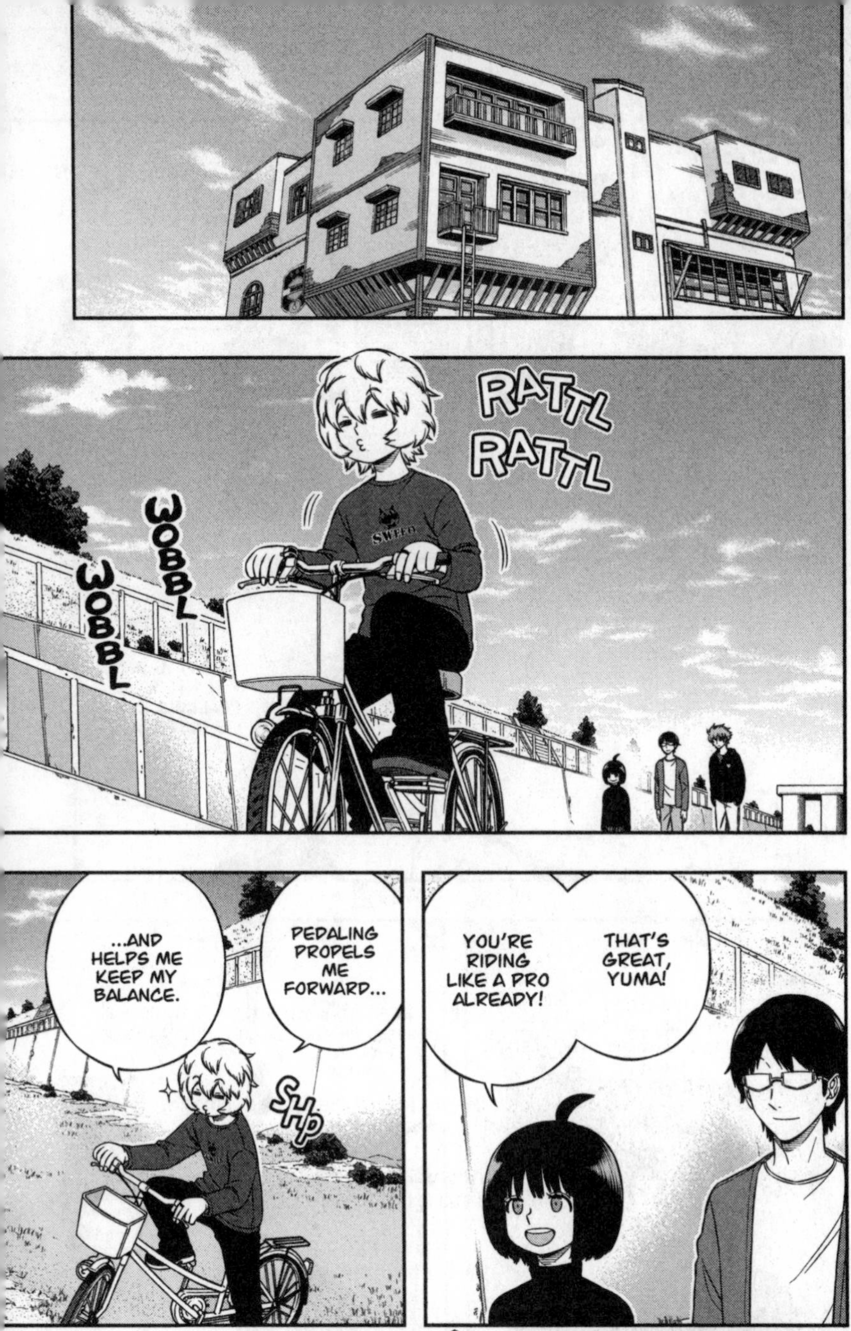
RATTL RATTL
WOBBL WOBBL
THAT'S GREAT, YUMA!
YOU'RE RIDING LIKE A PRO ALREADY!
PEDALING PROPELS ME FORWARD...
...AND HELPS ME KEEP MY BALANCE.
SHP

Chapter 203 The Away Mission Test

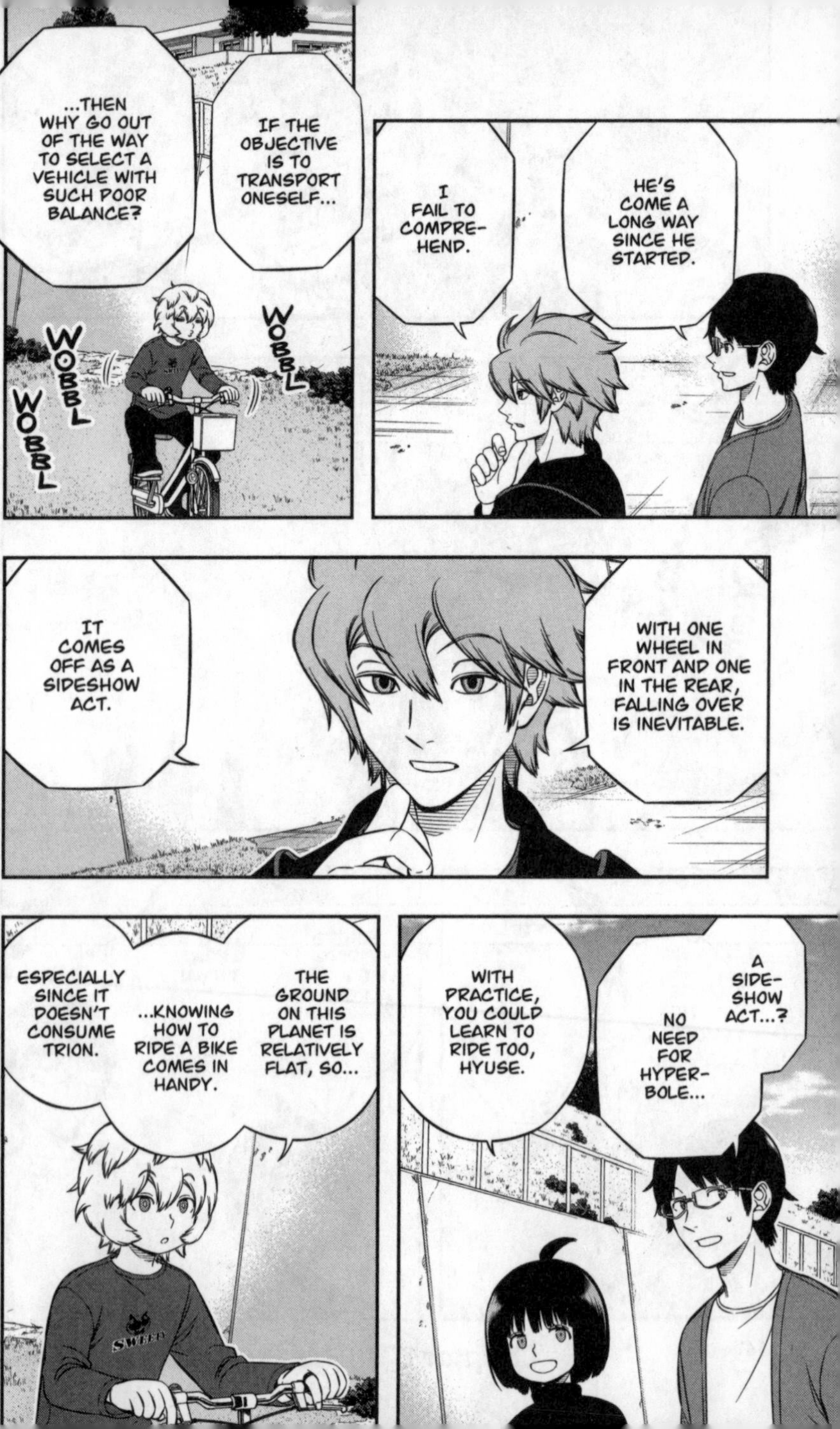
HE'S COME A LONG WAY SINCE HE STARTED.
I FAIL TO COMPRE-HEND.
IF THE OBJECTIVE IS TO TRANSPORT ONESELF...
...THEN WHY GO OUT OF THE WAY TO SELECT A VEHICLE WITH SUCH POOR BALANCE?
WOBBL
WOBBL
WOBBL
WITH ONE WHEEL IN FRONT AND ONE IN THE REAR, FALLING OVER IS INEVITABLE.
IT COMES OFF AS A SIDESHOW ACT.
A SIDE-SHOW ACT...?
NO NEED FOR HYPER-BOLE...
WITH PRACTICE, YOU COULD LEARN TO RIDE TOO, HYUSE.
THE GROUND ON THIS PLANET IS RELATIVELY FLAT, SO...
...KNOWING HOW TO RIDE A BIKE COMES IN HANDY.
ESPECIALLY SINCE IT DOESN'T CONSUME TRION.
SWEETY

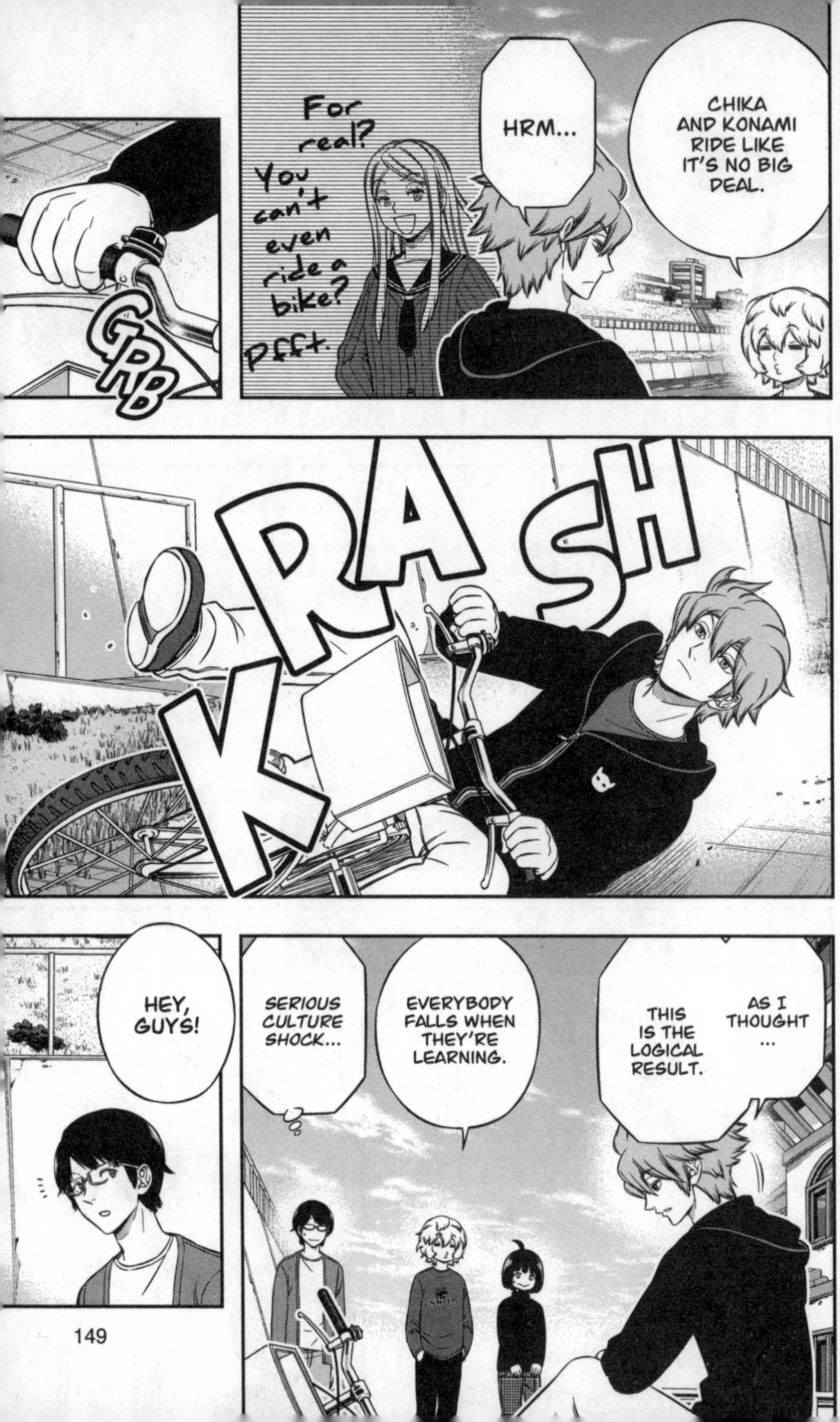
CHIKA AND KONAMI RIDE LIKE IT'S NO BIG DEAL.
HRM...
For real? You can't even ride a bike? Pfft.
GRB
KRASH
AS I THOUGHT...
THIS IS THE LOGICAL RESULT.
EVERYBODY FALLS WHEN THEY'RE LEARNING.
SERIOUS CULTURE SHOCK...
HEY, GUYS!

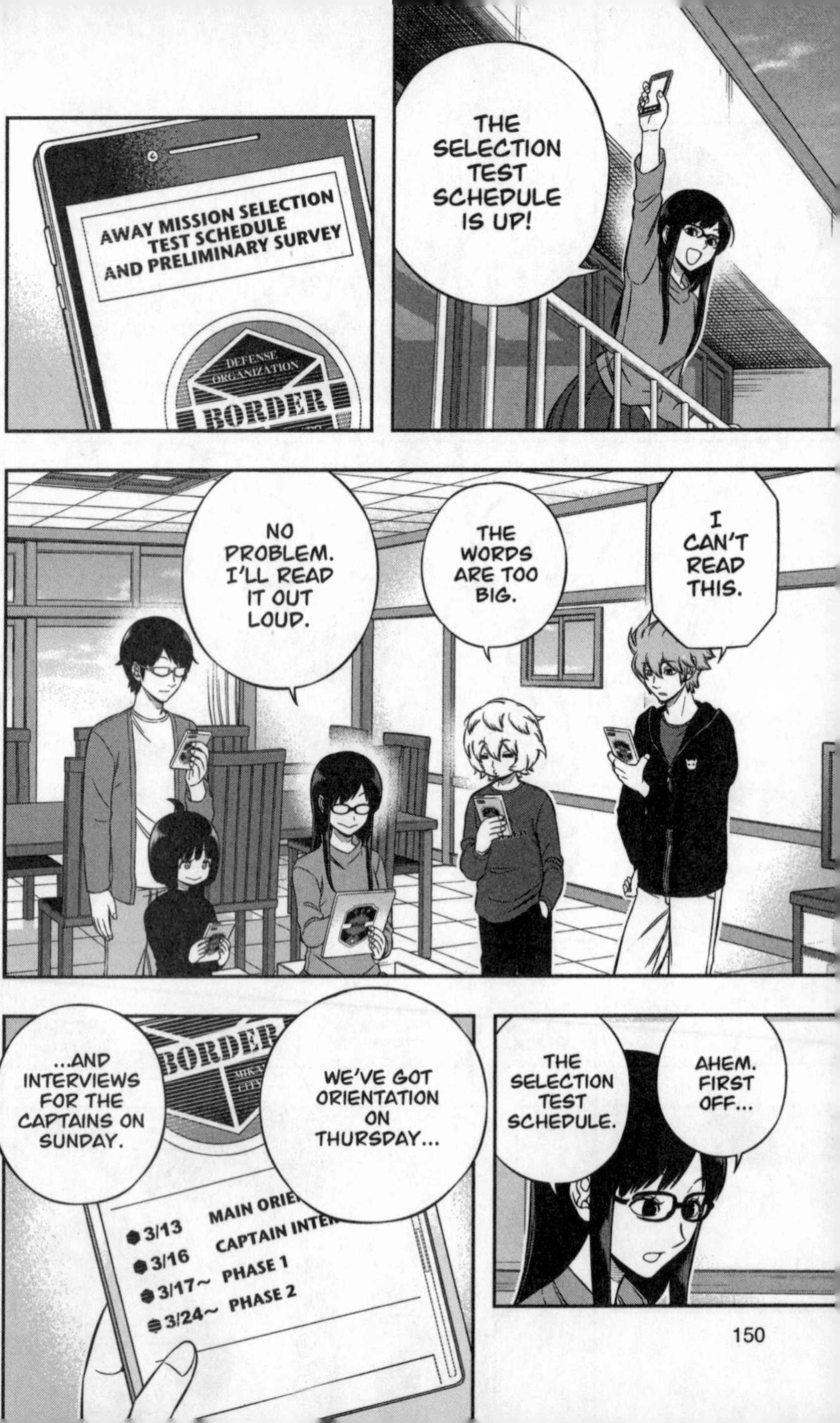
THE SELECTION TEST SCHEDULE IS UP!
AWAY MISSION SELECTION TEST SCHEDULE AND PRELIMINARY SURVEY
DEFENSE ORGANIZATION
BORDER
I CAN'T READ THIS.
THE WORDS ARE TOO BIG.
NO PROBLEM. I'LL READ IT OUT LOUD.
AHEM. FIRST OFF...
THE SELECTION TEST SCHEDULE.
WE'VE GOT ORIENTATION ON THURSDAY...
...AND INTERVIEWS FOR THE CAPTAINS ON SUNDAY.
BORDER
3/13 MAIN ORIE
3/16 CAPTAIN INTE
3/17~ PHASE 1
3/24~ PHASE 2

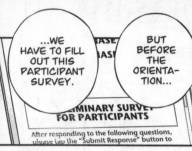

...WE HAVE TO FILL OUT THIS PARTICIPANT SURVEY.

BUT BEFORE THE ORIENTA- TION...

...IMINARY SURVEY FOR PARTICIPANTS

After responding to the following questions, please tap the "Submit Response" button to

AND IMMEDI- ATELY AFTER...

...WE MOVE TO PHASE 2, WHICH LASTS FOR TWO DAYS.

PHASE 1 OF THE TEST RUNS FOR A WEEK, STARTING NEXT MONDAY.

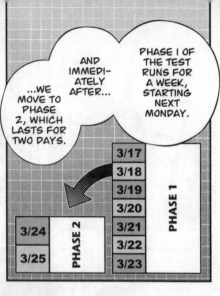

	PHASE 2		PHASE 1
		3/17	
		3/18	
		3/19	
		3/20	
3/24		3/21	
		3/22	
3/25		3/23	

HMM. A SURVEY?

JUST THREE QUEST- IONS.

② BESIDES THE MEMBERS OF YOUR OWN SQUAD, WHO WOULD YOU PREFER TO WORK WITH ON THE AWAY MISSION?

PICK UP TO FIVE OTHER AGENTS.

① DO YOU WISH TO JOIN THE AWAY MISSION?

THE CHOICES ARE: "YES," "YES, WITH MY SQUAD," OR "NO."

③ IS THERE ANYONE YOU'D PREFER NOT TO WORK WITH?

PICK UP TO TWO AGENTS.

151

WHO ELSE WE'D LIKE TO WORK WITH, HUH?

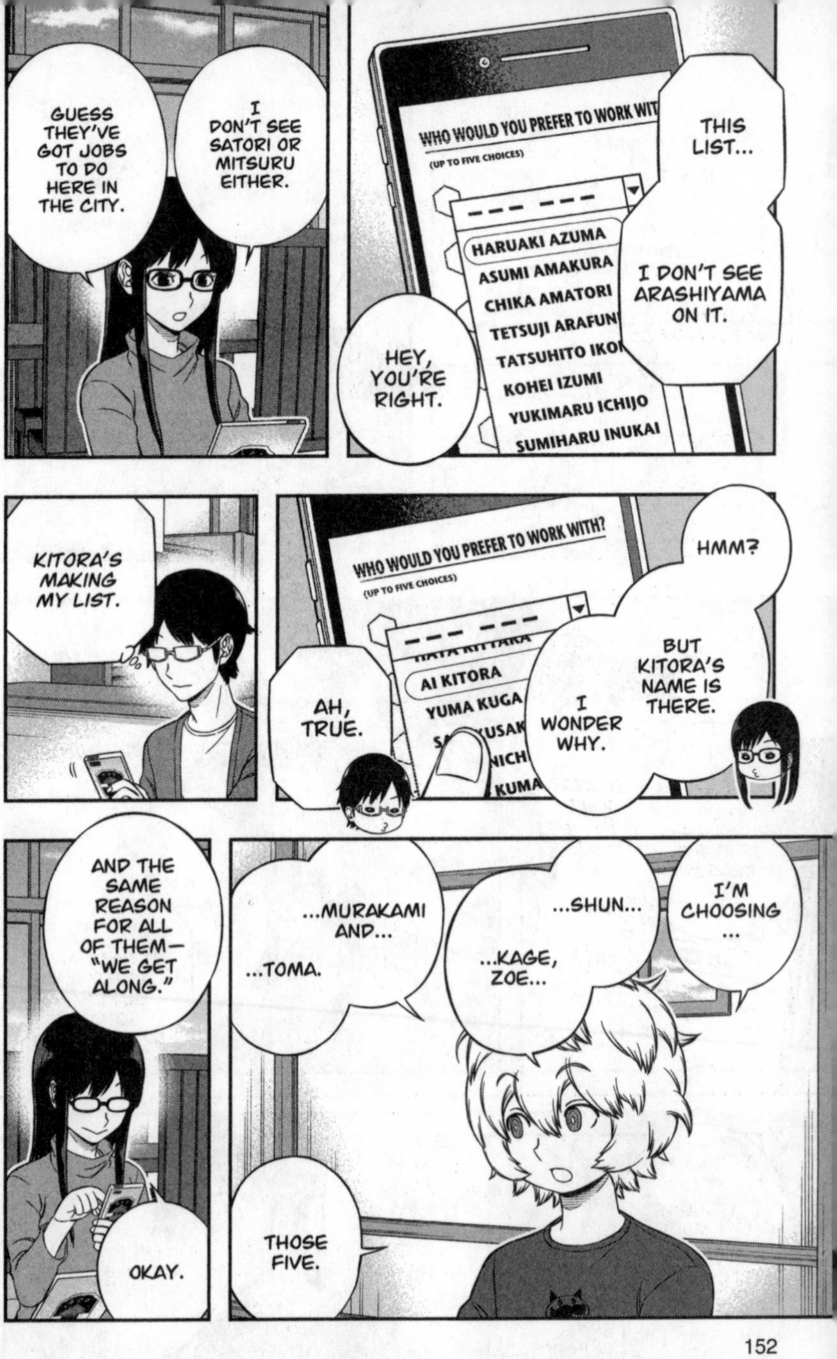
THIS LIST...
WHO WOULD YOU PREFER TO WORK WIT
(UP TO FIVE CHOICES)
HARUAKI AZUMA
ASUMI AMAKURA
CHIKA AMATORI
KOHEI IZUMI
YUKIMARU ICHIJO
SUMIHARU INUKAI
I DON'T SEE ARASHIYAMA ON IT.
HEY, YOU'RE RIGHT.
I DON'T SEE SATORI OR MITSURU EITHER.
GUESS THEY'VE GOT JOBS TO DO HERE IN THE CITY.
HMM?
WHO WOULD YOU PREFER TO WORK WITH?
(UP TO FIVE CHOICES)
AI KITORA
BUT KITORA'S NAME IS THERE.
I WONDER WHY.
AH, TRUE.
KITORA'S MAKING MY LIST.
I'M CHOOSING ...
...SHUN...
...KAGE, ZOE...
...MURAKAMI AND...
...TOMA.
THOSE FIVE.
AND THE SAME REASON FOR ALL OF THEM—"WE GET ALONG."
OKAY.

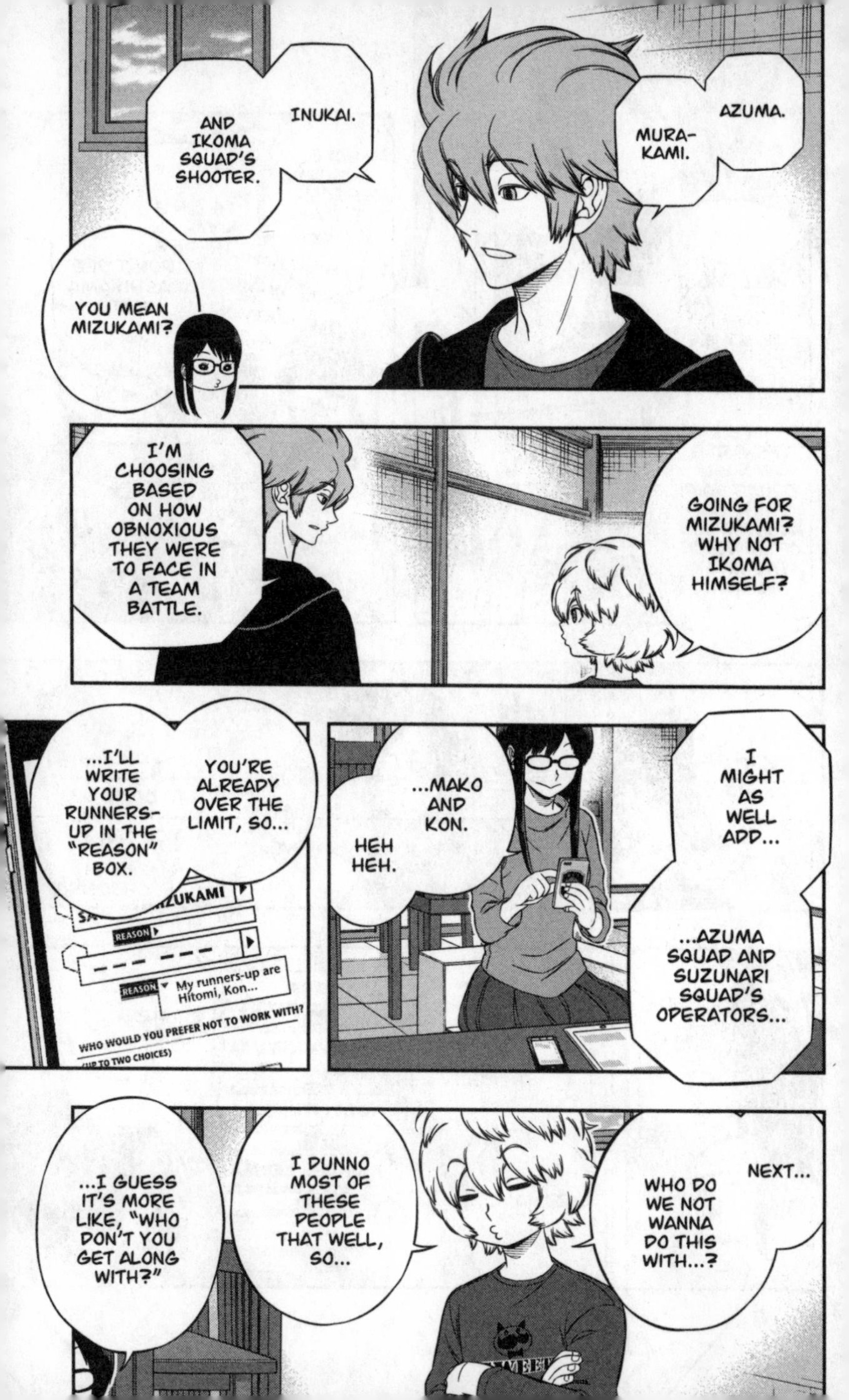
AZUMA.
MURA-KAMI.
INUKAI.
AND IKOMA SQUAD'S SHOOTER.
YOU MEAN MIZUKAMI?
GOING FOR MIZUKAMI? WHY NOT IKOMA HIMSELF?
I'M CHOOSING BASED ON HOW OBNOXIOUS THEY WERE TO FACE IN A TEAM BATTLE.
I MIGHT AS WELL ADD...
...AZUMA SQUAD AND SUZUNARI SQUAD'S OPERATORS...
...MAKO AND KON.
HEH HEH.
YOU'RE ALREADY OVER THE LIMIT, SO...
...I'LL WRITE YOUR RUNNERS-UP IN THE "REASON" BOX.
REASON
REASON
My runners-up are Hitomi, Kon...
WHO WOULD YOU PREFER NOT TO WORK WITH?
(UP TO TWO CHOICES)
NEXT...
WHO DO WE NOT WANNA DO THIS WITH...?
I DUNNO MOST OF THESE PEOPLE THAT WELL, SO...
...I GUESS IT'S MORE LIKE, "WHO DON'T YOU GET ALONG WITH?"

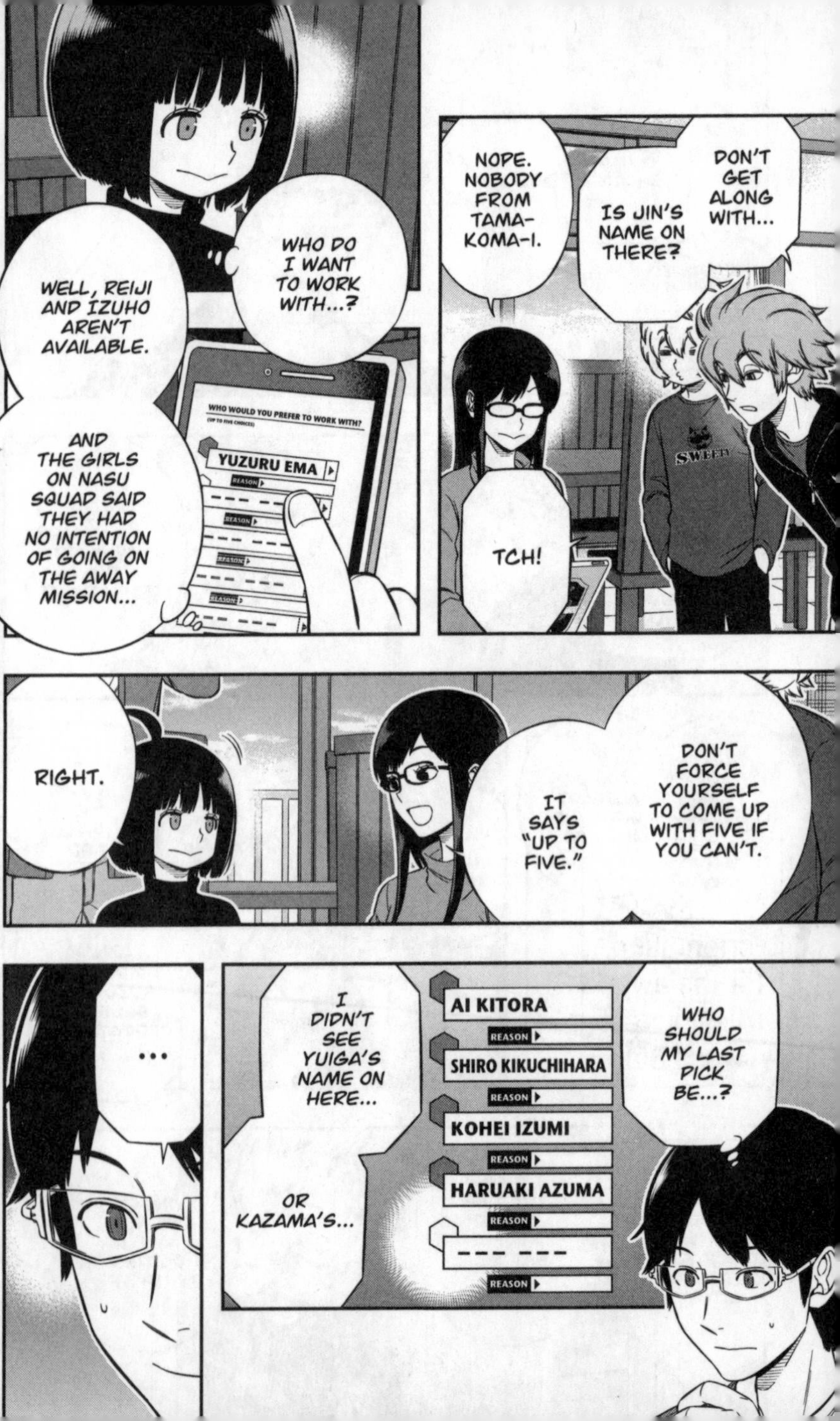
DON'T GET ALONG WITH...
IS JIN'S NAME ON THERE?
NOPE. NOBODY FROM TAMA-KOMA-1.
TCH!
WHO DO I WANT TO WORK WITH...?
WHO WOULD YOU PREFER TO WORK WITH?
YUZURU EMA
REASON
REASON
REASON
REASON
WELL, REIJI AND IZUHO AREN'T AVAILABLE.
AND THE GIRLS ON NASU SQUAD SAID THEY HAD NO INTENTION OF GOING ON THE AWAY MISSION...
DON'T FORCE YOURSELF TO COME UP WITH FIVE IF YOU CAN'T.
IT SAYS "UP TO FIVE."
RIGHT.
WHO SHOULD MY LAST PICK BE...?
AI KITORA
REASON
SHIRO KIKUCHIHARA
REASON
KOHEI IZUMI
REASON
HARUAKI AZUMA
REASON
REASON
I DIDN'T SEE YUIGA'S NAME ON HERE...
OR KAZAMA'S...
...

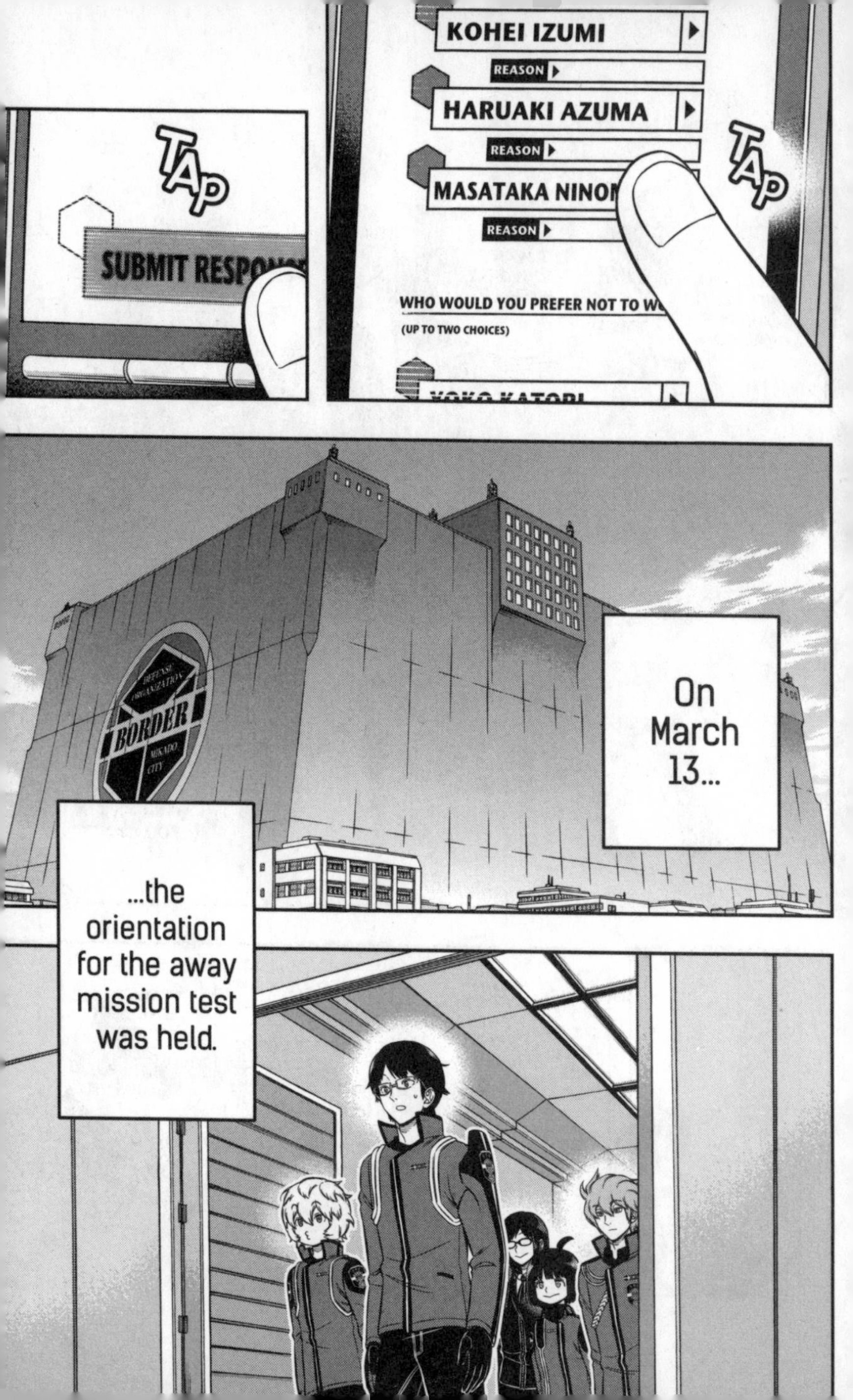
KOHEI IZUMI
REASON
HARUAKI AZUMA
REASON
MASATAKA NINOM
REASON
TAP
WHO WOULD YOU PREFER NOT TO W
(UP TO TWO CHOICES)
TAP
SUBMIT RESPON
On March 13...
...the orientation for the away mission test was held.

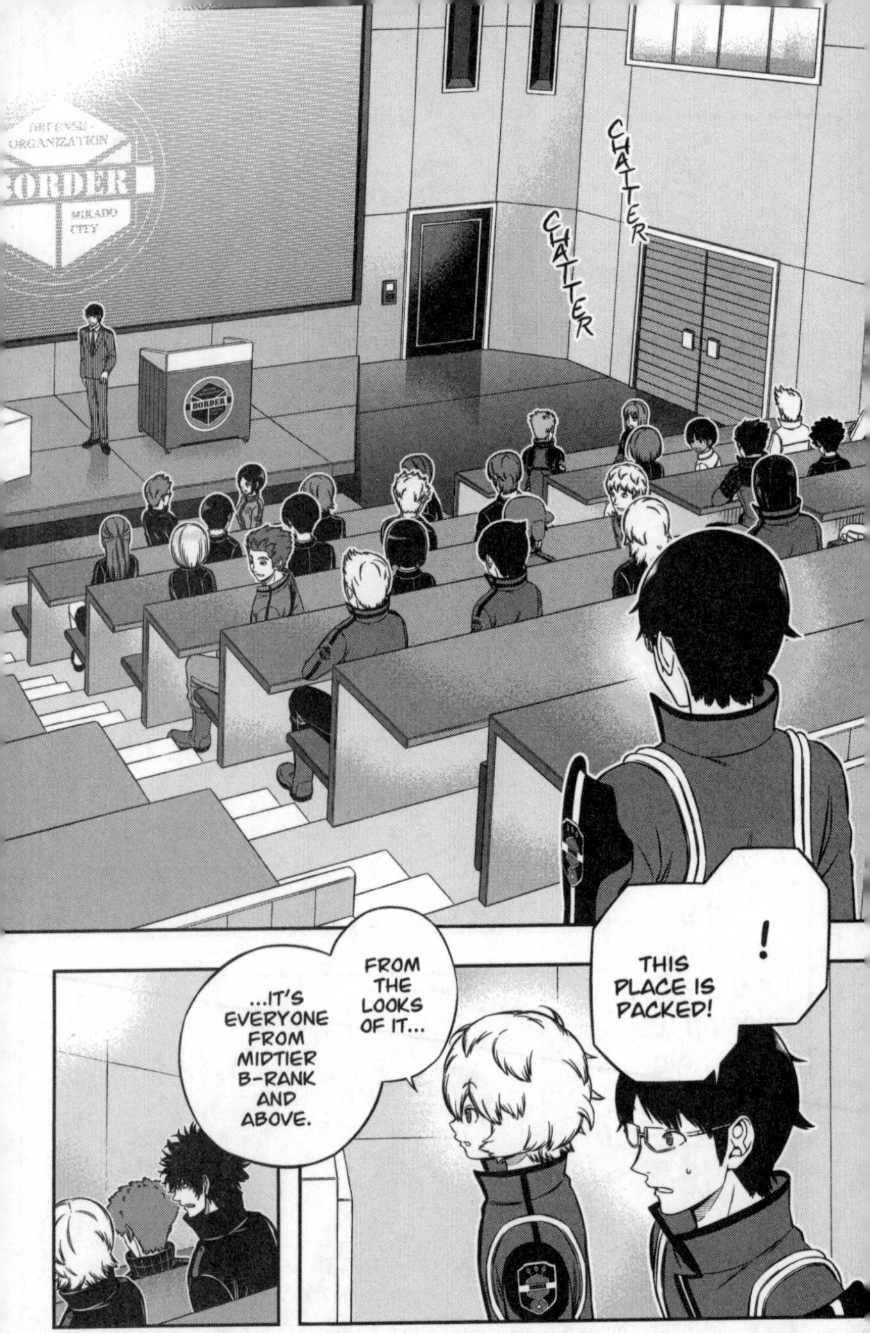
BORDER
CHATTER
CHATTER
!
THIS PLACE IS PACKED!
FROM THE LOOKS OF IT...
...IT'S EVERYONE FROM MIDTIER B-RANK AND ABOVE.

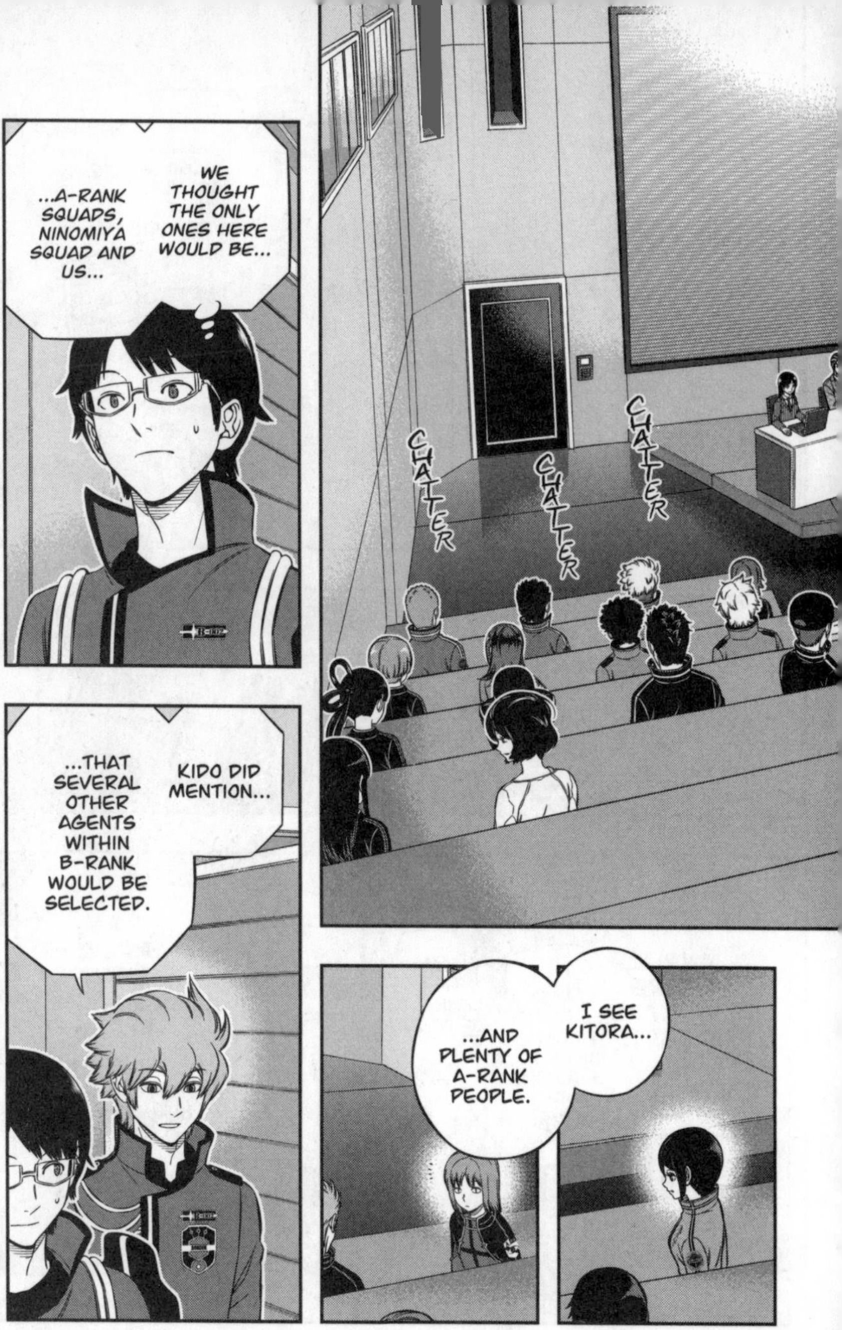
CHATTER
CHATTER
CHATTER
WE THOUGHT THE ONLY ONES HERE WOULD BE...
...A-RANK SQUADS, NINOMIYA SQUAD AND US...
KIDO DID MENTION...
...THAT SEVERAL OTHER AGENTS WITHIN B-RANK WOULD BE SELECTED.
I SEE KITORA...
...AND PLENTY OF A-RANK PEOPLE.

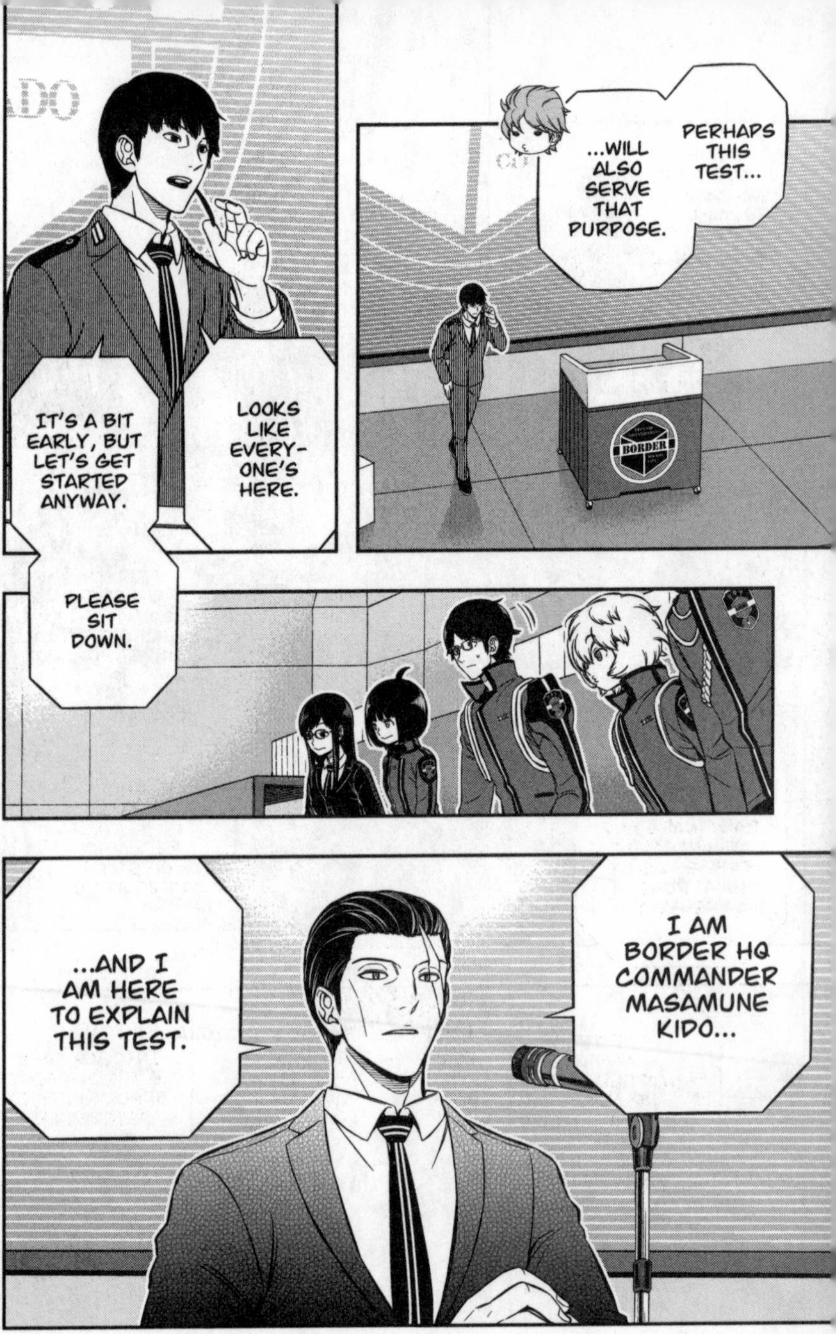
PERHAPS THIS TEST...
...WILL ALSO SERVE THAT PURPOSE.
BORDER
LOOKS LIKE EVERY-ONE'S HERE.
IT'S A BIT EARLY, BUT LET'S GET STARTED ANYWAY.
PLEASE SIT DOWN.
I AM BORDER HQ COMMANDER MASAMUNE KIDO...
...AND I AM HERE TO EXPLAIN THIS TEST.

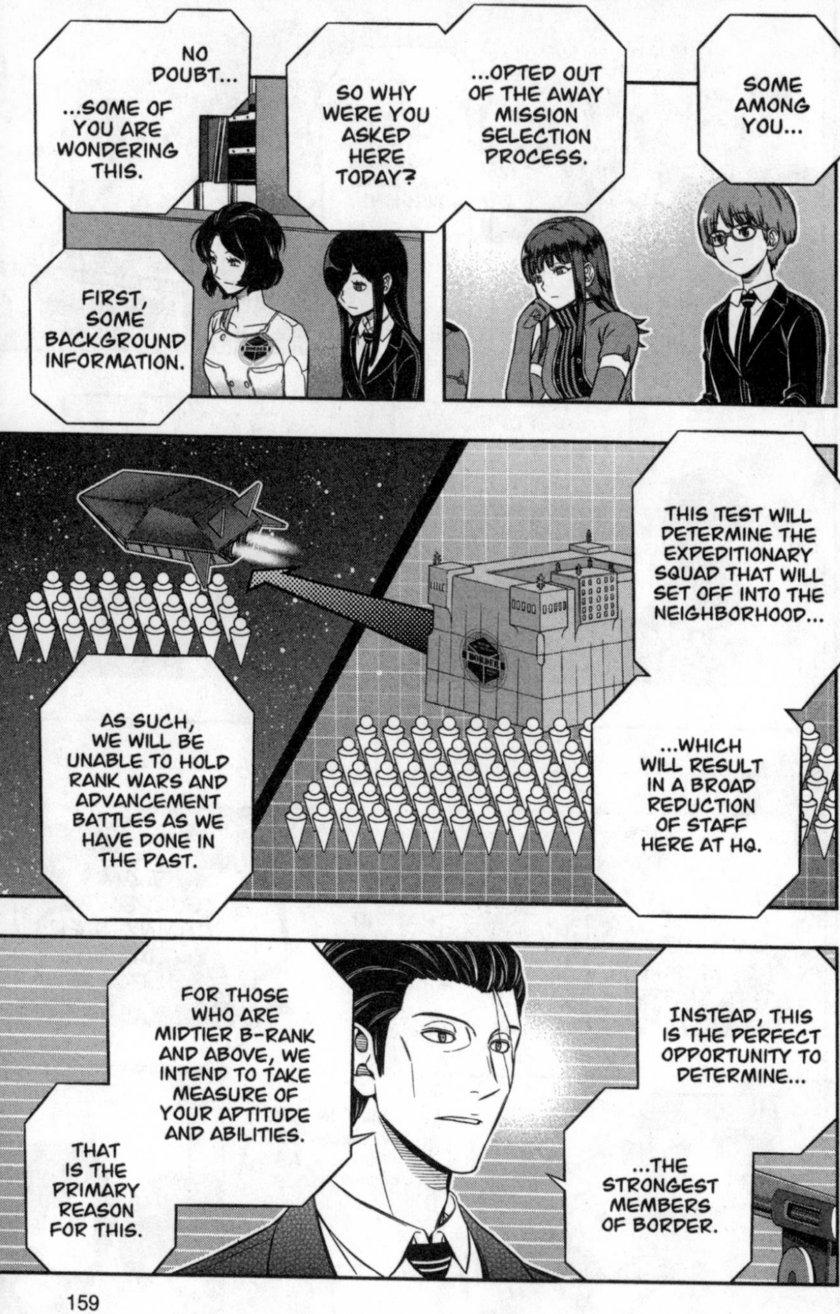
SOME AMONG YOU...
...OPTED OUT OF THE AWAY MISSION SELECTION PROCESS.
SO WHY WERE YOU ASKED HERE TODAY?
NO DOUBT...
...SOME OF YOU ARE WONDERING THIS.
FIRST, SOME BACKGROUND INFORMATION.
THIS TEST WILL DETERMINE THE EXPEDITIONARY SQUAD THAT WILL SET OFF INTO THE NEIGHBORHOOD...
...WHICH WILL RESULT IN A BROAD REDUCTION OF STAFF HERE AT HQ.
AS SUCH, WE WILL BE UNABLE TO HOLD RANK WARS AND ADVANCEMENT BATTLES AS WE HAVE DONE IN THE PAST.
INSTEAD, THIS IS THE PERFECT OPPORTUNITY TO DETERMINE...
...THE STRONGEST MEMBERS OF BORDER.
FOR THOSE WHO ARE MIDTIER B-RANK AND ABOVE, WE INTEND TO TAKE MEASURE OF YOUR APTITUDE AND ABILITIES.
THAT IS THE PRIMARY REASON FOR THIS.

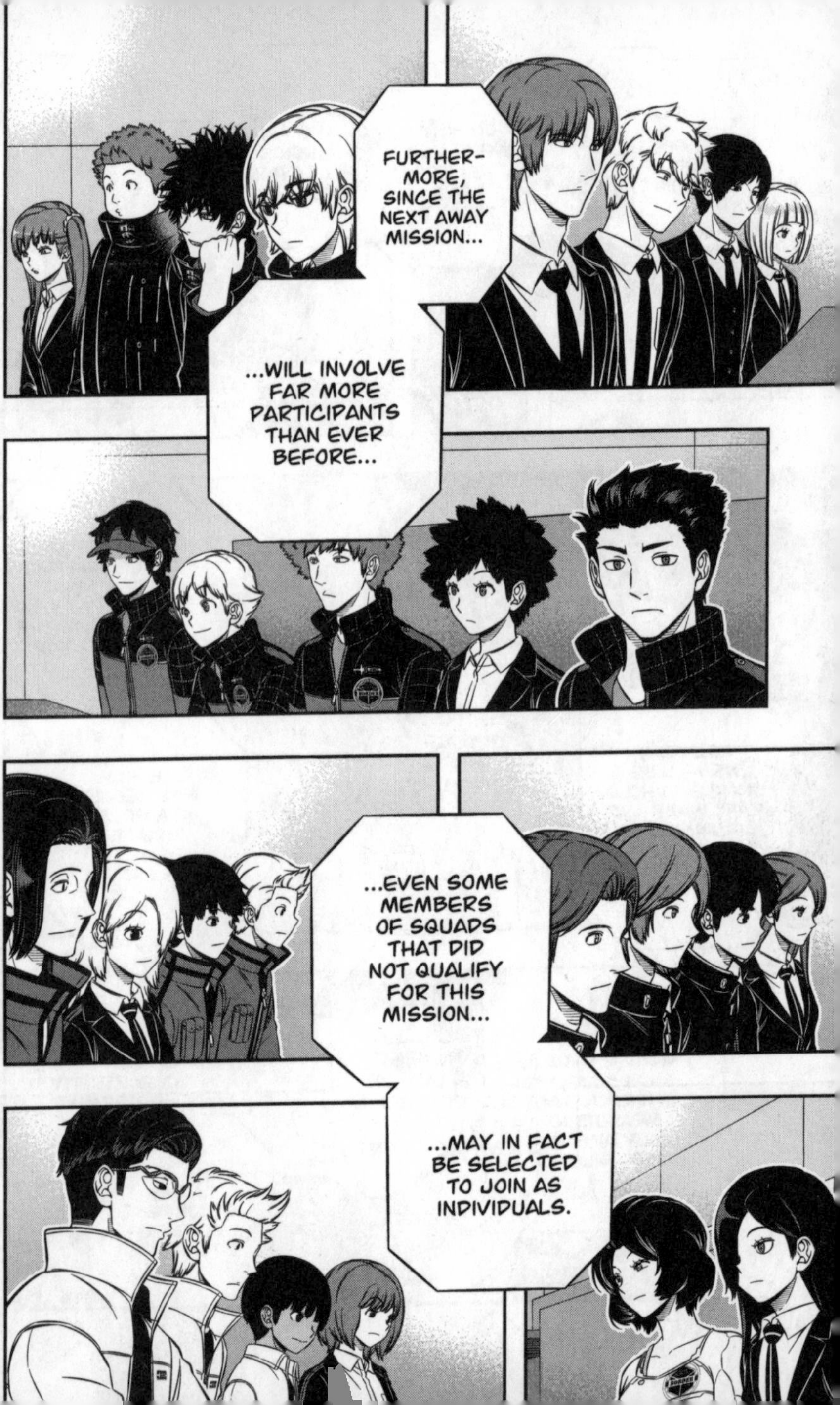
FURTHER-MORE, SINCE THE NEXT AWAY MISSION...
...WILL INVOLVE FAR MORE PARTICIPANTS THAN EVER BEFORE...
...EVEN SOME MEMBERS OF SQUADS THAT DID NOT QUALIFY FOR THIS MISSION...
...MAY IN FACT BE SELECTED TO JOIN AS INDIVIDUALS.

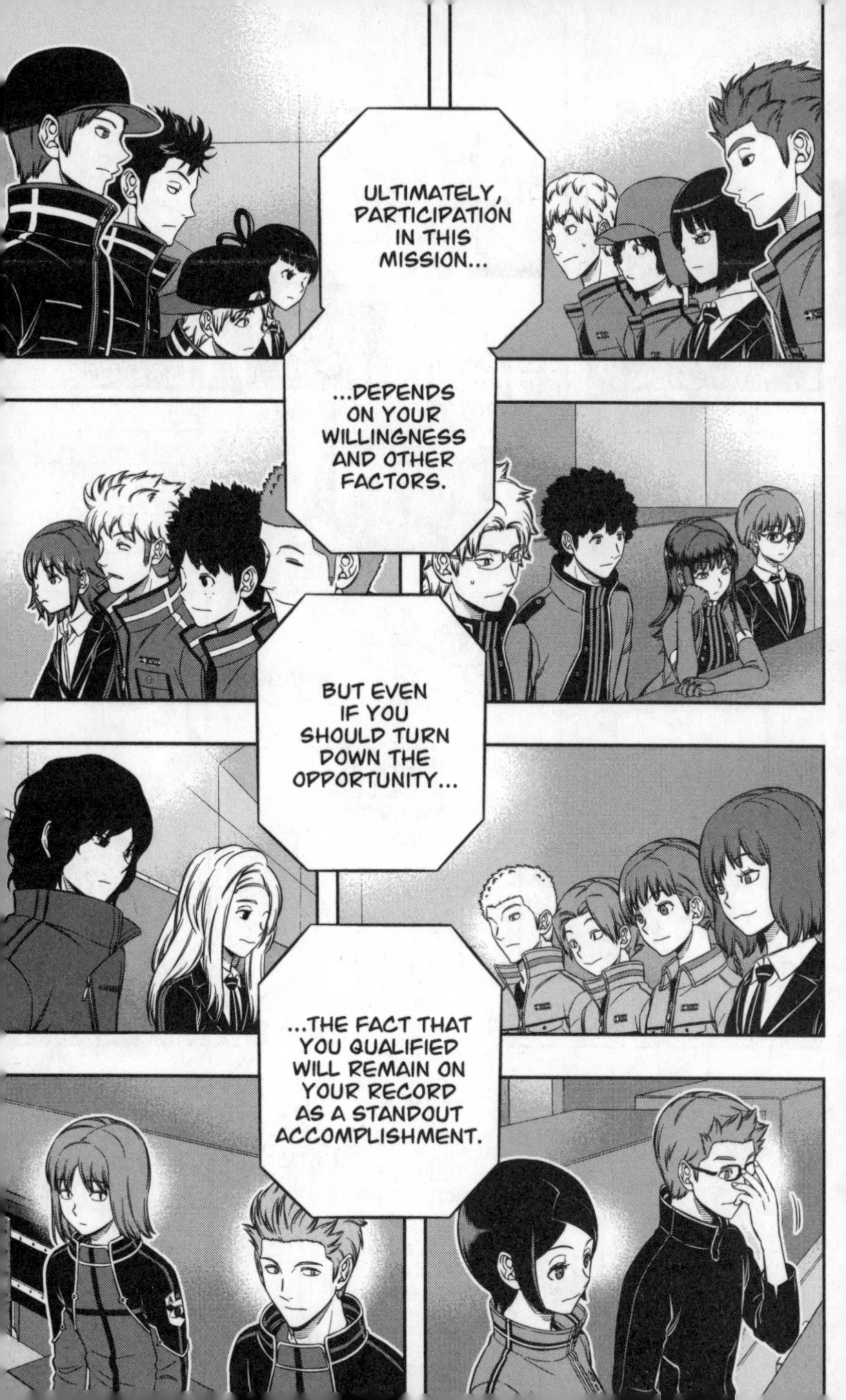
ULTIMATELY, PARTICIPATION IN THIS MISSION...
...DEPENDS ON YOUR WILLINGNESS AND OTHER FACTORS.
BUT EVEN IF YOU SHOULD TURN DOWN THE OPPORTUNITY...
...THE FACT THAT YOU QUALIFIED WILL REMAIN ON YOUR RECORD AS A STANDOUT ACCOMPLISHMENT.

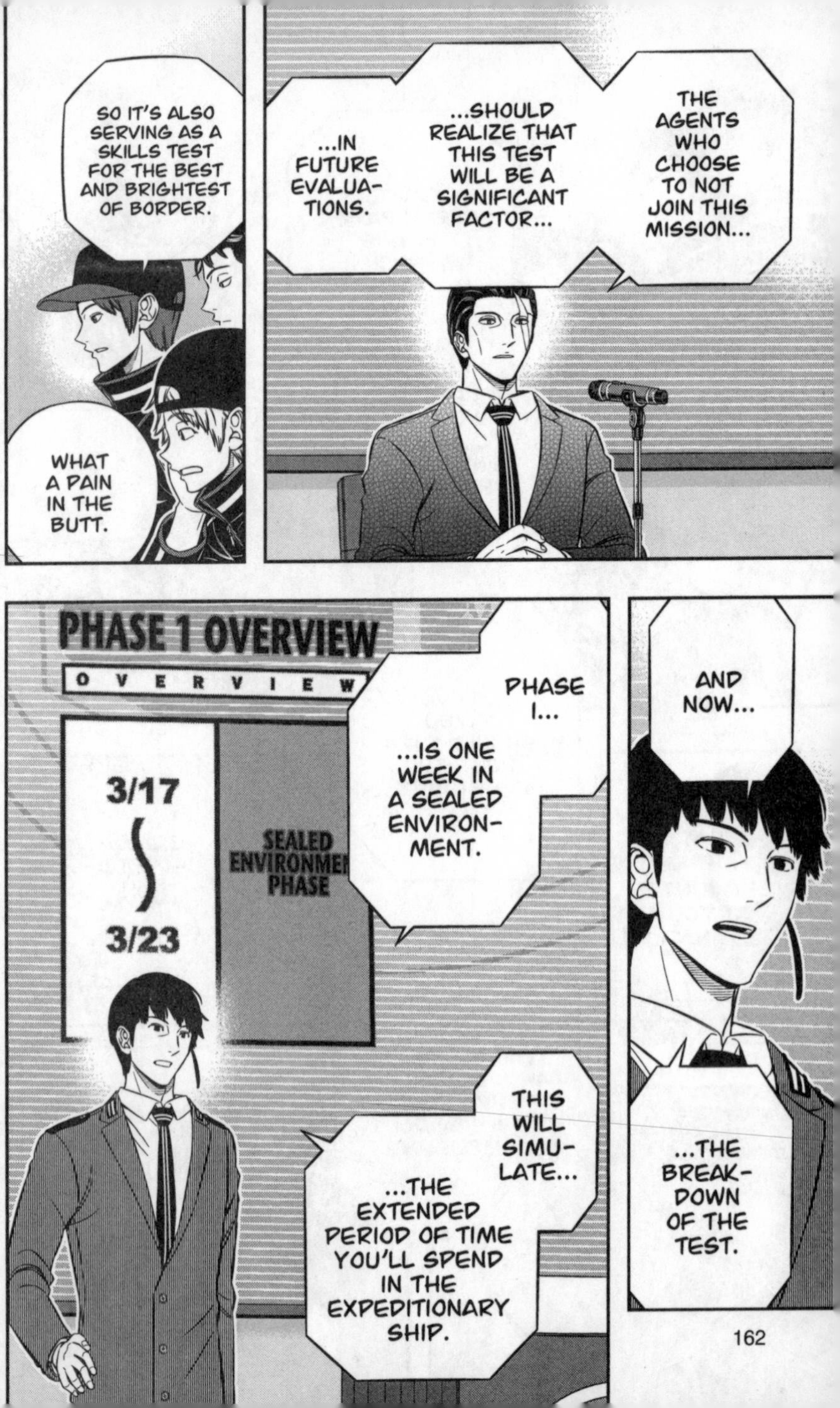
THE AGENTS WHO CHOOSE TO NOT JOIN THIS MISSION...
...SHOULD REALIZE THAT THIS TEST WILL BE A SIGNIFICANT FACTOR...
...IN FUTURE EVALUATIONS.
SO IT'S ALSO SERVING AS A SKILLS TEST FOR THE BEST AND BRIGHTEST OF BORDER.
WHAT A PAIN IN THE BUTT.
AND NOW...
...THE BREAKDOWN OF THE TEST.
PHASE 1 OVERVIEW
O V E R V I E W
3/17
3/23
SEALED ENVIRONME
PHASE
PHASE 1...
...IS ONE WEEK IN A SEALED ENVIRONMENT.
THIS WILL SIMULATE...
...THE EXTENDED PERIOD OF TIME YOU'LL SPEND IN THE EXPEDITIONARY SHIP.

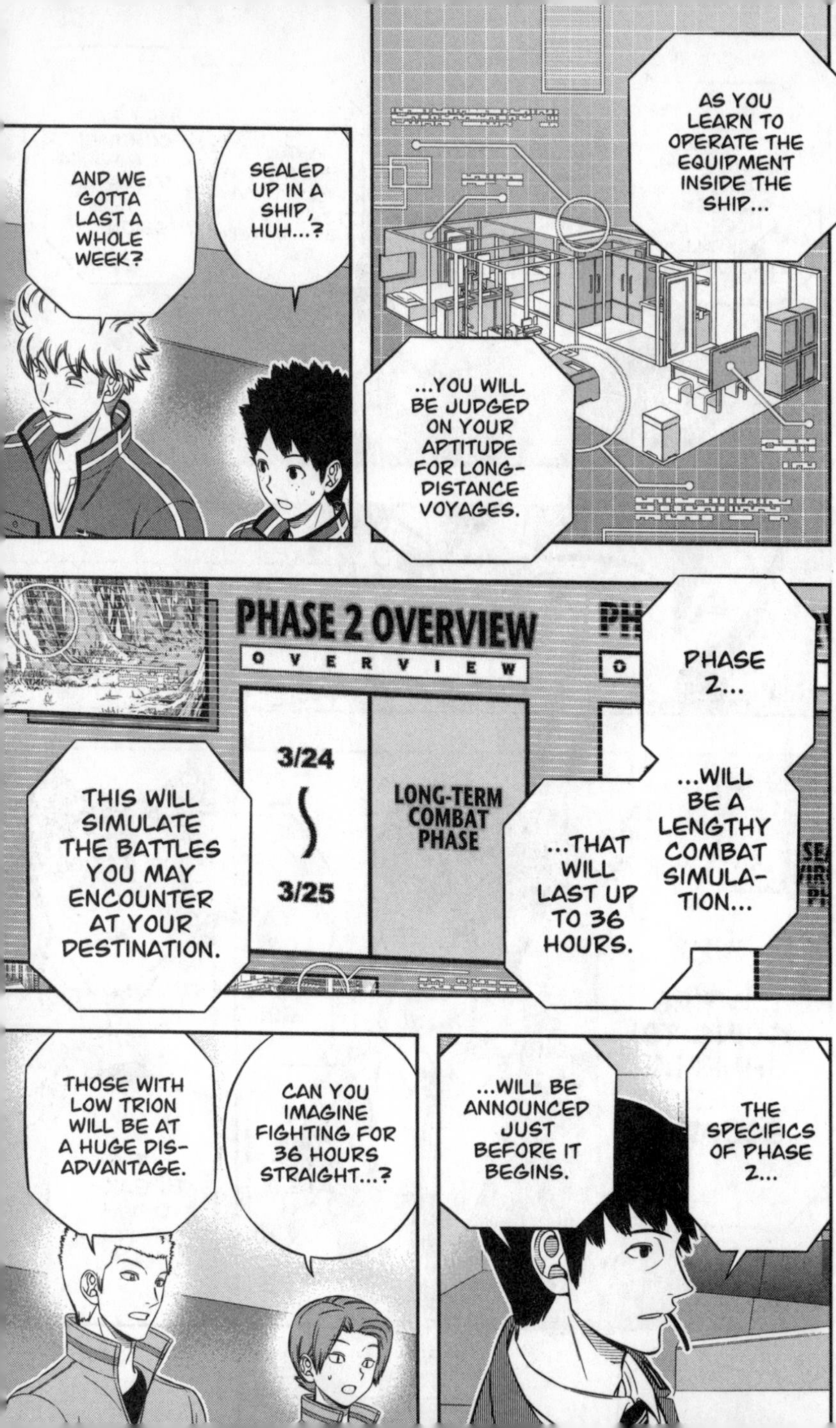
AS YOU LEARN TO OPERATE THE EQUIPMENT INSIDE THE SHIP...
...YOU WILL BE JUDGED ON YOUR APTITUDE FOR LONG-DISTANCE VOYAGES.
SEALED UP IN A SHIP, HUH...?
AND WE GOTTA LAST A WHOLE WEEK?
PHASE 2 OVERVIEW
OVERVIEW
3/24
3/25
LONG-TERM COMBAT PHASE
PHASE 2...
...WILL BE A LENGTHY COMBAT SIMULATION...
...THAT WILL LAST UP TO 36 HOURS.
THIS WILL SIMULATE THE BATTLES YOU MAY ENCOUNTER AT YOUR DESTINATION.
THE SPECIFICS OF PHASE 2...
...WILL BE ANNOUNCED JUST BEFORE IT BEGINS.
CAN YOU IMAGINE FIGHTING FOR 36 HOURS STRAIGHT...?
THOSE WITH LOW TRION WILL BE AT A HUGE DISADVANTAGE.

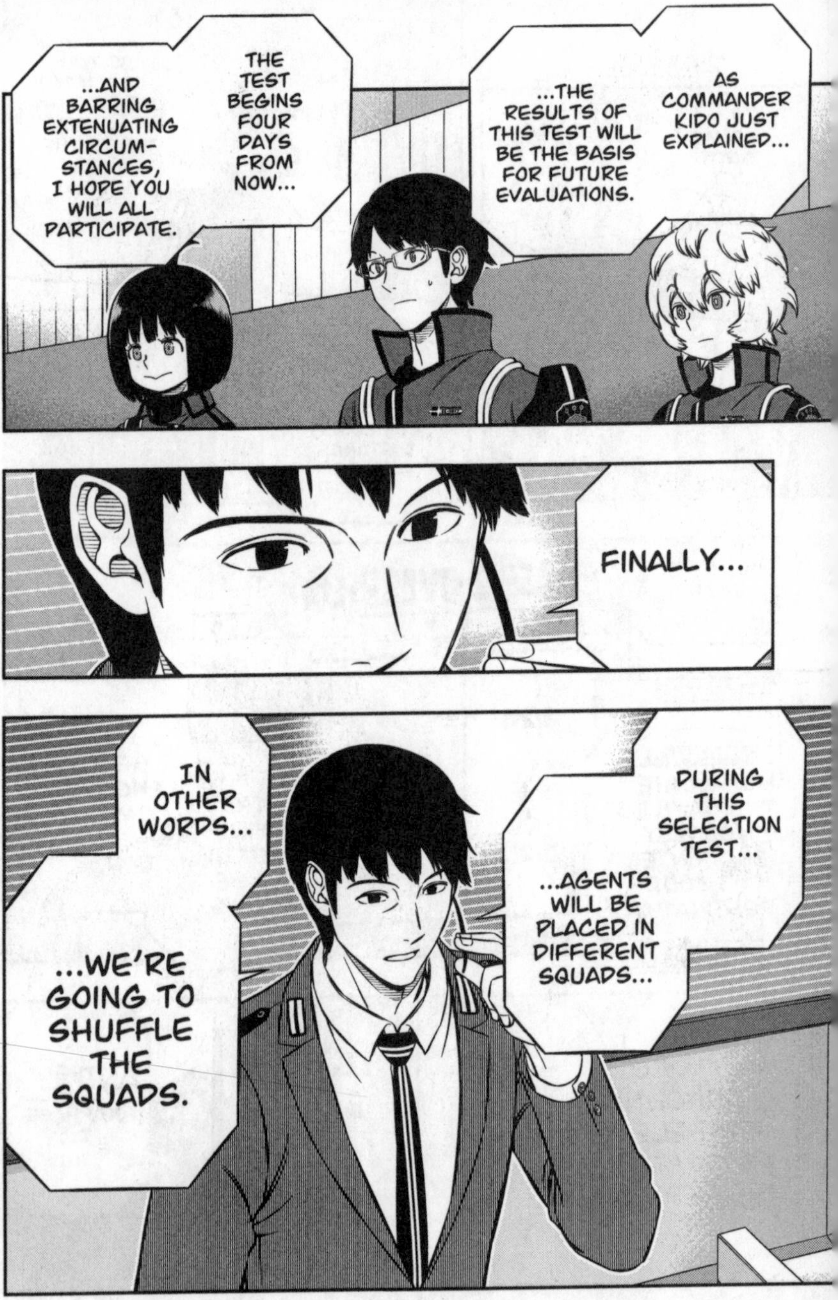
AS COMMANDER KIDO JUST EXPLAINED...
...THE RESULTS OF THIS TEST WILL BE THE BASIS FOR FUTURE EVALUATIONS.
THE TEST BEGINS FOUR DAYS FROM NOW...
...AND BARRING EXTENUATING CIRCUM-STANCES, I HOPE YOU WILL ALL PARTICIPATE.
FINALLY...
DURING THIS SELECTION TEST...
...AGENTS WILL BE PLACED IN DIFFERENT SQUADS...
IN OTHER WORDS...
...WE'RE GOING TO SHUFFLE THE SQUADS.

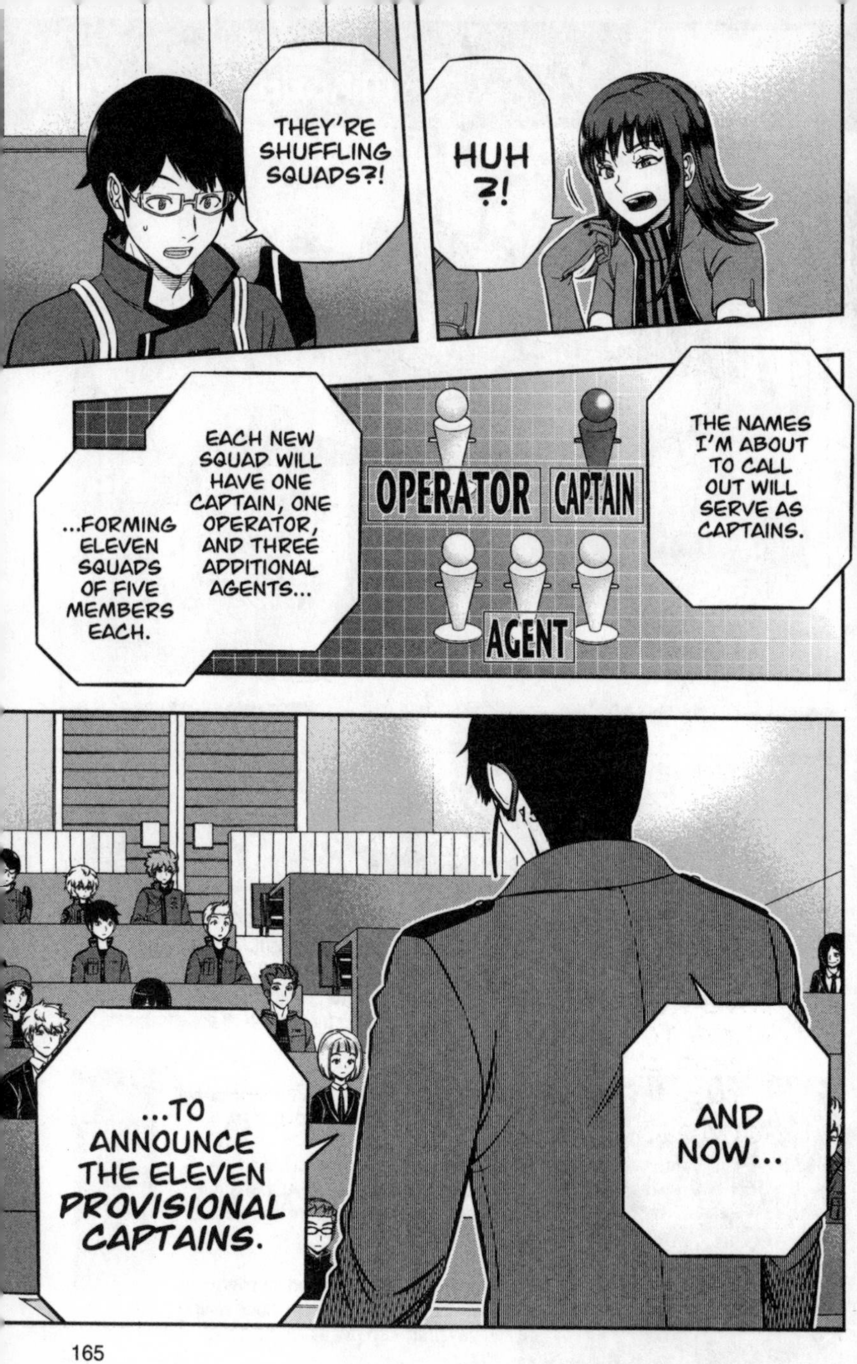
HUH ?!
THEY'RE SHUFFLING SQUADS?!
THE NAMES I'M ABOUT TO CALL OUT WILL SERVE AS CAPTAINS.
CAPTAIN
OPERATOR
EACH NEW SQUAD WILL HAVE ONE CAPTAIN, ONE OPERATOR, AND THREE ADDITIONAL AGENTS...
...FORMING ELEVEN SQUADS OF FIVE MEMBERS EACH.
AGENT
AND NOW...
...TO ANNOUNCE THE ELEVEN PROVISIONAL CAPTAINS.

Mikado Revealed

Saikoro [Chinese Restaurant]

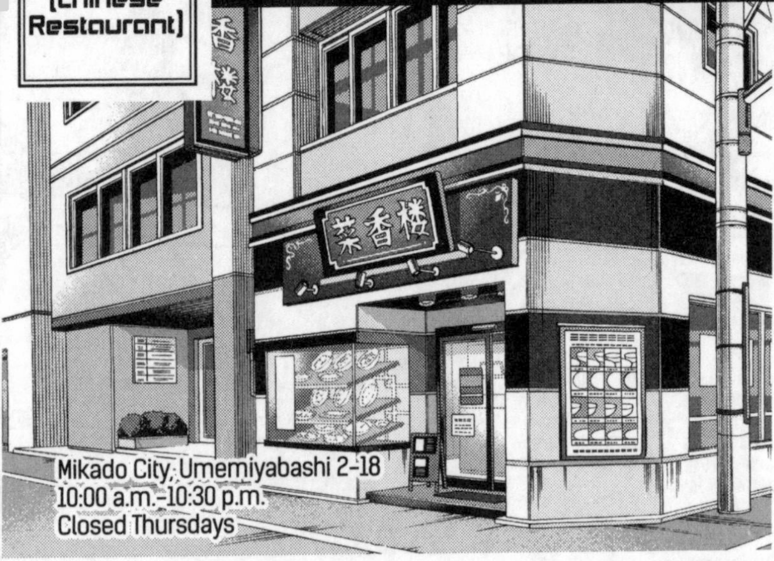
菜香楼

Mikado City, Umemiyabashi 2-18
10:00 a.m.–10:30 p.m.
Closed Thursdays

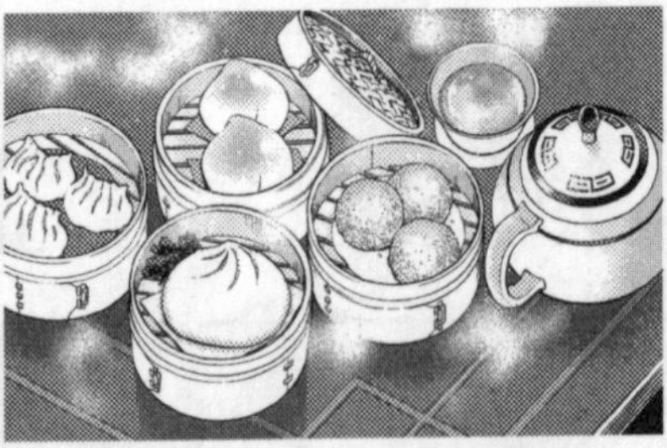

↑ All-you-can-eat dim sum for 2,200 yen per person. Chinese tea can also be purchased as a gift.

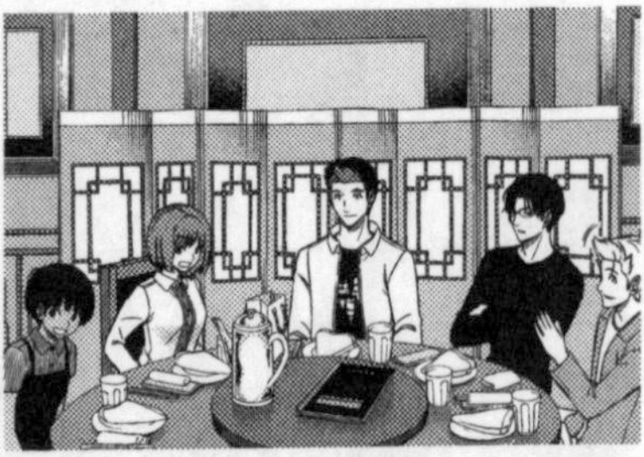

↑ Private dining room with a large, round table. Reservation required. Often used for welcome and send-off parties and other celebrations.

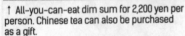

When I visited Osaka, I found this great Chinese place that offered amazing food for a real bargain. I think it's gone now. Maybe the low prices couldn't keep them in business? Time marches on, and I don't like it.

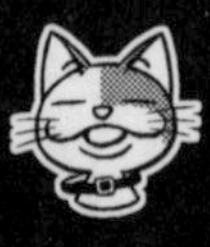

4,000 Years of History on a Plate

There's a restaurant chain with a similar name, but this one is family owned.

The Chinese owner modifies a wide variety of dishes to the Japanese palate, and the restaurant has a broad customer base.

There are offerings priced for everyone, from those on a budget to those willing to pay premium prices for the good stuff.

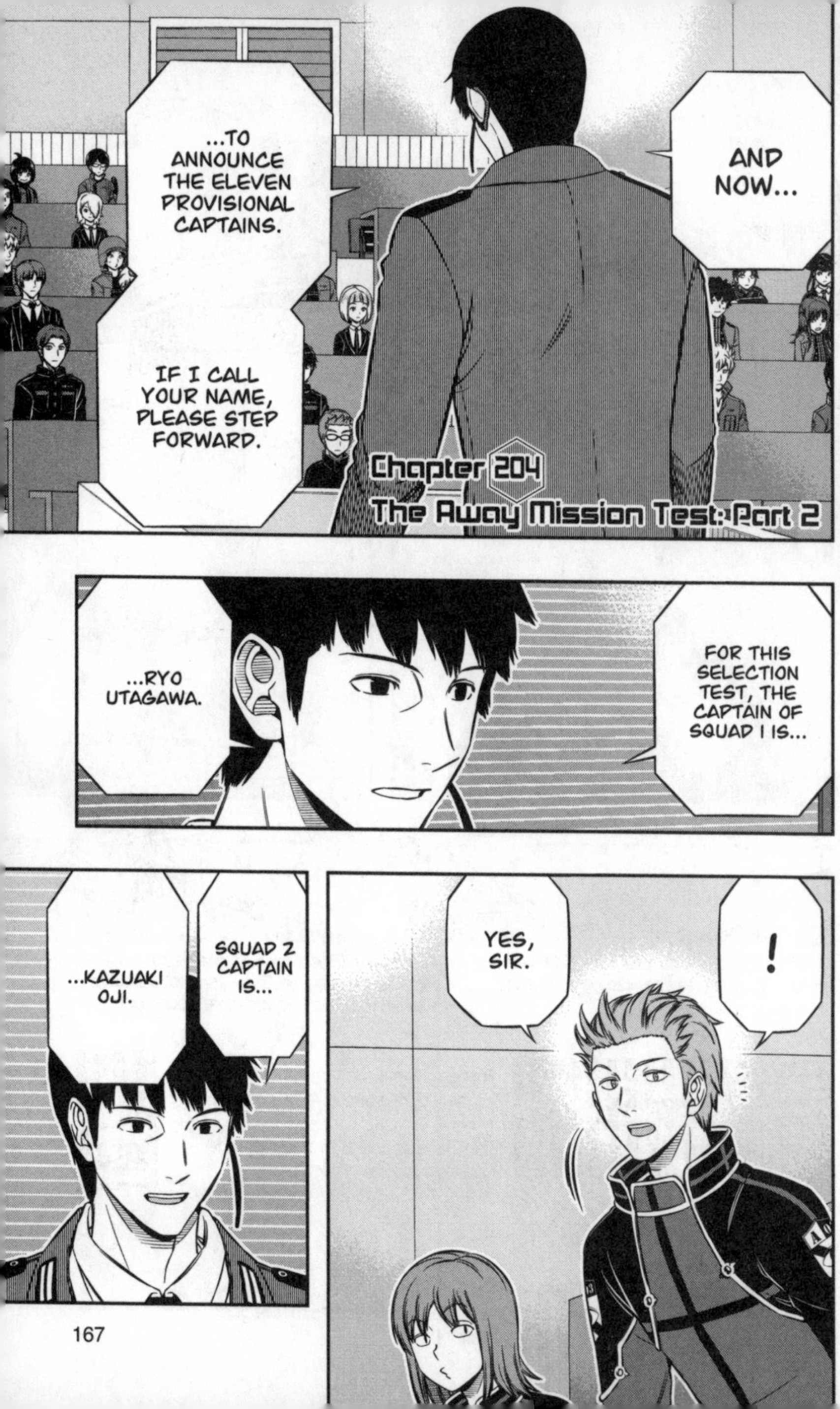
AND NOW...
...TO ANNOUNCE THE ELEVEN PROVISIONAL CAPTAINS.
IF I CALL YOUR NAME, PLEASE STEP FORWARD.
Chapter 204
The Away Mission Test: Part 2
FOR THIS SELECTION TEST, THE CAPTAIN OF SQUAD 1 IS...
...RYO UTAGAWA.
!
YES, SIR.
SQUAD 2 CAPTAIN IS...
...KAZUAKI OJI.

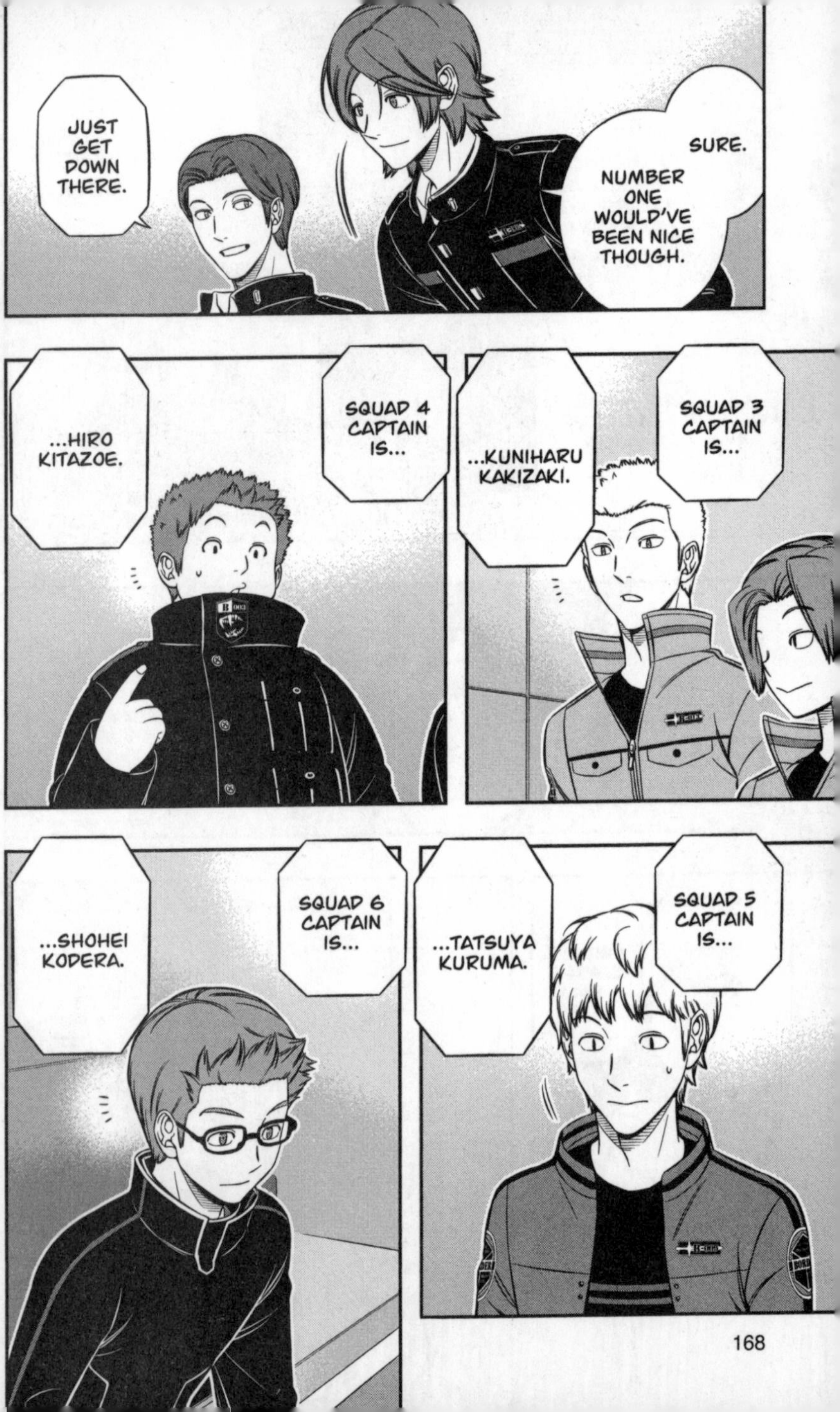
SURE.
NUMBER ONE WOULD'VE BEEN NICE THOUGH.
JUST GET DOWN THERE.
SQUAD 3 CAPTAIN IS...
...KUNIHARU KAKIZAKI.
SQUAD 4 CAPTAIN IS...
...HIRO KITAZOE.
SQUAD 5 CAPTAIN IS...
...TATSUYA KURUMA.
SQUAD 6 CAPTAIN IS...
...SHOHEI KODERA.

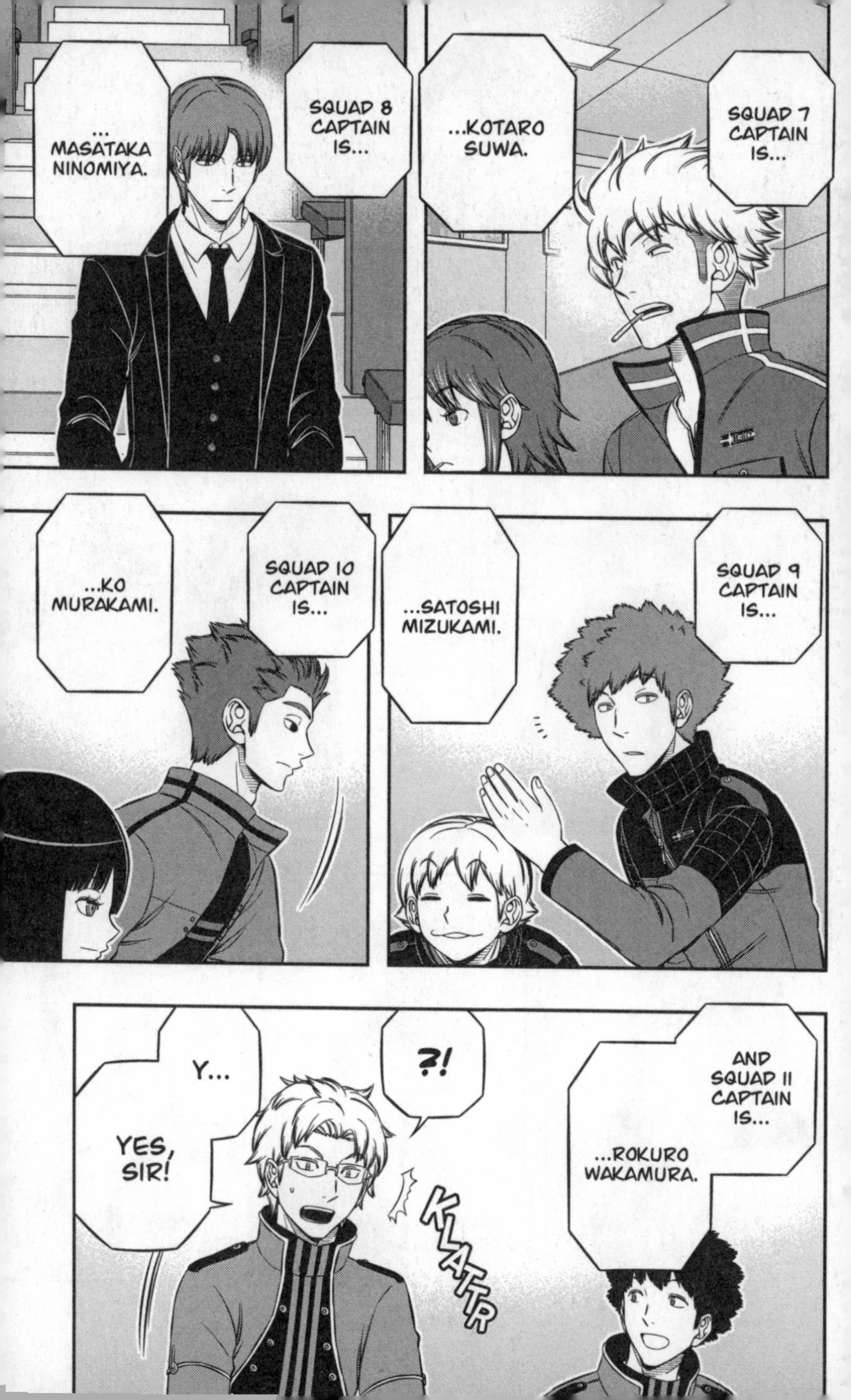
SQUAD 7 CAPTAIN IS...
...KOTARO SUWA.
SQUAD 8 CAPTAIN IS...
...MASATAKA NINOMIYA.
SQUAD 9 CAPTAIN IS...
...SATOSHI MIZUKAMI.
SQUAD 10 CAPTAIN IS...
...KO MURAKAMI.
AND SQUAD 11 CAPTAIN IS...
...ROKURO WAKAMURA.
KLATTR
?!
Y...
YES, SIR!

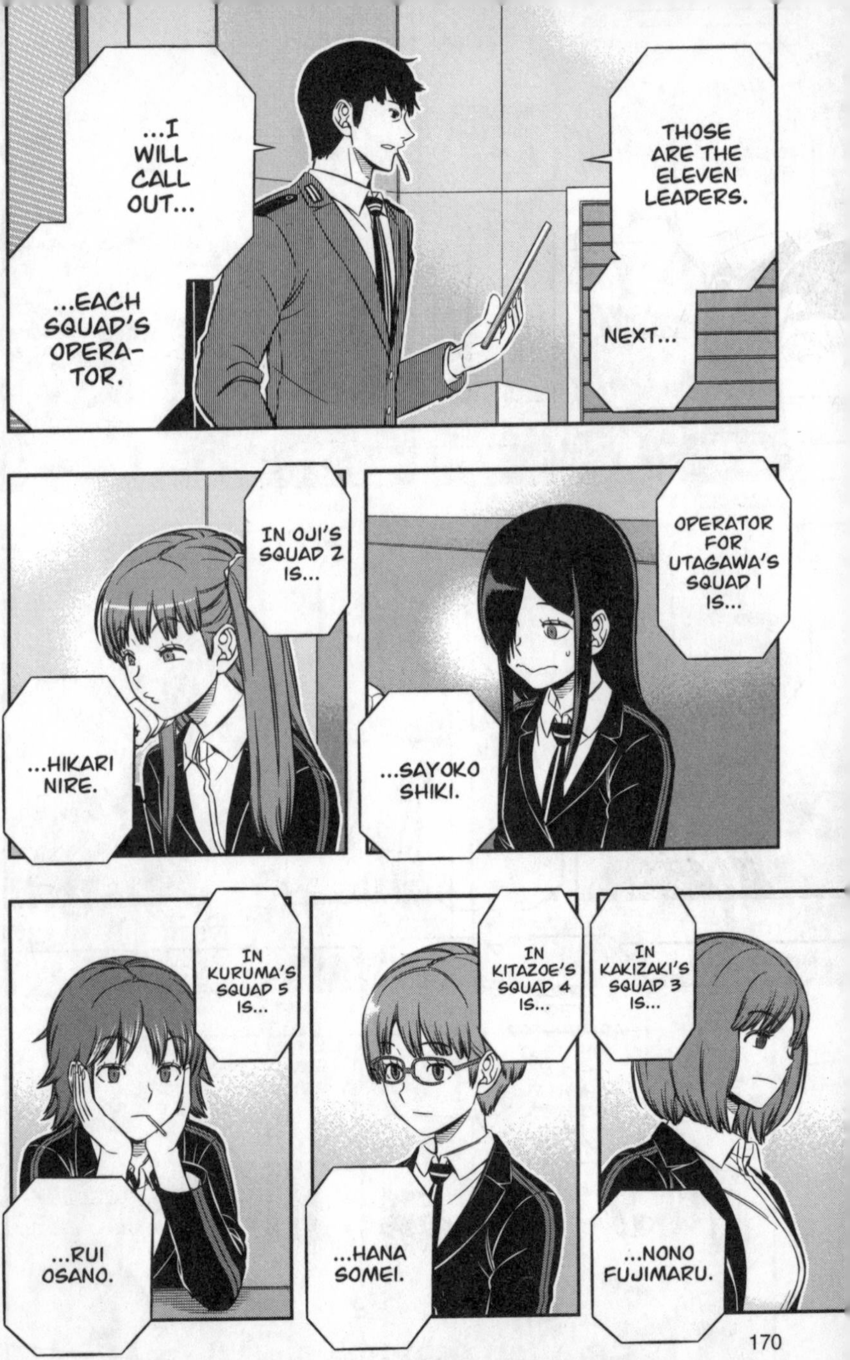
THOSE ARE THE ELEVEN LEADERS.
NEXT...
...I WILL CALL OUT...
...EACH SQUAD'S OPERA-TOR.
OPERATOR FOR UTAGAWA'S SQUAD 1 IS...
...SAYOKO SHIKI.
IN OJI'S SQUAD 2 IS...
...HIKARI NIRE.
IN KAKIZAKI'S SQUAD 3 IS...
...NONO FUJIMARU.
IN KITAZOE'S SQUAD 4 IS...
...HANA SOMEI.
IN KURUMA'S SQUAD 5 IS...
...RUI OSANO.

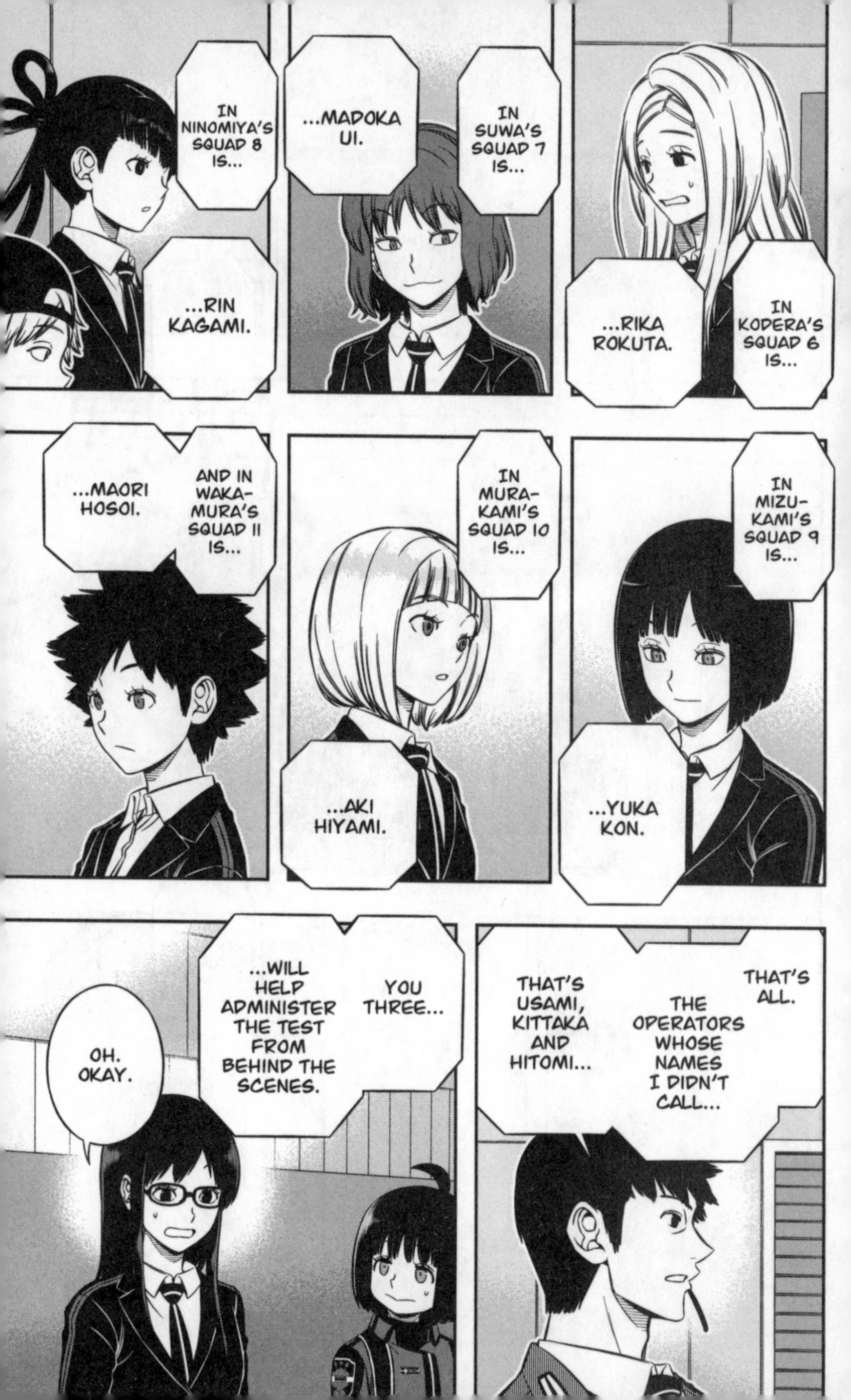
IN KODERA'S SQUAD 6 IS...
...RIKA ROKUTA.
IN SUWA'S SQUAD 7 IS...
...MADOKA UI.
IN NINOMIYA'S SQUAD 8 IS...
...RIN KAGAMI.
IN MIZU-KAMI'S SQUAD 9 IS...
...YUKA KON.
IN MURA-KAMI'S SQUAD 10 IS...
...AKI HIYAMI.
AND IN WAKA-MURA'S SQUAD 11 IS...
...MAORI HOSOI.
THAT'S ALL.
THE OPERATORS WHOSE NAMES I DIDN'T CALL...
THAT'S USAMI, KITTAKA AND HITOMI...
YOU THREE...
...WILL HELP ADMINISTER THE TEST FROM BEHIND THE SCENES.
OH. OKAY.

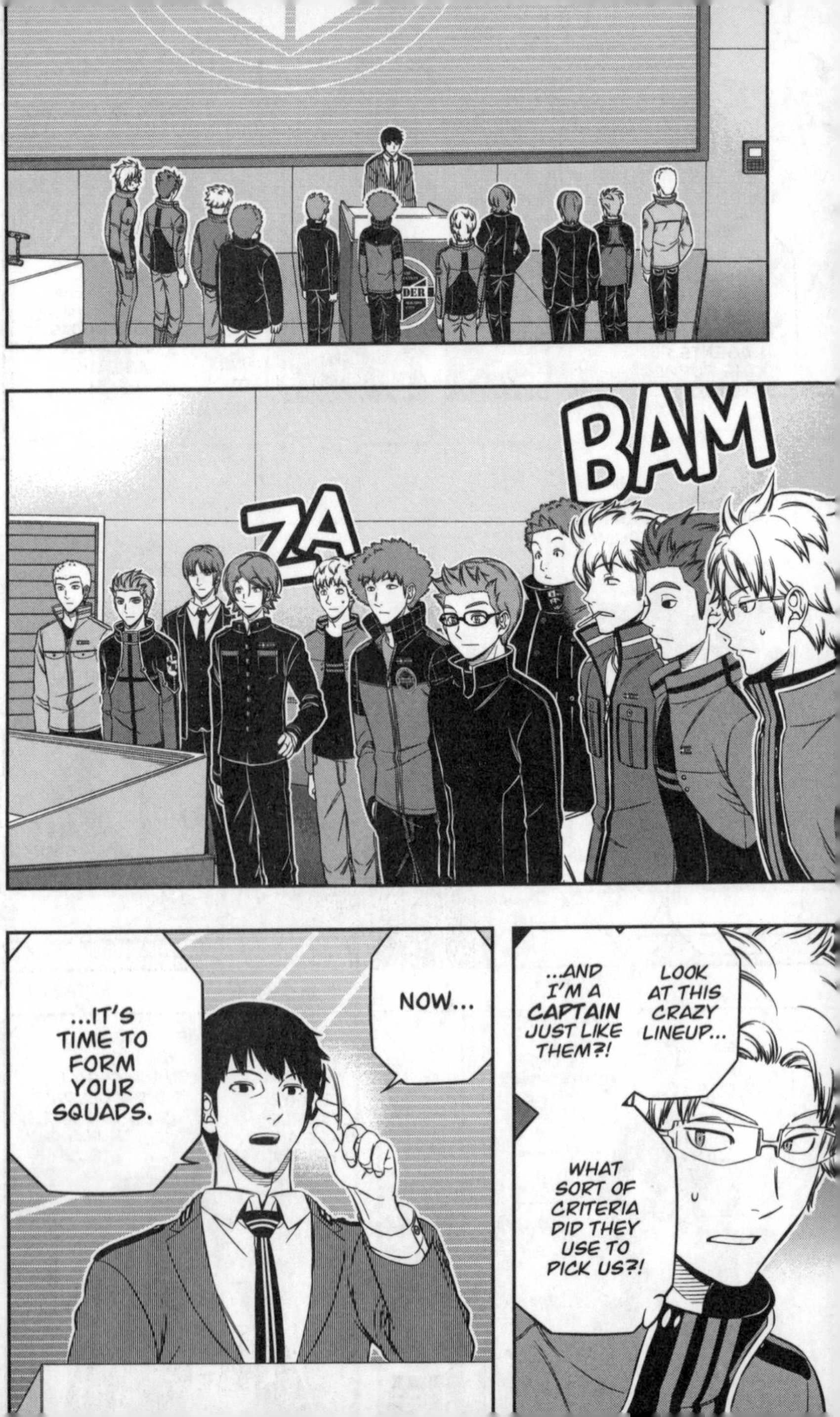
BAM
ZA
LOOK AT THIS CRAZY LINEUP...
...AND I'M A CAPTAIN JUST LIKE THEM?!
WHAT SORT OF CRITERIA DID THEY USE TO PICK US?!
NOW...
...IT'S TIME TO FORM YOUR SQUADS.

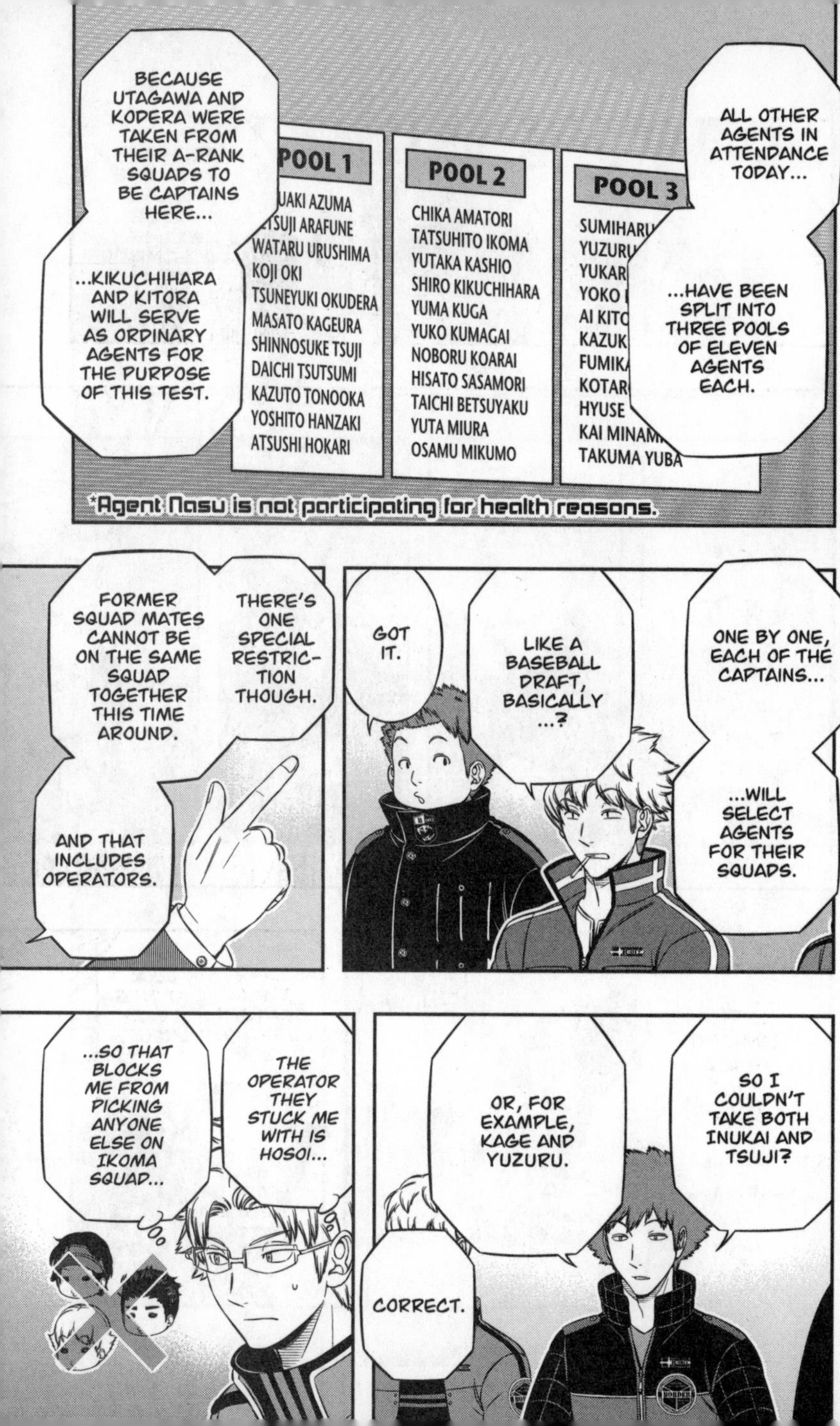
ALL OTHER AGENTS IN ATTENDANCE TODAY...
...HAVE BEEN SPLIT INTO THREE POOLS OF ELEVEN AGENTS EACH.
BECAUSE UTAGAWA AND KODERA WERE TAKEN FROM THEIR A-RANK SQUADS TO BE CAPTAINS HERE...
...KIKUCHIHARA AND KITORA WILL SERVE AS ORDINARY AGENTS FOR THE PURPOSE OF THIS TEST.
POOL 1
UAKI AZUMA
TSUJI ARAFUNE
WATARU URUSHIMA
KOJI OKI
TSUNEYUKI OKUDERA
MASATO KAGEURA
SHINNOSUKE TSUJI
DAICHI TSUTSUMI
KAZUTO TONOOKA
YOSHITO HANZAKI
ATSUSHI HOKARI
POOL 2
CHIKA AMATORI
TATSUHITO IKOMA
YUTAKA KASHIO
SHIRO KIKUCHIHARA
YUMA KUGA
YUKO KUMAGAI
NOBORU KOARAI
HISATO SASAMORI
TAICHI BETSUYAKU
YUTA MIURA
OSAMU MIKUMO
POOL 3
SUMIHARU
YUZURU
YUKAR
YOKO
AI KITO
KAZUK
FUMIKA
KOTAR
HYUSE
KAI MINAM
TAKUMA YUBA
*Agent Nasu is not participating for health reasons.
ONE BY ONE, EACH OF THE CAPTAINS...
...WILL SELECT AGENTS FOR THEIR SQUADS.
LIKE A BASEBALL DRAFT, BASICALLY...?
GOT IT.
THERE'S ONE SPECIAL RESTRICTION THOUGH.
FORMER SQUAD MATES CANNOT BE ON THE SAME SQUAD TOGETHER THIS TIME AROUND.
AND THAT INCLUDES OPERATORS.
SO I COULDN'T TAKE BOTH INUKAI AND TSUJI?
OR, FOR EXAMPLE, KAGE AND YUZURU.
CORRECT.
THE OPERATOR THEY STUCK ME WITH IS HOSOI...
...SO THAT BLOCKS ME FROM PICKING ANYONE ELSE ON IKOMA SQUAD...

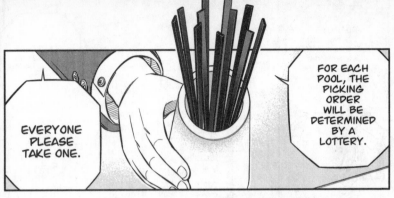

FOR EACH POOL, THE PICKING ORDER WILL BE DETERMINED BY A LOTTERY.

EVERYONE PLEASE TAKE ONE.

ELEV-ENTH!

I'M GOING DEAD LAST!

UGH...

174

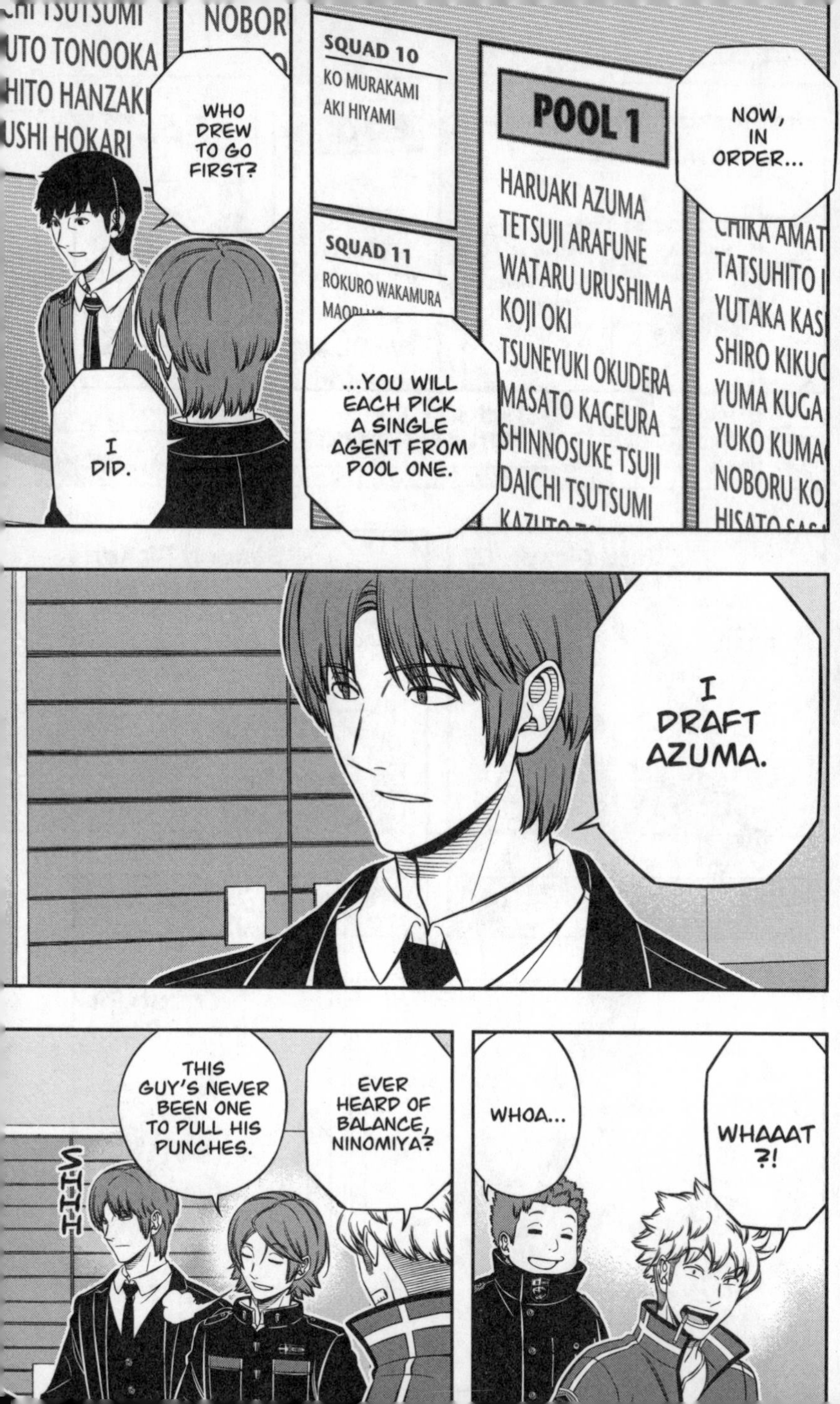
NOW, IN ORDER...
POOL 1
HARUAKI AZUMA
TETSUJI ARAFUNE
WATARU URUSHIMA
KOJI OKI
TSUNEYUKI OKUDERA
MASATO KAGEURA
SHINNOSUKE TSUJI
DAICHI TSUTSUMI
YUMA KUGA
SQUAD 10
KO MURAKAMI
AKI HIYAMI
SQUAD 11
ROKURO WAKAMURA
...YOU WILL EACH PICK A SINGLE AGENT FROM POOL ONE.
WHO DREW TO GO FIRST?
I DID.
I DRAFT AZUMA.
WHAAAT ?!
WHOA...
EVER HEARD OF BALANCE, NINOMIYA?
THIS GUY'S NEVER BEEN ONE TO PULL HIS PUNCHES.

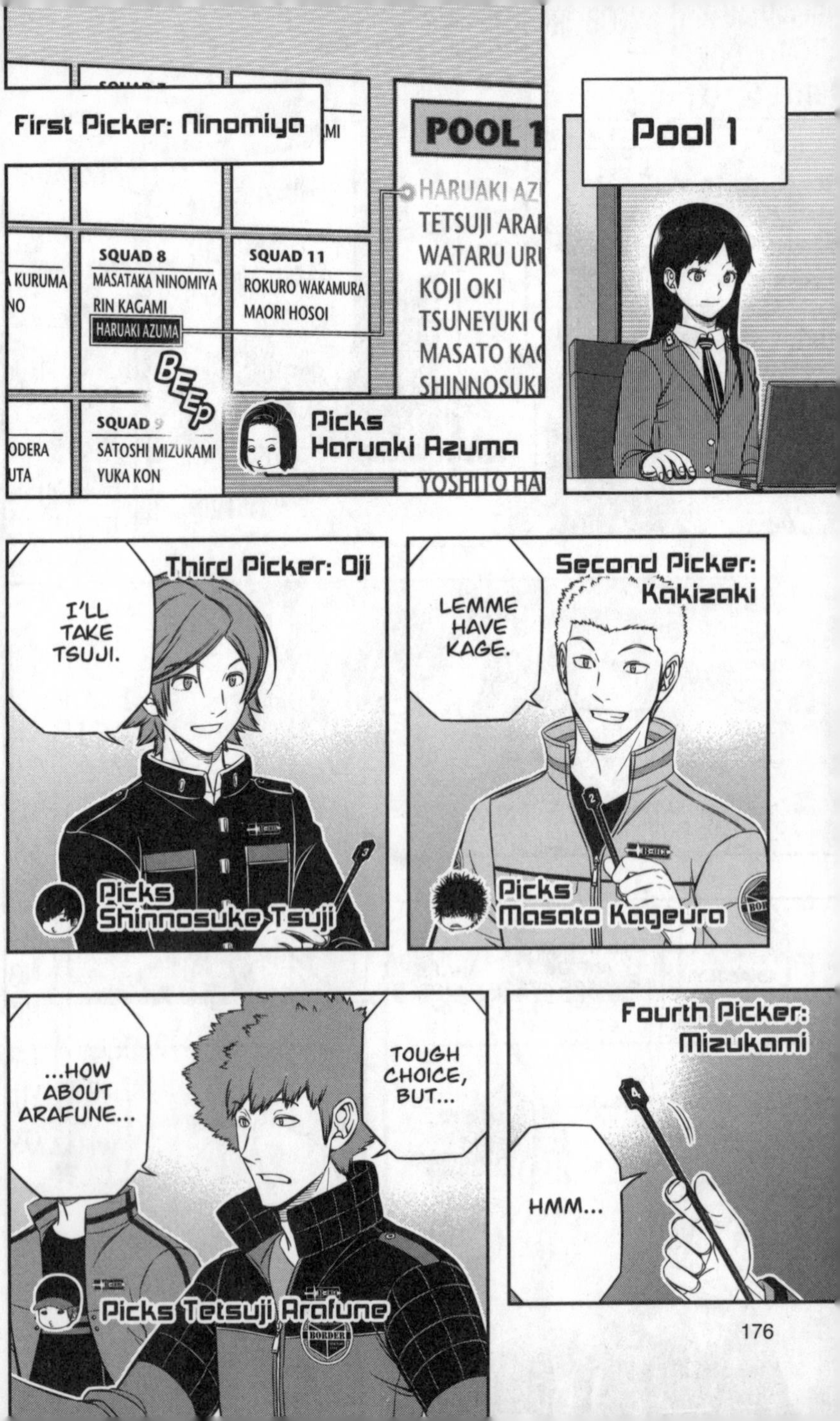
Pool 1
First Picker: Ninomiya
POOL 1
HARUAKI AZ
TETSUJI ARA
KOJI OKI
SQUAD 8
MASATAKA NINOMIYA
RIN KAGAMI
HARUAKI AZUMA
SQUAD 11
ROKURO WAKAMURA
MAORI HOSOI
SQUAD 9
SATOSHI MIZUKAMI
YUKA KON
BEEP
Picks Haruaki Azuma
Second Picker: Kakizaki
LEMME HAVE KAGE.
Picks Masato Kageura
Third Picker: Oji
I'LL TAKE TSUJI.
Picks Shinnosuke Tsuji
Fourth Picker: Mizukami
HMM...
TOUGH CHOICE, BUT...
...HOW ABOUT ARAFUNE...
Picks Tetsuji Arafune

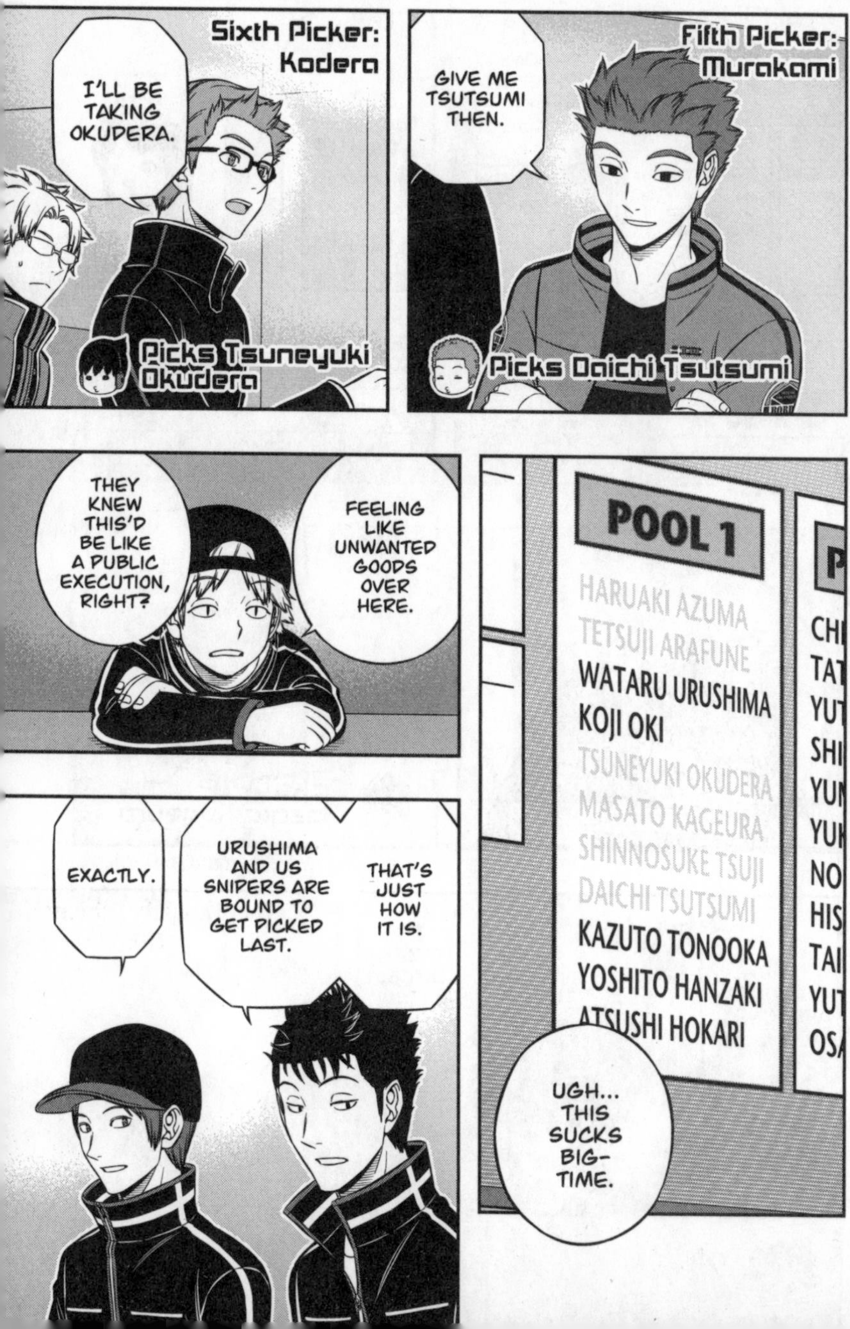
Fifth Picker: Murakami
GIVE ME TSUTSUMI THEN.
Picks Daichi Tsutsumi
Sixth Picker: Kodera
I'LL BE TAKING OKUDERA.
Picks Tsuneyuki Okudera
POOL 1
HARUAKI AZUMA
TETSUJI ARAFUNE
WATARU URUSHIMA
KOJI OKI
TSUNEYUKI OKUDERA
MASATO KAGEURA
SHINNOSUKE TSUJI
DAICHI TSUTSUMI
KAZUTO TONOOKA
YOSHITO HANZAKI
ATSUSHI HOKARI
UGH... THIS SUCKS BIG-TIME.
FEELING LIKE UNWANTED GOODS OVER HERE.
THEY KNEW THIS'D BE LIKE A PUBLIC EXECUTION, RIGHT?
THAT'S JUST HOW IT IS.
URUSHIMA AND US SNIPERS ARE BOUND TO GET PICKED LAST.
EXACTLY.

...THEN BAGWORM'S TRION DRAIN IS GONNA PUT US AT A BIG DISADVANTAGE.

IF THE BATTLE PHASE IS GONNA DRAG ON FOREVER...

CUZ OF BAGWORM, RIGHT?

YEAH, YEAH, I KNOW THAT.

SO THOSE OF US WHO TEND TO HIDE AND SNEAK AROUND WERE NEVER GONNA BE TOP PICKS...

Bagworm
A cape that prevents the user from being tracked on radar. Incurs minor trion drain over time.

RIN KAGAMI	KOKORO WAKAMURA	TSUNEYUKI OKUDERA	
HARUAKI AZUMA	MAORI HOSOI	MASATO KAGEURA	
		SHINNOSUKE TSUJI	
		DAICHI TSUTSUMI	
		KAZUTO TONOOKA	
		YOSHITO HANZAKI	YUTA MIURA
		ATSUSHI HOKARI	OSAMU MIKUMO

ESPECIALLY SINCE AZUMA AND ARAFUNE FLEW RIGHT OFF THE SHELF...

WHICH MAKES SENSE, BUT IT STILL SUCKS.

I'M OFF!

AWW, MAN...

I'LL TAKE HOKARI.

Seventh Picker: Kuruma

Picks Atsushi Hokari

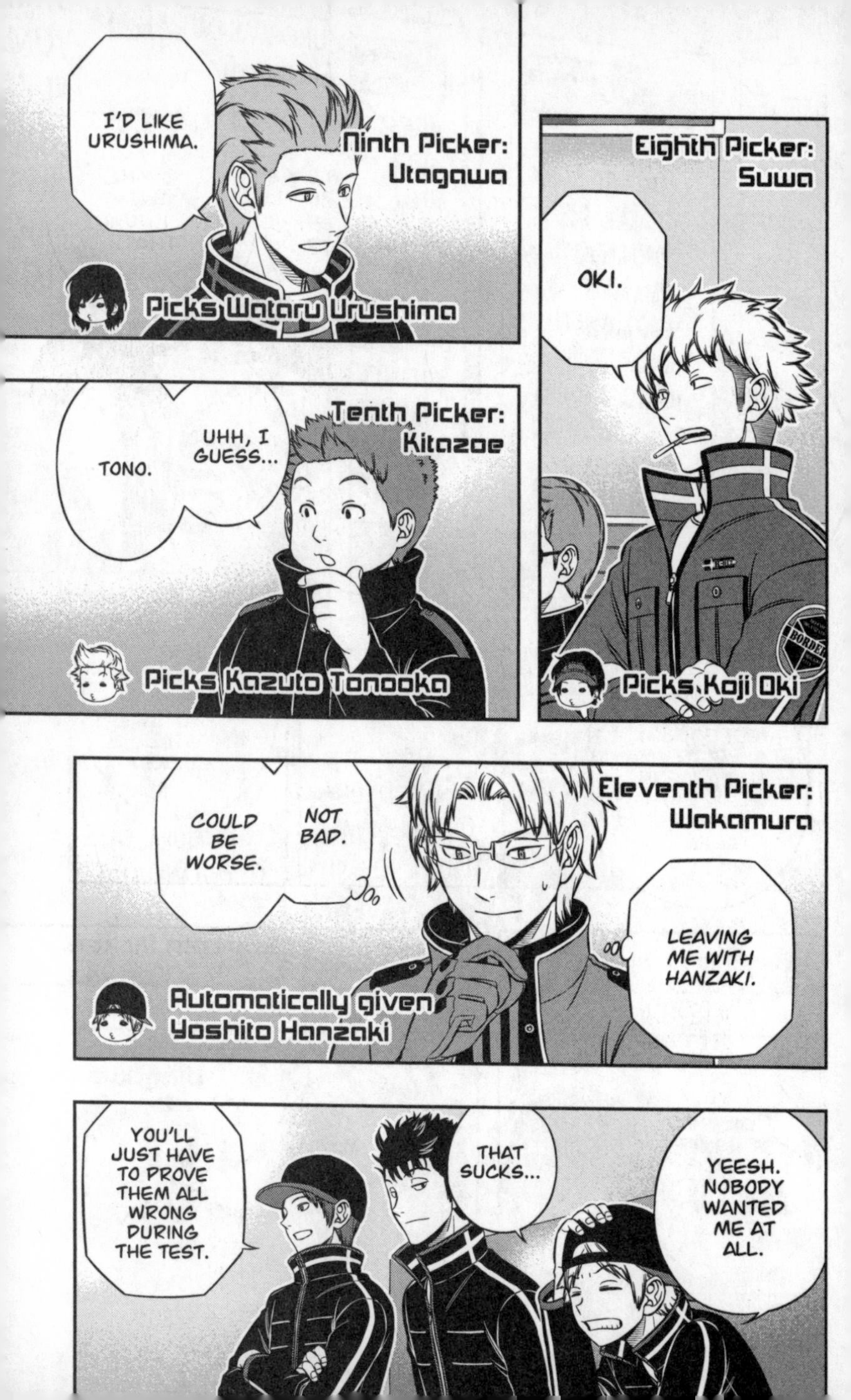
Eighth Picker: Suwa
OKI.
Picks Koji Oki
Ninth Picker: Utagawa
I'D LIKE URUSHIMA.
Picks Wataru Urushima
Tenth Picker: Kitazoe
UHH, I GUESS...
TONO.
Picks Kazuto Tonooka
Eleventh Picker: Wakamura
LEAVING ME WITH HANZAKI.
NOT BAD.
COULD BE WORSE.
Automatically given Yoshito Hanzaki
YEESH. NOBODY WANTED ME AT ALL.
THAT SUCKS...
YOU'LL JUST HAVE TO PROVE THEM ALL WRONG DURING THE TEST.

POOL 2

CHIKA AMATORI
TATSUHITO IKOMA
YUTAKA KASHIO
SHIRO KIKUCHIHARA
YUMA KUGA
YUKO KUMAGAI
NOBORU KOARAI
HISATO SASAMORI
TAICHI BETSUYAKU
YUTA MIURA
OSAMU MIKUMO

MURAKAMI
HIYAMI

URO WAKAMURA
RI HOSOI

POO

SUMIHA
YUZUR
YUKAR
YOKO
AI KITO
KAZUKI K
FUMIKA TER
KOTARO TO
HYUSE KRO
KAI MINAM
TAKUMA YU

URO WAKAMURA
RI HOSOI

PLEASE DRAW LOTS AGAIN.

MOVING RIGHT ALONG TO POOL TWO.

RTL RTL RTL

Pool 2

WAY BETTER THAN LAST TIME!

I'M SIXTH!

6

WELL...

...TAKING THE SQUAD BREAK-DOWN INTO CONSIDER-ATION...

First Picker:
Utagawa

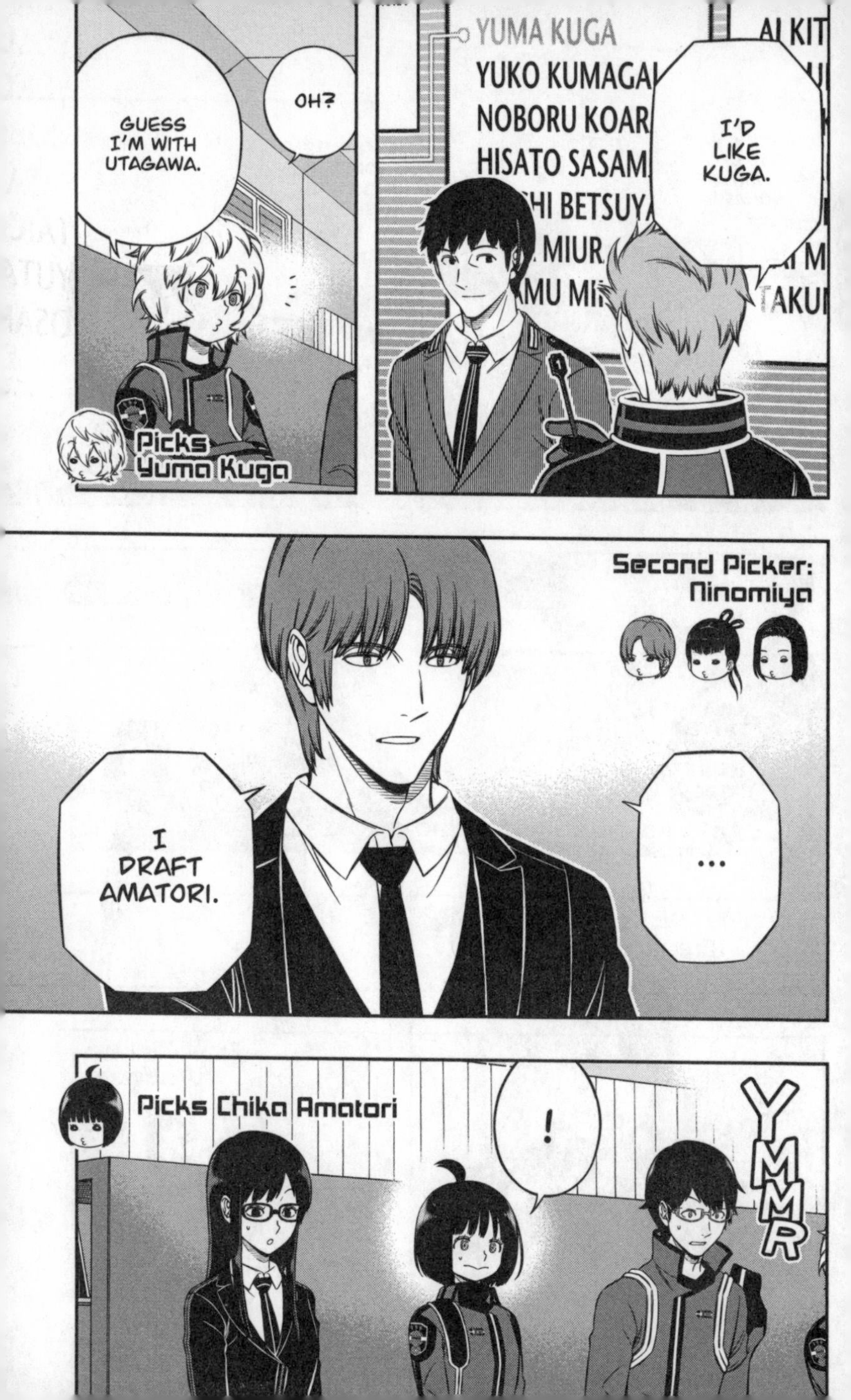
YUMA KUGA
YUKO KUMAGAI
NOBORU KOAR
HISATO SASAM
HI BETSUY
MIUR
MU MI
AI KIT
TAKU
I'D LIKE KUGA.
OH?
GUESS I'M WITH UTAGAWA.
Picks Yuma Kuga
Second Picker: Ninomiya
...
I DRAFT AMATORI.
YMMMR
!
Picks Chika Amatori

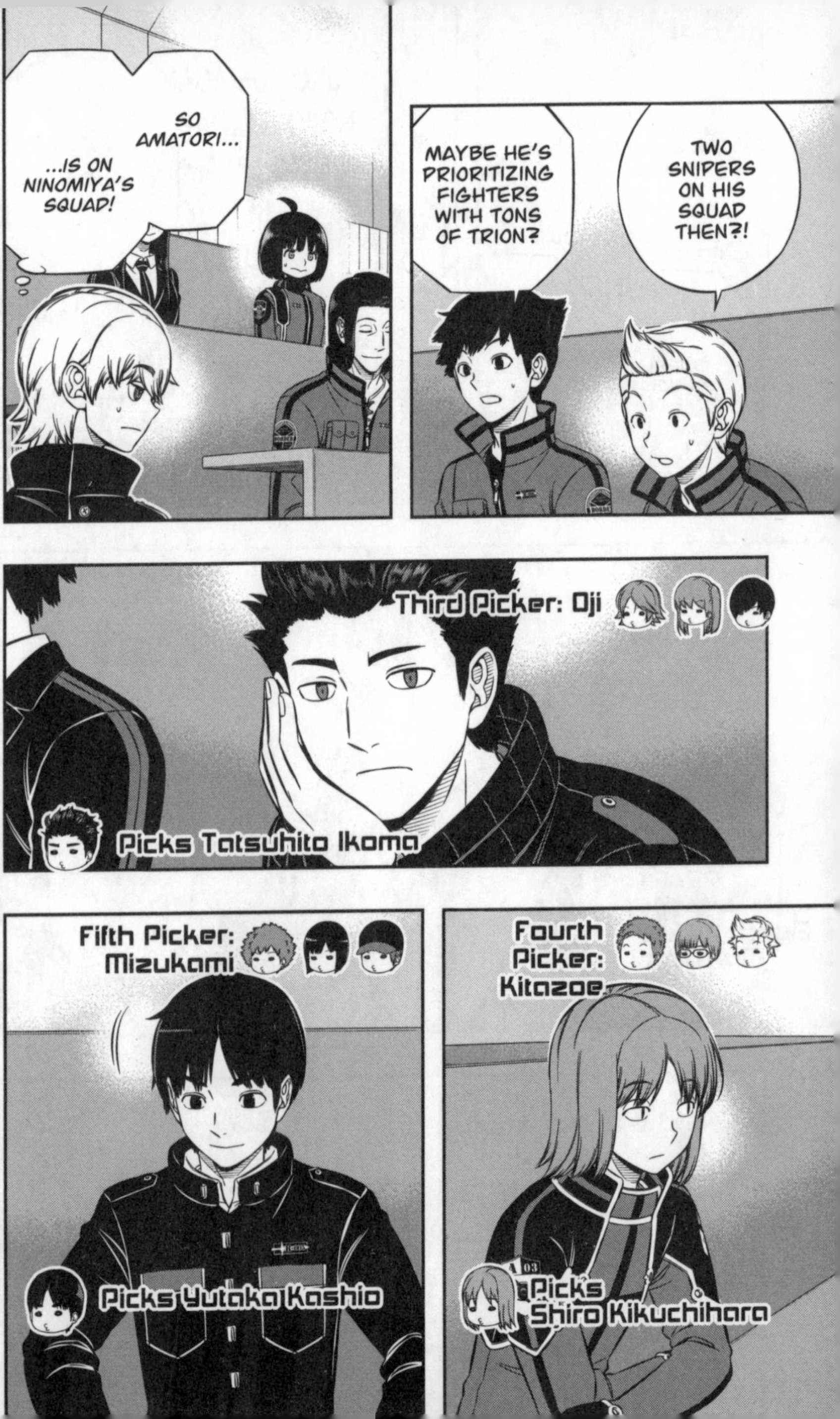
TWO SNIPERS ON HIS SQUAD THEN?!
MAYBE HE'S PRIORITIZING FIGHTERS WITH TONS OF TRION?
SO AMATORI...
...IS ON NINOMIYA'S SQUAD!
Third Picker: Oji
Picks Tatsuhito Ikoma
Fourth Picker: Kitazoe
Picks Shiro Kikuchihara
Fifth Picker: Mizukami
Picks Yutaka Kashio

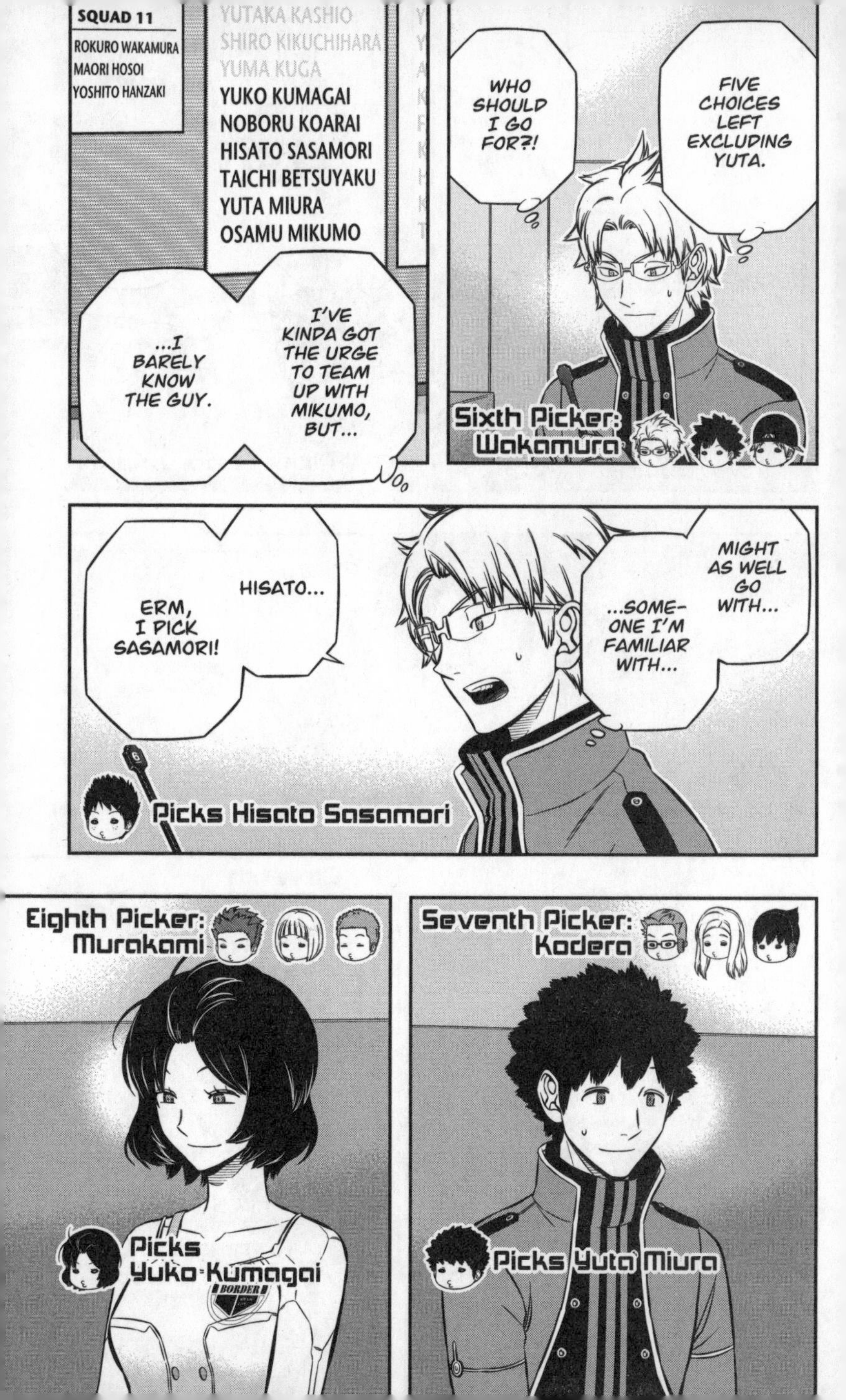
FIVE CHOICES LEFT EXCLUDING YUTA.
WHO SHOULD I GO FOR?!
Sixth Picker: Wakamura
SQUAD 11
ROKURO WAKAMURA
MAORI HOSOI
YOSHITO HANZAKI
YUTAKA KASHIO
SHIRO KIKUCHIHARA
YUMA KUGA
YUKO KUMAGAI
NOBORU KOARAI
HISATO SASAMORI
TAICHI BETSUYAKU
YUTA MIURA
OSAMU MIKUMO
I'VE KINDA GOT THE URGE TO TEAM UP WITH MIKUMO, BUT...
...I BARELY KNOW THE GUY.
MIGHT AS WELL GO WITH...
...SOME-ONE I'M FAMILIAR WITH...
HISATO...
ERM, I PICK SASAMORI!
Picks Hisato Sasamori
Seventh Picker: Kodera
Picks Yuta Miura
Eighth Picker: Murakami
Picks Yuko Kumagai
BORDER

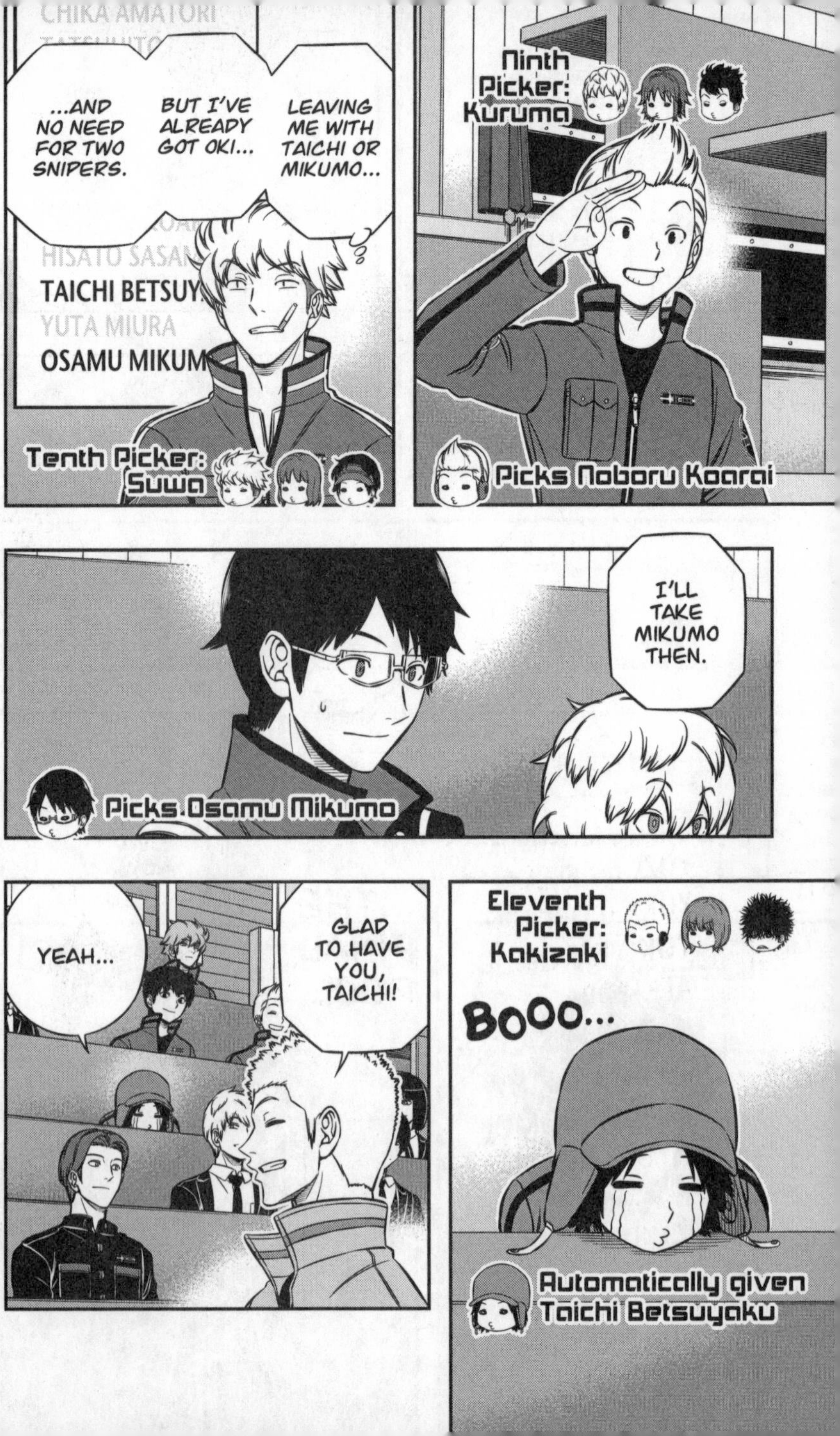
Ninth Picker: Kuruma
Picks Noboru Koarai
CHIKA AMATORI
HISATO SASAM
TAICHI BETSUY
YUTA MIURA
OSAMU MIKUM
LEAVING ME WITH TAICHI OR MIKUMO...
BUT I'VE ALREADY GOT OKI...
...AND NO NEED FOR TWO SNIPERS.
Tenth Picker: Suwa
I'LL TAKE MIKUMO THEN.
Picks Osamu Mikumo
Eleventh Picker: Kakizaki
BOOO...
Automatically given Taichi Betsuyaku
GLAD TO HAVE YOU, TAICHI!
YEAH...

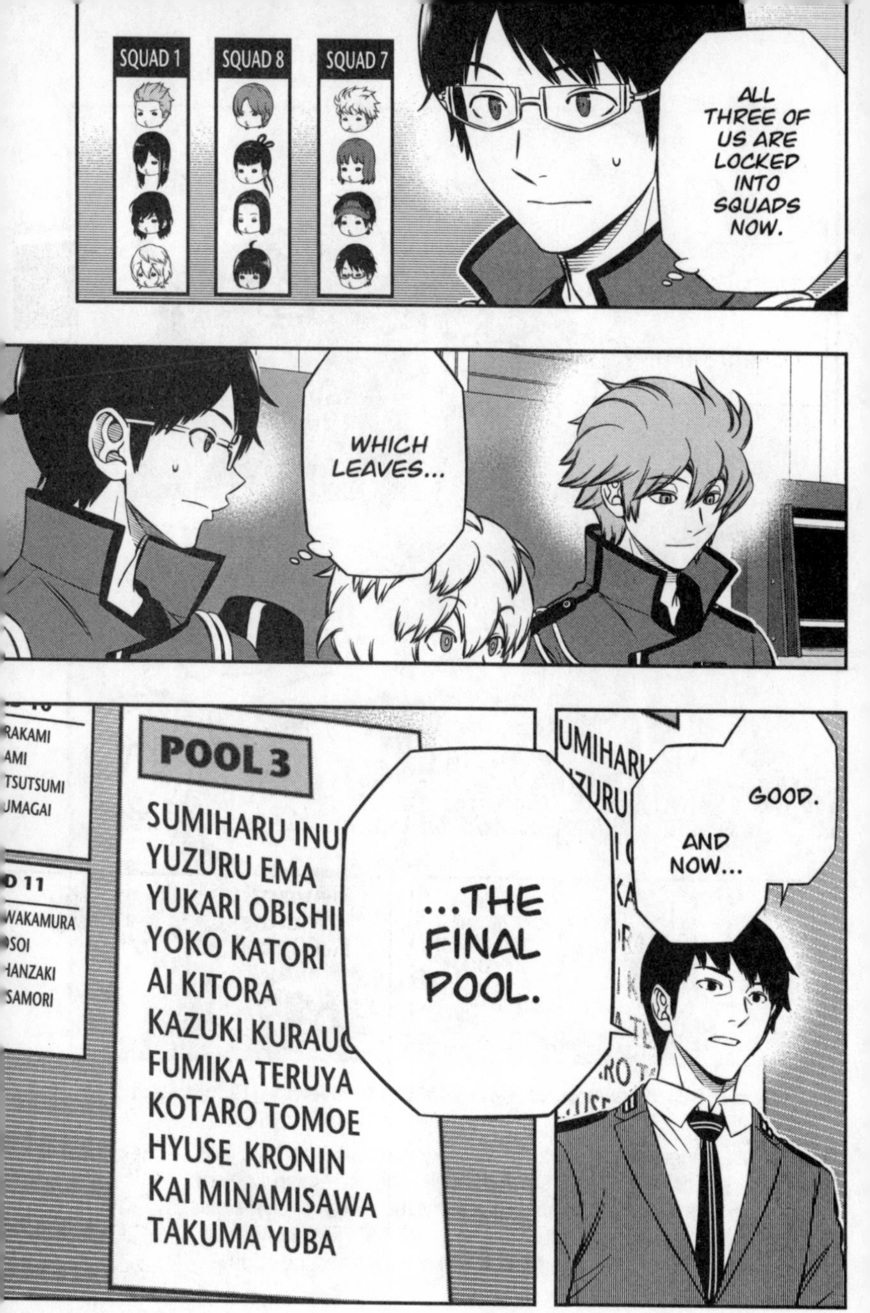
ALL THREE OF US ARE LOCKED INTO SQUADS NOW.
SQUAD 1
SQUAD 8
SQUAD 7
WHICH LEAVES...
GOOD.
AND NOW...
...THE FINAL POOL.
POOL 3
SUMIHARU INU
YUZURU EMA
YUKARI OBISHI
YOKO KATORI
AI KITORA
KAZUKI KURAU
FUMIKA TERUYA
KOTARO TOMOE
HYUSE KRONIN
KAI MINAMISAWA
TAKUMA YUBA

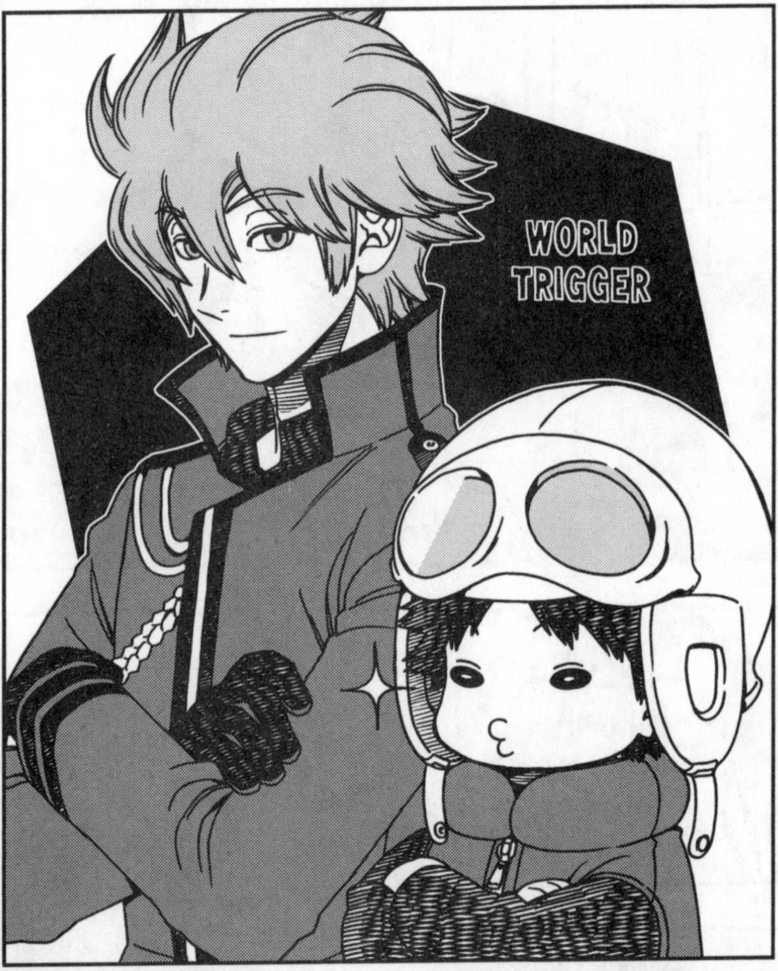
WORLD
TRIGGER

■ Autograph Board celebrating *Jump SQ*'s 13th Anniversary [Originally in color]

The good old autograph board, which I do every year. This time, I chose to feature Yotaro (who was recently in the limelight) and his minion. If you're wondering how the timing worked out such that the previous volume also included one of these, it's because I only released a single volume in all of 2020. Horrible, right? I'm hoping to produce at least a second volume for 2021. I'm trying.

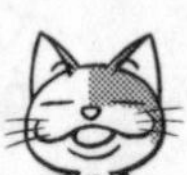

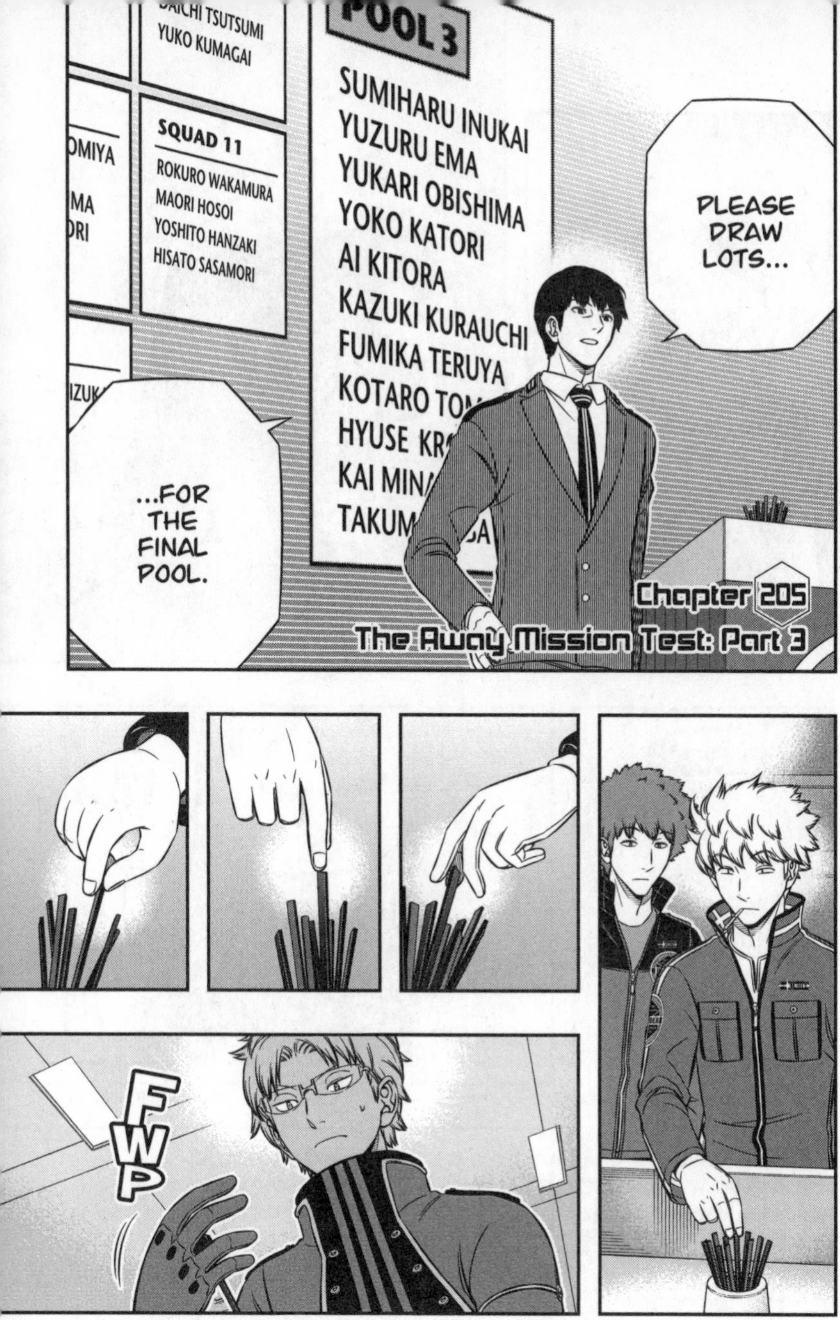
PLEASE DRAW LOTS...
POOL 3
SUMIHARU INUKAI
YUZURU EMA
YUKARI OBISHIMA
YOKO KATORI
AI KITORA
KAZUKI KURAUCHI
FUMIKA TERUYA
SQUAD 11
ROKURO WAKAMURA
MAORI HOSOI
YOSHITO HANZAKI
HISATO SASAMORI
YUKO KUMAGAI
...FOR THE FINAL POOL.
Chapter 205
The Away Mission Test: Part 3
FWP

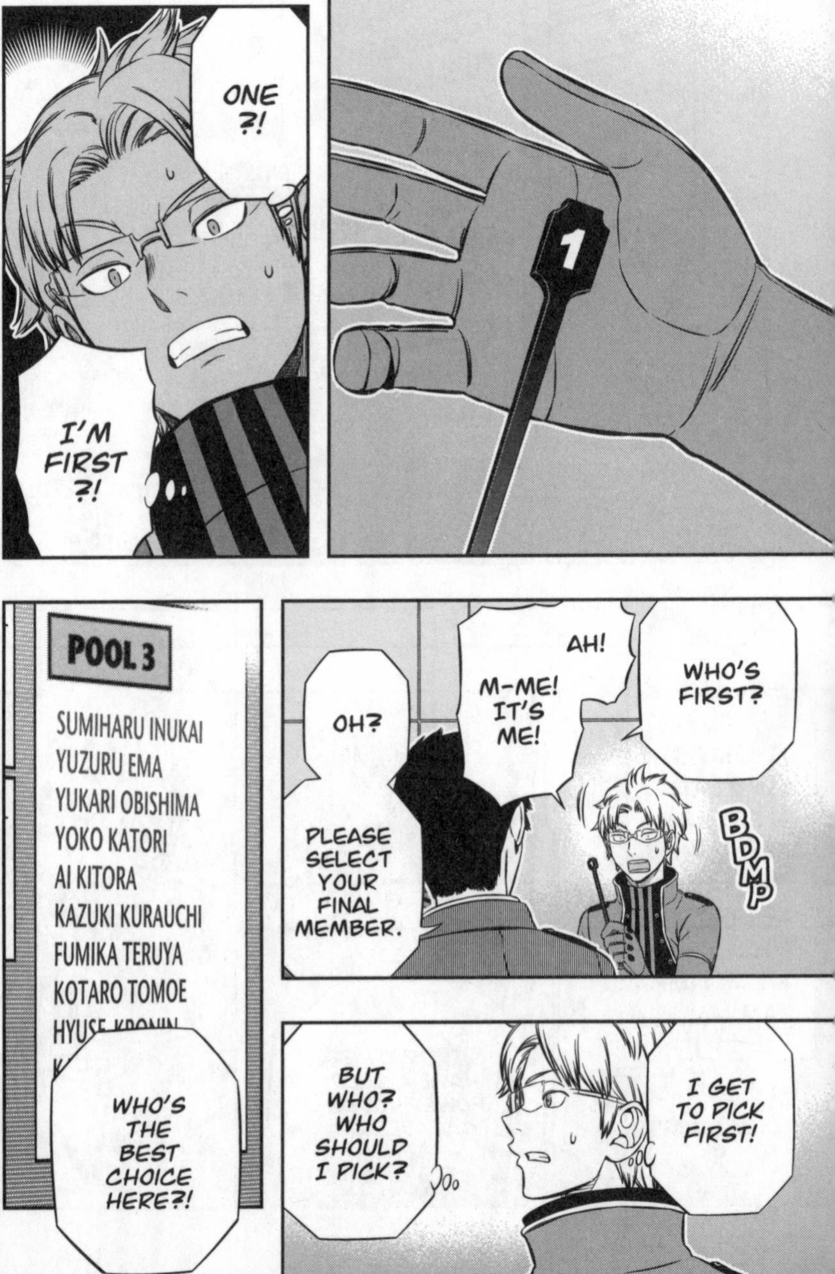
ONE ?!
I'M FIRST ?!
WHO'S FIRST?
AH!
M-ME! IT'S ME!
BDMP
OH?
PLEASE SELECT YOUR FINAL MEMBER.
POOL 3
SUMIHARU INUKAI
YUZURU EMA
YUKARI OBISHIMA
YOKO KATORI
AI KITORA
KAZUKI KURAUCHI
FUMIKA TERUYA
KOTARO TOMOE
I GET TO PICK FIRST!
BUT WHO? WHO SHOULD I PICK?
WHO'S THE BEST CHOICE HERE?!

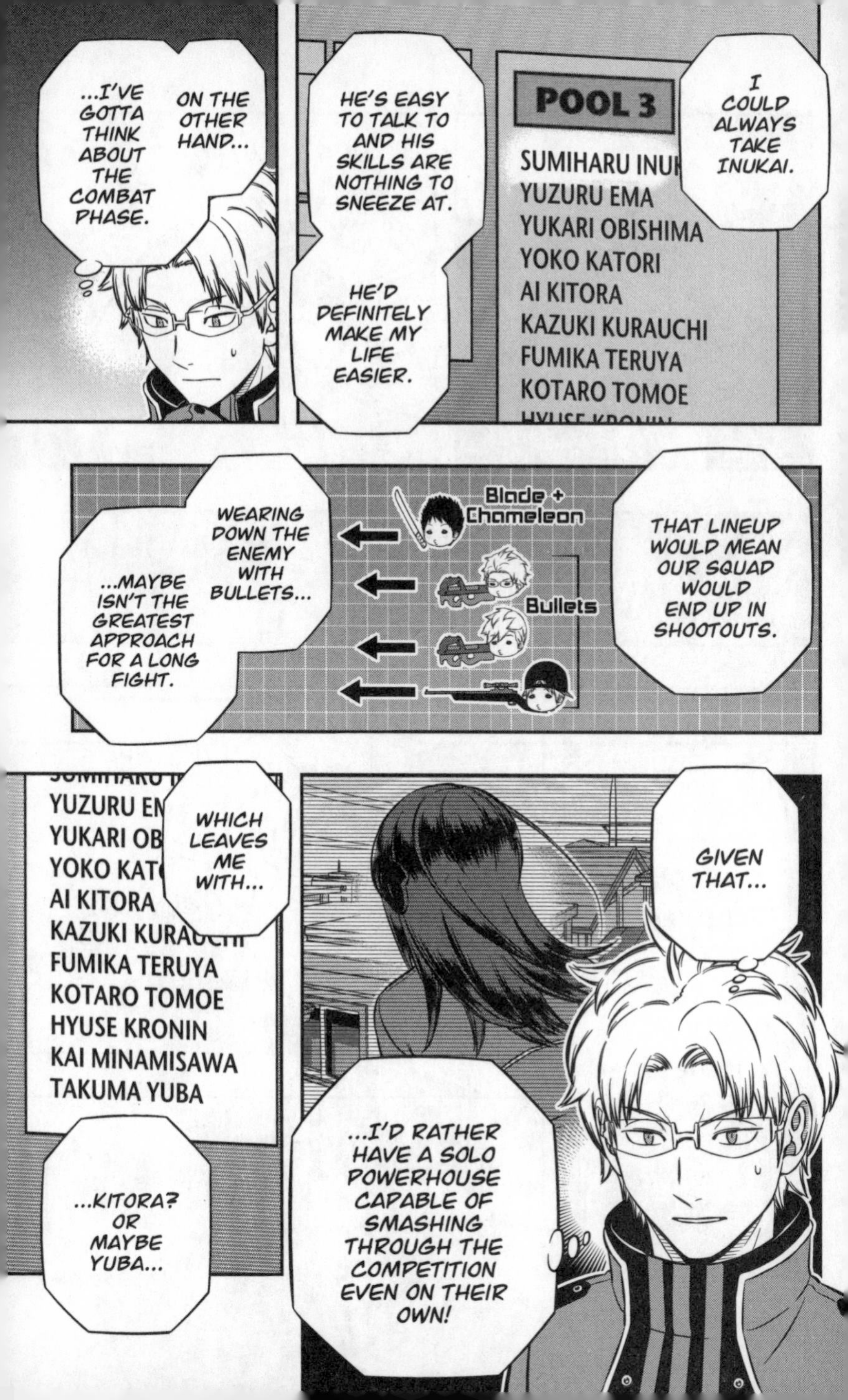
I COULD ALWAYS TAKE INUKAI.
POOL 3
SUMIHARU INUK
YUZURU EMA
YUKARI OBISHIMA
YOKO KATORI
AI KITORA
KAZUKI KURAUCHI
FUMIKA TERUYA
KOTARO TOMOE
HE'S EASY TO TALK TO AND HIS SKILLS ARE NOTHING TO SNEEZE AT.
HE'D DEFINITELY MAKE MY LIFE EASIER.
ON THE OTHER HAND...
...I'VE GOTTA THINK ABOUT THE COMBAT PHASE.
THAT LINEUP WOULD MEAN OUR SQUAD WOULD END UP IN SHOOTOUTS.
Blade + Chameleon
Bullets
WEARING DOWN THE ENEMY WITH BULLETS...
...MAYBE ISN'T THE GREATEST APPROACH FOR A LONG FIGHT.
GIVEN THAT...
...I'D RATHER HAVE A SOLO POWERHOUSE CAPABLE OF SMASHING THROUGH THE COMPETITION EVEN ON THEIR OWN!
AI KITORA
FUMIKA TERUYA
KOTARO TOMOE
HYUSE KRONIN
KAI MINAMISAWA
TAKUMA YUBA
WHICH LEAVES ME WITH...
...KITORA? OR MAYBE YUBA...

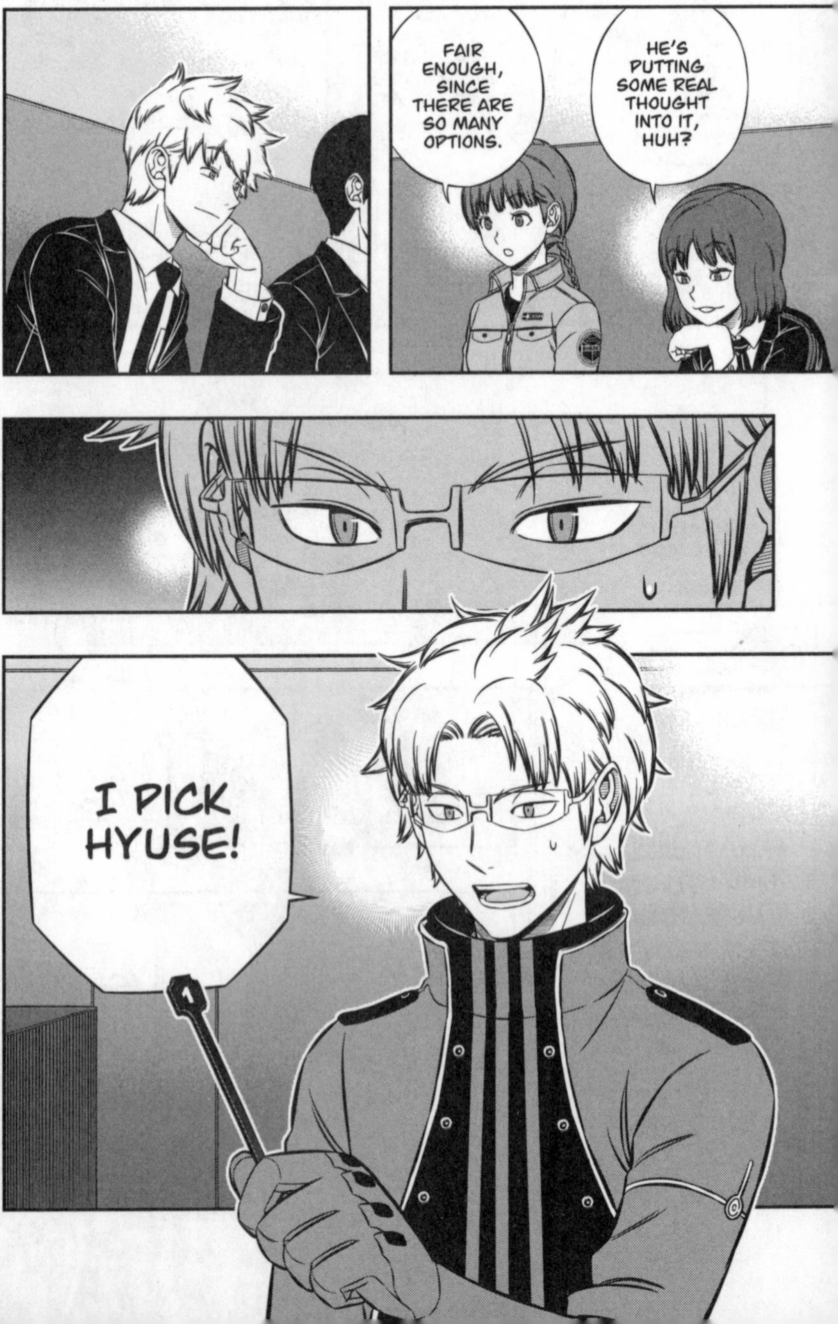
HE'S PUTTING SOME REAL THOUGHT INTO IT, HUH?
FAIR ENOUGH, SINCE THERE ARE SO MANY OPTIONS.
I PICK HYUSE!

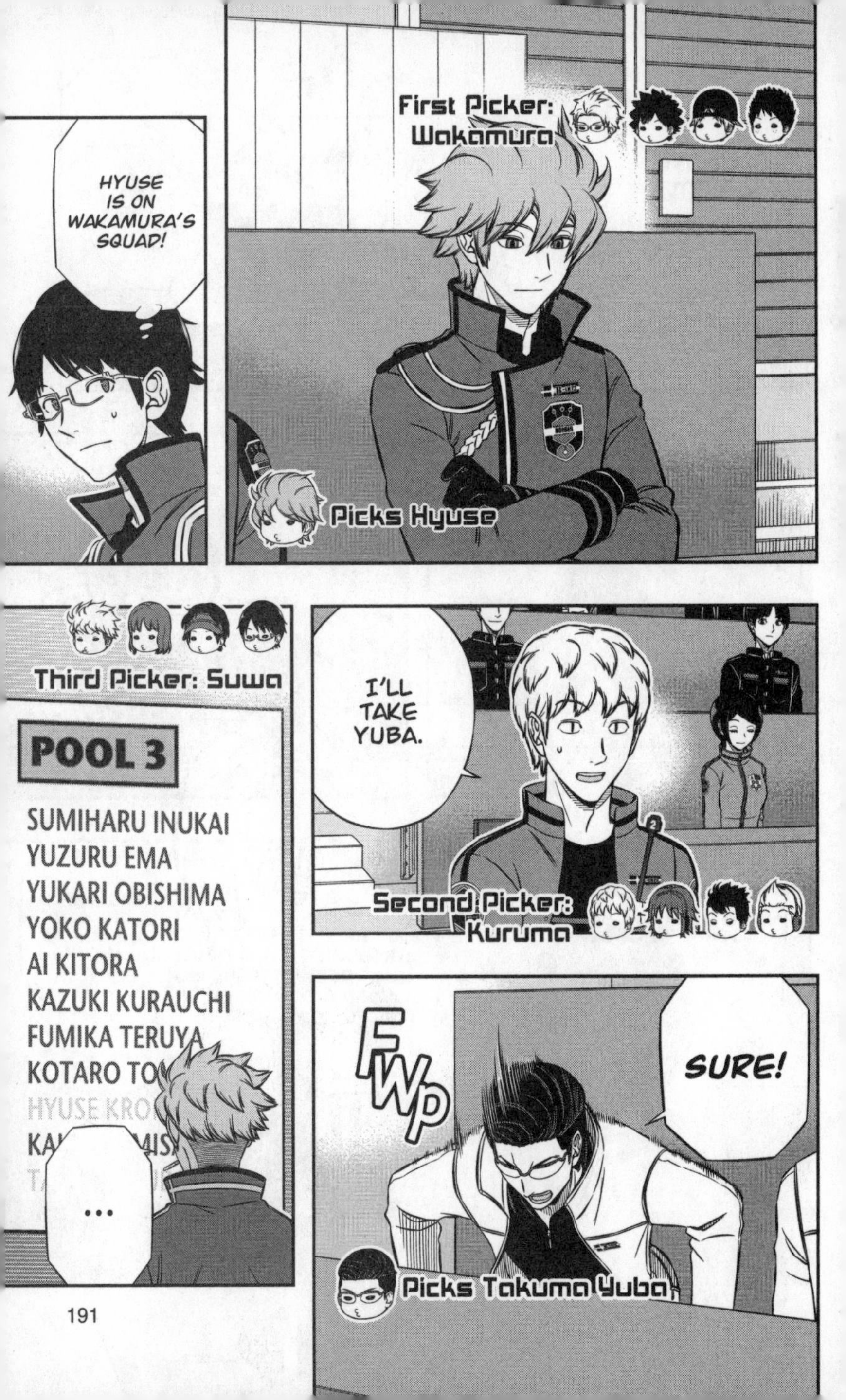
First Picker: Wakamura
Picks Hyuse
HYUSE IS ON WAKAMURA'S SQUAD!
I'LL TAKE YUBA.
Second Picker: Kuruma
SURE!
FWP
Picks Takuma Yuba
Third Picker: Suwa
POOL 3
SUMIHARU INUKAI
YUZURU EMA
YUKARI OBISHIMA
YOKO KATORI
AI KITORA
KAZUKI KURAUCHI
FUMIKA TERUYA
KOTARO TO
HYUSE KRO
...

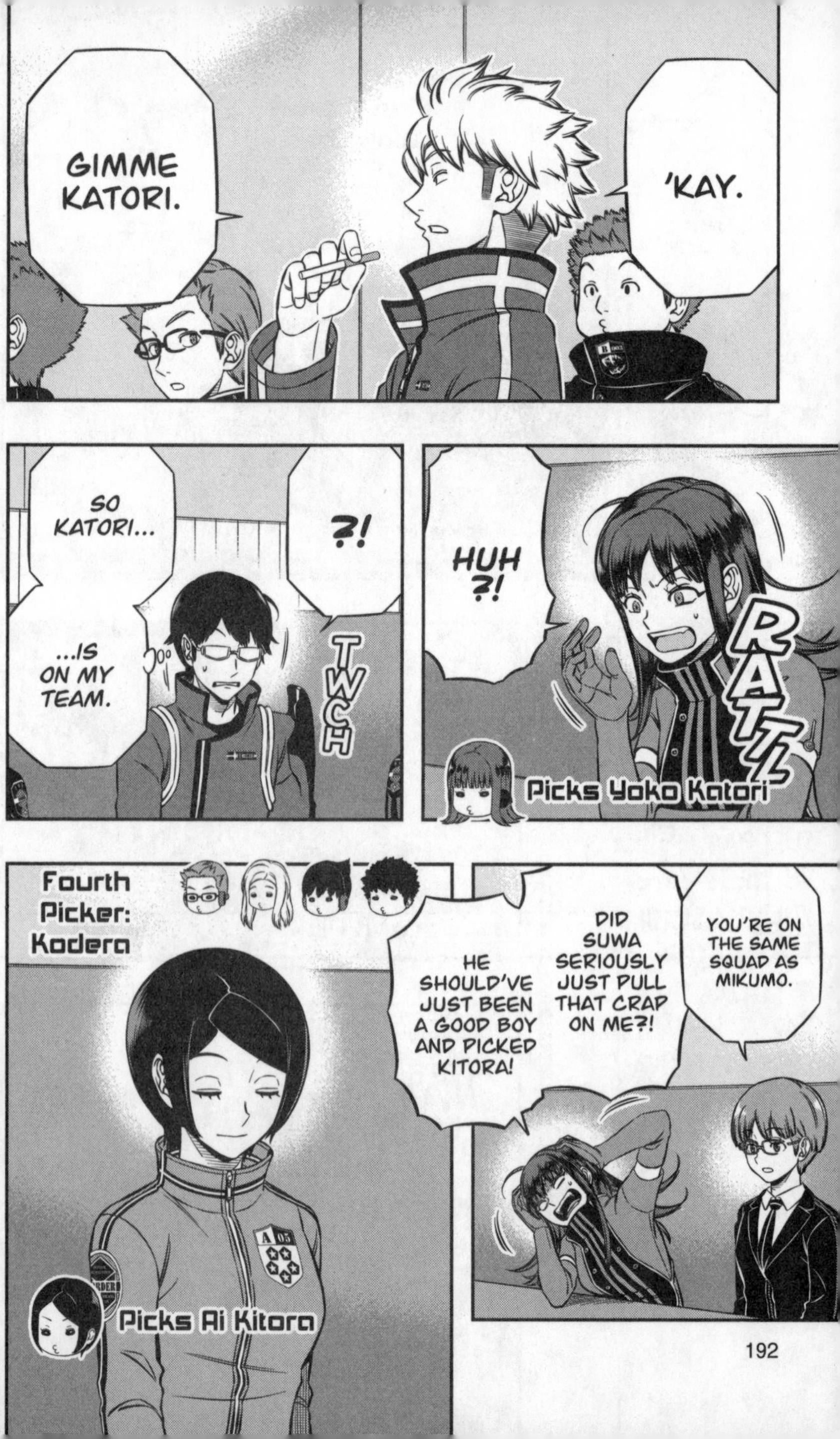
'KAY.
GIMME KATORI.
HUH ?!
RATTL
Picks Yoko Katori
?!
SO KATORI...
...IS ON MY TEAM.
TWCH
YOU'RE ON THE SAME SQUAD AS MIKUMO.
DID SUWA SERIOUSLY JUST PULL THAT CRAP ON ME?!
HE SHOULD'VE JUST BEEN A GOOD BOY AND PICKED KITORA!
Fourth Picker: Kodera
Picks Ai Kitora

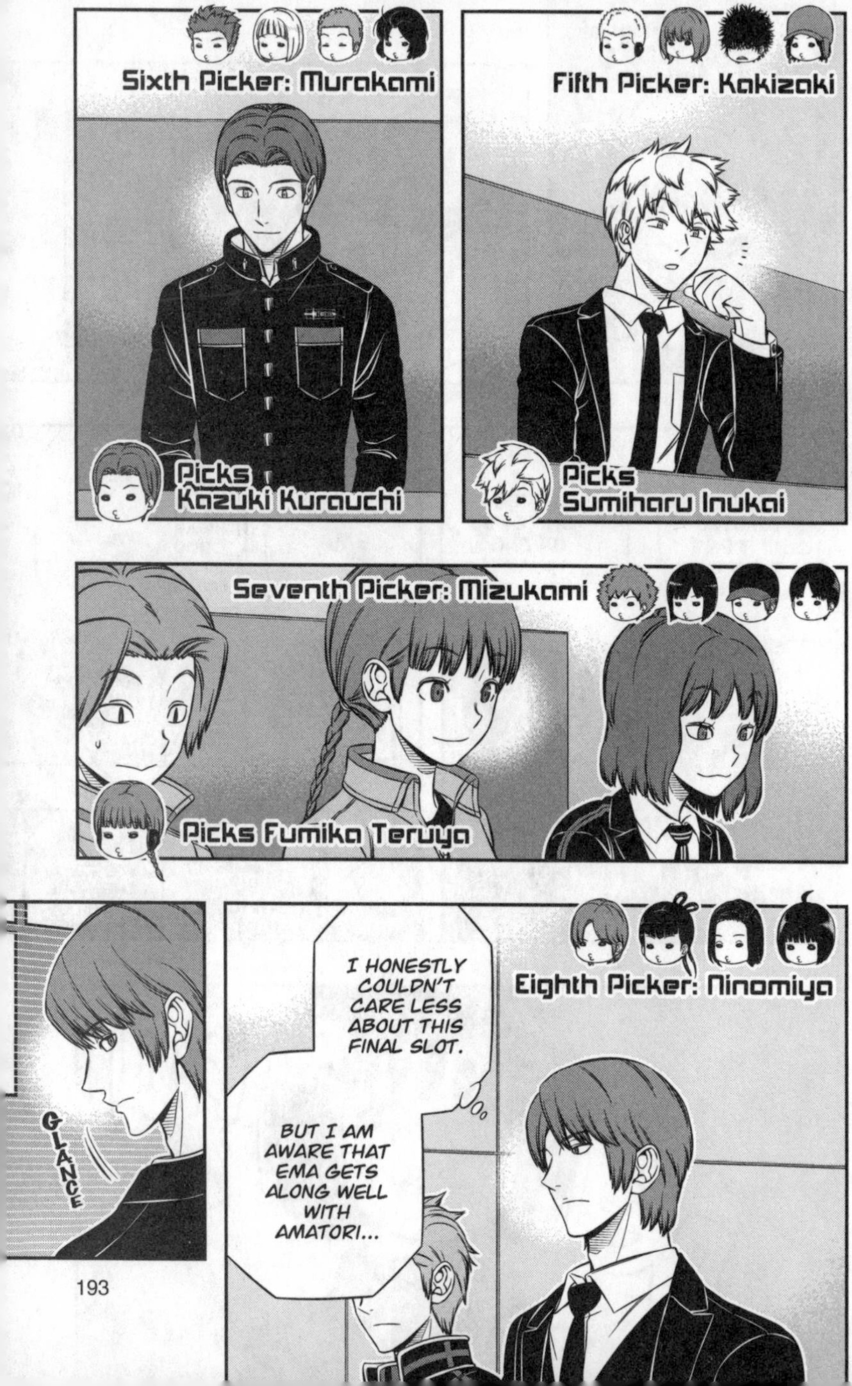
Fifth Picker: Kakizaki
Picks Sumiharu Inukai
Sixth Picker: Murakami
Picks Kazuki Kurauchi
Seventh Picker: Mizukami
Picks Fumika Teruya
Eighth Picker: Ninomiya
I HONESTLY COULDN'T CARE LESS ABOUT THIS FINAL SLOT.
BUT I AM AWARE THAT EMA GETS ALONG WELL WITH AMATORI...
GLANCE

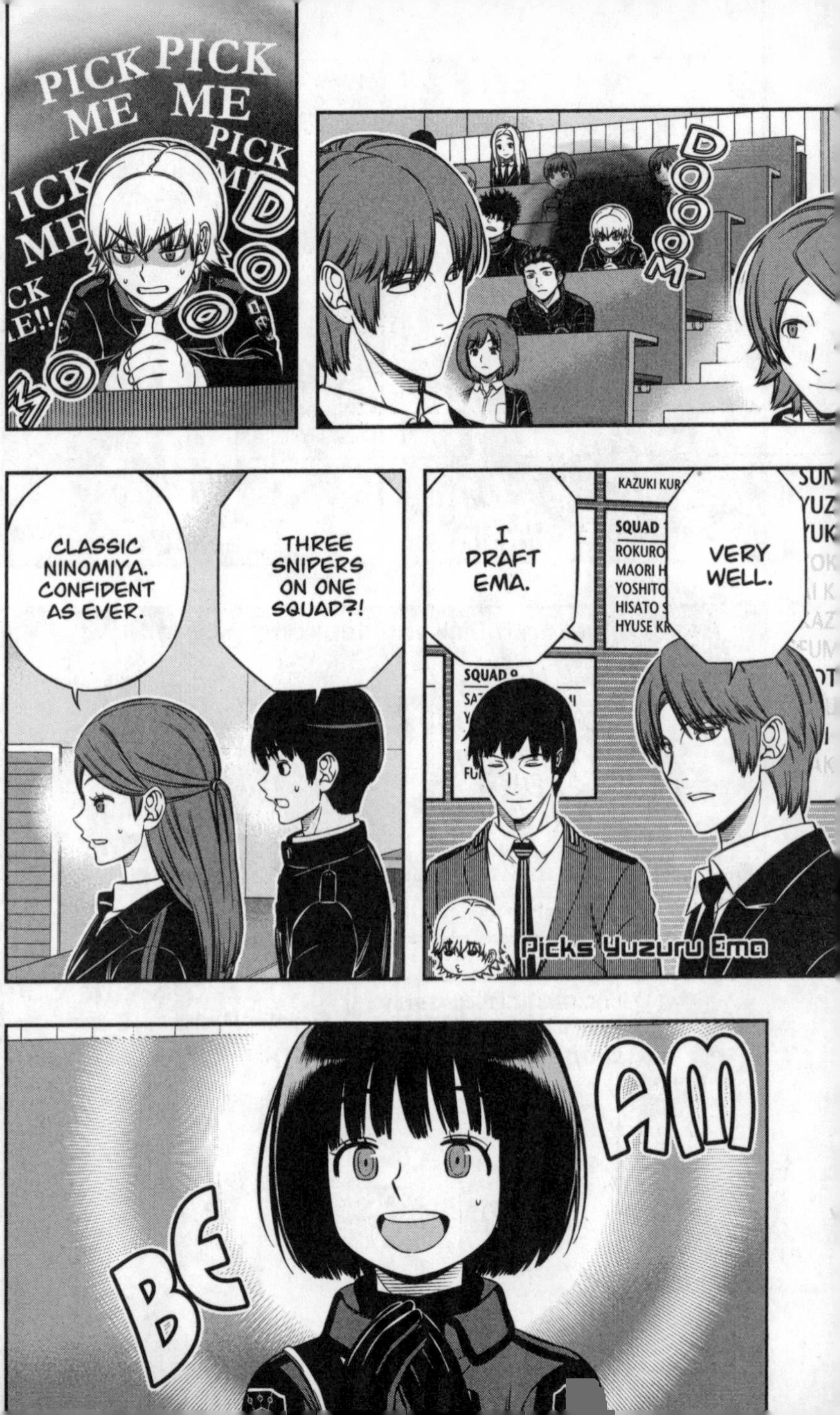
DOOOOM
PICK ME
PICK ME
PICK ME
PICK ME
PICK ME!!
DOOOOM
VERY WELL.
I DRAFT EMA.
SQUAD 1
SQUAD 9
Picks Yuzuru Ema
THREE SNIPERS ON ONE SQUAD?!
CLASSIC NINOMIYA. CONFIDENT AS EVER.
BEAM

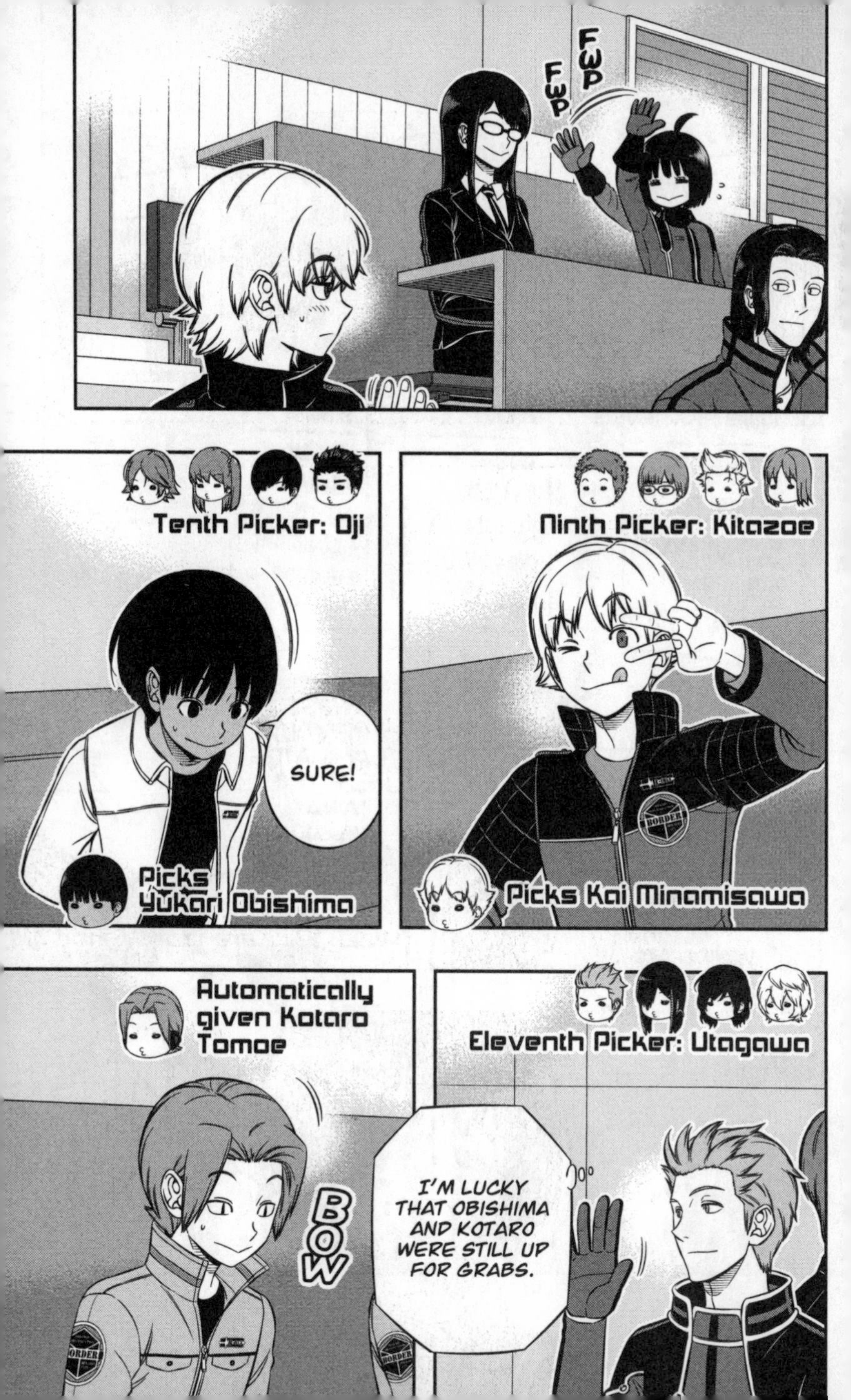
FWP
FWP
Ninth Picker: Kitazoe
Picks Kai Minamisawa
Tenth Picker: Oji
SURE!
Picks Yukari Obishima
Eleventh Picker: Utagawa
I'M LUCKY THAT OBISHIMA AND KOTARO WERE STILL UP FOR GRABS.
Automatically given Kotaro Tomoe
BOW

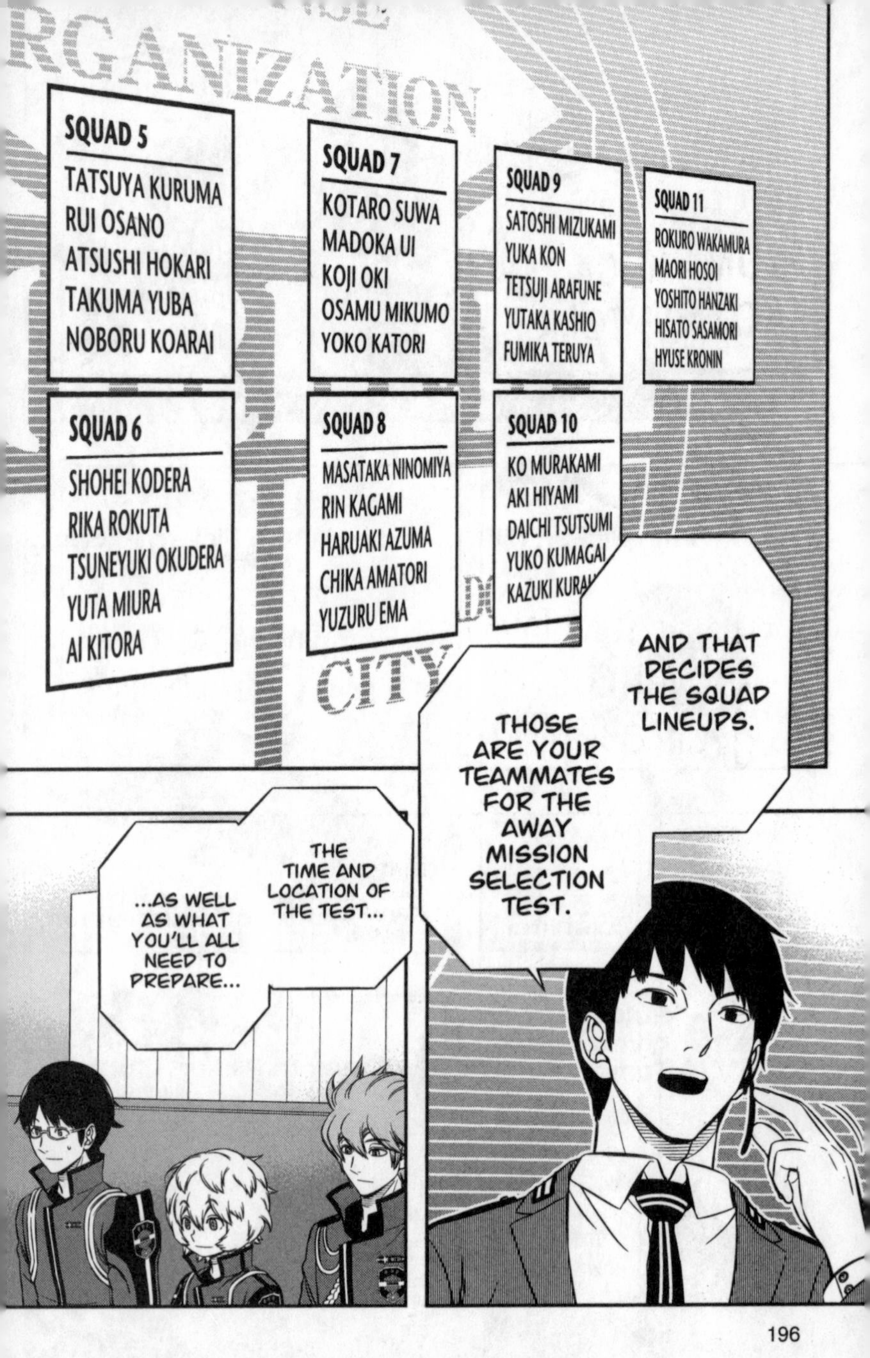
RGANIZATION
SQUAD 5
TATSUYA KURUMA
RUI OSANO
ATSUSHI HOKARI
TAKUMA YUBA
NOBORU KOARAI
SQUAD 7
KOTARO SUWA
MADOKA UI
KOJI OKI
OSAMU MIKUMO
YOKO KATORI
SQUAD 9
SATOSHI MIZUKAMI
YUKA KON
TETSUJI ARAFUNE
YUTAKA KASHIO
FUMIKA TERUYA
SQUAD 11
ROKURO WAKAMURA
MAORI HOSOI
YOSHITO HANZAKI
HISATO SASAMORI
HYUSE KRONIN
SQUAD 6
SHOHEI KODERA
RIKA ROKUTA
TSUNEYUKI OKUDERA
YUTA MIURA
AI KITORA
SQUAD 8
MASATAKA NINOMIYA
RIN KAGAMI
HARUAKI AZUMA
CHIKA AMATORI
YUZURU EMA
SQUAD 10
KO MURAKAMI
AKI HIYAMI
DAICHI TSUTSUMI
YUKO KUMAGAI
KAZUKI KURA
CITY
AND THAT DECIDES THE SQUAD LINEUPS.
THOSE ARE YOUR TEAMMATES FOR THE AWAY MISSION SELECTION TEST.
THE TIME AND LOCATION OF THE TEST...
...AS WELL AS WHAT YOU'LL ALL NEED TO PREPARE...

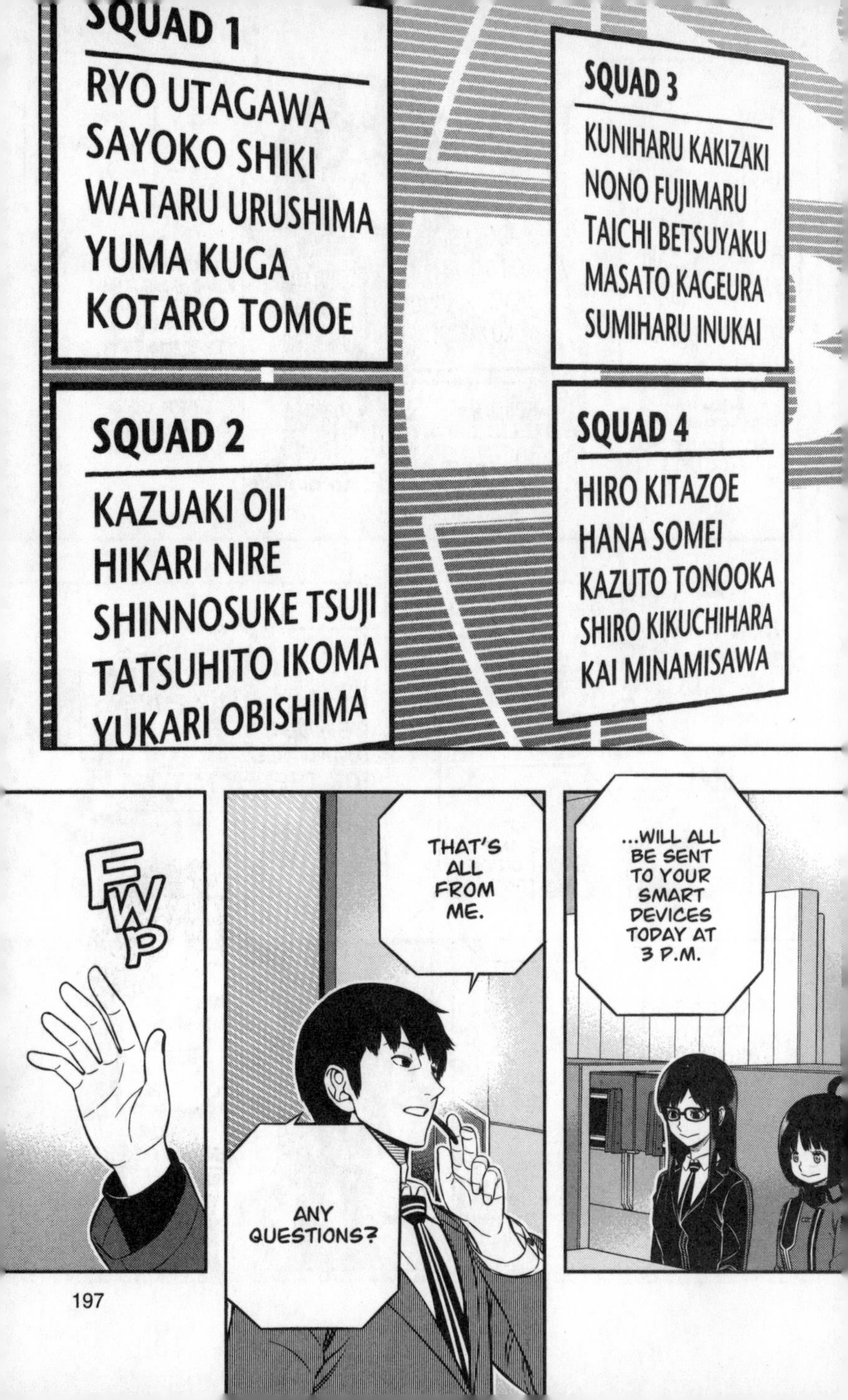
SQUAD 1
RYO UTAGAWA
SAYOKO SHIKI
WATARU URUSHIMA
YUMA KUGA
KOTARO TOMOE
SQUAD 2
KAZUAKI OJI
HIKARI NIRE
SHINNOSUKE TSUJI
TATSUHITO IKOMA
YUKARI OBISHIMA
SQUAD 3
KUNIHARU KAKIZAKI
NONO FUJIMARU
TAICHI BETSUYAKU
MASATO KAGEURA
SUMIHARU INUKAI
SQUAD 4
HIRO KITAZOE
HANA SOMEI
KAZUTO TONOOKA
SHIRO KIKUCHIHARA
KAI MINAMISAWA
...WILL ALL BE SENT TO YOUR SMART DEVICES TODAY AT 3 P.M.
THAT'S ALL FROM ME.
ANY QUESTIONS?
FWP

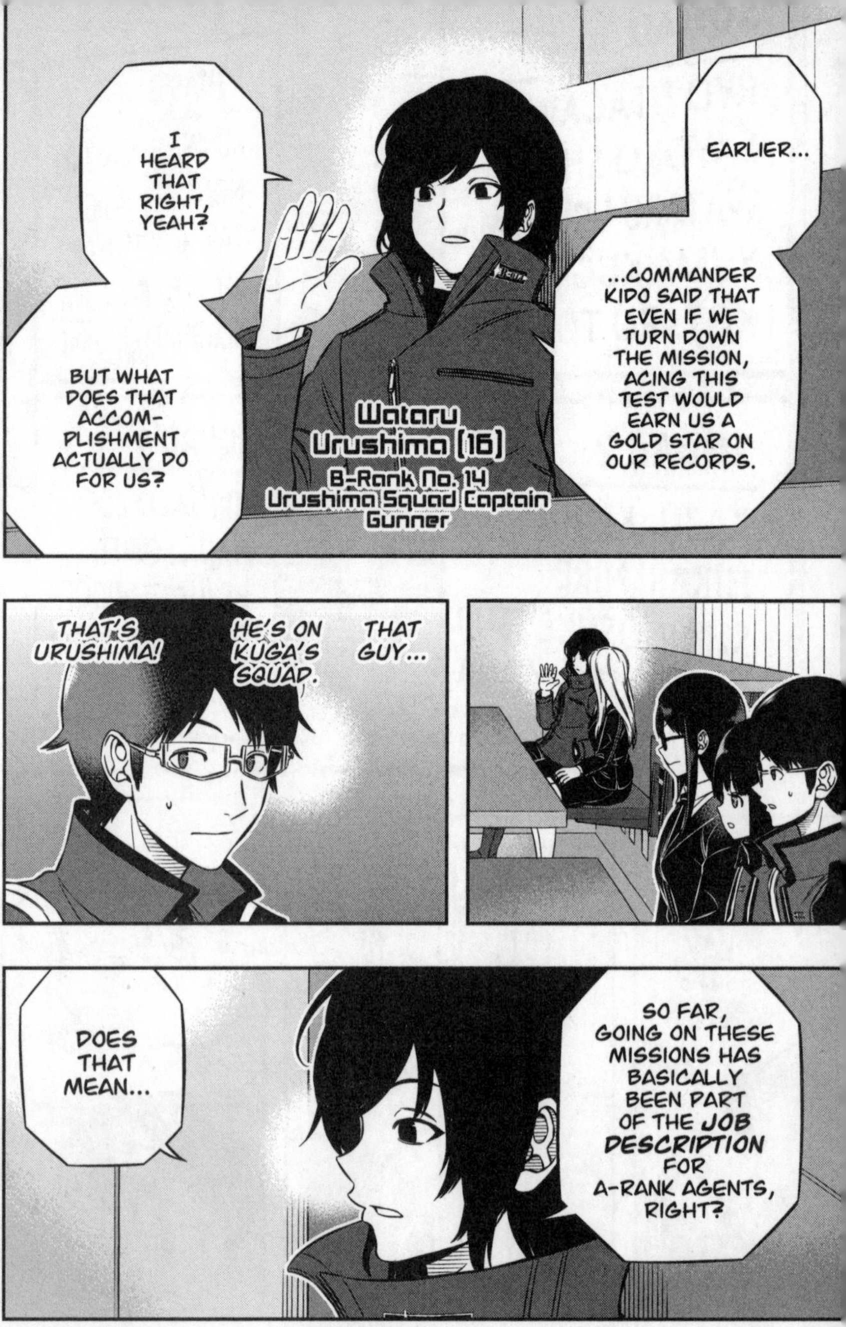
EARLIER...
...COMMANDER KIDO SAID THAT EVEN IF WE TURN DOWN THE MISSION, ACING THIS TEST WOULD EARN US A GOLD STAR ON OUR RECORDS.
Wataru Urushima (16)
B-Rank No. 14 Urushima Squad Captain Gunner
I HEARD THAT RIGHT, YEAH?
BUT WHAT DOES THAT ACCOM-PLISHMENT ACTUALLY DO FOR US?
THAT GUY...
HE'S ON KUGA'S SQUAD.
THAT'S URUSHIMA!
SO FAR, GOING ON THESE MISSIONS HAS BASICALLY BEEN PART OF THE JOB DESCRIPTION FOR A-RANK AGENTS, RIGHT?
DOES THAT MEAN...

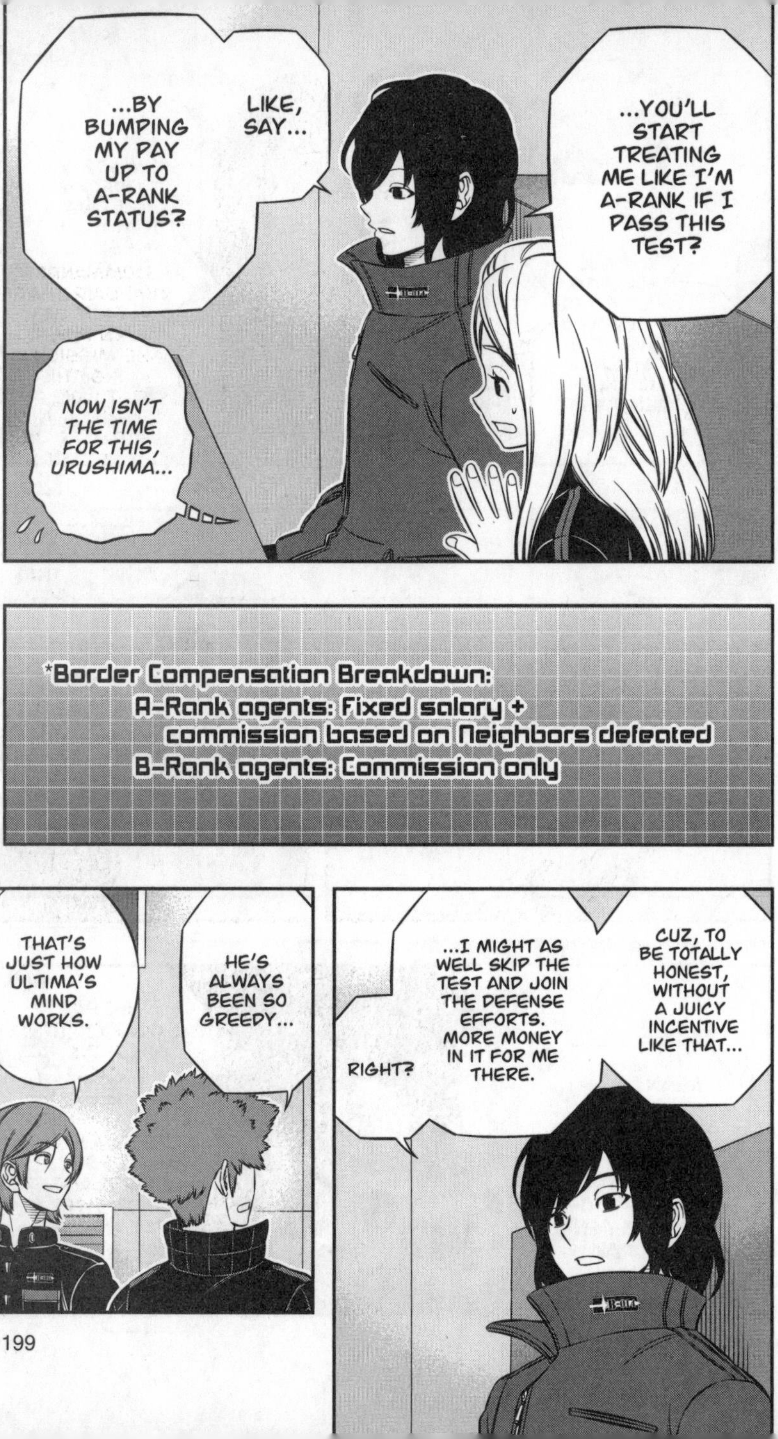
...YOU'LL START TREATING ME LIKE I'M A-RANK IF I PASS THIS TEST?
LIKE, SAY...
...BY BUMPING MY PAY UP TO A-RANK STATUS?
NOW ISN'T THE TIME FOR THIS, URUSHIMA...
*Border Compensation Breakdown:
A-Rank agents: Fixed salary + commission based on Neighbors defeated
B-Rank agents: Commission only
CUZ, TO BE TOTALLY HONEST, WITHOUT A JUICY INCENTIVE LIKE THAT...
...I MIGHT AS WELL SKIP THE TEST AND JOIN THE DEFENSE EFFORTS. MORE MONEY IN IT FOR ME THERE.
RIGHT?
HE'S ALWAYS BEEN SO GREEDY...
THAT'S JUST HOW ULTIMA'S MIND WORKS.

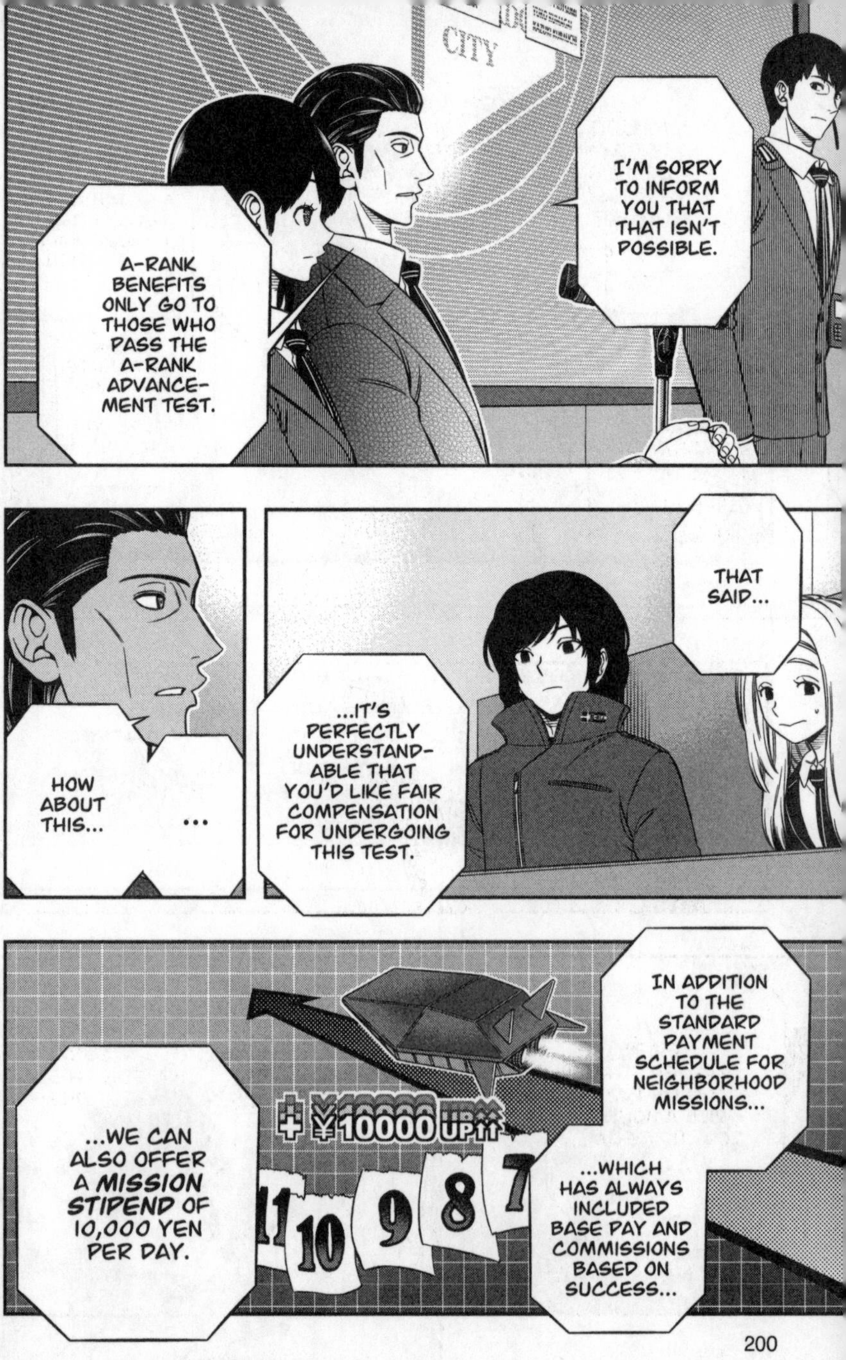
I'M SORRY TO INFORM YOU THAT THAT ISN'T POSSIBLE.
A-RANK BENEFITS ONLY GO TO THOSE WHO PASS THE A-RANK ADVANCEMENT TEST.
THAT SAID...
...IT'S PERFECTLY UNDERSTANDABLE THAT YOU'D LIKE FAIR COMPENSATION FOR UNDERGOING THIS TEST.
...
HOW ABOUT THIS...
IN ADDITION TO THE STANDARD PAYMENT SCHEDULE FOR NEIGHBORHOOD MISSIONS...
...WHICH HAS ALWAYS INCLUDED BASE PAY AND COMMISSIONS BASED ON SUCCESS...
+ ¥10000 UP
...WE CAN ALSO OFFER A *MISSION STIPEND* OF 10,000 YEN PER DAY.

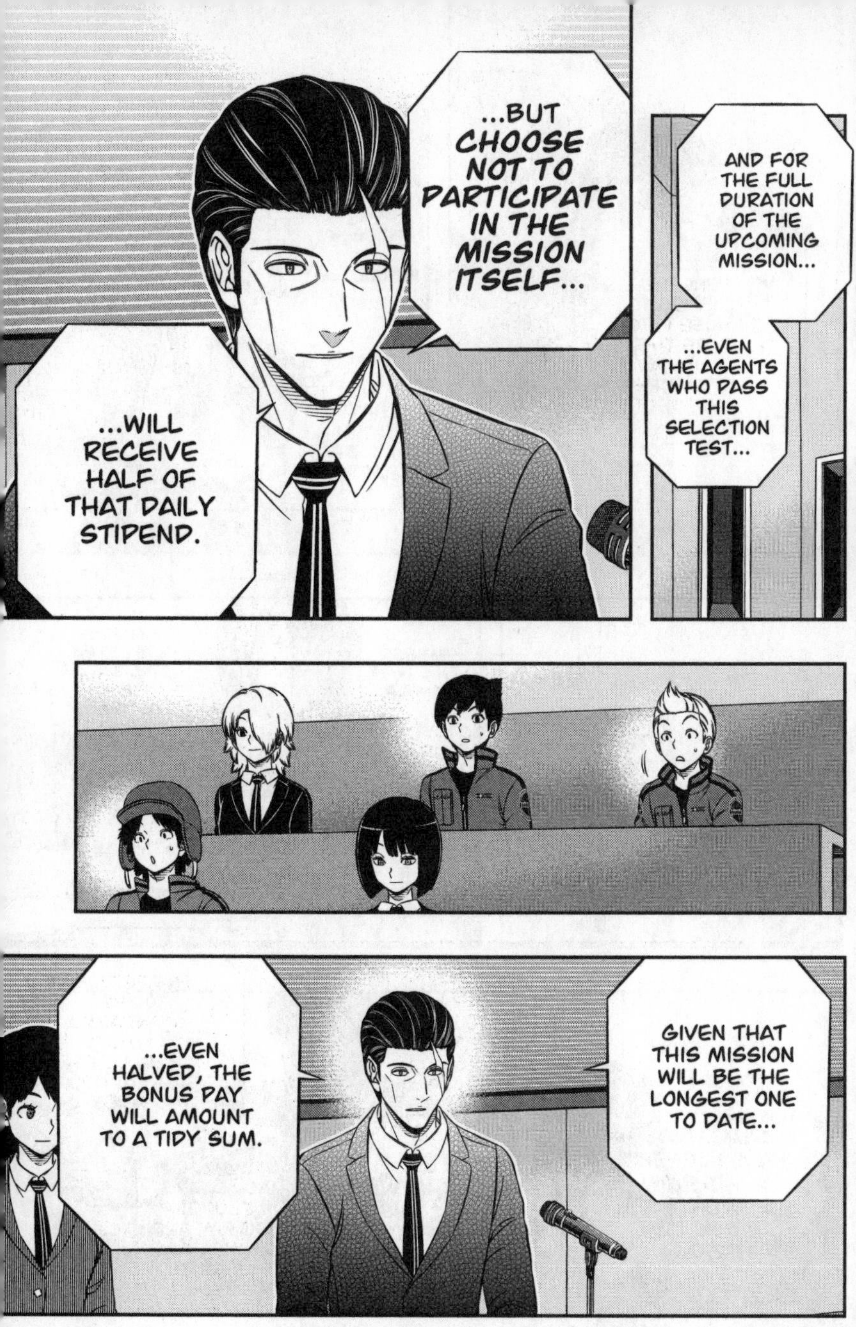
AND FOR THE FULL DURATION OF THE UPCOMING MISSION...
...EVEN THE AGENTS WHO PASS THIS SELECTION TEST...
...BUT CHOOSE NOT TO PARTICIPATE IN THE MISSION ITSELF...
...WILL RECEIVE HALF OF THAT DAILY STIPEND.
GIVEN THAT THIS MISSION WILL BE THE LONGEST ONE TO DATE...
...EVEN HALVED, THE BONUS PAY WILL AMOUNT TO A TIDY SUM.

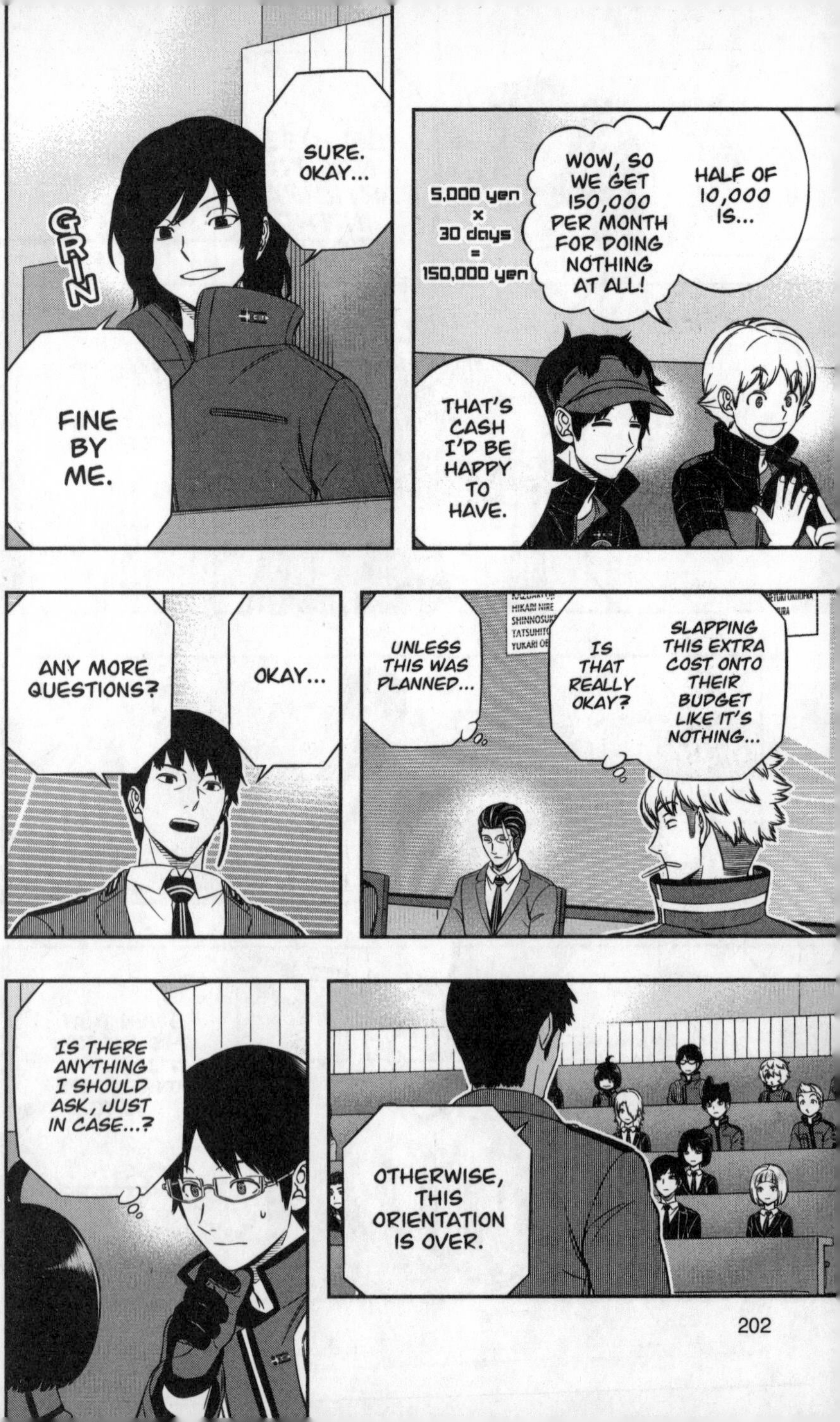
HALF OF 10,000 IS...
WOW, SO WE GET 150,000 PER MONTH FOR DOING NOTHING AT ALL!
5,000 yen x 30 days = 150,000 yen
THAT'S CASH I'D BE HAPPY TO HAVE.
SURE. OKAY...
GRIN
FINE BY ME.
SLAPPING THIS EXTRA COST ONTO THEIR BUDGET LIKE IT'S NOTHING...
IS THAT REALLY OKAY?
UNLESS THIS WAS PLANNED...
OKAY...
ANY MORE QUESTIONS?
OTHERWISE, THIS ORIENTATION IS OVER.
IS THERE ANYTHING I SHOULD ASK, JUST IN CASE...?

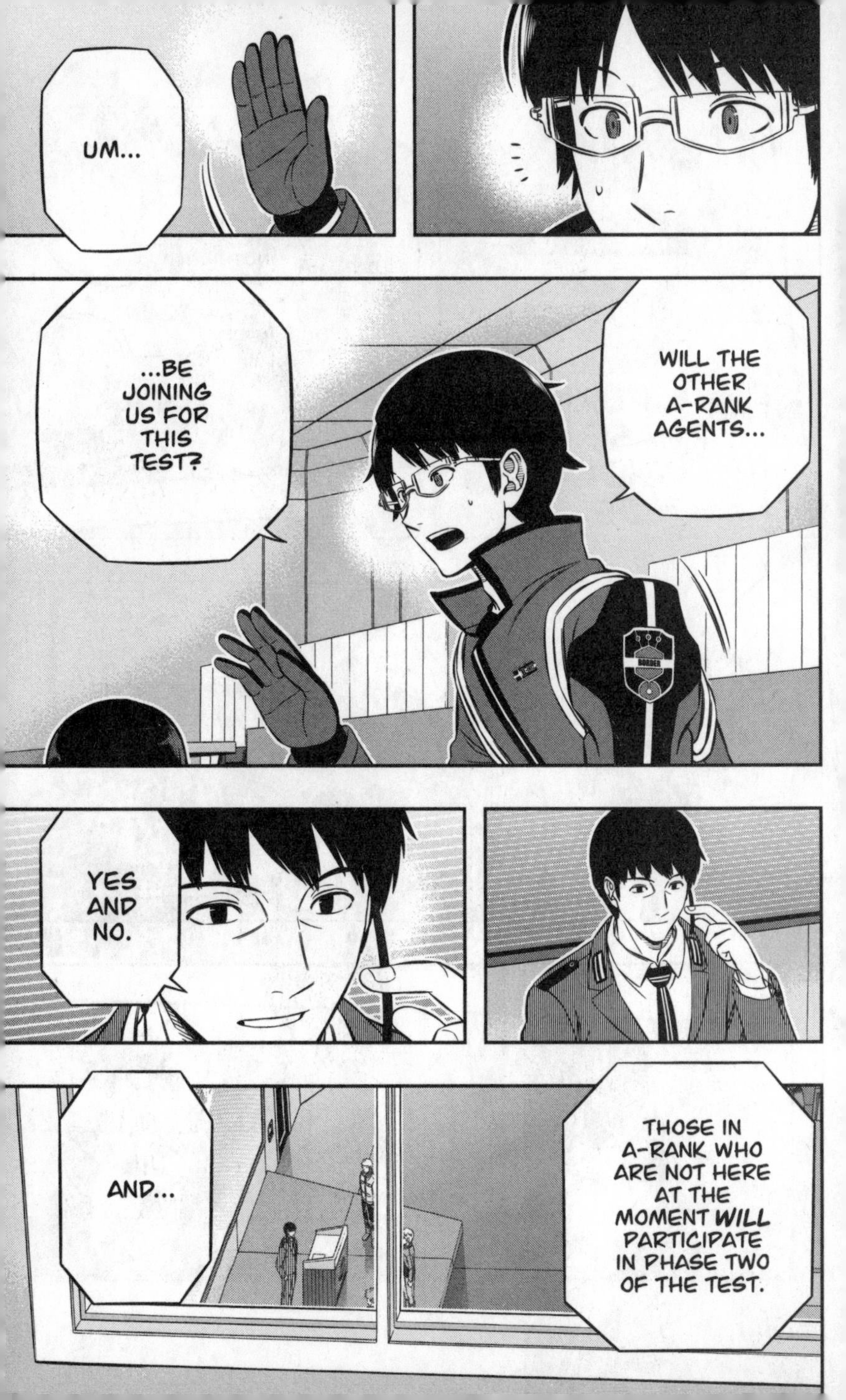
UM...
WILL THE OTHER A-RANK AGENTS...
...BE JOINING US FOR THIS TEST?
YES AND NO.
THOSE IN A-RANK WHO ARE NOT HERE AT THE MOMENT **WILL** PARTICIPATE IN PHASE TWO OF THE TEST.
AND...

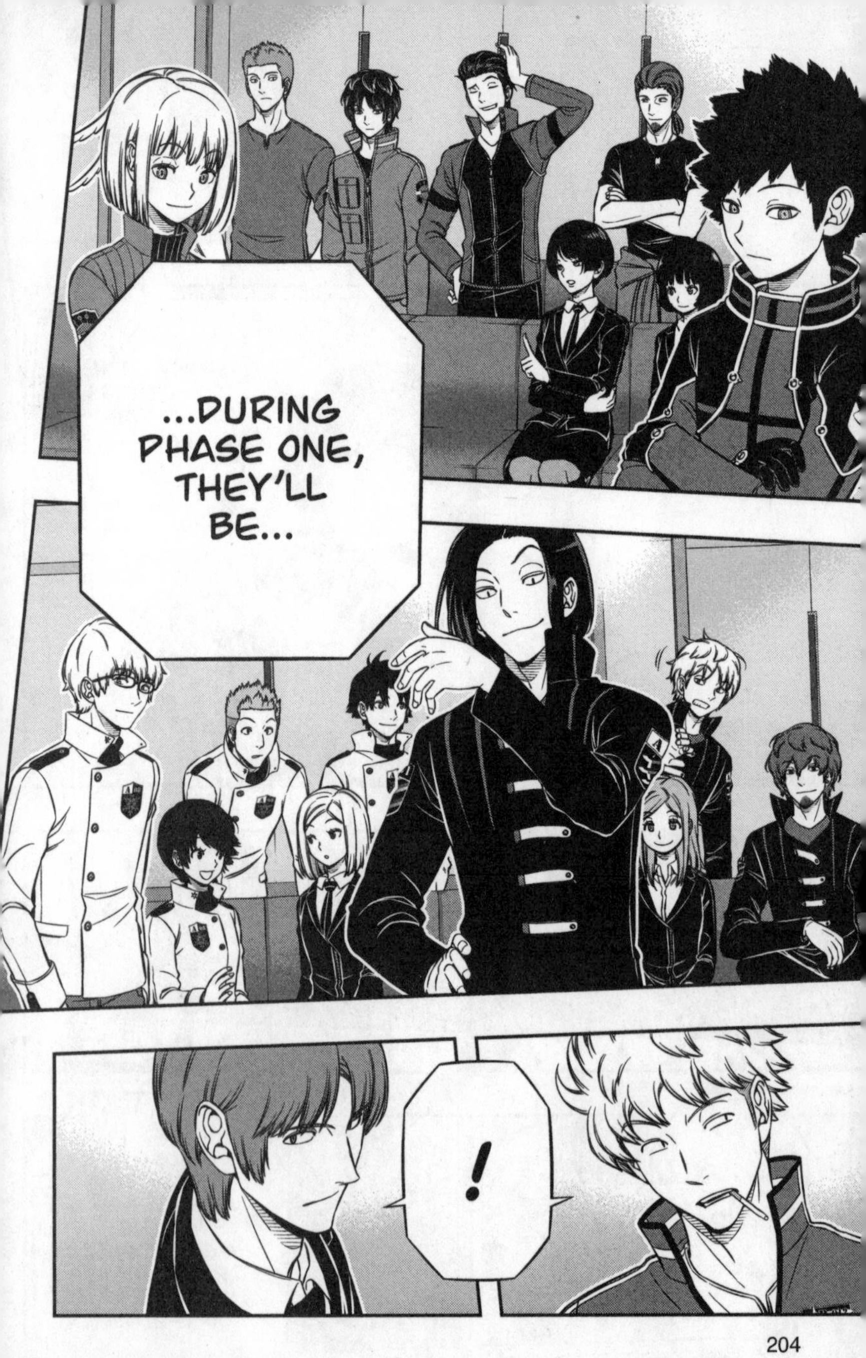
...DURING PHASE ONE, THEY'LL BE...
!

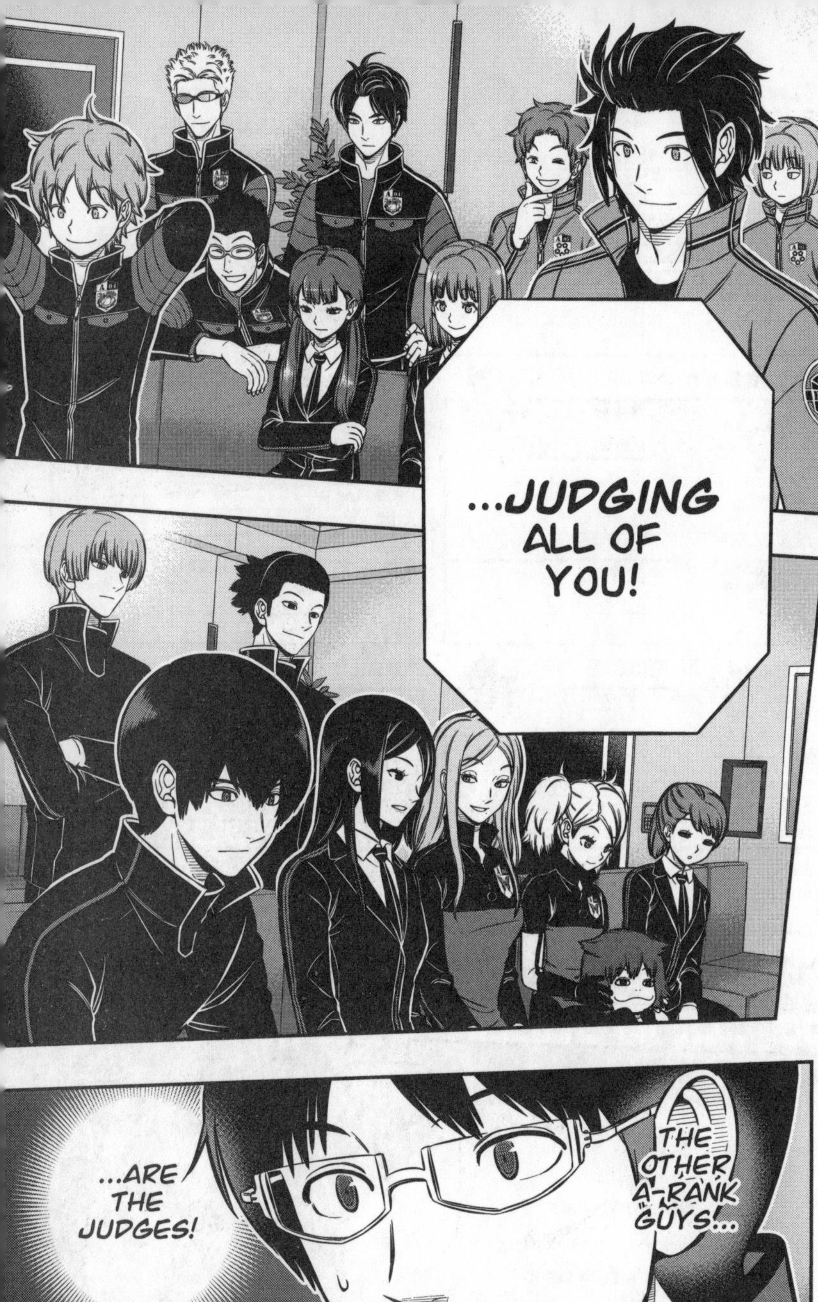
...JUDGING ALL OF YOU!
THE OTHER A-RANK GUYS...
...ARE THE JUDGES!

End of Volume Bonus Content

The much-demanded... Provisional Captains' Survey Answers Reveal

Squad 1: Ryo Utagawa

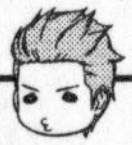

Who would you prefer to work with?	Reason
Shiori Usami	Excellent abilities/personality
Shohei Kodera	Diligent, trustworthy
Yukimaru Ichijo	Unique sense of freedom
Kazuto Tonooka	Naturally calm, highly focused
Kuniharu Kakizaki	Highly responsible, can be relied upon
Who would you prefer not to work with?	**Reason**
N/A	

Squad 2: Kazuaki Oji

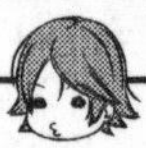

Who would you prefer to work with?	Reason
Tatsuhito Ikoma	Fun
Nozomi Kako	Fun
Ryuji Saeki	Fun
Hyuse Kronin	Seems fun
Chika Amatori	Legendary Trion levels
Who would you prefer not to work with?	**Reason**
Shuji Miwa	Impervious to my jokes

Squad 3: Kuniharu Kakizaki

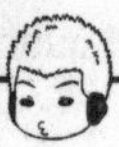

Who would you prefer to work with?	Reason
Takuma Yuba	Good guy, reliable
Tatsuhito Ikoma	Fun, reliable
Haruaki Azuma	Great leader
An Kobayakawa	Good personality, reliable
Takaaki Katagiri	Levelheaded, reliable
Who would you prefer not to work with?	**Reason**
N/A	

Squad 4: Hiro Kitazoe

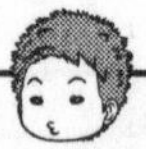

Who would you prefer to work with?	Reason
Tatsuya Kuruma	b/c I respect him
Yuka Kon	b/c she's smart and reliable
Kotaro Suwa	b/c he's a solid leader
Yuma Kuga	Strong and a fun kid
Kazuaki Oji	Notices things others don't
Who would you prefer not to work with?	**Reason**
Risa Maki	b/c she gets mad at me

Squad 5: Tatsuya Kuruma

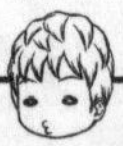

Who would you prefer to work with?	Reason
Haruaki Azuma	b/c he's levelheaded with a broad outlook
Daichi Tsutsumi	Gentle, quick thinker
Rokuro Wakamura	b/c good common sense, hard worker
Hikari Nire	b/c cheery, looks after others
Shinnosuke Tsuji	b/c serious, good at picking up slack
Who would you prefer not to work with?	**Reason**
N/A	

be out in Japan Autumn 2021!!

STAFF

Author:
Daisuke Ashihara

Manager/Art Assistant:
Koma

Squad 6: Shohei Kodera

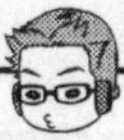

Who would you prefer to work with?	Reason
Haruaki Azuma	Good commander
Shiori Usami	Excellent skills and personality
Yoshito Hanzaki	Technical skills, tenacious
Hana Somei	Calm, intelligent
Soya Kazama	Excellent burst power and judgment
Who would you prefer not to work with?	**Reason**
Masato Kageura	Side effect is tricky
Wataru Urushima	Not a team player

Squad 7: Kotaro Suwa

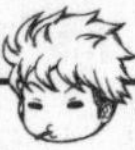

Who would you prefer to work with?	Reason
Haruaki Azuma	Top-choice mahjong player
Shiji Fuyushima	Second-choice mahjong player
Kuniharu Kakizaki	Takes command, good personality
Yuma Kuga	Sharp as a tack, good personality
Kaho Mikami	Skilled, good personality
Who would you prefer not to work with?	**Reason**
Soya Kazama	Depressing, nasty personality
Saki Kusakabe	Saucy, nasty personality

Squad 8: Masataka Ninomiya

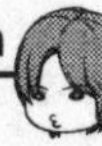

Who would you prefer to work with?	Reason
Haruaki Azuma	Good commander
Kohei Izumi	Good marksman
Ko Murakami	Good on defense, adaptable
Satoshi Mizukami	Good strategist
Ren Tsukimi	Excellent operator
Who would you prefer not to work with?	**Reason**
Nozomi Kako	Selfish
Kei Tachikawa	Unintelligent

Squad 9: Satoshi Mizukami

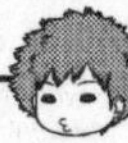

Who would you prefer to work with?	Reason
Hyuse Kronin	Seems strong and I could poke fun at him
Shiro Kikuchihara	Strong side effect
Yu Kunichika	Skilled, but can also goof off
Isami Toma	Skilled, but can also goof off
Kei Tachikawa	Skilled, but can also goof off
Who would you prefer not to work with?	**Reason**
Wataru Urushima	b/c bad personality
Ren Tsukimi	Seems scary, intense

Squad 6: Shohei Kodera

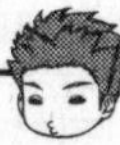

Who would you prefer to work with?	Reason
Tetsuji Arafune	Good consolidator, planner
Masato Kageura	Keen sense for things
Yuma Kuga	Inventive, adaptable
Kei Tachikawa	Strong, operates on a big scale
Hiro Kitazoe	Top-class firepower and personality
Who would you prefer not to work with?	**Reason**
Kotaro Tomoe	b/c I'd worry about him
Futaba Kuroe	b/c I'd worry about her

Squad 11: Rokuro Wakamura

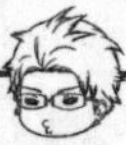

Who would you prefer to work with?	Reason
Sumiharu Inukai	Skilled, good communicator
Haruaki Azuma	Good supervisor, educator
Kazuma Satomi	Skilled, good communicator
Tatsuya Kuruma	Popular, reliable
Hiro Kitazoe	Skilled, good communicator
Who would you prefer not to work with?	**Reason**
Ai Kitora	Seems to think little of me
Risa Maki	Definitely thinks little of me

World Trigger Volume 24 will

Assistants:
Satoshi Watanabe
Haruto Nawashirowaza
Shingo Sasai
Daisuke Kakehi
Hiroi Horikoshi (Zodiac: Gladius)

Volume Editor:
Akihiro Katayama

Volume Designer:
Yuta Yuzawa

Third Magazine Release Editor:
Koji Yoshida

Fourth Magazine Release Editor:
Takuma Yui (Zodiac: Lupus)

WORLD TRIGGER

Bonus Character Pages

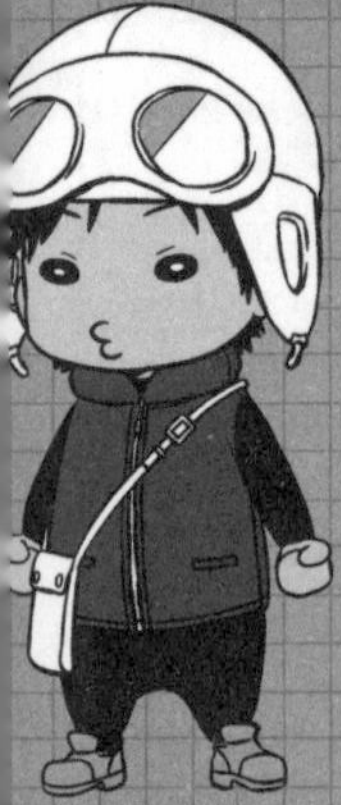

YOTARO

The Four-Eyes with Six Wounds

A boy whose true identity was revealed a mere 20 volumes after his debut. Upon seeing his sister for the first time in a few days, he immediately showed her a high-speed, three-dimensional acrobatics routine. More than any other scene in *World Trigger*, this scene made me think, "What the hell am I drawing here?" Ruka decided it'd be best to live separately from her little brother (and that worked out for the adults involved), but I have to wonder how Yotaro would've turned out if he'd been raised at HQ instead of Tamakoma Branch? How could you not wonder?

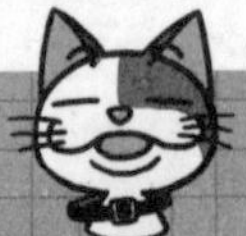

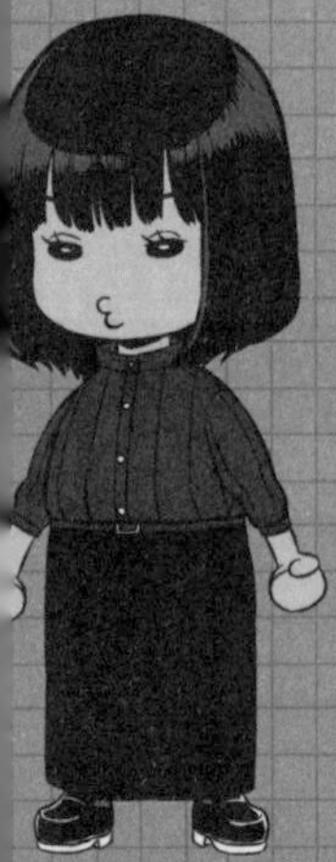

RUKA

Princess with Scorn in Her Eyes

The big sis who copped quite the attitude mere seconds after her debut in the story. Despite her being a key figure in the Border hierarchy, my own ineptitude kept her as a benchwarmer for basically forever. She's mostly confined to Border HQ, but she does go out shopping now and then with a bodyguard in tow. Perhaps Ruka's classy aura is what made Sawamura so awkward around Shinoda. At least until she was made assistant director. Is someone on the hunt for a hubby?

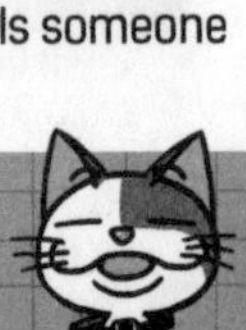

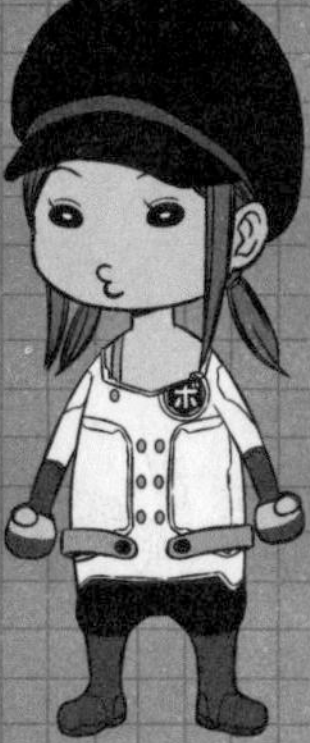

AKANE

Garduating from the Nasu 4

Her early retirement prompted discussion among the leadership team, but since this lover of fingerle gloves didn't know any top-level secrets, they didn see the need to wipe her memories. Everyone hop she's thriving in her new home, never forgetting her time with Nasu Squad. Her parting gift was basically a guarantee that Izuho (whose fate was y to be determined) will eventually make it onto Nas Squad. To the 107 of you out there in the "Put Izuho Fuyushima Squad" coalition, I say, "Move to a para world, because it ain't happening in this one."

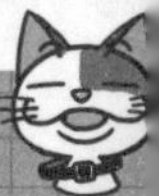

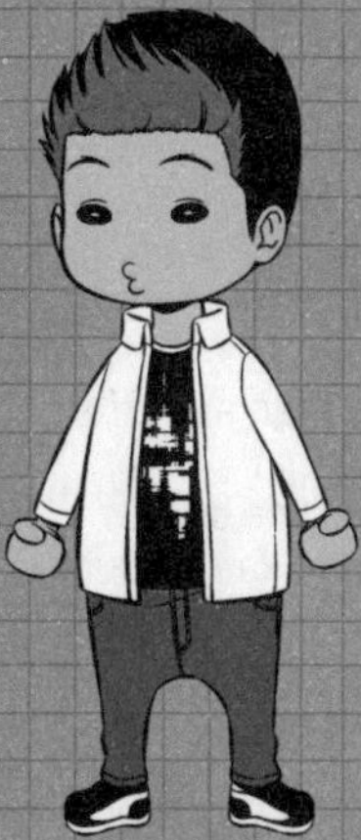

KANdATA

His First Appearance Is a Send-Off

For this former all-rounder of Yuba Squad, rumors are all that precede him. When he appeared in a flashback, I carelessly thought, "He probably won't show up again," and forgot to do something about his bangs, which led to an enigmatic hairstyle. He shows up later in the story eating Chinese food, which goes to show that even an author can't predict everything. He seems to be following in his dearly departed father's footsteps by becoming an architect. I wish him all the best.

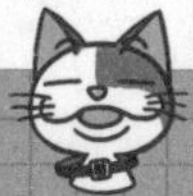

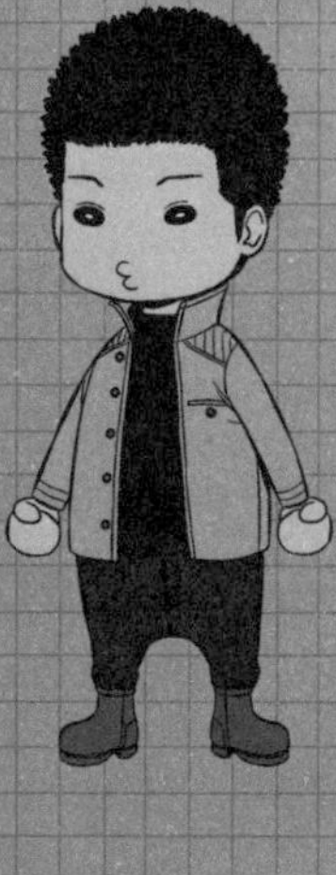

ORKAN

Crew Cut's True Identity

This royal crew cut guy was in disguise as a Japanese baseball-playing boy. It's been seven years since Galopoula High last made it to Koshi for nationals, but this shrewd guy is aiming for a second championship while managing to fool A at the same time. He thought he'd be negotiating with Jin, but somehow or other a certain four-ey joined the talks. Orkan wasn't impressed, but he was gracious enough not to let that show on his face. Expect exciting things from him.

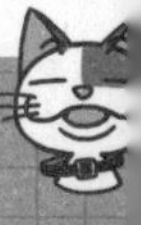

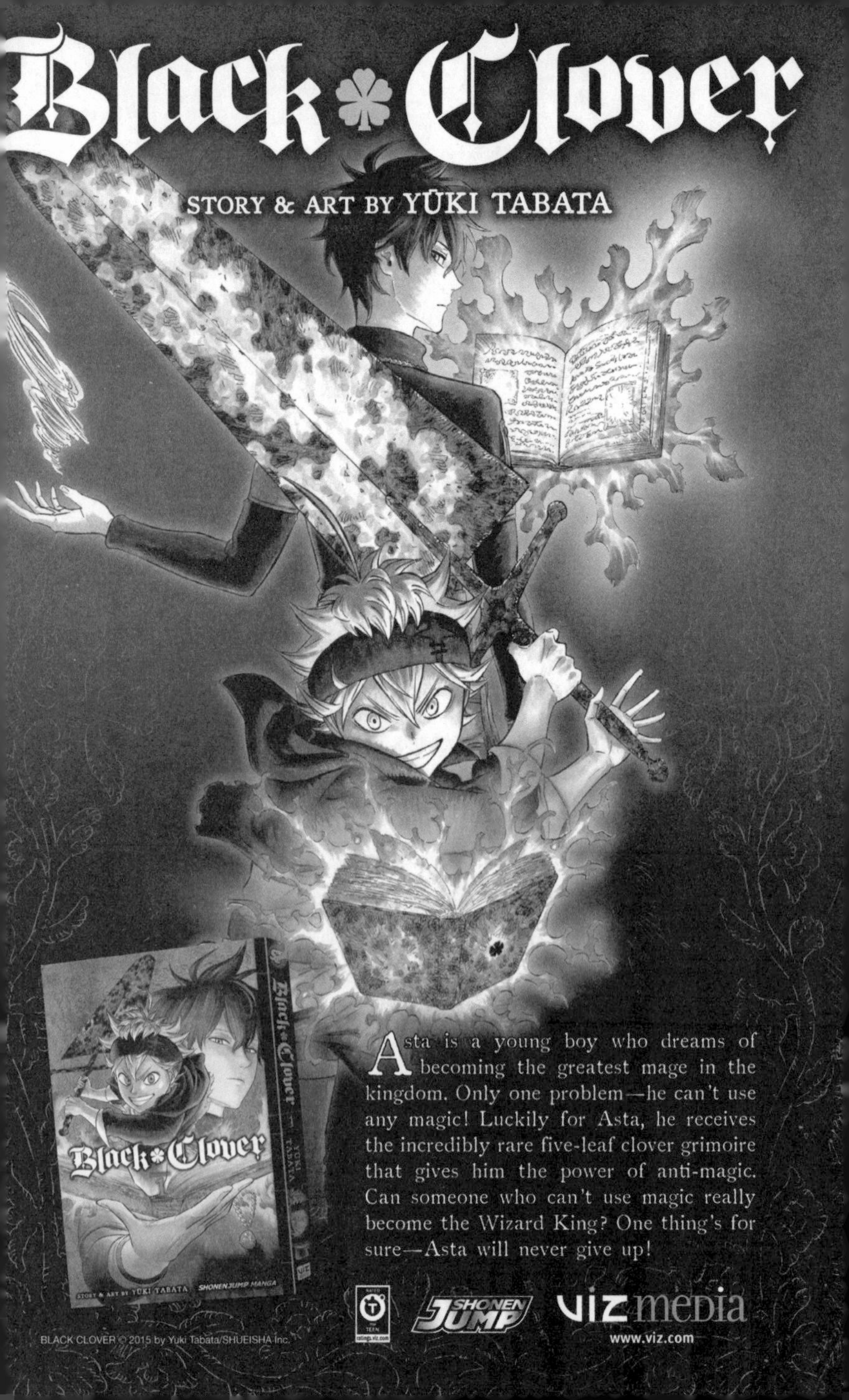

Black Clover
STORY & ART BY YŪKI TABATA
Asta is a young boy who dreams of becoming the greatest mage in the kingdom. Only one problem—he can't use any magic! Luckily for Asta, he receives the incredibly rare five-leaf clover grimoire that gives him the power of anti-magic. Can someone who can't use magic really become the Wizard King? One thing's for sure—Asta will never give up!
Black Clover
YUKI TABATA
STORY & ART BY YUKI TABATA
SHONEN JUMP MANGA
SHONEN JUMP
VIZ media
www.viz.com
BLACK CLOVER © 2015 by Yuki Tabata/SHUEISHA Inc.

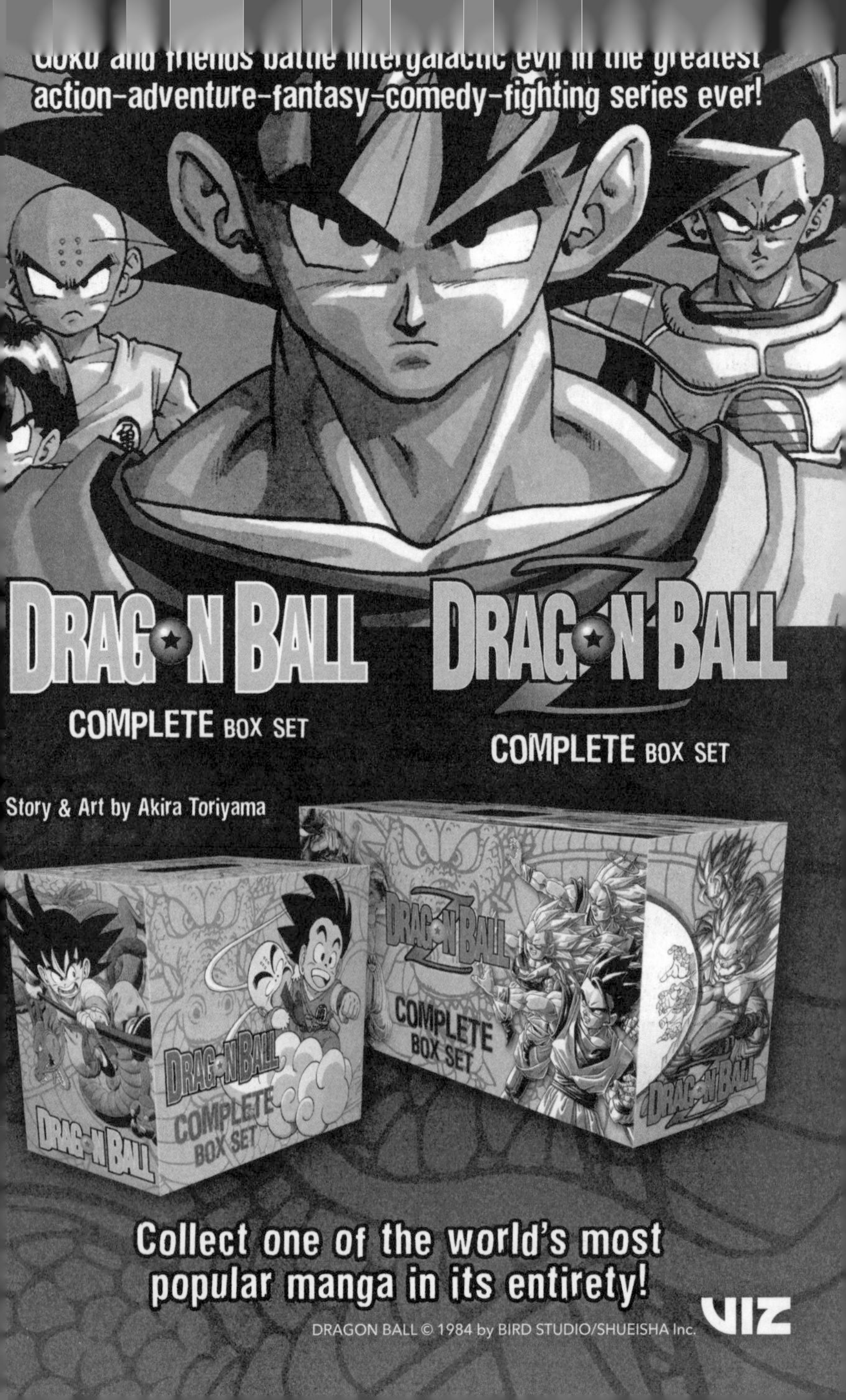

Goku and friends battle intergalactic evil in the greatest
action-adventure-fantasy-comedy-fighting series ever!
DRAGON BALL
COMPLETE BOX SET
DRAGON BALL Z
COMPLETE BOX SET
Story & Art by Akira Toriyama
Collect one of the world's most
popular manga in its entirety!
VIZ
DRAGON BALL © 1984 by BIRD STUDIO/SHUEISHA Inc.

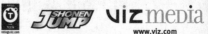

DEMON SLAYER
KIMETSU NO YAIBA

Story and Art by
KOYOHARU GOTOUGE

In Taisho-era Japan, kindhearted Tanjiro Kamado makes a living selling charcoal. But his peaceful life is shattered when a demon slaughters his entire family. His little sister Nezuko is the only survivor, but she has been transformed into a demon herself! Tanjiro sets out on a dangerous journey to find a way to return his sister to normal and destroy the demon who ruined his life.

ASTRA LOST IN SPACE

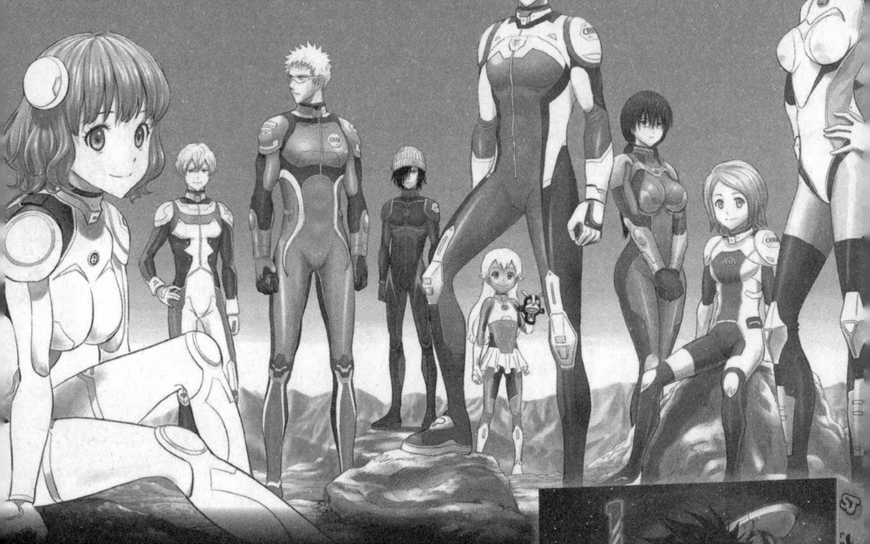

CAN EIGHT TEENAGERS FIND THEIR WAY HOME FROM 5,000 LIGHT-YEARS AWAY?

It's the year 2063, and interstellar space travel has become the norm. Eight students from Caird High School and one child set out on a routine planet camp excursion. While there, the students are mysteriously transported 5,000 light-years away to the middle of nowhere! Will they ever make it back home?!

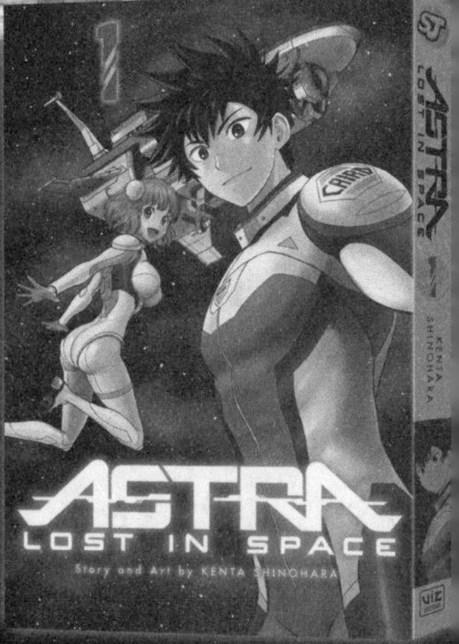
1
ASTRA
LOST IN SPACE
Story and Art by KENTA SHINOHARA
KENTA SHINOHARA
VIZ

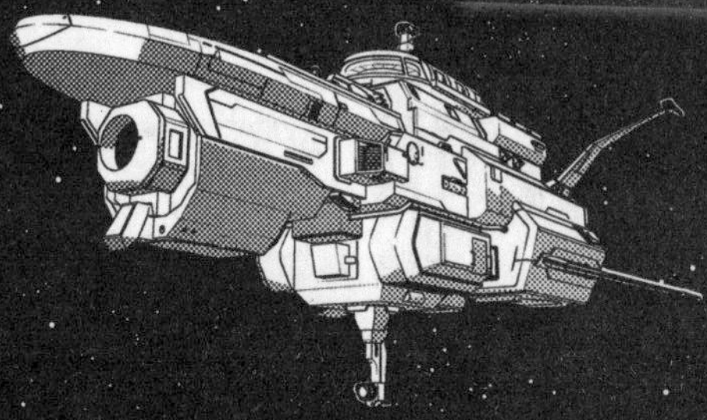

VIZ RATED T TEEN

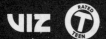

YOU'RE READING THE WRONG WAY!

World Trigger reads from right to left, starting in the upper-right corner. Japanese is read from right to left, meaning that action, sound effects, and word-balloon order are completely reversed from the English order.